HE CALLS ME BY
LIGHTNING

ALSO BY S. JONATHAN BASS

Blessed Are the Peacemakers: Martin Luther King, Jr.,
Eight White Religious Leaders, and the
"Letter from Birmingham Jail"

S. JONATHAN BASS

HE CALLS ME BY LIGHTNING

THE LIFE OF CALIPH WASHINGTON
AND THE FORGOTTEN SAGA OF
JIM CROW, SOUTHERN JUSTICE,
AND THE DEATH PENALTY

LIVERIGHT PUBLISHING CORPORATION

A Division of W. W. Norton & Company
Independent Publishers Since 1923
New York • London

For Kathleen, Caroline, and Nathaniel

For information about permission to reproduce selections from this book,
write to Permissions, Liveright Publishing Corporation,
a division of W. W. Norton & Company, Inc.,
500 Fifth Avenue, New York, NY 10110

For information about special discounts for bulk purchases, please contact
W. W. Norton Special Sales at specialsales@wwnorton.com or 800-233-4830

Manufacturing by Berryville Graphics
Book design by Ellen Cipriano
Production manager: Anna Oler

Library of Congress Cataloging-in-Publication Data

Names: Bass, S. Jonathan, author.
Title: He calls me by lightning : the life of Caliph Washington and the forgotten
saga of Jim Crow, southern justice, and the death penalty / S. Jonathan Bass.
Description: First edition. | New York ; London : Liveright Publishing Corporation,
[2017] | Includes bibliographical references and index.
Identifiers: LCCN 2017005135 | ISBN 9781631492372 (hardcover)
Subjects: LCSH: Washington, Caliph, 1939–2001. | Discrimination in
criminal justice administration—Alabama—History. | African American prisoners—
Alabama—Biography. | Death row inmates—Alabama—Biography. |
Alabama—Race relations—History.
Classification: LCC E185.93.A3 B37 2017 | DDC 305.8009761—dc23 LC record
available at https://lccn.loc.gov/2017005135

Liveright Publishing Corporation
500 Fifth Avenue, New York, N.Y. 10110
www.wwnorton.com

W. W. Norton & Company Ltd.
15 Carlisle Street, London W1D 3BS

1 2 3 4 5 6 7 8 9 0

CONTENTS

Muscoda Iron Ore miners in the early 1940s.

PREFACE

For hardship does not spring from the soil,
nor does trouble sprout from the ground.

—JOB 5:6

S HE WAS ALREADY lying in a coffin in the Bessemer Public Library
the first time I saw Hazel Farris. I was on an elementary school field
trip to see Bessemer, Alabama's most celebrated citizen: a leathery corpse
known as "Hazel the Mummy." When we arrived at the city's library,
located in the majestic old post office building on Nineteenth Street,
our hosts ushered us down the stairs to the basement and a makeshift
"hall of history" where Hazel was lying in state. Never before had I seen
a dead body, much less one that passed on over seventy years earlier. As I
gazed upon this grotesque artifact—faded ruddy hair, hollow eye sockets,
sunken cheekbones, and broken and missing teeth—my thoughts were
a mixture of horror and fascination. Her skin looked like an overcooked
Idaho potato, and every joint, rib, and bone was visible underneath.

Decades later, when I came across an old promotional poster for Ms.
Farris, her image came rushing back, as did the lore surrounding her
death. According to the story, she was a pint-sized, red-headed woman
in Louisville, Kentucky, who possessed a fierce temper, drank whiskey

straight from the bottle, and fought with her husband. At breakfast on the morning of August 16, 1905, she announced her intention to buy a new hat. When her husband objected to this latest spending spree, she pulled a six-gun and shot him dead. As she stood over her spouse's lifeless corpse and inspected the deed she had done, three city policemen rushed through the door. Farris turned and fired three more shots—killing each officer. Within minutes, a county sheriff's deputy arrived and slipped into the house. He saw the bodies littered across the floor, and as he tried to sneak up behind Hazel, she turned suddenly, and the pair tussled over the deputy's gun. His gun discharged, and a wayward bullet tore off Hazel's ring finger. She soon broke free from his grip, grabbed her pistol from the floor, and ended his life with a single shot.

Hazel Farris fled Kentucky and took refuge among the thieves, murderers, and whores living at the turn of the century in the wild young town of Bessemer, Alabama. She found work in a bordello in the red-light district and a new love—a police officer. It was short-lived, however. When she entrusted her cop-killing stories to her policeman, he opted for the $500 bounty on her head as opposed to her love. Rather than face the hangman's noose, Farris ended her life with a heady mixture of arsenic and whiskey on December 20, 1906. Her corpse was taken to a local furniture store, where it mummified and was later sold to a carnival show barker.

For over a hundred years, Bessemer residents recounted this sordid tale of Hazel Farris. Few locals, however, asked why a prostitute who murdered five men and took her own life was the city's most revered and celebrated citizen. The answer was undeniably obvious, even if it was lost upon the city's white residents: "Hazel the Mummy" was an all-too-fitting symbol of Bessemer—a small industrial town divided by race, labor, and ideology—where an incendiary brew of vice, violence, and corruption thrived. This was a city that counted among its population Communists, vigilantes, black revolutionaries, union thugs, pathological racists, scabs, mobsters, and criminals—all of whom used violence as a necessity to gain or maintain power. And this was a place where crooked politicians and lawless policemen lined their pockets with money and sin, where vice was plentiful and virtue was lacking, where murder and mayhem were essential elements of the culture, and where poor, itiner-

ant individuals like Hazel Farris looked to escape life's sorrows in a city
of strangers.

During the already fractious summer of 1957, fifty years after Hazel's
death, another downhearted resident searched for a way out of Bessemer. His name, unknown to history, was Caliph Washington. Just seventeen, he was the prime suspect in the shooting death of a policeman,
James B. "Cowboy" Clark. The racial element to the apparent murder—
Washington was black; Clark was white—fueled the sweltering fury
of Bessemer's all-white police force. Most of the city's population was
black, and race only intensified an already omnipresent feeling of danger
as the lawmen hunted mercilessly for young Washington. Alone and
abandoned, he hid in the woods and prayed for escape.

I first heard of Caliph Washington's story from David Murphy, who
brought a copy of an old handbill to my office at Samford University in
Birmingham, Alabama, and smacked it on top of my desk. "You've got
to read this," he proclaimed. Murphy, then an undergraduate, was working on his research project for my civil rights history class. In a packet
of materials he received from a far-away archive of the Roman Catholic
Josephites was a leaflet entitled "Wrongly Condemned Man Held Without Trial." The man was Caliph Washington. As I soon appreciated, it was
indeed a great untold story, but there were, of course, plenty of forgotten
tales from the civil rights era that needed telling. I slipped the article
into a "future projects" folder and hoped, perhaps, that I would look at it
again someday. Someday, however, came sooner than I expected.

One morning as I visited with Reverend Wilson Fallin, a Baptist
pastor, historian, and Bessemer native, I asked if he had known Caliph
Washington. In his rich, sonorous voice, he answered, "Oh yes," and proceeded to give me a soul-stirring sermon on Caliph Washington. The
minister had known him well and encouraged me to "dig a little deeper"
into his tragic experiences. A few days later, Dr. Fallin spoke at St. Francis of Assisi Catholic Church in Bessemer, and afterward a small woman
walked up to him and said, "You probably don't remember me, but my
husband's name was Caliph." Wilson responded, "Of course I remember you, and I know someone that you need to talk to." The next day I
received a message to call Mrs. Washington.

When I spoke with Christine Washington on the phone, she explained that she prayed for many years for someone to come along and tell Caliph Washington's tale. She paused for a second and added, "I think that someone is you." And I was taken.

AS I BEGAN to sort out Washington's tortuous life, I discovered that his story was inseparable from Bessemer—the dark city of "Hazel the Mummy." Yet I knew that average citizens, both black and white, helped the city maintain a fragile varnish of respectability. These peaceful, law-abiding residents worked hard, attended church, and lived quiet lives. Many were unaware of Bessemer's shadowy side. "I never knew," my Pollyannaish mother once told me, "that things were that bad."

I felt like I was in a slightly privileged position because my parents grew up in Bessemer. During the Great Depression, my grandparents and great-grandparents joined the migration of penniless farmers looking for a better life and a steady job in the city. My paternal grandfather, Samuel J. Bass, left his father-in-law's farm in the west Alabama community of Speed's Mill in Pickens County and found work in the Muscoda Iron Ore Mines on the outskirts of Bessemer. For almost twenty years, he toiled as a miner and safety officer, providing a hard-earned living for his wife Lillian and their three boys. My dad, Sam Jr., was the restless eldest son who escaped Bessemer at sixteen to join the Merchant Marines in 1943. When my grandfather took him to the Alabama Great Southern depot, he bade him goodbye and said, "You are on your own. There's nothing more I can do to help you." He turned and walked away as his son stood alone on the train platform. My dad and his brothers were products of the corrupting influences of Bessemer, which left all of them battling personal demons for the rest of their lives.

My mother's family had a similar background. My mother, Clara Faye, was raised by her grandparents, Collie and Ida Mae Lindsay Burroughs, who left their family's land in Buhl (west of Tuscaloosa) so that Collie could work as a wrought iron fabricator at Ingalls Iron Works in Bessemer. He had a third-grade education, and could read a little and sign his name, but Ida Mae never went to school and made an X mark in place of her signature. When I knew them, they were well into their eighties. Collie spent his days confined to a wheelchair listening to southern gospel music on an old radio, and when the song and the spirit moved him, he shook in a physical and spiritual earthquake. I often asked him if he was okay, and he always nodded his head, still riding the aftereffects of the band of holy angels who just visited him. His favorite song was Alfred E. Brumley's "I'll Fly Away." Brumley was inspired to write it while he was picking cotton and humming an old prison song, adapting the lyrics to include "When the shadows of this life have gone, I'll fly away; / Like a bird from prison bars has flown, I'll fly away."

BRUMLEY'S LYRICS FORESHADOWED the life and trials of Caliph Washington. Perhaps only in the dim shadow of death could he find a way home. As a young black man in the South of the 1950s, Washington found that the entire legal system—from local law enforcement to the Alabama Supreme Court—was stacked against him. Researching his hopeless cause, I discovered numerous personal connections with his story. Just like my white grandfather, Caliph Washington's black father moved from rural Pickens County to work as a miner in the Muscoda Mines, where they both joined the International Union of Mine, Mill, and Smelter Workers. Before joining the police force, Cowboy Clark worked, in fact, at Vanderburg's Gulf Super Hi-Way Service Station, where my uncle, G. W. "Dub" Burroughs, was the manager. When I asked Uncle Dub about Clark's death, he remembered that "he was killed by a retarded Negro." Dub's wife, my aunt Dorothy, was working the graveyard shift at Bessemer General Hospital the night the ambulance brought Clark's mortally wounded body to the emergency department. She recalled, "He was already dead when he arrived." And finally, I once worked at a small newspaper in Bessemer where a retired police officer, Lawton Grimes, Jr., served as a photographer. He gained his photo experience by snapping mug shots of prisoners, including Caliph Washington. Lawton spent every workday at lunch regaling us with his exploits on the Bessemer police force and those of his legendary father, Lawton "Stud" Grimes, Sr.

Although these personal connections add authenticity to the story, the broad historical significance of Caliph Washington's life and trials serve as an avenue to explore the measures used by white southern officials (lawmen, lawyers, judges, and juries) to enforce Jim Crow "justice" at the local level, especially through race-based jury exclusion. The broad focus of this book is on the search for racial justice and the equal application of laws in southern courtrooms, prison systems, and death chambers throughout the civil rights years (1957–72). Thousands of pages of trial transcripts and other legal documents provide unique insight into the southern legal environment from local, state, and federal perspectives. What is missing from the study of southern legal history during those years is a thorough examination of the workings of local- and state-level Jim Crow legal systems. This book is intended to help fill that void.

He Calls Me by Lightning then becomes, in many ways, Bessemer's story. Caliph Washington's life has come to symbolize the violence, corruption, and racism that dominated not only in this city but also in the larger South. Bessemer in particular was a worn-out, dirty city, whose most famous inhabitants included "Hazel the Mummy"; Virginia Hill, a Hollywood socialite and girlfriend to mobster Bugsy Siegel; and Joseph N. Gallo, the consigliere (counselor) to the Mafia bosses in New York's Gambino crime family. But Caliph Washington, a barely literate black man, remains the central character in this forgotten saga of Jim Crow, southern justice, and the racial implications of the death penalty. As one of Washington's friends once said, "Each and every one of us [should] remember that Caliph Washington is not just a name on a piece of paper or the central character in a story we've been told. Caliph Washington is a human being! And every human being deserves . . . honest thought and consideration."

HE CALLS ME BY
LIGHTNING

Seventeen-year-old Private Caliph Washington escaped
Bessemer in 1955 and served a tour of duty in the U.S. Army.

1

STEAL AWAY

CALIPH WASHINGTON STARED out the window of the Greyhound Scenic Cruiser as it rolled through bare Mississippi villages like Hickory Flat, Pott's Camp, Pumpkin Center, and Myrtle. This undisturbed Sunday morning, July 14, 1957, found a handful of quiet passengers scattered about the bus, a General Motors creation with an air-suspension ride and a sputtering air conditioner. A seventeen-year-old army private of average height, Washington had athletic shoulders, a gentle voice, and a sunshine grin that seemed all the brighter against his midnight black skin. Wearing wine-colored pants, a blue shirt, and a fuzzy gray wide-brimmed fedora too small for his head, he sat in the second to last row of the bus, near two other black passengers. A crumpled brown paper sack rested at his feet; it contained a change of clothes, a piece of cake, and a pearl-handled revolver that had just ended the life of a white Alabama policeman.

Over forty-eight hours earlier, just after midnight on Friday, July 12, a shooting incident occurred on an empty red-dirt street close to a row of run-down shotgun houses in Bessemer. Situated thirteen miles southwest of Birmingham, at the base of the red iron mountain that gave it life, Bessemer was a poisonous city consumed by vice, violence, and vigilantism, where an impoverished and powerless black majority was oppressively governed by a ruthless and corrupt white establishment. The shooting of policeman James B. "Cowboy" Clark looked like a homicide, and all evidence pointed to Caliph Washington as the triggerman. Before the shooting, the officer was in high-speed pursuit of a car driven by Washington. That car, left abandoned near the body of the officer, belonged to Washington's father. The few witnesses all agreed that the man fleeing the murder scene looked like Caliph Washington. From the time of the incident on Friday night, Washington eluded law enforcement officials. As police conducted an aggressive search for the armed fugitive, he slipped out of the state and caught the Greyhound leaving Amory, Mississippi, for Memphis.

Fear and instinct compelled him to run; the time and the place convinced him to escape; life's experiences and his family's history whispered for him to steal away. "Steal away in the midnight hour," urged the old spiritual. "Steal away when you need some power; steal away when your heart is heavy; steal away." Washington needed the big wheels of that silver Greyhound to take him a thousand miles away from Bessemer to the distant hope of freedom.

IN THE ALABAMA of 1957, Washington's alleged crime was the "supreme offense, on the same level of a white woman being raped by a black man," one sheriff's deputy noted. Such crimes, whether committed or not, collided with long-standing regional, state, and local racial codes of honor, shame, mastery, masculinity, and power. As historian Pete Daniel observed, "At any point, at any time, in any town, crossroads, house, or field, a short circuit in racial customs could spark violence." The ordeal of Caliph Washington reveals the savage and petty tyranny of law enforcement, criminal jurisprudence, and community vengeance in the Jim Crow South. In what would become a grim, decades-long odyssey, state and local officials ignored the Bill of Rights and denied

Washington due process and equal protection. "The entire system of white supremacy," as author Stetson Kennedy noted in 1946, "is predicated upon prefabricated prejudices against social equality, against which white southerners have been conditioned to react emotionally instead of rationally."

As Caliph Washington left Alabama on that Sunday bus, he could not escape this burden of irrational southern honor. It was a tangled society, as author Robert Penn Warren once explained, akin to a giant spider web, where even the slightest touch sent "vibration ripples" to the farthest reaches. "It does not matter whether or not you meant to brush the web of things," Warren wrote. "Your happy foot or your gay wing may have brushed it ever so lightly, but what happens always happens and there is the spider, bearded black and with his great faceted eyes glittering like mirrors in the sun, or like God's eye, and the fangs dripping." Washington's actions sent ripples to farthest corners of white society in Alabama. At worst, he murdered a police officer; at best, he dared to defend himself against a white man. Both would elicit rage and demand eye-for-an-eye vengeance. Caliph Washington's Alabama tragedy was similar to the Scottsboro Boys case a quarter century before, in which the southern justice system also "proved impotent." In that case, an all-white jury convicted nine young black men of raping two white women without any evidence that linked them to the alleged crime.

BORN ON NOVEMBER 14, 1939, Caliph was the sixth of eight children for Doug and Aslee Washington—sharecroppers working a tiny strip of bottomland near rural Aliceville, Alabama. Instituted after the Civil War, sharecropping was a form of modern feudalism where poor, landless blacks and whites farmed lands owned by other men. At the end of the season they gave a percentage of their harvest in return. Like many other poor people in Alabama, Doug Washington toiled each day raising cotton for a tight-fisted Pickens County white landowner. The family lived in a cropper's shack with no electrical power or indoor plumbing, but plenty of rotten boards; the family, as one observer once noted, "could study geology through the floor, botany through the walls, and astronomy through the roof." The landowner provided the Washingtons with the necessities for planting a cotton crop: an old mule, a rusty plow, and a sack of seeds—nothing else. At picking time, each family member, including young children, had to do their share of the back-breaking labor, with little respite even from the day's end or stormy weather.

When croppers like Doug Washington settled with the landowner at the end of the season, they often discovered they owed more than they earned. "You couldn't argue with them," one cropper recalled. "You couldn't ask no questions." A black man dared not challenge a white man's reckoning; they had to stand by and take what they got. Each year Washington worked harder, earned less, and slipped deeper in debt. "It was just like he was in prison," his son Caliph later recalled. "So they would always keep you and say you're going to have to stay another year or two before you can be relieved of this debt. So when the year would come up, you would never come up with what they wanted."

For the Washingtons and other blacks in Pickens County, conflict with the white landowners was constant. "If you didn't do exactly what they wanted you to do," Caliph said, "regardless of what your parents told you to do, then they would come out and riot at night and try and frighten us. Sometimes they would whip some, and sometimes they would kill some."

In the 1940s, Doug Washington quit farming and joined the exodus of rural folks looking for economic freedom in Birmingham's industrial district. He found a permanent job as an iron ore miner at U.S. Steel's Muscoda Mines in Bessemer. Muscoda was a slope mine that took advantage of the large outcrop of iron ore on Red Mountain by boring into the seam horizontally, at a downward angle. "The ore mines sorta grows on the men," one worker believed. Down in the mines, Doug found reprieve from some of the aboveground racial tensions. "Weren't no black nor white in the mines, just miners," one of Doug's fellow black workers later recalled. "There was no friction at all." Both races rode the skip down into the mines together, came back together, and ate together. Everybody brought their own lunch: biscuits and fried meat rolled up in the newspapers."

Still, Bessemer shared many of the same impoverished character-istics of other Alabama Black Belt towns. Blacks made up 61 percent of the city's population and held the lowest-paying jobs. The median income for all citizens in the city was among the lowest in Alabama, while the unemployment rate was one of the highest. Only 23 percent of Bessemer's citizens had a high school education, and on average most residents had attended just beyond the eighth grade. Most of the city's black population lived on unpaved streets in poorly constructed firetrap homes with inadequate plumbing. The 1950 census found two-thirds of the housing in the city substandard, with no indoor toilets. Public housing facilities in the city numbered zero.

From Caliph Washington's perspective, however, the move was a vast improvement from the hard living in rural Pickens County. For the first time in his life, he lived in a house with electric lights, a reliable coal-burning furnace, running water, and unlike most blacks in Besse-mer, indoor plumbing. The Washington children now had enough food to eat, a warm place to live, and clothes without patches all over and shoes without holes and worn soles. The move to Bessemer also gave Caliph Washington hope for a better life. "When we got up here," he remembered, "I could see all types of opportunities before my eyes," especially in education.

In the 1950s, Washington attended the all-black Dunbar High School. Originally named Bessemer Colored High School, the school opened in 1923 in a stately brick building located at 2715 Sixth Avenue North. Five years later, local educator Pearl Shelton Blevins suggested renaming the high school for the black poet Paul Laurence Dunbar, whose writings, at times, gently and ironically bespoke the tragedy of black life in America. "I know why the caged bird sings," he wrote in "Sympathy," "ah me / When his wing is bruised and his bosom sore,— / When he beats his bars and he would be free; / It is not a carol of joy or glee." In "The Haunted Oak" he wrote from the perspective of a tree used to lynch a guiltless man: "I feel the rope against my bark / And the weight of him in my grain / I feel in the throe of his final woe / The touch of my own last pain."

Despite the promise of a high school education, Caliph Washington dropped out of school at fourteen, and like his father before him, he worked hard, earned little, and clashed with the white people. His opportunities for a better life soon slipped away. On July 14, 1957, his only hope was to run away from Bessemer and avoid a possible death on the branches of some haunted oak tree.

In the early afternoon, the Greyhound bus entered the densely wooded Holly Springs National Forest and crossed Mississippi's muddy Tallahatchie River. Only three more stops remained on the schedule: Holly Springs, Byhalia, and Olive Branch. In two hours or so, Washington hoped to arrive at the bus terminal in Memphis—a major transfer station located on Union Street, near the banks of the Mississippi River—where he would begin the next leg of his journey. For the first time in days, he relaxed just a little, and he chatted with a few fellow Greyhound travelers. Washington's thoughts, however, never drifted far from the death of the white lawman—he knew from personal experience what would await him if he ever returned to Bessemer. "It was pretty hard growing up as a colored person in Bessemer," he once said. "The white folks made you feel so . . . so small."

TWO YEARS BEFORE, on a late summer evening in 1955, Caliph and his older brother Joseph were at home while the rest of the family attended a church service. The weather that summer seemed downright tropical, as a suffocating heat wave sapped the energy from nearly every living thing. Caliph tried to keep cool by stripping down to his white cotton boxer shorts and matching T-shirt. He dozed fitfully in his bed—trying to get comfortable in ways you never can when it's that hot—while Joseph, or "Doogie" as he was called, took a cold shower in the cramped bathroom adjacent to the enclosed back porch.

The Washingtons lived at 418 Short Fifteenth Street, in a tiny shack located on the south side of Bessemer in the Thompson Town settlement. The area, one of Bessemer's original land tracts from the 1880s, was once a respectable working-class neighborhood filled with miners and other industrial workers. Located on a level scrap of land near the base of Red Mountain, Thompson Town was once a center of union activities during the Great Depression, but by the 1950s it was a used-up community made up of Bessemer's poorest black residents.

The Washingtons resided in one of sixteen dilapidated shotgun shacks, all spaced close together, one room wide, one story high, and five rooms deep. Shotgun houses took their name from their simple, narrow design: a shotgun shell fired through the front door would come out the back without touching a wall. But the name was also a reminder that in the South, and especially in towns like Bessemer, guns were more than just architectural metaphors—they were rooted in everyday life.

These shotgun houses were situated on a small tract of land in the center of a square block accessible only by a dusty unpaved back alley. Bessemer zoning regulations prohibited blacks from living in white-designated residential areas. "It shall be unlawful," the code mandated, "for any person, other than persons of the white race, to reside within the areas described." The boundary lines between black and white neighborhoods ran willy-nilly throughout Bessemer and separated the races along streets, alleys, blocks, and even lots. "They would separate us," Caliph Washington later recalled, "and they had a square around you" that kept the races apart. In spite of the laws, the two races still lived in close proximity; the Washingtons resided in a tiny black island of homes surrounded by nearby white neighbors.

Out the back door of the Washington home and across an over-grown field covered in tall summer weeds lived their nearest white neighbors, Margaret S. Parsons and her two teenage daughters, located at 428 Sixteenth Street. The manager of the nearby American Deluxe Cleaners, Margaret was the estranged wife of Ira "Dick" Parsons, a patrolman on the Bessemer police force. On the evening of August 29, this same Parsons, an ill-humored, hot-headed Irishman, was visiting his two daughters when he heard some noise behind the house. What happened that night would later be debated in court. "I looked out of my window and saw two boys whistling and waving at my daughters," Parsons recalled. "I told one of my daughters to parade by the window to keep the boys' attention until I could go downstairs and see who they were. They were Caliph and Joseph Washington, both had nothing on but their underwear."

Parsons called the police department, and although off duty, he grabbed his gun and handcuffs and headed across the field. It was 10 p.m. Unaware of the coming trouble, Joseph walked onto the back porch and hung the mop he used to clean the bathroom over the rail to dry. As he turned to go back through the screen door inside, he caught a glimpse of a white man coming out of the darkness. Parsons leaped onto the porch and pistol-whipped Joseph on the head, back, and shoulders. He fell hard onto the rough-hewn plank floor. Parsons cocked back his dusty boots and began kicking Joseph in the ribs.

When Joseph was lying half-conscious in the doorway, Parsons stepped over him and entered the house. He jerked Caliph out of bed and began hitting him over the head with the pistol. Caliph begged the officer to stop, but the pistol kept coming down again and again like a miner's nine-pound hammer. Caliph was on his knees in front of Parsons. Blood flowed from the cuts on his head and stained his white T-shirt with a crimson hue. He tried to fall forward onto the floor and curl into a fetal position, but Parsons stood in the way, huffing, sweating, and cursing. The best Caliph Washington could do was grab the policeman around the legs and rest his head on Parsons's kneecaps. When he felt the teenager received enough punishment, Parsons pulled the handcuffs out and placed them around the young man's wrists. Just then, Bessemer police officers J. I. Jones and Herman Lowery entered the front door. They watched as Parsons struck Caliph another hammer blow to the head. Parsons stepped back, and the young man crumpled to the floor.

Lowery and Jones, patrolmen working the three-to-eleven evening shift, picked the bloody and bruised Washington brothers off the floor, placed them under arrest, and transported them to the city jail. At 10:40 p.m., the desk sergeant on duty, Lawton Grimes, Jr., a tough-talking, chain-smoking lawman, charged the lads with indecent exposure, disorderly conduct, and resisting arrest. Grimes, in charge of the department's photographic services, snapped the pair's mug shots (with Caliph's head wrapped in bandages), took their fingerprints, and placed the boys in one of the windowless jail cells—cagelike structures with heavy iron bars, two metal bunk beds, and a slop bucket. The boys spent a long, sleepless night in the cell.

Many whites, like Dick Parsons, hated the thought of black men having any contact with white women. "You couldn't look at a white woman, not hard," Washington later remembered. "Therefore if you looked at them and they said anything, the men would come out and beat you up. That's what they used to try to do. They were telling us that they were keeping us in our place."

THE WASHINGTON BROTHERS were not the only ones facing the wrath of white men "protecting their women." Even as they awaited trial in Bessemer, Robert Hodges, a Mississippi fisherman, discovered the body of young Emmett Till in the waters of the meandering Tallahatchie River. In August 1955, the fourteen-year-old Till, just a few months younger than Caliph Washington, violated southern social customs by innocently flirting with an older white woman. Two white men pulled Till from his uncle's home, beat him, shot him through the head, tied a 125-pound cast-iron cotton gin wheel to his body, and dumped his corpse in the river. Washington and others of his generation understood that committing real or perceived crimes against whites would bring swift and deadly vigilante justice—something young Till, a northerner from Chicago, did not realize.

On the morning of August 31, 1955, the Washington brothers, with bloody bandaged heads, entered a modest municipal courtroom. On the bench sat somber-faced, high-strung James Hamrick, a magistrate who was once reprimanded by the Bessemer City Commission for using profanity from the bench in earshot of a fashionable lady of high community standing. Defending the two brothers was Bessemer's only black lawyer, David Hood, Jr. The husband of Caliph's elementary school teacher, Hood was a tall, distinguished man with a soft voice and a quiet, gentle nature. Born on October 5, 1919, in Bessemer, Hood attended Dunbar High School, where he became a protégé of Principal Arthur Shores, who was studying and practicing law on the side and would one day become the state's most respected civil rights attorney. Shores inspired Hood to follow in his footsteps, because the legal field in the South provided unlimited prospects for black lawyers. "No greater opportunity,"

Shores said, "is offered anywhere in the country to raise the level of the Negro through the efforts of the Negro lawyer and be amply compensated, than here in the Deep South." When David Hood graduated from Howard University School of Law, he joined Shores's law firm, where he specialized in civil rights and constitutional issues.

In the late summer of 1955, Hood was sitting across the courtroom from Bessemer city attorney Lee Bains, who prosecuted the complaint for the city. He called Officer Dick Parsons as the first witness. Parsons testified that the Washington boys "came out on the back porch of the Washington home dressed in only their under clothing, whistled 'wolf calls' and waved at my two daughters," who could be seen in the second-story window of the home across the field. Officer J. I. Jones testified next, explaining that he saw the Washington boys in their shorts and T-shirts but he did not "see any exposure of their privates." Jones added that he saw Parsons "strike at Caliph, but I don't know whether he struck him." Herman Lowery was next on the witness stand, testifying that neither of the boys resisted arrest while he was in their presence. "Both were bleeding about their heads," he added, "when Officer Jones and I arrived on the scene."

Attorney Hood called Caliph to the stand in his own defense. "Officer Parsons came into the house and jerked me out of bed," he testified, "and started hitting me over my head with a pistol. He hit me again after I was handcuffed." Both Washington boys denied being outside the house whistling at anyone that night.

Called back to the stand, Officer Parsons admitted that when Caliph grabbed him around the legs, "I struck Caliph more than one time with my pistol." Hood also compelled Parsons to admit that "at first I did not know nor could I tell who the boys were from that distance away." The *Birmingham World*, the area's largest-circulation black newspaper, reported that tall weeds and a giant, unmovable, rusted, broken-down truck obstructed Dick Parsons's view of the back porch of the Washington home. The porch was over two hundred feet away, a reporter for the paper observed, "and was built-in-side-of-the-house . . . which cannot be seen from the Parsons' home." Hood also called several of the Washingtons' neighbors, Willie Mae Dean, Mary Dean, Annie Jones, and

Reverend J. C. Snider, all of whom testified that they did not hear any-one whistling or calling anybody that night. The *World* concluded that Lawyer Hood presented a "terrific, rugged, brilliant argument for the defense," contending that Officer Parsons could not see who the boys were from that distance.

Following testimony, Judge Hamrick threw out the indecent expo-sure charge against Caliph and Joseph Washington but divided the two remaining counts between the boys. He found Joseph guilty of resisting arrest and gave him a $60 fine and court costs. The court convicted Caliph of disorderly conduct and ordered him to pay a fine of $100 plus court costs and to serve a nine-day hard-labor jail sentence.

The Washington brothers paid their fines, and Caliph served his time on a city work crew, but the physical and mental scars from the incident remained. "We didn't leave it alone," he later recalled, "'cause we had skull cracks and everything." With the help of David Hood, the brothers sued the City of Bessemer for use of excessive force. The suit only inflamed local politicians, lawmen, and vigilantes. Harassment and intimidation by local whites became more frequent, and the Washing-tons moved to a home in the "Pipe Shop" community on the north side of Bessemer, away from the watchful eye of Dick Parsons.

In the fall of 1955, the entire state seemed on edge. U.S. Steel had recently shut down many of the iron ore mines along Red Mountain, sending Doug Washington and others looking for work. Civil rights emerged as an important issue as Birmingham's federal district judge Harlan H. Grooms ruled that the University of Alabama must admit a qualified black applicant, Autherine Lucy. At the time, Lucy propheti-cally warned, "I know there is going to be some unpleasantness." When she began classes in February 1956, the resulting riots infuriated her legal defense team, and they filed a complaint that accused the university of conspiring with unruly mobs to prevent integration. The university board of trustees responded by expelling Lucy. No further attempt to integrate the university would come until 1963.

In the Bessemer public school system, blacks made up almost 70 per-cent of the school-age population. In light of the U.S. Supreme Court's recent decisions in *Brown v. Board of Education*, integration seemed a looming reality. The previous May, in the second *Brown* ruling, the high court announced that integration should proceed at "all deliberate speed." For most whites in Bessemer, integration at any speed, slow or fast, was unacceptable.

Not much in the city suggested moderation. Bessemer was a city of extremes and stark contrasts. On most issues, especially race, no middle ground existed, no shades of gray—only black and white. Even Bessemer's tiny two-color traffic lights gave no signs of caution, only red or green, stop or go.

Living with the threat of retaliation and their lawsuit at a dead end, Caliph and Joseph Washington decided it was time to leave Bessemer. "Right after all of that stuff took place," Caliph recalled, "we left." The quickest way out of town, the brothers believed, was to join the army. Joseph was eighteen and clear to join, but Caliph at sixteen was too young. At five-foot-nine and a rugged 187 pounds, however, Caliph Washington easily convinced the enlistment officer that he was old enough to serve in the U.S. Army. He was well practiced at lying about his age since dropping out of school at fourteen to help the family earn more money. For two years he secured jobs at a bottling plant, a milk company, a tire plant, and a car wash—work usually reserved for adults.

In 1956, with the Parsons incident hanging over him, Caliph Washington left Bessemer, for the first time, on a big bus bound for the U.S. Army Training Facility at Fort Jackson, near Columbia, South Carolina. For eight weeks, he went through basic training. He learned to walk, talk, think, and act like a soldier. He prepared for combat by completing the "baptism of fire" simulation, where trainees crawled through sand, barbed wire entanglements, and other obstacles while machine guns and artillery were fired overhead. With basic training completed, he took additional instruction in light vehicle operation and maintenance. Pvt. Caliph Washington was then assigned to the Twenty-Ninth Tank Battalion, stationed in Bremerhaven, West Germany. Years before, the Twenty-Ninth was one of the first tank units created at the beginning of World War II and trained personally by Gen. George S. Patton, who once observed that this group of men were the "most highly specialized bunch of killers this army has turned out thus far."

Ironically, for southern black men in the postwar U.S. Army, tours of duty in Germany provided opportunities to experience more freedom than they could back home. *Ebony* magazine reported that many black GIs discovered that "democracy had more meaning" there, and they were "finding more friendship, more respect and more equality." Perhaps Washington enjoyed some of this freedom and the grown-up independence of army life, but he was not well suited for the command structure and strict discipline of the military.

Immature and far from home, he often defied authority and was, on at least one occasion, insubordinate to an officer. He spent twenty-four days in the stockade in Germany and was brought before a board of officers who were to evaluate his less-than-desirable conduct. They concluded that it was "unlikely that he can be rehabilitated to the extent where he may be expected to become a satisfactory soldier." The board recommended that Caliph Washington be discharged for "habits and traits of character manifested by misconduct."

On July 1, 1957, the army deactivated the Twenty-Ninth Tank Battalion in Germany, and the unit traveled to Fort Hamilton in Brooklyn, New York, where Pvt. Caliph Washington received a discharge under "other than honorable conditions." Wearing his dress uniform, he then traveled to Alabama on a southbound Greyhound and arrived in Bessemer on Sunday, July 7, 1957. A crowd of family and friends gathered to celebrate his homecoming. It had been almost two years since the beating by Dick Parsons, and this was Caliph Washington's first opportunity to return to Bessemer in fifteen months. The young soldier hoped his troubles with local police were over, but four days later, he was once again looking to escape Bessemer, Alabama.

A Bessemer street scene in the early twentieth century where
Old Joe whiskey was a popular choice at local saloons.

2

A HELL OF A PLACE

And he opened the bottomless pit; and there arose
a smoke out of the pit, as the smoke of a great furnace;
and the sun and the air were darkened.

—REVELATION 9:2

THE BESSEMER OF Caliph Washington's youth was filled with thick smoke from iron and steel furnaces, rolling mills, pipe and foundry companies, mining operations, brick manufacturers, and railway freight car producers. The impenetrable, smoldering air obscured the sun and covered the town in a veil of soot and dinginess. The foul city of thirty thousand people rested in the southern end of a soiled six-mile-wide valley, next to a tired, overworked mountain of inferior-grade iron ore. All day and all night, the roaring inharmonious symphony of heavy industry was the song of iron and steel, which left Bessemer, as one observer wrote, "red-eyed with sleepless fires" and surrounded by "smoke-belching" industry.

Bessemer's grit and grime, however, went far beyond industrial smoke and soot. While most residents, black and white, went about their daily lives, a shadow city existed: edgy, hard-boiled, and dirty. As a local police officer once explained, "Illegal goings-on are wide open. It's always been wide open, and corruption don't start at the bottom."

In 1915, a magazine writer described the city as the "grim child" of the New South, "sturdy and honorably stained" with the sweat, violence, and soot that gave the central business district its distinct "smoke begrimed" appearance.

Years earlier, Bessemer's founder, Henry Fairchild DeBardeleben, believed this black smoke meant money—and lots of it. While searching for investors for his new city in the late nineteenth century, DeBardeleben proclaimed that "no stockholder will be allowed to come in who can't make smoke . . . and the man who can make the most smoke will have the most stock."

An Alabama native, DeBardeleben was born on his parents' farm in Autauga County on July 22, 1840. Following the death of his father, the young DeBardeleben became the legal ward of Alabama's first major industrial entrepreneur, Daniel Pratt. Pratt, who made his fortune manufacturing and selling cotton gins throughout the world, imparted to his young ward his passion for business development. Combined with his abounding enthusiasm and natural intelligence, DeBardeleben emerged as the model of a New South entrepreneur following the Civil War. The young industrialist invested early in Birmingham's iron ore-mining and steel-making activities and was hailed by newspapers as a "pioneering master" and the city's own Christopher Columbus.

In the 1880s, when DeBardeleben failed to acquire land to build new blast furnaces around Birmingham, he decided to carve a new city out of the piney woods in western Jefferson County and build his industrial complex around it. With persuasive skills known to be "fatal" to anyone with money in their pocket, he convinced a handful of individuals to invest a minimum of $100,000 apiece. "Here is where we are going to establish a young city," he told his investors, pointing to a spot on a geological map between the Black Warrior and the Cahaba coalfields. It was near limestone deposits and within "gunshot" of the great "mass of red fossiliferous iron ores" on Red Mountain— it had all the elements necessary for iron and steel production. The spot under DeBardeleben's finger was the hamlet of Jonesboro, a settlement of roughneck farmers on the old rocky road between Huntsville and Tuscaloosa.

SOME SEVENTY YEARS earlier, the Creek War brought young men from Tennessee, Kentucky, Georgia, and the Carolinas to the Alabama wilderness to fight under the command of Andrew Jackson. In 1814, Jackson decisively defeated the Creeks at the Battle of Horseshoe Bend, then forced the tribes to sign the Treaty of Fort Jackson, which ceded 23 million acres to the United States. The land that would one day become central Alabama was opened for settlement.

Among the first whites to arrive in 1816 were a handful of people from South Carolina and Kentucky who settled along a muddy creek near the Old Huntsville Road. They cleared land, planted crops, propped up several hundred rickety logs, and named the place Fort Jonesboro in honor of their leader, a wild-eyed Indian fighter with "reckless courage," named "Devil" John Jones. The hell-blazing nickname seemed to fit the man, the people, and the place. Jones grew corn, brewed whiskey, and raised hell with his neighbors—beating one so badly that the fellow sold his land, packed his wagons, and moved twenty miles to the south to avoid contact with the roughhousing son of a bitch. By the time Jones moved on to settle elsewhere in the state, the entire valley that extends from Bessemer through Birmingham was called Jones Valley.

Devil John Jones and many like him were the descendants of immigrants from Scotland and Northern Ireland—common people who brought to America a culture based on kinship, violence, honor, and hedonism. Historian David Hackett Fischer wrote that these settlers had a "penchant for family feuds, a love of whiskey and a warrior ethic that demanded vengeance." Devil John and his fellow migrants brought this culture to the southwestern frontier, where the isolated pioneer lifestyle reinforced it. Journalist W. J. Cash once described these trail-blazing men as pleasure-seeking hell-of-a-fellows—southerners who were able "to stand on [their] heads in a bar, to toss down a pint of raw-whiskey at a gulp, to fiddle and dance all night, to bite off the nose or gorge out the eyes of a favorite enemy, to fight harder and love harder than the next man, to be known eventually far and wide as a hell-of-a-fellow." In Alabama, Scots-Irish families who occupied the land near the "shanty" fort in Jonesboro often feuded over minor disagreements and never attended any community gathering, as one writer noted, "without breaking it up with fighting." The land was poor, and so were the people.

This area of the state, one Alabama politician pointed out during those years, was so forsaken and pitiable that a "buzzard would have to carry provisions on his back or starve to death on his passage." But during the 1880s, Henry DeBardeleben boasted that his new town would become the greatest in all Alabama. "Life is one big poker game," he once said, and the thrill of investment meant an opportunity to "savor the melodramatic and to dream of millions." With over $2 million in capital investments, DeBardeleben set about building his new town. "There's nothing like taking a wild piece of land all rock and woods," he proclaimed, "and turning it into a settlement of men and women; bringing railroads in, making payroll, starting things going; nothing like boring a hillside through and turning over a mountain."

The stockholders proposed naming the town after Sir Henry Bessemer, the inventor of the process that made possible the mass production of steel. As the president of the Iron and Steel Institute noted in 1890, Henry Bessemer's discovery changed the face of Western civilization, helping prevent the West from a "relapse into barbarism," and it would lead the way to higher civilization in the twentieth century. "The name of Bessemer will therefore be added to the honorable roll of men who have succeeded in spreading the gospel of 'Peace on earth and goodwill toward men,' which our Divine Master came on earth to teach and encourage." It was a high-minded legacy for a mean, barbaric start-up city in an area prone to violence.

Founded on April 12, 1887, Bessemer, Alabama, its promoters boasted, had a future "brighter than any city in the South" and showed promise "without parallel in the history of American towns." They touted the city as a burgeoning garden paradise. "Nature has done some of her most charming work here," one optimistic early report noted, "and the region is ready for those finishing touches that are the work of the architect and landscape."

If you desire a home in an equable, healthy, attractive climate, in an unusually favored country with pure water, good soil, rich products, picturesque scenery, devoid of rugged winters as well as tropical summers, except from visitations of tornadoes or cyclones, or of epidemic diseases, or of unusual natural pests, you will find such a place or locality centering at Bessemer.

Even though the area was prone to unpredictable storms, widespread illnesses (cholera, pellagra, tuberculosis), and mosquitoes as big as cottonwood blossoms, its boosters proclaimed Bessemer the "Marvel City," a place where "home and prosperity" were within the grasp of the humblest and lowliest.

Seeking the promise of a better life, it was the poorest folks in Alabama society, especially debt-ridden sharecroppers and tenant farmers like Caliph Washington's family, who moved to Bessemer. Soon the local chamber of commerce promoted the city as having "labor in great abundance, skilled and unskilled, white and black, male and female, but all native born, content and efficient." A constant stream of rural southerners poured into the city looking for jobs. "These people," a Bessemer resident observed, "worked hard, lived hard, and in many instances died hard."

What Bessemer actually became was nothing more than an overgrown mining town with an affinity for violence and iniquity. Although the mine villages themselves had no "shot houses, or houses that sold whiskey," one miner later recalled, "If they wanted to get drunk, they went somewhere else to get drunk." And that place lay just outside Bessemer, at the three-mile limit on the city's eastern border known as Whiskeytown. Every evening miners and steel workers, both black and white, poured out of their camps and mineshafts searching for sin there, and they found plenty. Out of some measure of necessity, entrepreneurship, and thirst, locals opened a dozen or so hooch houses in Whiskeytown. The tosspot area became a "notorious center" of liquor, prostitution, and criminal activities.

The flood of rural men (single or separated from families) into urban areas for work and industry was an old story and always a recipe for violence and unrest. In Bessemer, Scots-Irish migrants carried with them an old streak of rural savagery into the vice-ridden boomtown and reveled in the sadistic violence that emerged as the city's defining feature.

"New arrivals from the countryside," historian Pete Daniel concluded, "brought their penchant for violence with them; in many ways the South outdid the Wild West in the frequency of shootouts and general gunplay. Indeed, urbanization and adjustments to new routines throughout the country seemed to breed violence." From the 1880s on, journalist W. J. Cash noted, some southerners found great pleasure in the "infliction of the most devilish and prolonged agonies."

Like other cities in the region, Bessemer grew too fast to provide safety or public services. At night, pedestrians walked dim lit streets at their own peril, as the risk of robbery, assault, or murder lurked in the darkness. As a local writer noted, "Murders, robberies, stickups, flimflam, pickpockets, gamblers, and other undesirable elements made it a dangerous place for a decent citizen to visit." For a time, the area averaged one killing per night. "In many cases," Bessemer police officer Lawton Grimes, Jr., wrote, "a human life was taken for no reason other than the excitement of taking a life."

Companies imposed oppressive controls and regulations, and security officers enforced strict prohibitions. And much to the chagrin of many locals, an 1874 state law prohibited the "sale, giving away, or other disposition of spirituous liquors, intoxicating bitters, or other intoxicating beverages" within three miles of the Jonesboro Methodist Church. But with crime, vice, and violence so widespread in Bessemer, police officers could do little to enforce the laws. The effort seemed so pointless that some of the lawmen participated in the city's debauchery. A local newspaper reported that a "spectacle for the angels" occurred one evening when the chief of police was seen "indulging in a carriage ride" through the streets of Bessemer with the "Queen of Whiskeytown," the city's most notorious prostitute. In addition, when police officers entered the sin-filled area, they were often seen, one newspaper observed, "complacently sunning themselves in tippled chairs, feet elevated, and batons at rest."

Blind-eyed local boosters ignored these problems and praised the "guardians of the peace" in hopes of luring more workers to Bessemer. "No city in all the South," a hyperbolic writer for the *Bessemer Weekly* noted, "can boast a police corps more efficient, reliable, and faithful; nor one better disciplined or more zealous and attentive in the performance of arduous and exacting duty." In reality, with crime high and pay low, the city found few individuals willing to protect and to serve the citizens. Turnover in personnel was constant. In 1897 frustrated officials fired the police chief for "neglect of duty and cowardice" and replaced him with Thomas Benjamin Wallace, a former supervisor at the Alabama Insane Hospital in Tuscaloosa. Wallace worked for mental health pioneer Peter Bryce, who believed in a "moral treatment" to heal the mind through the creation of a normal environment (no physical restraints) that required regular work for able-bodied patients. Perhaps with that background, Bessemer leaders believed the new chief could curb the city's pathological criminal culture.

Wallace's job got even tougher, however, when Bessemer politicians overturned the prohibition law that confined most illegal activities to Whiskeytown. Once the zoning levee was erased, alcohol, gambling, debauchery, violence, and murder flooded the city proper. The former police chief of Tuscaloosa, Louis Napoleon Ball, came to this marvel of a city not to bring law and order but to establish a "palatial pleasure resort." Ball's Bank Saloon, located at the corner of Second Avenue and Nineteenth Street—the central business corner of Bessemer—boasted "elegant fixtures, superb appointments, the best service, and the finest liquors." Nearby, the three Nordman brothers operated the Palace Saloon. A newspaper noted that the "triumvirate of Nordmans" maintained a large clientele by serving only the finest liquors, beer on tap and in bottle, and all the most "modern drinks," including new cocktails like the Sazerac and the Tom Collins. A few blocks away, the Bickart brothers operated the Metropolitan Bar, which enjoyed, as one writer observed, "a popularity and patronage exceptionally gratifying." The Bickarts also distributed all products "known to the whiskey trade," with names like Old Joe, Four Roses, and Three Feathers. Customers could order a finger of High Ball Rye or an "unexcelled extra pale" beer at a nickel a glass, twenty-five cents for a half pint, and a dollar for a quart.

More than eighteen saloons operated in the Bessemer business district during these years, and most of them were infested with the rotten sins of gambling and prostitution. Lawbreaking stalked at the doorways of such evil, a resident complained, and made violent crimes "doubly sure and greater." Gatherings of whiskey drinkers, fallen women, and cardsharps led to frequent bloodlettings. To minimize the violence occurring inside the ornate saloons, burly bartenders forced the ruckus out onto Bessemer's streets, where ruffians brawled, punched, kicked, gouged, bit, sliced, stabbed, shot, and died in a stew of slag, mud, blood, and whiskey.

When these rowdy men from the mining villages and steel mills were not fighting, they were watching other beasts kill each other, flocking to dog, bear, cock, and wildcat fights held in pits near the center of town, where they placed bets with their hard-earned wages. Professional gamblers set up shop in this frontier atmosphere and profited mightily from games of blackjack, craps, and five-card stud. Each day, trains arrived from Birmingham and other areas of the South with "gambling dandies" aboard; travelers hoped to participate in the city's free-flowing "sporting activities" and the "unusual array of corruption and wickedness." All this activity thrived in spite of city ordinances outlawing gambling houses, cockfighting, and all games and sports of an "indecent character." One Bessemer citizen demanded city officials impose severe penalties on the men who ran the gambling rooms "before it was too late" and God's wrath destroyed this modern Sodom and Gomorrah.

A few reform-minded citizens blamed Bessemer's lawlessness on its distance from the county's governmental, judicial, and political center in Birmingham. Residents resented the inconvenience of having to travel over poor roads to take care of business in Birmingham or use the seventy-five-minute one-way ride on the slow-moving dummy train line—the forerunner of the streetcar line between the two cities. Bessemer maintained a begrudging and uneasy relationship with Birmingham. The two cities shared similar virtues, vices, fortunes, and misfortunes. Like Birmingham, Bessemer was a blend of western brutality, northern capital, and New South hype. Both fought to become the South's greatest industrial city, and both promoted themselves as the "Pittsburgh of the South." But it was Birmingham, nicknamed the Magic City, that emerged as the region's industrial giant, while Bessemer lagged far behind. This calamity convinced Bessemer's political leaders that Birmingham stood in the way of the path to greatness for the Marvel City. "For many years," one politician proclaimed, "Bessemer has been . . . the south end of a northbound mule to the rest of the county."

With this butt-of-a-mule inferiority complex in concert with crime and corruption, Bessemer struggled with status anxiety, poor civic self-esteem, and an identity crisis. Hoping to alleviate these problems, the Alabama legislature in 1893 established a separate judicial territory in western Jefferson County, excluded Birmingham's circuit court authority, and created the Bessemer Division of the Jefferson County Circuit Court or the "Bessemer Cutoff."

Residents were less than satisfied. "Jefferson County has long ago ceased to have a government representative of her people," the *Bessemer Workman* opined in 1901. The alternative, the newspaper proposed, was to carve out a Bessemer County and provide citizens with "the right of local self-government." Bessemer politicians pressed for it, but the idea failed to gain support. "Aside from the giving of several men good offices, it is hard to see the advantage of a division," a journalist observed, "it would be doubling the expense of county government without advantage of the governed." In 1901, Birmingham politicians constitutionally restricted the formation of new counties in Alabama.

This "final" resolution, however, did little to quell Bessemer's quest for secession and independence. For decades more, local antipathy toward Birmingham compelled politicians to keep up the fight for a new county. Only that way, they felt, could Bessemer establish an identity separate from Birmingham. Politicians tapped into this festering resentment by promising to lead Bessemer out of Birmingham's shadow, but Bessemer's widespread violence, crooked politicians, and illegal activities made some folks in the Magic City long for greater distance between the two locales.

The Bessemer Cutoff arrangement did little to bring law and order to the area or reduce its vice and violence. Even when these vices were conducted in private, they would disgrace any community, but in Bessemer the debauchery took place in the center of town. City laws prohibited "houses of ill fame" and barred "lewd women" from visiting saloons or living within fifty feet of one, but as a politician once quipped, "You can make prostitution illegal, but you can't make it unpopular." Residents complained that prostitutes promenaded along every Bessemer street and solicited customers "over, in, under, and about" all downtown businesses in the "most flagrant and outrageous violations" of city and state laws—

statutes that the mayor, town marshal, and the entire police force knew as well as the "sun which rose each morning." This was "worse than a crime," another citizen observed, because it degraded the moral standing of "those whom the community had selected to protect it from such inflictions." Still another local demanded that officials "remove these lewd women" because of the "shame and disgrace" of allowing "these women to live where they do and go at will upon the main streets. It should be stopped. It must be stopped." But during Bessemer's first two decades, politicians and lawmen ignored community pleas to enforce the laws.

In the early twentieth century, local newspapers headlined the incessant and sadistic violence: "L. F. Duff Found Stabbed on Street," "Fight in Bank Saloon," "Fatal Blow Dealt by Whisky Flask," "A Negro Killed in Bloody Encounter." On December 23, 1906, a writer for the *Birmingham Age-Herald* reported that police "came upon one of the most horrible and bloody scenes that has ever been known to the local force." They discovered Albert Gray, a laborer, at his home lying on the floor "cold in death" with his jugular vein cut out and a puncture wound through the heart. "There was hardly a spot on the floor of the two rooms that was not covered with blood," an observer noted. "It was also splattered over the walls and ceiling."

Had he lived that long, even old Devil John Jones might have found the level of violence beyond the norms of Scots-Irish frontier life. Bessemer's murder rate was one of the highest in the country, and the victims were often innocent citizens who happened to stroll by when the bullets commenced to flying.

TEMPERANCE REFORMERS BELIEVED they had the answer to the high crime rates in Bessemer and Birmingham: shut down the saloons, and Satan shall be subdued. Saloons, one overzealous Alabamian argued in 1907, resulted in crime, poverty, insanity, and murders; they brutalized manhood, degraded womanhood, and resulted in suffering childhood. But closing the saloons would bring about prosperous homes, contented wives, joyful mothers, happy children, useful men, peaceful communities, prosperous businesses, reduced crime, and fewer criminals. With Bessemer as the example, it would be hard to argue with their assessment.

Following a 1907 vote in favor of countywide prohibition, these reformers succeeded in restricting legal alcohol sales in Alabama, but they failed to end the heavy consumption of liquor in the state, especially in Bessemer. "Blind Tigers," "Blind Pigs," roadhouses, speakeasies, and shot houses served illegal hooch at locations in or near the Marvel City. Some locals became walking "Blind Tigers" and served up liquor hidden in traveling bags, in fruit crates, or inside an overcoat or bathrobe. One Bessemer police officer described one of these dispensaries:

> Weaving along the sidewalk came an apparition presaging trouble and dressed in an old bath robe designed for someone several sizes larger, its onetime blue expanse unacquainted with soap and water, oversized bedroom slippers, and a once gay-colored handkerchief around her head. Wrinkled, toothless, always repulsive looking, old Rachel was coming . . . talking to herself. Rachel made a precarious living selling a concoction of canned heat, denatured alcohol, embalming fluid, and any other ill-smelling liquid that came to hand, which she called whiskey. Proving that she believed her sales talk, Rachel had become her own best customer.

Old Rachel had plenty of help in meeting the demand of the alcohol-deprived citizens, as moonshiners produced increasing quantities of corn liquor, which one Bessemer citizen described as some of "the best made" in the United States.

With easy access to such resources, the closing of Bessemer's saloons also had little effect on the area's crime, violence, and debauchery. In 1911, Jefferson County citizens voted to repeal prohibition and reopen the saloons. The next year, as Bessemer celebrated its twenty-fifth birthday, the editor of the *Weekly* complained that the city was still "one of the most lawless" in the South. "The precentage [*sic*] of shootings and killings being notably high has long been acknowledged even by the most loyal citizens and also that this is due largely to the indiscriminate carrying of firearms."

To mention just one example: in 1912 Will Smith, a black man accused of shooting a Bessemer police officer, barricaded himself in the home of a white resident, J. G. Bruce. More than 150 armed whites from all over town surrounded the house and unleashed a "rain of bullets" into the residence. When the bloody Smith appeared on the back porch, the *Weekly* reported, "a perfect fusillade of shots followed and he fell and a rush was made on him and his body was hauled out. . . . The negro . . . was an ugly dirty looking specimen about 30 or 35." In 1916, Police Chief Thomas Benjamin Wallace died of a gunshot wound as he and Bessemer deputies wrestled with a farmer who resisted arrest.

During the 1920s, a booming economy and more workers living in close proximity led to more murders and more demands for whiskey— even with nationwide prohibition throughout the decade. When the economy went bust in the 1930s, the culture of violence intensified further. The Great Depression brought strikes and other direct challenges to the economic status quo from those seeking better wages, collective bargaining, union recognition, and voting rights for working-class whites and blacks. On the left, Communist Party officials and labor union organizers seized upon the local economic downturn to try to expand support among workers. "The time was ripe," one laborer later recalled, "for organizations to rise up and struggle against oppressive conditions."

But such efforts brought down a reign of terror. Officials of U.S. Steel's Tennessee Coal and Iron division (TCI) brought in strikebreakers and hired gunhands, while Alabama governor Benjamin Meek Miller deployed the National Guard to repress the rebellion and restore order and stability. On Red Mountain, one Bessemer resident recalled, "it was just like a battleground sometimes. And they would have to send the guards to quell them." The ACLU reported that repression and violence in the area was "continuous, not incidental." To maintain the status quo, one observer noted, the steel industry in the area "fostered a climate of opinion in which violence against radicals flourished."

Intimidation took various forms. Sheriff's deputies and city police raided homes and enforced an antisedition law that made it a crime to "possess more than one copy of any material advocating overthrow of the government." Urban vigilantes, like the Ku Klux Klan, resorted to kidnappings, beatings, bombings, floggings, and shootings in defense of the "existing order." Any perceived threat to the racial and economic establishment compelled this new southern vigilantism. Steel company officials, to maximize profits, needed a docile black workforce that would accept low pay and long hours without question. Enforcing racial codes and strict company rules through violence kept blacks in a subservient role and separate from whites. Vigilantism in Alabama had a long tradition stretching back to the frontier days of Devil John Jones and other rough-hewn men who enforced their own laws in preservation of the status quo.

Many whites in Bessemer, as in other areas of the South, saw violence as the first, and best, method to preserve regional traditions and the southern way of life. "From a generally narrow concern with the classic frontier problems of horse thieves and counterfeiters," wrote a keen observer of the southern scene, "vigilantism broadened its scope to include a variety of targets connected with the tension of the new America: Catholics, Jews, Negroes, immigrants, laboring men and labor leaders, political radicals, advocates of civil liberties, and nonconformists in general." When one union organizer complained about the violence and extralegal activities, a lawyer in the Bessemer circuit solicitor's office told him, "I know it's not constitutional, but some things are laws that are not constitutional. That's the way we do [things] in Bessemer."

The Bessemer Klavern of the Ku Klux Klan was one of the largest in the South—so powerful that they erected this sign at the Bessemer city limits in 1959.

3

"THESE WHITE FOLKS
WILL KILL YOU"

CALIPH WASHINGTON'S MIND was elsewhere. As he drove down South Bessemer Road just after midnight on Friday, July 12, 1957, his thoughts drifted to the evening's fun with a pretty young woman from Birmingham. Several hours earlier, he borrowed his father's shiny two-tone, crystal-green-metallic-over-mist-green 1950 Chevrolet Styleline sedan to take his buddy Robert Shields on a double date with sisters Mary and Birdie Robinson. Washington left his parents' home in northern Bessemer about 4:30 p.m. and drove the five miles to Shields's house in an area of southwestern Birmingham called Travellick. Shields climbed into the car, and the duo drove to pick up the Robinson sisters, who lived on Avenue T in the smoggy industrial suburb of Ensley.

With no particular place to go, the four teenagers (Mary paired with Washington and Birdie with Shields) spent the evening engaged in aimless fun and distraction: laughing, talking, and driving. They stopped at the Dairy Frost in Smithfield in northwestern Birmingham for ice cream; paid a call on the sisters' aunt in Bessemer; then dropped in on Washington's older brother George, who lived nearby. On the way back to Ensley, the quartet stopped at Grant Judkins's Blue Gardenia nightclub in Brighton for sandwiches, Cokes, and dancing. About ten minutes before midnight, Washington and Shields dropped the girls off at their Ensley home and drove back to Travellick.

In front of Shields's house on Park Avenue Southwest, the teenagers chatted about the girls. Washington seemed to be smitten by Mary Robinson. "I need to see her again," he told Shields. "I really do like her." Shields stepped out of the car and told his dreamy-eyed friend to be careful while driving home that time of night. It was late, after midnight, and the seventeen-year-old promised his mama that he would be home at a decent hour. Washington supposed that she might make a fuss about the time, so he decided to spend the night with his brother George in southern Bessemer.

But as he drove the Chevrolet down the hill from Shields's house, Washington's mind focused mostly on the young lady, and at the time little else mattered. He turned left onto near-deserted South Bessemer Road and headed west toward home. He rested his elbow out the window and tapped his fingers on the steering wheel in rhythm with the R&B music on the radio. A few late cars drifted by as he drove down the dimly lit road. Traveling southwest, Washington soon crossed from Birmingham into the small municipality of Brownville and then along the narrow path through Lipscomb. In 1957, Lipscomb was virtually all white, and blacks from outside the cloistered village were expected, as one observer later noted, "to come through but not stop." This vengeful spirit was about to intersect with the life of Caliph Washington.

FEWER THAN THREE thousand people lived in Lipscomb's three square miles. A quiet mining village once known as East End, the insulated town grew up around the old Lipscomb Station stop on the Birmingham-to-Bessemer dummy train line. In the 1920s, Lipscomb was along the original 1,696-mile U.S. Highway 11 route that stretched from Rouses Point, New York, to New Orleans, Louisiana. On its thirteen-mile run from Birmingham to Bessemer, U.S. 11 followed a snaking, narrow path along the northern base of Red Mountain and crossed a dozen or more heavily used railroad lines—delays and police speed traps were just around any curve of this dangerous road.

Soon after the route opened in 1927, Alabama highway officials designed plans to build a new road, patterned after the German Auto-bahn, to connect Jefferson County's two largest cities. The result was a straight and wide four-lane road that local residents dubbed the "Bes-semer Super Highway." With the addition of streetlights in 1940, locals boasted that this super road was the longest "white way" east of the Rocky Mountains. It seemed an apt description when a few years later, the Ku Klux Klan erected a welcome sign at the city limits that showed a horse-riding, hooded Klansman holding a Confederate battle flag. When the Bessemer Ministerial Association refused to demand the removal of the sign, the president of the organization quit in protest and proclaimed that "erecting that sign was an un-Christian act that pierced the heart of every Negro who saw it." That was but one of the many sins being committed up and down what some locals began referring to as the "Klan Highway."

Lipscomb officials fought to keep Bessemer's un-Christian acts from corrupting their tiny kingdom. One evening, police officers discovered a car just inside Lipscomb's city limits with an inebriated woman passed out in the front seat. They knew that she had her fill of sin in Bessemer, so the lawmen pushed the car a few feet across the city line and reported the inci-dent to the Bessemer Police Department. When they arrived, Bessemer officers shoved the car into Lipscomb and called back and told Lipscomb police to deal with the drunk. According to one officer, this went back and forth for quite a while until the woman sobered up and drove off.

Lipscomb's ministers preached often on sin and prayed to the Lord to keep pure the souls of the city's residents. "Lord, thank you for this little town of Lipscomb," a pastor prayed one evening. "Thank you Lord, that we don't have no gambling joints in Lipscomb. And thank you Lord that we don't have no bawdy houses in Lipscomb, and Lord thank you that we don't have no beer joints in Lipscomb. Lord thank you that we don't have no dance halls in Lipscomb." In the congregation, one churchgoer mumbled in response, "Lord, we ain't got nothing."

By the early 1950s, Lipscomb had plenty of nothing. The iron ore mines had shut down, businesses closed, families moved, and the town slipped into a quiet despair. Lipscomb's limited tax base provided residents with only a few poorly funded community services: a meager street and sanitation department, a crew of dedicated volunteer firefighters, and a seedy group of police officers. Low pay, political infighting, no training, and few opportunities for advancement gave the police force a poor reputation and led to consistent turnover in personnel.

In 1952, Mayor Roland F. Owen fired Police Chief Melvin Little without approval of the city council and with no explanation. "I'm not obligated to explain unless I want to," Owen said at the time, "and I don't want to." Chief Little later claimed that the mayor disliked him because he refused to drive Owen around in a Lipscomb police car "like a taxi-cab." Less than a year later, Owen forced Little's replacement, Robert L. Payne, to resign for what the former chief called pure politics. "Unfair as it may be," Payne said, "I had no recourse other than to fulfill his demands. I have been, am at present, and will be in the future, on the opposite side of the political fence from him."

Within weeks of the resignation, Owen hired three new policemen (James Wilson, John Henderson, and Frank Oakley) and appointed R. C. Douglas as chief—all in violation of city law that required approval by the city council. By the end of 1953, all four resigned after being charged with negligence in the death of a prisoner, Vera Fikes Teer, who was found unconscious outside a Lipscomb nightspot and thrown in jail by the policemen. The next morning, officers found Teer dead in her cell. An autopsy revealed that the woman's unconscious condition, and later death, was a result of a severe blow to the head and not alcohol. Bessemer deputy coroner T. J. McCollom said there was "no question" of the officers' negligence. "They should have sent her to the hospital or had a doctor examine her," he added.

In 1957, Thurman P. Avery, a slow-talking Alabamian with ties to the Ku Klux Klan, served as Lipscomb's police chief. On July 11, Avery received an anonymous tip: a fearless, high-speed, "devil-driving" whiskey runner in a souped-up coupe equipped with a racing motor, heavy springs, and extra tanks for whiskey storage would deliver a carload of moonshine to a house near the intersection of Thirty-third Street and

South Bessemer Road, on the dividing line between Lipscomb and Bessemer, in the shot house haven once known as Whiskeytown.

By 1956, the production, transportation, and consumption of illegal whiskey reemerged as a major law enforcement problem. The seizure of moonshine stills in Alabama and other southern states was approaching Prohibition-era levels. Folks with a taste for hooch could purchase a gallon for $3 to $4 and avoid the whopping $10.50-a-gallon federal whiskey tax and the always increasing state taxes. Most thirsty souls ignored the danger of moonshine poisoning from lead, methyl alcohol, or paint thinner. "If death does not occur from such exposure," author Jess Carr wrote, "blindness is often the result."

In spite of the dangers, the bargain prices were too great a temptation to switch to the more refined store-bought brands. After World War II, many Alabama shiners moved stills out of the rural deep woods and set up operations in secluded areas near Bessemer to better serve an urban-industrial clientele. During the 1950s, law enforcement officials estimated that moonshine accounted for over 50 percent of all alcohol consumption. In the Bessemer area, some politicians and lawmen ignored bootlegging activities, so those involved in selling and transporting white lightning made big profits. Chief Avery and his partner, James Barney "Cowboy" Clark, hoped to arrest one of these moonshine runners as he made a delivery to a clandestine shot house.

Earlier that July evening, Cowboy Clark dressed for work at his modest home on Avenue F in Lipscomb. His shift began at 5 p.m. He wore his stiffly starched and crisply pressed summer police uniform: a short-sleeve midnight blue shirt and matching long trousers. Once dressed, Clark drove over to police headquarters in patrol car number thirteen—a late model, black Ford Fairlane sedan with a thundering V-8 engine. A Lipscomb patrolman for just a few months, Cowboy was Thurman Avery's hometown buddy from the untempered mining town of Searles, southwest of Bessemer, in northern Tuscaloosa County. At the time of his hiring, Clark worked for cigar-chomping G. W. Burroughs as a grease-monkey mechanic and a fill-'er-up attendant at a Gulf gas station on the Bessemer Super Highway.

A likable, backslapping country boy with a fourth-grade education,

Clark was a tall, fleshy thirty-seven-year-old with dark blond hair, lubricated and combed in an Elvis Presley wave, and overgrown buckteeth with a wide-cut gap between the two front ones. The aptly nicknamed Cowboy had an affinity for horses, cowboy boots, gaudy Texas belt buckles, and sweat-stained Gene Autry Stetsons. According to his sister, Dorothy, his wide-ranging talent and big-toothed grin were legendary: He could rope a steer, bull-whip a cigarette into two pieces from the lips of some fearless soul, shoot buzzing flies from forty yards away, and sing a mournful ballad about laying to rest a poor cowpoke beneath the lone prairie—all skills that might help him capture the imagination of a sin-loaded honky-tonk girl.

A lonesome drifter right out of one of his ballads, Clark learned his western skills and earned his nickname during the Depression as a young circus performer, doing trick pony riding, fancy roping and lassoing, and skillful six-gun shooting. Clark sent most of the money he earned back home to his impoverished, widowed, arthritis-crippled, stroke-ridden mother and his two fatherless siblings. When he quit the circus and came back to Alabama to work as a laborer for the Works Progress Administration (WPA) digging ditches for fifty cents a day, Cowboy also brought an old flat-top guitar and began singing sad songs to the hardworking white folks who frequented dimly lit honky-tonks—with swinging doors, barstools, and sawdust floors—in and around Tuscaloosa and Bessemer. "He came by it naturally," Dorothy later remembered. "He just picked that thing up, learned a few chords, and went on." In those smoke-filled joints, Clark earned a meager living singing traditional cowboy ballads and imitating the popular western performers of his day, including Tex Ritter, Gene Autry, Rex Allen, Roy Rogers, and Marty Robbins.

Throughout the 1940s and 1950s, Cowboy Clark worked all day as a laborer, mechanic, carpenter, or some other hands-on job (he never stayed in one place too long), and at night he sang those lonesome western ballads, including one of his favorites, "The Cowboy's Lament (Streets of Laredo)," which included the lyrics:

I spied a poor cowboy wrapped up in white linen,
Wrapped in white linen as cold as the clay.

"I see by your outfit that you are a cowboy."
These words he did say as I boldly stepped by.
"Come sit down beside me and hear my sad story
I'm shot in the breast and I know I must die."

The good looks and bravado of this singing cowboy attracted the attention of several fun-loving honky-tonk angels, and in 1941, Cowboy began a stormy five-year marriage to Gladys Josephine Green that ended in divorce in 1946. Soon afterward he married an overbearing divorcee, Linann Elledge Orr. They divorced in January 1957.

When Thurman Avery asked Cowboy Clark to join the Lipscomb police force in 1956, he seemed to find the perfect job to fit his western persona. Clark drove to the Bank Pawn Shop (so named because the building once housed the Citizens Bank) in downtown Bessemer and purchased a new Smith and Wesson Combat Masterpiece: a nickel-plated, pearl-handled, .38-caliber revolver with a reputation for deadly accuracy. The total cost was $88.05, which he would pay in weekly installments, and it included a leather "quick-draw" holster for prominent display. Everyone around town, at least the white folks, seemed to like Clark, and he often showed off his gun-twirling skills to Lipscomb's young and old alike.

Sometime after he became an officer in Lipscomb, Clark stopped a vivacious twenty-seven-year-old raven-haired widow, Florence Hobson Talley, for speeding through his territory. When she went to city hall to pay her fine, Talley, the mother of two young daughters, handed the clerk her money and left a note with her telephone number for the lawman who gave her a ticket. The two began a whirlwind courtship and were married within days of his divorce in January 1957. During the summer of that year, Cowboy drove his new family up to Toledo, Ohio, to visit his mother, brother, and sister, who all moved north in search of a better life.

Always the performer, Clark wanted to show off his pretty young wife, his new car, and his crisp, pristine lawman's clothes, with badge and gun. "Oh, he always loved to dress immaculate and look just perfect," his sister Dorothy later recalled, but that day when he modeled his new uniform and twirled his guns, a foreboding spirit washed over her and she began to cry. She ran to the bathroom to hide her tears. Clark found her sobbing and asked, "What's the matter with you?" She responded, "Oh Barney, I'll never see you alive again. I just know it." He told her that she was just being silly.

Clark was back at work from his vacation in Ohio just a few days when Chief Avery told him about the bootlegger stakeout. The assignment had ominous and personal undertones for Cowboy. His late father, Dick Clark, was a mean-spirited, no-count moonshiner who lived near the murky waters of the Black Warrior River in the far western reaches of Jefferson County. Born in 1893, in the nearby mining town of Adger (so named for Andrew Moffett Adger, the secretary and treasurer for the DeBardeleben Coal and Iron Company), Dick Clark worked for several years as a coal miner and supported his wife Lula Luella Townson, a pious, spirit-filled Pentecostal Holiness believer, and three children. But the long hours, low pay, and dungeon-dark work were too much for him. He began moonshining, quit mining, and ran afoul of the law, gamblers, and his devout wife.

The stiff-necked Lula kicked him out of the house soon after Dorothy's birth, and Dick took up residence with a like-minded river woman in a handcrafted shiner's shack on the banks of one of the tributaries of the Black Warrior. The pair made and sold corn liquor for several years, until Dick met an untimely death from drinking a pint of his own ill-brewed poison whiskey. His brothers drove a logging truck down to his shanty, loaded Dick's body into the back, and hauled his pickled corpse to the old family home in Adger; there the Clark women groomed and dressed him in clean clothes, while the menfolk made a coffin out of cedar. They laid him to rest in an unmarked grave in the Adger cemetery.

CLARK AND AVERY had whiskey on their minds that evening in July 1957. As they approached their destination, the houses along the street became cheaper and meaner, but all appeared quiet. Cowboy Clark stopped the patrol car in the curve above Thirty-third Street, where the pair had a clear view in every direction. He shut off the engine and turned off the lights. Where Avery and Clark were sitting, they could see that two corners of the intersection were empty neglected lots with tall weeds growing. Across the road on the southeastern corner was a dried-out, brown, $20-a-month rental house with unlevel floors, out-of-sort windows, a sagging roof, a leaning chimney, and a chicken coop in the backyard. Across Thirty-Third Street was a five-room bungalow with a poor roof and no bathroom facilities that rented for $12 a month.

Avery grew restless and decided to take a look around the area on foot, breaking a basic rule of a two-member surveillance team: stick together. "Do not split up a team," one investigator wrote in 1951. "They are more effective both in observation and in apprehending the criminal when working together." Avery opened the car door. As he stood, he reached down and grabbed a flashlight. He closed the door and leaned through the open window in front of Clark and spoke in a low voice: "You wait here. If you see anything, honk the horn three times."

With a prominent limp in his left leg from a coal mining accident in Searles, Avery slowly wandered up the steep hill, around the sharp curve, and disappeared behind the houses. Avery peered around corners and shined his meager light into the dark shadows of the neighborhood. A few minutes later, the chief heard a car crank and speed off. He heard no siren, and at the time, he thought nothing of it. He continued looking for the shot house and the whiskey runners for another thirty minutes, before walking back to wait with Clark again.

As Avery walked down to the bottom of the hill, he realized that the patrol car was gone and that the sound of the speeding car he heard earlier was Clark. The chief stood in the middle of the street unsure where to go. After a few moments of indecision, a befuddled Avery began searching for a telephone to contact the dispatcher. Lipscomb shared the radio frequency with Bessemer, and Avery hoped the dispatcher on duty that evening, Sergeant H. E. Williamson, could reach Clark and send him back to Thirty-Third Street.

A half hour before, as Cowboy Clark began pursuit of the two-tone Chevy, he lifted the microphone from the hook on the dashboard and reported his position on Dartmouth Avenue (South Bessemer Road) and Twenty-Ninth Street coming into Bessemer city limits. Williamson acknowledged Clark's radio transmission.

CALIPH WASHINGTON GLANCED in his rearview mirror and saw a car fall in behind him with bright round headlights glowing. He looked back at it without much interest, until the lights suddenly grew larger as the car closed in on his bumper. The young man stepped on the gas, but the other car matched his speed. He grew concerned.

Violent reprisals against blacks in the area were an ever-present danger, especially in the late 1950s. In the wake of an economic downturn in heavy industry following World War II and the U.S. Supreme Court's attack on the foundation of segregation in its *Brown v. Board of Education* decisions in 1954 and 1955, many working class whites in and around Bessemer, and throughout the South, felt threatened and pushed to the margins of society. With the "southern way of life" and the industrial economy collapsing around them, white supremacist organizations like the Ku Klux Klan provided these whites an opportunity to vent their "frustration and insecurity" through ritual and violence. Bessemer's Klan Klavern was large, powerful, and particularly violent. The Klan's "repressive influence" seemed omnipresent, not just in its overt expressions of violence but also in the terror engendered in the knowledge that the Klan's distinct form of vigilante justice, lynching, "lurked around every corner." With so many Bessemer law enforcement officials also members of the Klan, the hidden hands of terror and law enforcement were one and the same.

Washington understood this as he studied the car in the rearview mirror. No red lights flashed; no siren wailed. This was not a police car, he assured himself. He had done nothing wrong. Still, he didn't like the look of it, because blacks lived, as historian Pete Daniel observed, "in a world of uncertainty, bound to careful behavior that still did not guarantee safety." Then Washington heard the crack of gunshots and the sound of bullets whizzing by his open window. Someone was shooting at his car, but who? "It scared me," Caliph later recalled. "The first thing I thought was, Ku Klux Klan—some night gang or something—somebody after me." He stomped on the accelerator, and the straight-six Chevy lurched forward as it gained speed. The other car stayed right on its tail.

While fear told Caliph Washington that Klan hoodlums were on his bumper, Cowboy Clark's bravado informed him that he was tailgating a moonshine whiskey runner in a two-tone 1950 Chevrolet. For reasons still unknown, perhaps in his excitement, he failed to switch on his siren.

Washington, looking in his rearview and side mirrors, could see nothing but bright round headlights. He sped down Dartmouth Avenue, a broad street lined mostly with large, well-built homes occupied by the city's elite. At Sixteenth Street, he took a hard left. His tires squealed as he rounded the corner and drove up the hill in the direction of his brother's house.

Clark, on his bumper, yelled into the microphone where he thought his location was. Several Bessemer patrolmen, including A. J. Wood and his partner, J. R. Pace, heard Clark's radio transmissions. Officer Wood thought Clark was lost. "He didn't know the city streets too well." Regardless, Wood and Pace, in patrol car number eight, were writing a speeding ticket almost thirty blocks away, on the north side of Bessemer near the intersection of Fourteenth Avenue and Thirteenth Street. "It is customary on a call coming in like that," Wood explained, "where they are chasing a car, we all give assistance without being asked." Wood made a U-turn and began traveling at a high rate of speed southeast toward the chase.

Caliph tried to elude the car on his tail. He swung the big car wildly as he took a hard right on Exeter Avenue and then a quick right on Short Fifteenth Street. He sped past the shotgun shack where he once lived. "I wasn't going to stop," Caliph later recalled. "I couldn't see nobody. All I could see was a bright light." He turned right on unpaved Dartmouth Alley and kicked up a cloud of dust on his way back to Sixteenth Street, where he turned right and then right again on Exeter and back down to Short Fifteenth Street. This time he honked the horn as he drove through the neighborhood. "I wanted people to come out," he remembered. "In that neighborhood down there, there was some bad black people, and they didn't take nothing off of nobody. I was honking the horn to get them woke up. I knew they would come out and have something to protect themselves with."

After passing by two or three times, he got back on Sixteenth Street and sped up the steep grade to Fairfax Avenue and took a right. Just before the Atlantic Coast railway underpass at Fourteenth Street, he took a fast right on to the unpaved Exeter Alley. Halfway up the alley, he looked in his mirrors again, and through a cloud of dust he saw a red light revolving on top of the car. He pulled hard to the left, slammed on his brakes, and came to a stop against a chinaberry tree near the corner of John Adams's house at 1502 Exeter Alley.

JOHN ADAMS WAS a sound sleeper. A mover for Continental Van Lines, he worked ten- to twelve-hour days beginning at 6 a.m. "We moves [sic] everywhere," Adams once said. "There ain't no telling where we'll be if we are on the job." That July night, Adams pushed his full-size bed next to the open, front bedroom window, hoping to gain some relief from the sweat-soaking heat wave. He lived in one side of a dried-up old double tenant house, with rotten pine siding and a steep, rusted tin roof. Located at 1502 Exeter Alley in Bessemer, Adams shared his side of the shack with his longtime live-in girlfriend, Mary Davidson.

That evening, the sound of car engines and metal hitting wood jolted him from a deep sleep. Never leaving his bed, the groggy Adams peered out the window. The street was aglow from two cars' headlights and a red police light atop one of the cars turning around and around. The other car had a bent chrome bumper that had peeled the bark off the trunk of the chinaberry tree growing at the corner of the house near his bedroom window. That summer, Adams's mature chinaberry looked like a giant umbrella with yellowish-green leaves, a thick, long, sturdy hardwood trunk, and a hearty root system—the kind of tree that wouldn't budge when hit by a two-ton, chrome-laden 1950 Chevrolet.

Adams laid his head on the windowsill and watched sleepy-eyed as Cowboy Clark stomped up to the other car and in a hard voice yelled, "Get out, boy." When the driver hesitated, Clark shouted again, "Get out, boy." The car door opened, and a young black man stood up. Adams squinted and rocked his head to and fro to make out the face. He recognized the young man standing beside the car as Caliph Washington.

Adams watched Washington and Clark standing silent and motionless. They stood less than a yard apart and stared—one imposing, pale, and erect; the other dark, tall, and lean. During these long, dragged-out moments, there were no sounds except their breathing and the thousands of unseen summer night bugs. "Them fellows didn't say nothing," Adams later recalled, no cussing and no fussing. "Didn't nary a word pass—nary a forceful word. Nothing."

Finally, Cowboy Clark told Caliph Washington to place his hands over his head. He complied, and the officer then carefully patted down the suspect. When he finished, Clark, in his usual unhurried gait, escorted Washington from the driver's side of the Chevrolet to the rear of the Lipscomb patrol car and out of Adams's prone line of sight. Two or three minutes later, Adams heard three gunshots in rapid succession—*Bam! Bam! Bam!* And like a turtle emerging from a shell, he craned his neck farther out the window to see what had happened.

Fearful, Adams was not about to get out of bed. "I didn't go," he remembered. "I say I was scairt [*sic*], and I ain't going out there. I ain't going to be in that mess. I ain't going out there."

Washington tried to get in his daddy's car and go home. From the darkness, someone yelled, "Boy, you get out. You better get from out of that car. You better get away from here. These white folks will kill you." Caliph left the driver's door open and ran into the shadows, holding Cowboy Clark's pearl-handled pistol and flashlight. Adams looked for him. "I didn't see Caliph no more," Adams later recalled. "Caliph disappeared, I guess."

A FEW BLOCKS away, Bessemer policemen Wood and Pace heard a distorted radio call from Cowboy Clark in patrol car number thirteen. "We weren't able to understand what he was saying," Wood remembered. "He was shouting in the mic. Apparently he had it too close to his mouth." Clark never radioed his position, leaving Bessemer patrolmen searching the Dartmouth area for him. Clark made one last radio transmission.

"He told us that he'd been shot in the stomach and then he groaned," Wood said.

Wood and Pace drove the patrol car straight up Fourteenth Street, crossing Clarendon, Dartmouth, Exeter, and Fairfax Avenues; they turned left onto Fairfax and left again on Sixteenth Street and drove back down the alphabet and turned left on Dartmouth. As they crossed Fifteenth Street, Pace thought he saw something to his left down an unpaved alley. Wood made a U-turn and turned right onto the dirt street. Through a veil of thin red dust clinging to the muggy summer air, the officers spotted a flashing red light reflecting off of a whitewashed cinder-block building. It was car number thirteen.

It took almost twenty minutes for Wood and Pace to locate Clark's patrol car at the 1500 block of Exeter Alley. As they slowly drove up the narrow path, headlights shining, the duo spotted Cowboy Clark on the dirt roadway kneeling like a drunkard in prayer. He was on the passenger side of the car—his head and left arm resting on the vinyl-covered front bench seat and the microphone a hand-length away. Wood stopped the car, radioed their position, and both officers rushed over to Clark. "He was in extreme pain," Wood later remembered. "His legs were continuously thrashing—just like a chicken that had been killed. We could hardly hold him."

Clark tried to say something to Wood and Pace, but they couldn't make out his pained, mumbled words. The two officers took a removable seat cushion and a long piece of cardboard from Clark's car and placed them in the dirt next to the open door. As if in slow motion, they eased Clark onto the makeshift pallet, then knelt beside him and spoke comforting words.

From his crouched position, Wood looked through the dusty haze illuminated only by the glow of headlights and saw a crowd of black faces gathered in the shadows, some standing on John Adams's front porch. Within a few minutes, an ambulance and several other Bessemer police cars arrived on the scene. The ambulance driver and officers Pace and Wood helped place Clark on a stretcher and load him into the vehicle. The ambulance rushed off, with Pace and Wood following behind in their patrol car, to Bessemer General Hospital—a poorly equipped, outdated, and understaffed facility that looked more like a run-down three-story apartment building than a hospital.

One of the nurses on duty that night in the emergency room was Dorothy Burroughs, the wife of G. W., Clark's former employer at the Gulf gas station. When the ambulance crew rolled the gurney with Clark's blood-soaked body into one of the cramped examination rooms, the ER doctor declared him dead on arrival. Nurse Burroughs covered his body with a white sheet and went to the nearest phone and dialed Hamilton 5-3925. She said to her husband as he answered: "G. W., Cowboy Clark is laying up here dead at the hospital. Someone shot him down." Just like in the lyrics of "The Cowboy's Lament," Cowboy Clark had passed on:

> Go bring me a cup, a cup of cold water,
> To cool my parched lips," the cowboy said;
> Before I turned, the spirit had left him
> And gone to its Giver—the cowboy was dead.

Across town, Caliph Washington was still running in the darkness. He dashed through the cornfield behind John Adams's house, scaled a chicken-wire fence, and jumped into the drainage ditch where Fifteenth Street came to an abrupt dead end. He climbed out of the ditch near Exeter Avenue, ran to Sixteenth Street, and climbed the steep grade to Brickyard Hill. At some point in the early morning hours, he slipped back down the hill and traveled north to the area around the Pullman Train Car Plant and the home of his acquaintance Elijah Honeycutt, who lived at 2803 Arlington Avenue. Between 2 and 2:30 a.m., Washington knocked on the screen door and awakened Honeycutt and his girlfriend, Rosie Merritt.

"Who is it?" a groggy Honeycutt yelled. "Caliph," a voice answered. "Caliph who?" he asked.

"Caliph Washington."

Honeycutt sat on the side of the bed for a few minutes, yawning and rubbing his eyes. When he opened the door, the young man asked, "Don't you remember me?" He told him yes and asked what was wrong.

Washington explained that his car had broken down, and he needed a ride over to Travellick. Honeycutt and his girlfriend dressed and drove Caliph over to the western edge of Birmingham. It all seemed like a dream for the foggy-minded Honeycutt, and he later barely remembered driving him. "Well, we left there and went straight over the hill there," he recalled. "We went around and down one road, and I don't know, we come up on the one and then we done come up the other road."

When they got up to a deserted area of Travellick, Honeycutt pulled the car over at the entrance to a dark dirt road heading up along the slopes of Red Mountain. Washington said, "I'll get out here." He thanked them for the ride and told the couple, "I'll see you," and disappeared into the darkness.

Washington hid in the dense, kudzu-infested woods near the Wenonah Iron Ore Mines that clung to the side of the mountain. July in Alabama was no time to be sleeping out in the woods. The night was warm, humid, and clear; a waning moon cast shadows through the tall pines and hardwood trees; no comforting wind could be found; countless bugs made a symphony of sounds. All this only added to the horror of Washington's hellish quandary. He was scared, confused, and alone. He spent a fitful night going over and over, again and again, the deadly events of just a few hours before. He knew not what to do.

At some point during the day that Friday, he hiked out of the woods and walked over to Robert Shields's house on Park Avenue. Dirty, sweaty, tired, and hungry, he knocked on the door. When Shields opened it, he saw Caliph, still wearing his pleated black dress pants and dirty white sport shirt. Caliph Washington recounted the entire incident to a stunned Robert Shields. "I need your help," he meekly asked. Shields and his mother gave the weary young man two ham sandwiches and a clean shirt. Washington then walked back in the Wenonah woods and hid the rest of the day.

CALIPH WASHINGTON WAS not the only American hiding that Friday, July 12, 1957. Across the country, citizens in more than one hundred cities prepared to take shelter during Operation Alert 1957, the annual program for preparing citizens and government for the "real thing"—

an "imaginary torrent of nuclear death and destruction." Near 10 a.m. that morning, civil defense sirens echoed throughout Birmingham and Bessemer, warning of an immediate nuclear attack. Enemy planes—presumably Soviet—were flying south from Canada and carrying hydrogen bombs five times more powerful than the one that had hit Hiroshima almost twelve years before. Civil defense officials warned citizens to take cover immediately. Washington, undoubtedly, heard the sirens.

At 1:58 p.m. the imaginary bomb "exploded" at the intersection of Vanderbilt Road and the Southern Railroad Tracks in North Birmingham. An Alabama newspaper reported that the "theoretical" blast "gouged out the heart of the city" by severely damaging buildings and leaving the streets impassible. The faux nuclear holocaust rained down "a shower of death-dealing radioactive particles," civil defense officials supposed. Yet local observers predicted the death of only 2,100 people, the injury of 11,000 more, and the survival of over 80 percent of the population—exaggerated numbers for an imaginary scenario to protect the public from the harsh realities of a nuclear war.

The next day, Saturday morning, staying alive remained Caliph Washington's top priority. He walked to a small grocery store and bought a pack of cigarettes, a cold drink, a block of cheese, and a slice of cake. Just outside the door was a newspaper rack stuffed with the morning's *Post-Herald*. If the fugitive had stopped to look at the paper, he would have seen a half-page spread devoted to James B. "Cowboy" Clark and his death. Large photographs showed the crime scene and investigators sifting through evidence. A picture of Cowboy Clark revealed a broad somber face, a small thick-lipped mouth, a prominent jaw, cold dark eyes, and a too-tight collar on his police uniform. Just below was Caliph Washington's picture, an unflattering police mug shot from 1955 with his head in bandages. To the right of Clark's and Washington's photos was a heart-tugging picture of Clark's sorrowful widow and his two fatherless stepdaughters.

The story of the incident was uncomplicated. Early Friday morning, James Clark had been shot "near the heart" and found dying alongside his patrol car in Bessemer. The shooting had taken place in the 1500 block of Exeter Alley in Bessemer. Residents of the community told police they heard cars speeding around the area before they heard three gunshots. An intensive manhunt was under way for a Negro in connection with the officer's fatal shooting. The fugitive was Caliph Washington, and Bessemer police warned that the suspect was armed and dangerous.

That Saturday evening, Washington once again walked down to Robert Shields's house. He asked Shields's stepfather, Tommy Lee Silmon, to drive him to his cousin's house in Adamsville, a small municipality on the Memphis Highway northwest of Birmingham. "What kind of trouble you in?" Silmon asked, and Caliph recounted the incident with the police officer. He pulled a shiny nickel-plated pistol from a brown paper sack and said, "That was the police's gun."

Silmon looked at the gun and then glared at Caliph and said, "That officer is dead."

Washington sat in cold silence. He understood that a black man involved in the killing of a white man—whether by accident or not—would bring a swift and harsh reprisal in the Jim Crow South. Washington's own living memory bespoke the horrors of violating the code of racial justice. Almost all black families in the South, an observer noted, had a story of an ancestor who "come up missing" and "vanished into that empty place—the rural crossroads or rail siding, the bayou or jail cell—where the white South at times sought to resolve its most intractable 'problem.'" When Washington was a little boy, as the family told the story, a maternal uncle left home one evening bound for a community dance. He never returned. At the hands of persons unknown, he was chained to railroad tracks along an isolated stretch of the Alabama Great Southern Railroad. When an AGS locomotive came roaring out of Meridian, Mississippi, bound for Birmingham and then on to Chattanooga, the giant iron wheels sliced his body into tiny pieces.

Caliph Washington feared an equally violent death from Bessemer vigilantes. He had to get out. He had to put distance between himself and the brutal white establishment in Bessemer. "I left," he later recalled, "because I knew what they would probably do." He decided that his only opportunity for freedom and safety was to leave Alabama and get to his brother Wilbert in Albuquerque, New Mexico. But how? He needed help and his options were few.

Washington again asked Silmon to drive him to Adamsville. He said no. "I'm too drunk," he told Caliph. Silmon had been drinking most of the day, and the short, wiry man could not hold his liquor. "I was scared to go that far away," he later explained. "You see, my tires wasn't no good, and then I was drinking anyway. When I am drinking, I don't drive my own car."

Washington and Silmon both later claimed that a stranger drove the pair out to Adamsville in a late-model Ford sedan. According to their account, when Silmon refused to give Washington a ride, the fugitive walked out of Silmon's house and stood on the front porch. As he contemplated his predicament, he claimed that he spotted a man working under the hood of a Ford sedan. "I don't know this fellow's name," Caliph later recalled. "I seen him up the road there and I done asked him" to drive me to Adamsville. He offered to pay for the ride, and the two men climbed into the car and drove down the street and picked up Silmon. The promise of more beer convinced a drunken Silmon to ride in the car. "I don't know who he was because I didn't ask him," Silmon remembered. "He asked me to come on and go up there. He knew there was a beer joint up there, and he was going to buy some more beer."

It was after 9 p.m. when they arrived at the Adamsville home of Caliph Washington's one-eyed cousin, Earnest Cross, and his wife Hattie. Cross was a seventy-two-year-old retired coal miner, and although illiterate, he spied Caliph's picture in the Saturday evening paper and realized that the lad was in serious trouble. As he exited the car, Washington handed either Silmon or the unnamed driver three dollars and said thanks and goodbye. Cousin Earnest, who saw only one person in the car besides Caliph, stood in the doorway and welcomed the troubled young man into his home as the car sped away.

Inside the house, Washington clutched a crumpled brown paper sack and recounted the incident with the policeman. As he told the story, he reached into the bag and pulled out a shiny pistol to show Cross. The old man grew concerned and his mind drifted. "I got scared then," he remembered. "I don't know hardly what he did say." When he snapped out of his haze, he realized the dangers of having the fugitive in his home. He picked up the telephone and called Fred Patterson, who lived nearby in the old Alden mining camp, and arranged for Washington to spend the night.

After taking Washington over to Patterson's house, Cross devised a plan to get his cousin out of state and on the road to New Mexico under the guise of a fishing trip, but he needed help from someone with a car more reliable than his old oil-burning Buick. Cross also believed a car filled with black men gone fishing would attract less attention than two people taking a drive; there would also be support if they ran into trouble. He turned to two reliable friends, Zack Graham, who owned a trusty dark green Studebaker, and Grover Pearson.

Early Sunday morning before 7 a.m., the men tied four fishing poles to the top of the Studebaker and placed tackle boxes in the floorboard. They drove over to Patterson's house and picked up Washington, who was clean shaven that morning and wearing a mismatched assortment of borrowed clothes. The crowning touch was a well-used, ill-fitting fuzzy gray fedora that he could pull down low over his eyes.

It was a hazy July Alabama morning as the group drove northwest on U.S. 78 toward the Mississippi border. They passed Walker County coalfields around Carbon Hill and Texas. At Guin in Marion County, they turned southwest on U.S. 278, passing through Beaverton and Crews before exiting the state after Sulligent. They entered Mississippi at Gattman, and the road turned north to Amory—a sleepy railroad town near the banks of the Tombigbee River. If traveling by rail, Amory marked the halfway point, approximately 125 miles, between Birmingham and Memphis. In 1887, when executives from the Kansas City, Memphis & Birmingham Railroad decided to build a new rail line from Memphis to Birmingham, they drew an X on the map at the exact center of the route and sold land for a new settlement named after railroad tycoon Harcourt Amory.

Around 10 a.m. on July 14, Cross, Pearson, Graham, and Washington arrived in Amory, at a time when most good citizens of the quiet hamlet were attending church services. They drove along the town's empty wide avenues and parked near the Greyhound bus stop located at a small city diner. Washington handed Grover Pearson a handful of cash, and he walked inside and bought the fugitive a bus ticket to Memphis. When the bus pulled up in front of the diner and opened its doors, Graham started the Studebaker and pulled to the curb behind the bus. Washington jumped out of the car, handed the driver the ticket, boarded the bus, and walked to the back as mandated by law and custom. The other three men left Amory, driving south toward Aberdeen.

Caliph Washington was now out of Bessemer and out of Alabama. Perhaps there was a chance he would get to New Mexico after all.

Caliph Washington arriving at the Jefferson County jail in
Bessemer—escorted by deputy sheriff Clyde Morris (*left*)
and police chief George Barron (*right*).

4

"IN BESSEMER, ANYTHING CAN HAPPEN"

MORE THAN ONE hundred law enforcement officials throughout central Alabama searched for Caliph Washington. With the assistance of federal, state, and military officials, police followed every lead on the fugitive's whereabouts. On Saturday morning, July 13, Birmingham lawmen pulled "two suspicious Negroes" off a Greyhound bus bound for Nashville and handed them over to Bessemer officials for interrogation. Birmingham and Lipscomb officers searched inbound and outbound passenger trains at the Terminal Station in downtown Birmingham. Lawmen warned the public that the suspect was dangerous and "armed with the dead officer's .38 service revolver."

Officers in the Bessemer Police Department were a ragtag crew of poorly paid, ill-trained, and hot-tempered individuals. The department's annual operating budget was only $44,270, well below that of other departments. On average, the city's thirty or so officers earned about $350 a month, less than Bessemer street and sanitation workers. In 1950, one Bessemer politician complained that the salaries of the "street department" were more than the combined salaries of the police and fire departments. "Street department employees work eight hours a day," he noted, "while employees of the Police Department have one day off every two weeks. . . . This condition should be corrected immediately." For unknown reasons, the city commission kept the pay low and the hours long.

Most policemen walked one of the three beats (upper, lower, back) in the business district. These foot patrollers often faced "untold dangers," one observer noted, because they had no radio communication with headquarters. "On the midnight shift," an officer later recalled, "there were only two locations where the beat men could contact headquarters by telephone." When a policeman made an arrest, he had to walk his prisoner several blocks to the jail, located on the second floor of city hall. If the jail warden ever had trouble with a rowdy prisoner, he could turn on a red light mounted atop a four-story building nearby and pray that one of the beat men would come to the rescue.

The officers walking the city's dimly lit streets were witness to the seedier elements of Bessemer's grim, desperate, and helpless culture. "The new cop was weary of the endless grind," one Bessemer beat walker wrote in 1934. "Last night it had been a riot among the celebrants at a birthday party. Some dusky swain had looked twice at a woman other than his own." His woman, fearful of losing her man, offered a protest in the form of "sudden, violent, and ghastly efficient flourishes" from a switchblade knife. "When the din of battle quieted enough to count the casualties," he continued, "the chocolate-colored disciple of Mae West whose overabundance of feminine allure had caused all the trouble, was out of the picture, permanently.

> Most of the others present, having allied themselves with one of the other contestants, and joined gleefully in the row, were in jail nursing sundry cuts and bruises—not to mention a healthy respect for the new cop. That queer person [the Bessemer police officer], feeling that a fight of such proportions should not be a private affair, but open to all comers of descent social position, had joined in with a baseball bat.

Those not walking the beat rode in one of Bessemer's two patrol cars. By the early 1950s, the city installed one-way radios in the cars. If an emergency call came into police headquarters, the warden would call the Birmingham Police Department and give the dispatcher the information to send out to the Bessemer officers. "The only way to determine if the call had been received," a lawman later recalled, "was when the officers . . . brought a prisoner to headquarters and informed the warden the arrest arose from their last complaint." By 1957, however, Bessemer had installed its own two-way radio equipment and hired a dispatcher.

It took little skill or training to become a police officer in Bessemer. In the 1950s, regulations required the applicant to have a high school education or equivalent, be at least twenty-one years of age, and score 70 or above on the civil service examination. In the decades before the department elevated its standards, any white man willing to bust heads and hate blacks was eligible. "If you looked right and acted right," one officer later recalled, "you got the job." Too few men, too little money, and too much crime led to constant turnover in personnel. Those with seniority were former railroad bulls or steel company security officials who practiced the same two-fisted violence they used in removing hobos from boxcars and breaking up union meetings in the mining camps. An editorial writer for the *Birmingham News* complained in the 1940s that Bessemer policemen were "so used to aiming their clubs at helpless skulls that they instinctively use them before they had time to take stock."

Violence and corruption dogged the department throughout the twentieth century. Officers considered Bessemer's majority black population a "bad lot" and justified vicious beatings in a manner so cruel, one observer noted in 1915, "that it would bring discredit and shame upon the most uncivilized and barbarous community." That same year the Birmingham-based Jefferson County circuit solicitor (the term then used for district attorney) ignored the dividing line between the two judicial districts and crossed into the Bessemer Cutoff to conduct a grand jury investigation of the racial brutality of the city police department. The high-minded Hugo Lafayette Black was the twenty-nine-year-old crusading solicitor who looked to bring law, order, and justice to a city that had never embraced those concepts. Black, who would one day serve as a U.S. senator from Alabama and as an associate justice on the U.S. Supreme Court, discovered that Bessemer police officers, who had sworn to uphold the law, chronically violated the "fundamental rights and constitutional privileges of its citizens."

Bessemer's lawmen, however, had a different perspective. Those who testified before Black's grand jury viewed beatings, whippings, and other forms of torture of black suspects as such a routine part of police duty that they saw nothing morally wrong with such treatment. "I have slapped some of them pretty hard," one officer said. "I slapped them because you can slap harder and you don't hurt your fist." Black suspects could do nothing to defend themselves, the officer admitted, but he was never cruel enough to "hit any with a pistol." Another officer described how police would beat the blacks and then whip them with a thick strap. "It was a belly-band strap," he added. "It had a buckle at one end and a strap, or 'cracker' on the other. They usually had that at hand."

Tobe McCoy was one of the few blacks brave enough to appear before the grand jury to tell the story of his violent encounter with Bessemer police officers. According to McCoy, he was out for a Sunday afternoon stroll when officers raided a gaming house near to where he was walking. One of the lawmen, an officer with a nasty reputation for shooting black suspects, took aim at McCoy, and the bystander took off running. "I didn't hear him say to stop," McCoy recalled, and as he ran, the officer shot the "fleeing suspect" in the buttocks. "I wasn't in the game at all," he added. "I didn't have any weapon of any kind. I never owned a pistol."

In the end, the grand jurors and Hugo Black agreed that Bessemer police officers routinely took "helpless prisoners in the late hours of night, into a secluded room . . . and there beat them until they were red with their own blood, in the efforts to obtain confessions." Black's report added:

We find that this cowardly practice in which four big officers with pistols safely strapped on their bodies would thus take advantage of ignorance and helplessness has been continuously in operation for a long number of years. A leather strap with a buckle on one end, and a big flap on the other, was invested for this purpose. . . . In this room were none present but the officers and the helpless prisoner, often innocent of the crime of which he was charged, arrested without a warrant, on vague suspicion.

It was a scathing indictment on the city and its police force, but Bessemer's political establishment rejected it. "It would have been more manly," Mayor I. A. Lewis proclaimed, "had the grand jury reported the good they saw. I know there is much more good than bad in every officer."

In the decades that followed, the lawlessness of Bessemer's policemen continued unabated. A few officers took payoffs and ignored places like the Blue Bird, the Southern Night Club, Club Reo, the Barn, and Hollywood Plaza, as well as shot houses, gambling establishments, and prostitution rings, especially one run by an elderly black woman who kept a .38 Special in the front pocket of her apron. "There may not be any more vice in Bessemer than other places," another officer explained, "but it sure is easier to find."

During the 1950s, when one investigator from the circuit solicitor's office probed shot house payoffs, someone tossed a dummy grenade into the front seat of his automobile as a warning. "This is Bessemer," Police Chief George Barron once proclaimed, "and experience has taught us that in Bessemer, anything can happen."

GEORGE BARRON JOINED the Bessemer Police Department in 1947 as motorcycle patrolman after working for a time as an electric bridge crane operator at U.S. Steel's Ensley works. In 1954, he earned promotion to lieutenant and was named chief in late 1956 at the age of thirty-three. Barron, a fit, 6-foot-2 and 180-pound former World War II marine, possessed somber gray eyes, a stone face, and a close crop of rapidly retreating brown hair. Born on August 3, 1924, in Jefferson County, he was the son of Rondle and Myrtle Barron of Adamsville.

Most whites in Bessemer held Chief Barron in high regard for his "good moral character" and excellent leadership skills. One local judge believed the department under his leadership was free of scandals and "unusually well administered," perhaps the best the city had ever known. In 1959, an FBI agent noted that Barron dressed neatly, was well groomed, and made a "fine appearance." The chief was "friendly by nature" and easily made friends and quickly established rapport. "His personality reflects a maturity based on a varied background," he wrote, and exhibited "all the necessary qualifications of an efficient officer and has sufficient administrative ability to command a small department."

Barron was also a steadfast segregationist who had no qualms about violating the civil rights of black citizens. At times, an FBI agent suggested, the racial climate in Bessemer necessitated this practice and justified violence. "Chief Barron is a police executive in a city which has a very large percentage of Negro population," the agent wrote, "and it is most politic for him to keep this segment of the population in line and not permit it at any time to rise to a position of prominence."

Black citizens seemed to be a frequent target of Bessemer police officers' belligerent inclinations. "When the police arrested a black man," civil rights leader and union activist Asbury Howard later recalled, "they were known for whipping up on them." A frequent technique was to kick suspects down the backstairs of the city jail, which allowed officers to claim they had never "laid a hand" on a bruised and battered prisoner. Bessemer policemen also enforced a "regular departmental policy" of requiring blacks to walk in the middle of the downtown streets, not on the sidewalks, after dark—presumably to keep them from any close contact with white women.

In 1944, Bessemer policemen forced black prisoners to participate in an Independence Day watermelon run. As sociologist Charles S. Johnson reported, white citizens cheered as firefighters blasted the inmates with high-pressure hoses to make the race more challenging. Winners received reduced sentences and the watermelons.

Adding to the violence and intimidation was the strength of the Ku Klux Klan in western Jefferson County. Local FBI agents made note of members of the Bessemer department "giving information to Klan officials." One FBI agent during the civil rights era emphasized that most of the older city police officers and county sheriff's deputies working in Bessemer were "former or present Klan members."

ON THIRD AVENUE North in Bessemer, directly across the street from city hall and police headquarters, stood the Jefferson County Courthouse and the sheriff's office. In 1957, Clyde W. Morris was the chief sheriff's deputy for the Bessemer area. A hard-living lawman with an affinity for Tampa Nugget Cigars, Morris supervised a small staff of seventeen deputies ("guardians of human rights," the *Birmingham News* called them) to serve and protect ninety thousand people living in the four hundred square miles of the western end of Jefferson County.

This area included the steel-driving municipalities of Bessemer, Lipscomb, Fairfield, Brighton, Midfield, Brownsville, and Johns, as well as dozens of unincorporated communities. "While it is true that residential areas of the Bessemer Cutoff are not getting the patrolling needed," Morris once said, "we feel we are doing a good job." Nevertheless, he agreed that the Cutoff had an unusually high number of capital and felony cases to investigate. "There is not a Saturday night," the chief deputy added, "that we do not get so many calls we cannot answer them all." In 1955, one local leader told the *Birmingham News* that the Bessemer Cutoff had more major crimes each year than any other county in the state and, in some cases, more than a dozen counties combined. Morris estimated that it would take at least one hundred lawmen to "adequately patrol" the crime-ridden Bessemer Cutoff.

IN THE MINDS of most whites in 1957, crime was not the most serious threat to law and order in Alabama; it was the prospect of black political and social equality and the loss of white status and power. In a place like Bessemer, with a sizable black majority, any threat to the social order, as in Caliph Washington's case, would elicit a swift and brutal response. Just like every other officer in the county, sheriff's deputy David Orange wanted in on capturing the presumed police killer. "We followed every report that Caliph Washington might be hiding here or there," he recalled, "and searched many places trying to find him." The twenty-six-year-old Orange was on the force for less than seven months, and the intensity of the manhunt unnerved him. The deputy's superiors warned Orange that Caliph Washington was a desperate, violent, armed fugitive who would shoot any officer who got near him. As he searched abandoned houses for Washington, the deputy expected to hear a gunshot and see a bullet whizzing toward his head.

Adding to his anxiety, Orange found himself riding in a car driven by Murphy Farley, an officer for the Alabama State Beverage Control Board. Murphy drove a black late-model Ford police interceptor with a 312 cubic-inch V-8 engine that he used to chase down fast cars hauling moonshine. When a call came over the radio that Caliph Washington was spotted on the other side of the county, the big, red-faced Murphy stomped the accelerator. Orange hung on tight. "We hurtled down the curving hillside on Rock Creek Road," Orange remembered, "reaching speeds close to one hundred miles an hour, where fifty was breathtaking. I knew what anxiety really was . . . a euphemism for fear." Murphy's cross-county race, however, proved to be for naught—just one of many false sightings of the suspect. Late Saturday evening, July 13, Orange's colleague Walter Dean announced that "if Washington is not found by Monday, a nationwide search will be started."

According to black residents in and around Bessemer, city police officers and Jefferson County sheriff's deputies bullied, beat, and arrested Washington's friends, family members, and potential witnesses. As one attorney later proclaimed sardonically, the police harassed and intimidated "every black person in Jefferson County who had ever known Caliph Washington."

On Friday evening, July 12, when Elijah Honeycutt stopped by the Washington home in Pipe Shop to console Caliph's mother, he found no one at home. As he got back in his automobile, "police cars came from everywhere," he later recalled, and Honeycutt found himself surrounded by ten or more officers. "I got out of the car, and they went to searching me and asking me what I was going to that house for," he said. "I broke down and told them." The officers grabbed Honeycutt, handcuffed him, and pushed him into the back of a squad car. For the next two hours they drove him around Bessemer, Lipscomb, and southwestern Birmingham as he showed the lawmen the route he used to help Caliph Washington make his initial escape. When the officers finished with him, they drove him to the Bessemer City Jail and held him for several more days.

Information from Honeycutt, in combination with other sources, led police to Tommy Silmon's home on Park Avenue in southwestern Birmingham. That Saturday evening, a dozen or so officers surrounded the house and waited in darkness. A heavily armed "police posse," the *Birmingham News* reported, was "pulling the net close around" Washington. "Officers at the search scene believe an arrest will be forthcoming shortly."

A few hours later, in the wee hours of Sunday morning, Silmon returned—presumably from the drive to Adamsville and a subsequent stop for a few beers. He was alone in his own car and not with a stranger in a Ford sedan. Officers watched as Silmon's Buick crept down the street and stopped in front of his home. The engine shut down and the headlights went out. The lone figure leaned over and picked up an item from the front seat, wobbled to a standing position on the side of the car, and closed the door. A voice pierced the night silence: "Stand still and drop what is in your hand." Silmon froze in a drunken stupor, unable to find where the voice was coming from. The voice repeated the command. Silmon raised the object in his hand, flicked on the switch, and shined Cowboy Clark's flashlight into the eyes of the shotgun-toting officer barking the orders. The officer fired, and shotgun pellets struck Silmon in the legs, sending him to the pavement, screaming in pain. Chief Barron defended his officer's trigger happiness as proper protocol, arguing that he had no choice, "not knowing what move Silmon might take next."

Someone, presumably Silmon, told officers that Washington was at a relative's home in Adamsville. Within a few hours, seven carloads of policemen arrived in the black area of Adamsville and engaged in a sadistic house-to-house romp, kicking doors in along Oakwood Drive. Hattie Cross was behind her home milking a goat when officers stomped through her vegetable garden and demanded to know where Caliph Washington was hiding. When she failed to answer, a policeman struck her in the face. She screamed and fell in the dirt as the officer pulled his gun and shot the goat. Everywhere Washington went on his escape, police left a terrible imprint, marking everyone he crossed paths with and starting a countdown to when they would come to collect.

Bessemer city police, miles from their jurisdiction but with the assistance of Jefferson County sheriff's deputies, spread throughout the neighborhood. Next door to Cross, they kicked open the door at William "Burley" Merritt's house, snatched him out of bed, dragged him behind his house, and beat him as his wife Ernestine looked on in horror. When the officers finished the beating, they slapped handcuffs on Burley, put him in the back of a patrol car with blood dripping from his nose and head, and took him to the Bessemer City Jail. Before they left the Merritt house, officers knocked Burley's elderly mother, Elizabeth Eaton, in the head with a rifle butt, and she lay bleeding and unconscious on the floor. She later died from the head trauma.

Jessie Kyser was in a house nearby when a pistol-wielding policeman kicked open the front door and entered. "Stop right there," Officer J. E. McGee screamed, but Kyser dropped his coffee cup and bolted out the back door. In a flash, McGee grabbed Kyser by the collar and tackled him to the ground. Apparently the officer thought he had Caliph Washington in his clutches. Gunshots rang out, and Kyser lay mortally wounded. The *Birmingham News* reported that McGee's gun "accidently discharged" when the suspect "grabbed the officer and they struggled in the garden." Officers on the scene also suggested that Kyser "grabbed the officer's gun and it went off." No matter how it happened, Kyser was dead. At a hearing on July 15, the shooting death was ruled justifiable.

According to witnesses, the officers continued terrorizing the residents for two and a half hours. This was war, and Bessemer police were on a search-and-destroy mission. When they were unable to locate Washington, they allegedly shot chickens, goats, and pigs in pens behind houses. They soon learned that they had missed Cross, Pearson, Graham, and Caliph Washington driving northwest in a green Studebaker by less than ten minutes. Law enforcement officials put out a three-state alert (Alabama, Mississippi, and Tennessee) for the fugitive and the other three men. Four of the dozen or so Bessemer officers in Adamsville began the trek down U.S. 78 to Mississippi: Jefferson County sheriff's deputies Arvel Doss and Charlie Stamps (the duo's primary assignment was to investigate "liquor violations"), the Bessemer city commissioner of public safety Herman Thompson, and Bessemer detective Lawton Grimes, Sr.

LAWTON "STUD" GRIMES was Bessemer's most colorful and feared lawman. He joined the force in 1940 after working a handful of industrial jobs and serving as a "special service agent" for a local firm—presumably an antiunion head buster for one of the iron and steel companies. Stocky, sweat-soaked, and tobacco-stained, Grimes looked, talked, and acted like the stereotypical southern lawman with a well-fed stomach and a flattop haircut that looked like fuzz from a pipe cleaner; when he talked, his hard-edged voice rattled like an old pickup truck riding along a gravel road. As a teenager at nearby Hueytown High School, he earned his nickname "Stud" as a fearless head-butting running back on the football team. His iron-fisted approach to law enforcement reinforced his nickname as hard-boiled as a 20-minute egg and his reputation for breeding bold-faced violence in Bessemer. He was a Klansman in one of the most active and violent chapters in the South. On one occasion, while wearing his robe and hooded mask, a photographer snapped a picture of Grimes at a Klan rally. When the photo appeared in a local paper, Grimes's police officer's uniform and identifiable potbelly showed from underneath his robe, much to the chagrin of his supervisors.

A little after noon, sheriff's deputies in Monroe County, Mississippi, pulled over Zack Graham's southbound Studebaker and arrested the trio. Officers took Cross, Pearson, and Graham to Aberdeen for questioning, and either one, two, or all three told of their fishing expedition in Amory to help Washington catch a northwest-bound Greyhound bus. The next day, Bessemer police brought the three men to Bessemer and charged them with aiding an escaping felon—if convicted, they would face a $500 fine and a year in prison.

Back in Amory, deputies stopped at the bus station and questioned Billy May, the ticket agent, who remembered selling the ticket to a nervous black man. May gave the lawmen a detailed description of Washington and the "number of the bus on which he left Amory." Within minutes, county officials radioed the Mississippi Highway Patrol that a U.S. Army soldier, "a negro male named Caliph Washington, approximately 18 to 19 years old, was thought to be on a Greyhound bus that left Amory, Mississippi at 10:30 en route to Memphis." They warned that the suspect would be toting a loaded .38 Special concealed in a brown paper sack.

When Washington boarded the bus in Amory, the Greyhound was making its first stop in Mississippi after having left Atlanta around 6:15 a.m. It also stopped in Anniston and Birmingham, following the same U.S. 78 route that the Freedom Riders would travel almost four years later. The bus was less than half full, and only two blacks occupied seats in the segregated back rows. Washington chose a driver's side window seat on the second to last row and placed the brown paper sack under the seat in front of him occupied by Furman Jones, a black uniformed army sergeant who was returning to Fort Hood, Texas, from his home in South Carolina.

In just a few minutes, the bus left Amory heading north toward Tupelo. For the first time in days, Washington felt at ease. He chatted for a while with a young woman across the aisle and then leaned forward and asked Jones if he could sit with him. He agreed, and the two talked about army life and Caliph's time overseas. A weary Furman Jones began his westward trek that day on the 12:55 a.m. Greyhound from Spartanburg to Atlanta, where he changed buses and began the ride through Alabama and into Mississippi. The bus made several stops along the route: Tupelo, New Albany, and Holly Springs.

As the Greyhound traveled west from Holly Springs toward Memphis, Mississippi state troopers J. W. Warren and Pete Connell arrived at the town's bus station looking for Washington. The counter clerk informed the pair that the bus pulled out just five minutes before. They jumped back into their patrol car and hurried down U.S. 78 in pursuit of the Greyhound. The bus traveled only 15 miles to Byhalia when the troopers caught up with it. Pronounced *Bu-hell-ya*, the hamlet was a wide place in the road that derived its name from a Chickasaw word meaning "great oaks." Before the Civil War, Byhalia boasted a thriving population and was a center of plantation culture for northern Mississippi and southwestern Tennessee. By 1957, however, only a handful of people remained in the isolated and impoverished area. The town's most noteworthy event was that some five years ahead, on July 6, 1962, the author William Faulkner would die from a heart attack while in Wright's Sanitarium in Byhalia.

When the troopers overtook the bus around 2 p.m., Trooper Warren recalled that the Greyhound was on the side of the road at a filling station just off U.S. 78. The driver was exiting the station and walking back toward the bus when the officers pulled up. "I told him we were looking for a Negro who had killed a policeman . . . in Alabama," Warren recalled. But both Caliph Washington and Furman Jones remembered that the troopers chased the Greyhound down and made the bus driver pull over. Whatever the case, Warren walked up the three short steps to the interior of the bus and spotted Furman Jones and Caliph Washington sitting side by side near the back. Heads turned and eyes trained on the trooper as he silently strode down the aisle, his eyes focused on the two black men. He walked just beyond the seat with Jones and Washington, leaned over, and whispered in a forceful tone, "Both of you put your hands behind your head, get up, and get off this bus." The pair complied. Caliph walked down the aisle first, with Jones and Trooper Warren close behind.

With the suspects off the Greyhound, Warren turned around and climbed back inside to search for the brown paper sack. Trooper Connell ordered Washington and Jones to stand with their backs against the side of the bus. The lawman focused on Jones first, seeing the army uniform and knowing that the suspect was a soldier. "Show us some I.D., boy," Connell barked at the nervous Jones. Jones handed the officer his military identification and explained that he was returning from leave in South Carolina to his base in Texas. Satisfied, the officers allowed him to return to his seat.

Caliph Washington stood silently and tried not to look guilty. When Connell asked where he was from, Washington answered that he was from Amory, Mississippi, on his way to Chicago. When he explained to the officer that he had no identification, Connell spun him around and began patting him down. When Washington spread his legs, his wallet slipped from its hiding place in his boxer shorts, slid down his leg, out the bottom of his trousers, and onto the ground. The Mississippi trooper picked it up, opened it, and read the name Caliph Washington on the driver's license. He climbed up the stairs to the bus and proclaimed to his partner, "We've got the right one," just as Warren reached the front holding the brown paper sack.

The state troopers exited the Greyhound and stood in front of Washington. Warren opened the bag and pulled out Cowboy Clark's fully loaded, pearl-handled, nickel-plated pistol. The silver .38 shimmered in the light of the heartless Mississippi sun. Warren checked the serial number. "K239435," he said out loud—a match. Also in the sack, he found a pair of pants, a shirt, and a piece of cake. They handcuffed Washington and placed him in the back of patrol car. The bus proceeded west to Memphis, where Shelby County sheriff's deputies arrested Furman Jones and held him for questioning until 10 the next morning.

Heading the opposite way, Connell drove east on U.S. 78, while Warren sat in the passenger seat talking over his left shoulder, trying to coax a statement out of Washington. Warren later told a newspaper reporter that the suspect at first admitted he had killed Clark, but Washington later denied it. It took over an hour to drive the fifty miles to the state trooper station in New Albany, Mississippi. There Arvel Doss, Charlie Stamps, Herman Thompson, and Stud Grimes were waiting.

That Sunday in New Albany, Caliph Washington stood with Bessemer police detective Grimes in front of the state trooper station. Apparently Grimes knew Washington well, later claiming that the young man "was raised right in my back yard, almost." Leaning against his unmarked Oldsmobile, Stud puffed on his ever-present pipe and peppered the suspect with questions. "Caliph, what happened?" he demanded. "How come you to shoot him?" He pulled the revolver out of the sack and asked, "Whose gun is this?"

Within a few minutes, Grimes and Monroe County deputies transported Washington to the courthouse in New Albany. Washington appeared before a local judge and waived extradition to Alabama. With all the legalities and paperwork taken care of, deputies escorted the suspect from the courthouse and officially handed him over to Stud Grimes. The Bessemer detective placed the handcuffed Washington in the back of his unmarked Oldsmobile and drove east toward home, with Doss, Stamps, and Thompson following in a Jefferson County patrol car. At Jasper, Alabama, Grimes transferred Washington to Chief Barron and Chief Deputy Sheriff Morris's black sedan for the final leg of the journey.

AFTER NEARLY SEVENTY straight hours of nonstop police work, which left Silmon's legs peppered with buckshot, an innocent man dead from a bullet and a woman from a blow to the head, and dozens more beaten and terrorized, the prime suspect would soon be behind bars. For Stud Grimes, the case had become an obsession. He was the first detective at the crime scene in the early morning hours of July 12 (having just completed a twelve-hour shift), participated in every stage of the head-cracking manhunt for Caliph Washington, and brought the suspect back to Bessemer late in the evening of July 14. Grimes's son later recalled that his father worked eighty-four hours "without letting up." A fireplug of a man, Stud lived for the manhunt and often found himself tangling with Bessemer's roughest characters. During his years on the force, he received knife and gunshot wounds, including one shooting that left him paralyzed for a while, and numerous assaults. His hard-boiled reputation was known throughout Alabama. A fellow Bessemer policeman once bragged that Grimes killed more people in the line of duty than any other officer in the state's history. Whether truth or legend, Stud Grimes was just as rough as the town he represented.

It was after 9 p.m. when Caliph Washington arrived at the Jefferson County Courthouse in Bessemer. A least a dozen white lawmen milled about the area as George Barron and Clyde Morris escorted the handcuffed suspect through the loading area behind the courthouse and into a small freight elevator and up to the main floor for fifteen minutes of booking, fingerprinting, and mug-shot making. Deputies then took him to the Law Library on the third floor of the courthouse, just across the hall from the district attorney's office, for questioning. The white interrogators, men associated with the Jefferson County sheriff's office, were Clyde Morris, Clarence. E. "Dixie" Walker, James W. Thompson, Wilton H. Hogan, and Walter C. Dean. The five bitter-eyed lawmen gathered around a long wooden oak library table in the hot, airless room, thick with humidity and intimidation. Caliph Washington sat in an unforgiving stiff-backed chair and watched the eyes of those men staring at him, cold and hateful. Most said not a word. Lead investigator Walter Dean did most of the talking.

"Caliph," he began in a calm voice, "tell what happened in your own words."

The suspect was too tired to show hesitance or fear, so he talked, and Dean wrote down his answers in longhand. "I had him to tell me what happened," Dean later recalled. "I asked him to start back at the beginning of the afternoon when he first got his daddy's automobile and to tell me where all he had been and what he had done up to the time after the officer was shot."

Almost an hour later, they finished, and Dean placed the five-page written document before an exhausted, intimidated, and overwhelmed Washington. "Put your initials here, boy," Dean said as he pointed to a spot on the paper. When Caliph scribbled "CW" on a page, Dean flipped to the next sheet and placed his index finger on the place for Washington to initial again. When he finished, Dean told him to print the phrase "I have read this statement and it is true," and then sign his name. He complied, and Dean picked up the document. Dean, Morris, Walker, Thompson, and Hogan all signed the statement as witnesses.

Dated July 14, 1957, at 10:20 p.m., the document began with the simple sentence: "My name is Caliph Washington." The defendant explained that he was born November 14, 1939, and was seventeen years old. He claimed to be home on leave from the U.S. Army, although he already received an "other than honorable" discharge. While on "leave," he was living with his mother and father in Bessemer. "I have not been mistreated in any way since I was arrested, nor promised any help or reward to make this statement, and I know it may be used in court at my trial for killing a policeman." In his statement, Washington recounted how he borrowed his daddy's 1950 two-tone sedan the previous Thursday evening and drove from Pipe Shop to Thompson Town to visit with friends in his old neighborhood. He then picked up Robert Shields and drove to Avenue T in Ensley to Birdie and Mary Robinson's house. "We stayed there a little while," he recalled, and then the group went to eat ice cream at the Dairy Frost. In less than half an hour, they returned to the girls' house and stayed for a few minutes. "Then all four of us left there," Caliph remembered, and drove to Lula Rice's house at 2000 Exeter Avenue in Bessemer. "We sat around and talked." They stayed for an hour until 10 p.m. On the way back to the girls' home in Ensley, they stopped at the Blue Gardenia in Fairfield for sandwiches. They dropped the girls off, and Robert and Caliph returned to Travellick. "We sat in front of his house and talked a while," the suspect said. "I left Robert's house, I think, about 12:30 in the morning and was on my way home."

Washington recalled that as he crossed Thirty-Third Street on the South Bessemer Road, a car came "out of the bushes" and started to follow him. "I was going about 40 miles an hour," the statement read, "which was too fast." The car followed about five or six blocks with no siren or red flashing light on top. "He shot at me two times," Caliph recounted, "and I speeded up and he turned on the red blinker light." By this time, Caliph was circling in the alleyways between Dartmouth, Exeter, and Fairfax avenues.

> I knew by this time it was a police car chasing me then I stopped in front of Bessie Mae Johnson's house. Time I got out of my daddy's car the policeman was standing by me. He had his gun in his hand. He said where is that whiskey. And I said I don't have anything. He was pretty close to me and I started to jerk the pistol out of his hand and we fumbled around and the pistol went off two or three times and I layed the policeman on the front seat of his car. I got his pistol; there was some bullets on the seat. I got them. And then I run to Exeter Avenue and saw the police; then I got in the ditch and then got back on Exeter Avenue.

Washington remembered knocking on the door of a house between Fairfax and Exeter: "Wouldn't anybody come to the door." He then ran to Elijah Honeycutt's house on Brickyard Hill. "He come to the door, I told him I wanted him to take me off apiece. He ask me what I was doing up there that time of morning. He didn't want to take me and I begged him to take me." Honeycutt and his girlfriend drove Caliph Washington to Travellick, near Robert Shields's house, where he hid in the woods the rest of the night. The next morning, he went to Robert's house and his mother gave him a sandwich and he returned to the woods and stayed there until the next day. On Saturday, he returned to Robert's house and asked his father "if he could take me off apiece" toward Highway 78 west.

> I didn't tell him then what I had done. . . . I paid Robert's daddy 3 bucks for taking me over there. I got over there about 10:30 last night. Then I went to a guy's house who had a Studebaker. I ask him if he would take me off apiece. He said it was too late but he was going on a fishing trip tomorrow down the highway and I could go along then.

Washington told the interrogators that he went and slept in the woods until early Sunday morning. He went back to "this man's house" at 7 o'clock and left with him and two other men in the Studebaker. In Amory, Mississippi, one of the men in the car, "a tall guy with a white t-shirt," purchased a bus ticket for Memphis. "And they left me there," Caliph recalled. He gave the man who had the Studebaker $5 or $6 for driving him to Amory.

The suspect explained to the officers that on the Greyhound bus, he sat with a soldier. "He was not with me in Bessemer," the statement read. "When I shot the officer, I was by myself. I still had the policeman's gun with me when I was arrested."

After Washington signed the document, the sheriff's deputies took him to a cell in the nearby Jefferson County Jail, and he fell asleep.

The next afternoon, the *Birmingham Post-Herald* arrived on the local newsstands with a bold-faced headline: NEGRO IS ARRESTED IN POLICE

SLAYING. Washington was carrying the "still-loaded service revolver of slain Lipscomb Police Sergeant James Clark," the paper reported. Investigators told reporter Jerry Upton that Clark spotted a "speeding car, driving recklessly," and chased the car into Bessemer. He pulled the driver over to the side of the road and arrested him. "The driver," Upton wrote, "apparently grabbed the officer's pistol and shot him."

For years, David Hood served as Bessemer's only black attorney,
and he played a pivotal role in each of Caliph Washington's trials.

5

A "WELL BOUND BOOK"

CALIPH WASHINGTON FEARED for his life. Within hours of his arrest, sheriff's deputies pulled him from his cell, placed him in handcuffs, led him outside, and pushed him into the back of an awaiting patrol car. A tip, a threat, or Bessemer's general climate of violence compelled county officials to quietly move Washington from the county jail in Bessemer to the one in Birmingham. Klansmen in the Marvel City, Washington recalled, "wanted to hang me," so the deputies "slipped me out" of town.

The deputies delivered the suspect to the basement of the county courthouse located on Twenty-First Street in downtown Birmingham, where the admitting warden recorded his name, color, sex, age, and the charges against him. Guards then led him into the secure compartment of a fortified elevator designed for safekeeping the "dangerous prisoner." They handcuffed his arm to an iron bar in the cagelike structure, closed the door, and sent Washington up to the county jail on the seventh floor. When the elevator stopped, guards opened the cage, unchained his arm, and led him through a series of heavy iron doors to the office of the chief warden, where Caliph was again interviewed.

Guards then escorted Washington to the receiving room, where he stripped from his freeman's clothes and donned a prison-issue blue convict's uniform—the color jail officials required all black inmates to wear. White prisoners wore white. Customs and laws of gender and race divided the jail's sixteen cellblocks into four parts: black men, white men, black women, white women. On July 15, guards led Caliph to a cell in the black men's section. Behind one of these cold, battleship-gray steel doors, Washington found scant furnishing: a double-decker bed, a toilet, and a drinking fountain that spouted chilled water. Outside his door, a long steel dining table and benches ran the length of a brightly lit, cream-colored tile corridor. At the far end of the cellblock was what the wardens called a "sun parlor" and what the prisoners termed "the pit"—a two-story, brick-walled enclosure, open to the sky (except for the overhead bars). Here Caliph Washington and the other inmates paced from "dead end to dead end," as one visitor described the scene, and "worked up appetites and worked off pent-up steam."

This new "escape-proof" Jefferson County Jail opened in 1931 and replaced the aged, crowded, and unsanitary "Big Rock"—a fifty-year-old facility constructed of stone that housed the area's oft-used gallows and was the site of frequent jailbreak attempts. High above the courthouse, the new jail was safe, secure, and sanitary. As Washington arrived in the summer of 1957, only one prisoner had escaped from the facility. "And all that," author James Saxon Childers told the county sheriff, "is why I don't like your jail. There's no glamour about this place. There's no chance for excitement. And, frankly, I consider it extremely unsporting. The prisoner simply has no chance [to escape] at all." So Caliph Washington, like many other prisoners housed in this penthouse penitentiary, waited for a formal indictment and subsequent trial by an "impartial jury" of his "peers."

His formal indictment would come when the next grand jury convened in Bessemer. Alabama law required county jury commissions to meet annually between the first day of August and the twentieth day of December and to compile the names of every male citizen and record the list in a "well bound book." Those male citizens qualified to serve (the names that would fill the jury box) were "generally reputed to be honest and intelligent men . . . esteemed in the community for their integrity, good character and sound judgment." At the time, Alabama law excluded a large segment of the population: women (regardless of race), anyone under twenty-one, anyone over sixty-one, habitual drunkards, those disease afflicted, those physically weakened, illiterates, and any-one convicted of offenses "involving moral turpitude," which included adultery, fornication, bigamy, and miscegenation—the latter a set public policy to "prevent race amalgamation and to safeguard the racial integrity of white and negro peoples."

The Birmingham-based, three-member, countywide jury commis-sion met the last Tuesday in August on every odd-numbered year (includ-ing 1957) to fill the jury box for both the Bessemer Cutoff and the rest of Jefferson County. Clerks for the commission used city directories, tele-phone listings, tax rolls, voting lists, and interviews to select the names for the list. Workers for the commission collected names and investigated possible jurors for possible criminal records. George W. Clayton, a Jef-ferson County jury commissioner, claimed that the three-member group wouldn't know which of the potential jurors were of the "colored race, Jew race, the Italian, the Greek or anybody." In other words, the commis-sioner claimed no discrimination based on race or color.

The names of potential jurors from the Cutoff were written on small cards and placed in a wooden box by the jury commissioners in Birming-ham. County officials transported the filled box to the county clerk's office in the Bessemer Cutoff and locked it in a safe. In 1957, the two cir-cuit judges in the Bessemer courthouse, Freelin R. Mathews and Gardner F. Goodwyn, Jr., had the only keys to the safe. At least two weeks prior to convening a trial jury, one of the two judges would open the safe and take the box into the courtroom. Someone on the clerk's staff would shake the box to mix up the cards and then the judge would open the wooden lid and grab a fistful of cards and count out however many he felt was necessary for a jury pool. In other words, if the judge decided it would take eighty jurors, he would deal out the cards until he reached eighty. If he had too few, he picked up more; if he had too many, he dropped the rest back into the box for the next jury selection. They drew names out of the same box for two years, and then the jury commissioners retrieved the box and filled it again with new names.

Following the Clark shooting in July, the next Bessemer grand jury was set to convene on September 9. A couple of weeks prior to that date, Judge Freelin Mathews retrieved the box and drew out the names of fifty-two men—four blacks and forty-eight whites—from the seven thousand names stuffed inside. He handed the cards to Elmore McAdory, the clerk for the Cutoff. McAdory arranged the cards in alphabetical order by last name, and included the juror's addresses and occupations. The clerk then took the list downstairs to Chief Deputy Clyde Morris's office, who issued the summons and, in the fall of 1957, assigned two deputies—Joe Moore and David Orange—to serve the papers.

Moore and Orange spent days driving their unmarked black sheriff's car all over the Cutoff serving the summonses. If they found a potential juror at home, they would report back to the court that the summons had been served; if no one was at home, they wrote "not found" or "nf" on their list. Orange, having served on the force for only nine months, quickly learned the rules of the jury venire game in the county. "To my great surprise," he later recalled, "when we went to an address that was on the envelope and it was evident that black folks lived at the address, the summons was marked, 'not found,' and returned without exception." Only whites were served jury summonses, and it had always been that way and would continue that way for years to come. "This was an unspoken rule," Orange added, "that was known by judges, lawyers, and prosecutors alike."

The morning of September 9 thirty-two of the fifty-two possible jurors arrived at the courthouse. Of the missing twenty, twelve were not found, seven were excused, and one failed to appear. Of the thirty-two in court that morning, Judge Freelin Mathews excused a few and rejected others; then the juror cards were shuffled, and the judge drew the names of seventeen white men: Edwin Walker Berry, Jr. (a bank manager), Howard Flournoy Bryan (a structural engineer), Oscar Emmett Chastain (a draftsman), Charles A. Allen (an electrician), Porter Cowan (a timekeeper), Samuel Lee Hallman (a clerk), Charles C. Heinton (a fabricator),

Clarence Joseph Hitchfield (a millwright), Garland Lee Hood (a pump-man), Elmer Leonard Ingram (a metallurgical observer), T. J. Ingram (a loader operator comptometer), William Ivy Ingram (an operator and timekeeper), Obie Bruce Johnson (a crane man), John W. McBeath (a stock clerk), James Hoyt Wine (a truck driver), William Edwin Whiten (a dry cleaner), and Frank C. Waldrop (a machinist).

The eighteenth man selected was black: Willis Nesbit (a laborer). Nesbit's selection for this particular case, David Orange believed, was an error at some level of the venire game. "If a black happened to get a jury subpoena," he recalled, "it was just a total mistake. In those days, no one would have ever deliberately delivered one to a black person—no way." Notwithstanding, it was perhaps an attempt by unscrupulous county officials to thwart any attempts by the defense attorneys to claim race-based jury exclusion in an appeal. This strategy rested on the presumption of Caliph Washington's guilt in the case.

For whatever reason, Willis Nesbit examined the evidence along with the seventeen other men in the grand jury room on the third floor of the courthouse annex in Bessemer. Nesbit and his fellow jurors returned a bill of indictment or a "true bill" in open court on September 12. They concluded that the strong evidence against Caliph Washington mandated a trial by a *petit* or petty jury (also referred to as a trial jury or common jury) made up of twelve persons summoned and empaneled for the trial of a specific case. "The Grand Jury of the said County," the indictment read, "charges that before finding of this indictment Caliph Washington, whose name to the Grand Jury is otherwise unknown, unlawfully and with malice aforethought, killed James B. Clark, by shooting him with a pistol, against the peace and dignity of the State of Alabama." In other words, Washington's indictment carried the charge of murder in the first degree. To convict him of that crime, the state had to prove that he had murdered James Clark with willful (without yielding to reason), malicious (without just cause or legal excuse), premeditated and deliberate (with intent and knowledge) aforethought.

The "true bill" was signed by Howard H. Sullinger, the deputy circuit solicitor (the term for a district attorney in Alabama)—the person responsible for prosecuting the state's case against Caliph Washington.

Born June 29, 1901, in the eastern Tennessee hamlet of Maryville, Sullinger graduated from Maryville College in 1923 and, after spending a few years as an educator, earned a law degree from the University of Michigan in 1930. He moved to Bessemer that same year and began the practice of law with Freelin Mathews—the men developed a deep, close father-son relationship that lasted for over thirty years. In 1937, Sullinger was named city attorney in Bessemer and held the position for ten years until Alabama governor Chauncey Sparks appointed him circuit solicitor following the death of Arthur Green in 1947. "I shall at all times," he said soon afterward, "strive with the aid of the law enforcement agencies to give our people the fullest possible protection in their lives and in their homes and properties, from the criminal element in our society."

A JEFFERSON COUNTY sheriff's deputy served the indictment to Caliph Washington in the county lock-up in Birmingham and informed him that no bond would be granted in this capital crime. The case would be *State of Alabama v. Caliph Washington*, and the trial was scheduled for the week of October 7 in Judge Mathews's Bessemer courtroom of the Circuit Court of the Tenth Judicial Circuit of Alabama.

Bespectacled, flabby-jowled, seam-faced, and broad-bellied, the seventy-eight-year-old Mathews was nearing the end of his long and powerful legal career in Bessemer. One author described him as "preeminent among the older generation" in Bessemer and an honored, able, and faithful public servant, who was "held in high regard throughout that section of Alabama by his colleagues in the legal profession." Born in Hanceville on May 14, 1879, Mathews was the son and grandson of well-to-do planters in Cullman County, located in the north-central part of the state. After receiving a bachelor of laws from Southwestern Baptist University in Jackson, Tennessee, Mathews opened a law practice with his brother in Bessemer in 1907. He served as an assistant circuit solicitor and a city judge before Bessemer Cutoff voters sent him to the bench in 1950 as one of the two county circuit judges. In the courtroom, Mathews was sedate, humorless, efficient, and conservative. Off the bench, he spent most of his day pondering the law, receiving visitors, and catnapping in his chambers located on the cramped second floor of the courthouse annex.

While the slumbering Mathews awaited Caliph Washington's day in court, David Hood, Jr., still Bessemer's only black lawyer, prepared the defense's case for trial. Hood solicited the help of another civil rights attorney, and a fellow Howard Law School graduate, Orzell Billingsley, Jr., of Birmingham. As lawyers, both men fought for equal rights for blacks. Stylistically, however, they were an odd duo: Hood was staid, bookish, and aristocratic; Billingsley was brash, tornadic, and fearless. One colleague described him as a "consummate actor" who moved "his face from rage to a broad smile with a looseness which belies his intelligence." At every opportunity, Billingsley fought the Jim Crow establishment. In a case in rural Sumter County, Alabama, the lawyer's client dropped dead soon after the judge in the case pronounced a harsh sentence. Much to the chagrin of local whites, Billingsley filed a wrongful death lawsuit against the judge.

Hood and Billingsley worked steadily in preparation for Washington's trial, but even with all this labor, they avoided service as the lead attorneys because they had no hope of receiving compensation for their efforts. Many blacks expected that a lawyer of their own race would offer unlimited pro bono legal representation, but an attorney needed a source of income to earn a meager living. For Washington's case, Hood and Billingsley recommended that the poverty-stricken defendant petition for a court-appointed attorney—who would be white, since white judges rarely appointed black lawyers to indigent cases.

Jim Crow customs affected the attitudes of both races toward black attorneys in the South. In southern society of 1957, black lawyers defending a black client who was accused of committing a crime against a white man, in a courtroom with a white prosecutor, a white judge, and an all-white jury, would be seen as an affront to southern traditions. As one writer observed, a black man or woman practicing law in the South needed extraordinary tact and fearless courage to stand up for his or her dignity "as a member of the legal profession in a court where opposing attorneys often refer to members of your race as 'darkies' or 'niggers' or . . . other epithets." In the minds of many blacks, as scholar Gunnar Myrdal wrote in the 1940s, "a Negro lawyer is not much use in a southern courtroom." Many members of the black community believed that Jim Crow laws prohibited a black attorney from even entering a courtroom, much less defending someone of the same skin color.

Birmingham attorney, and David Hood mentor, Arthur Shores believed that black lawyers needed to gain notoriety for success "in order to live down the deep set conviction of many Negroes, that the Negro lawyer hasn't a chance against whites in the courts." Shores gained his own reputation as a defender of civil rights in the late 1930s, when he represented Will Hall, who filed charges against a white Birmingham police officer for a brutal beating with a ten-inch piece of rubber hose. Klan members threatened Shores with violence if he refused to drop the case, but he "chose to suffer the consequence" and won a striking victory. The local personnel board found the officer guilty of using excessive force, gave him a public reprimand, suspended him from the force, and placed him on probation. Following the verdict, as the diminutive Shores was leaving the hearing, a black man assaulted him, but several friends knocked the assailant to the floor. His attacker later confessed that whites paid him to start the ruckus as a reminder to the attorney to avoid civil rights cases. But Shores's boldness endeared him to the black community, and from that moment forward, his legal practice boomed. "The adversities that have confronted the Negro lawyer of the South," he wrote a few years later, "have only served to make him stronger, more skillful and more serviceable."

Although Hood and Billingsley were strong and successful attorneys, Bessemer, where white supremacy and racial superiority were so deeply ingrained, was no place for a black lawyer to defend a black man. So on September 23, 1957, Judge Mathews appointed Kermit Charles Edwards "to defend one Caliph Washington, an indigent defendant, on trial for murder." Edwards had fourteen days to prepare a defense for a capital crime.

A sullen man with a tired oval face and dark eyes, K. C., as he preferred to be called, was a 1932 graduate of the University of Alabama with a bachelor of laws. Born on May 6, 1909, the Summerland, Mississippi, native became a lawyer, as he wrote in 1931, because of a "desire on my part to engage in an honorable profession for the benefit of the public with a fair compensation for myself." This quest for cash, however, led Edwards to push the boundaries of ethical conduct throughout his legal career in Birmingham. He frequently solicited cases in the black community, especially personal injury claims, and gained a reputation as an opportunist and an "ambulance chaser." In 1938, a lawyer complained to the Alabama State Bar Association that Edwards was engaged in some of the "most damaging cases of solicitation" he had ever witnessed.

Nonetheless, on this day in open court, K. C. Edwards stood with Caliph Washington as Judge Mathews read out the charge of murder in the first degree. "How do you plead?" Mathews asked.

Washington pleaded not guilty by reason of self-defense. It was now up to the prosecution to prove beyond a reasonable doubt that the defendant should be convicted of murder in the first degree.

Four days later, on September 27, attorney David Hood filed motions to delay the trial. He first moved to "quash the venire" (to annul and void the jury pool) and "quash the indictment" (to void the accusation of the crime issued by the grand jury) because the systematic exclusion of blacks from jury service would deprive Caliph Washington of his rights guaranteed under the constitution and laws of Alabama and the Fourteenth Amendment of the U.S. Constitution. Hood also asked the court to suspend the trial because Caliph was insane at the time of the alleged crime, and an inquiry was needed into his mental condition.

At the pretrial hearing on September 30, attorneys Hood, Billingsley, and Edwards showed the court that in spite of making up a majority of the city's population, almost no black names were listed on Bessemer's jury rolls since its founding. Hood pointed out a special notation beside the name of Willis Nesbit, the only black on the jury roll for September 9—the letters "C.O.L." He argued that the calling of Nesbit and the other blacks for the September 9 jury pool was a fluke or a deliberate attempt to undermine one of the key aspects of the defense's court case. Several white Bessemer attorneys testified that they never struck a black man from a jury roll or seen one on a jury. William C. Smithson began practicing law in Bessemer in 1917, and he testified that "I just didn't see them [blacks on juries] or come in contact with them in my work."

In response, prosecutor Howard Sullinger argued that there was no systematic exclusion of black men from juries, and that the defense's arguments were so broad that they were frivolous and provided no answer to the question of whether Caliph Washington could get a fair trial. "He's covering everything from Genesis to Revelation," Sullinger proclaimed, "just on the theory that he might be able to prove something somewhere down the line." Blacks, Sullinger believed, "don't come in here with constitutional rights to sit on any case. I think the attorneys have a right to select their own juries." Judge Mathews agreed.

Nonetheless, David Hood continued to hammer his point about race-based jury exclusion. Washington's defense team called dozens of black men from the Bessemer Cutoff who met the qualifications but had never been called to serve on a jury. "No persons of negro blood," Hood concluded, "have been called to serve on the jury venires" from the community where they lived. The attorneys knew that the conservative white judge would never grant the motions they requested, but they demonstrated for a future appeal that the defendant would be neither indicted nor tried by a jury of his black peers.

This was the same legal strategy behind Hood's decision to test the waters of an insanity plea. He hoped to delay or sidestep what he believed to be an inevitable guilty verdict from an all-white Bessemer jury. But Dr. Frank A. Kay, head of the psychiatric department at the University of Alabama Medical College of Alabama in Birmingham, testified that Washington was not psychotic or insane. "There is nothing in his history to suggest that he has ever had any mental disturbance that would affect his mental competency," Kay concluded. David Hood quietly dropped the idea of the insanity defense, as all of his attempts to delay or postpone the trial failed.

IN THE FALL of 1957, as Caliph Washington's trial grew closer, Bessemer police detective Stud Grimes and his partner Andrew M. "Andy" Eubanks trailed defense attorneys Hood and Billingsley to their homes, offices, and "wherever they went," Billingsley later recalled. They were an intimidating presence. Andy Eubanks was a slack-jawed sourpuss detective with bright-white, slicked-down-comb-over hair. At seventy-two, Eubanks had worked in law enforcement for over fifty years, having begun his career as a Birmingham police patrolman with a horse and wagon in 1906. When Grimes and Eubanks teamed as crime-solving partners in 1949, they quickly gained a hard-boiled reputation. "Safe crackers, murderers, burglars with reputable names in the Cutoff are all known to these keen veterans," the *Birmingham News* reported in 1955. They were the type of flatfoots that solved crimes with a slap, a kick, a knee, a fist, and a nightstick. When necessary, they used a revolver.

In the days and weeks leading up to Washington's trial, Grimes and Eubanks put on street clothes and tailed the two lawyers in an unmarked Oldsmobile. They seldom said a word or left their car. They watched, waited, and smoked. "You should get in that car when both of our pipes are going full blast," Grimes once said. "It's quite a sight and smell also."

On Saturday, October 5, two days before Washington's trial, Grimes and Eubanks approached attorney Hood as he exited his law office with an employee, Betty Fears. For whatever reason, the crime-fighting duo decided to search Hood and Fears. Grimes snatched Hood's briefcase from his hand and opened the latches. Inside, on top of a stack of legal documents and notes, was the lawyer's pistol. Eubanks rumbled through Fears's purse and pulled out a switchblade knife. Given the rough nature of Bessemer politics, most lawyers, black and white, carried a weapon for protection. Regardless, in the days before this racially charged trial, Bessemer police badgered anyone who dared defend Caliph Washington. Grimes and Eubanks arrested Fears and Hood. Police charged Fears with carrying a switchblade knife or a knife longer than three inches, and Hood with a violation of the state firearms act. A judge later fined Hood $100 and sentenced him to ninety days in jail.

Hood believed these tactics were retaliation for his involvement in the Caliph Washington case as well as civil rights lawsuits. A few weeks earlier, Hood filed a federal lawsuit against the City of Bessemer on behalf of two black residents, William Thomas and Bleven Stout, who were denied admission to all-white Roosevelt Park. When the two men attempted to use a tennis court at the park, an irate mob of armed white men confronted them, and one yelled, "We plan to keep our community white." Bessemer police arrested the men for their own protection. Attorney Hood claimed in the suit that the Bessemer city code, which denied blacks the use of parks and swimming pools, was unconstitutional under the Fourteenth Amendment. Bessemer officials promised to build a separate but equal park for the city's black residents, whereupon Thomas and Stout dropped the lawsuit. As soon as the federal judge dismissed the case, Judge Gardner F. Goodwyn, Jr., reduced the sentence for Hood's concealed-weapons charge to a fine of $10 and no prison time. Although the forces of segregation won this fight, the intimidation of David Hood continued from police officers and the Klan, who were often one and the same.

During Washington's trial, Hood would discover two unexploded sticks of dynamite behind his home, and he received threatening phone calls night and day. Persons unknown broke into his home one day and stole $500, and that night they robbed his office of another $700—Hood never trusted banks and kept large sums of cash in a desk drawer at work and under his mattress at home. He installed large security lights around his home, but the harassment seemed to grow worse. Hood then hired three men to guard his house at night but soon dismissed them because of the cost. He decided to guard the house himself and began sleeping on the couch in the front room while clutching a loaded rifle.

Early one morning at 1:30 a.m., someone tossed several sticks of dynamite toward the front porch but missed the target. The bomb rolled away from the porch and exploded—dislodging bricks from the house and showering Hood with glass. He ran outside with the gun but found no one to shoot. "In my opinion," the attorney said soon afterward, "whoever threw the dynamite was afraid to get close to the house and stood across the street and didn't throw it as far [as] intended." His wife and two children, asleep in a back bedroom, were uninjured. Although Hood feared for his life and the safety of his family, he remained undeterred in the quest for integration in Bessemer and civil rights for its black community.

IN 1957, AN end to racial segregation in Bessemer seemed inevitable, but most whites resisted the change. They joined other communities throughout the South and organized a local White Citizens' Council chapter to preserve the laws and customs of segregation through a "lawful and logical" program of raising public awareness and disseminating information. The Bessemer Citizens' Council distributed segregationist literature that included such titles as *God Laughs at the Race-Mixers, We've Reached Era of Judicial Tyranny, The Supreme Court Must Be Curbed, God the Original Segregationist,* and *Let's Restore to Africa Her Stolen Children.* The rhetoric in these pamphlets was unmistakably clear. Black Christians, as one writer believed, should remain content with being "our brothers in Christ without also wanting to become our brothers-in-law." Another essayist wrote that cannibalism persisted in parts of Africa because the natives had no contact with white civilization. "That is still the way the Africans act," he supposed, "when they don't have one single Southern White man around to hold them back."

The Bessemer Citizens' Council held a number of community forums during 1957, one featuring a fiery speech by Judge George Corley Wallace. The thirty-seven-year-old Wallace was just beginning his first campaign for governor. As a circuit judge in Barbour County, he was a populist showman with shifting political convictions. In 1948, he remained a loyalist to the national Democratic Party at a moment when most Alabama delegates bolted the convention over civil rights. As historian Dan Carter concluded, Wallace was a segregationist, "but he wasn't a *stupid* segregationist." But his stance on segregation was immovable.

By the mid-1950s, he was a vocal opponent of federal government attempts to end segregation, and he urged white southerners to resist these intrusions. Addressing four hundred whites in the auditorium at Bessemer High School, Wallace warned listeners not to be lulled into a belief that integration was inevitable. "It definitely is not," he said. "We should keep telling the Supreme Court, the Congress, the President, and the Communist·Party that we are not going to integrate, and that's that." The only way that forced integration would occur, Wallace insisted, was to "subvert by force" the constitutional rights of the majority of the southerners. "Therefore, the fight that you and I and other southerners are making against unlawful and unjustified interference by the federal government in local affairs," he said, "is a fight to preserve constitutional government in this country and to guarantee that all citizens of this nation remain free."

For many whites in the Alabama of 1957 and 1958, Wallace's rhetoric was too flaccid. When he criticized primary opponent John Patterson's connections to the Ku Klux Klan, he picked up the endorsement of
the state's chapter of the NAACP. With this unwelcome support from
the state's leading civil rights organization, he finished a distant second
to Patterson in statewide balloting. Judge Wallace returned to the bench,
where he focused on ways to defy federal court orders for his own political gain.

Wallace's call for the end of federal interference must have seemed
prophetic in September 1957, when President Dwight Eisenhower
ordered riot-trained units from the 101st Airborne Division to enforce
integration at Central High School in Little Rock, Arkansas. Senator
John Sparkman (D-AL) called on Eisenhower to withdraw the troops as
a "first step toward restoring the principle of States Rights, and rebuilding the confidence and goodwill between the two races so essential to
the well-being of both." Local papers reprinted a telegram Sparkman
sent to Eisenhower in which he argued that one of the "great tragedies"
of *Brown v. Board of Education* was the "destruction of friendly relations
between Negro and White in the South and the engendering of hatred
and intolerance." The tremendous gains of both races were now "lost or
endangered."

These nationwide tensions served as a volatile backdrop and further poisoned the racial climate in Bessemer as Caliph Washington's
trial began at 9 a.m. on October 7, 1957, with defense attorney K. C.
Edwards and prosecutor Howard Sullinger striking the jury. In the end,
twelve white men from the Bessemer Cutoff area were the final selection. When all the witnesses in the case were sworn in, Judge Mathews
turned to Sullinger and Edwards and proclaimed, "All right, gentlemen,
state your case."

IN THE WEEKS leading up to the trial, Sullinger built a strong case
against Caliph Washington based on forensic and ballistics reports
obtained from the Bessemer Police Department. Chief Barron, following Cowboy Clark's death, ordered a detailed autopsy and a thorough

scientific investigation. This modern approach to crime solving was part of Barron's meager effort to establish professional standards for his force, but he did little to teach his men that a suspect, even a black one like Caliph Washington, was presumed innocent until proven guilty. But in a racial crime, especially when a black man was accused of murdering a white lawman, whether in 1907 or 1957, the assumption of guilt permeated the investigation, trial, verdict, and sentencing. This preordained conclusion empowered Sullinger to portray seventeen-year-old Caliph Washington as a cold-blooded, ruthless murderer.

Testimony on behalf of the state began with Dr. Lun Hsun Kwong, the pathologist at West End Baptist Hospital in Birmingham who performed the autopsy on Cowboy Clark around 2 a.m. on Friday, July 12. A native of Beijing, Kwong passed the examinations administered by the Alabama Board of Medical Examiners a month before performing Clark's autopsy. During the exam, he was asked to describe the "gluteus maximus muscle" and to give its "origin, insertion, and relationship to other structures." In response, Kwong described the buttocks as a "powerful muscle." A few weeks later, as the now-licensed pathologist sat in the witness chair, he told the court that after removing Clark's clothes, he noticed a small opening on the dead man's chest, three to four inches below the nipple on the left side; the wound corresponded with a hole in Clark's bloody blue shirt. He opened the abdomen to locate the object inside. He worked his way through the extensive internal hemorrhaging, examined each organ, and discovered two holes in the stomach made by the object that penetrated the skin. As he searched further, he found that the projectile had cut into the pancreas and punctured the aorta, the main blood vessel. "An aorta is like a water pipe or garden hose . . . a rounded tube," Kwong explained. Once it was ruptured, Clark went into immediate shock and was dead in twenty minutes.

As the pathologist continued to trace the path of destruction, he discovered a bullet lodged in Cowboy Clark's lumbar vertebrae. Removing it was tedious, but Kwong chiseled around Clark's vertebrae and made certain the bullet remained in its original condition, without any added scratches or deformities. Deputy coroner James Thompson carefully pulled it out and wrapped it in cotton gauze. This lone bullet, Kwong testified, was flattened on one side, having followed a straight, diagonal path of destruction through Clark's body.

Kwong noted that the bullet first nicked Clark's left forearm, then entered below his nipple at a 45-degree descending angle. It traveled six to seven inches before lodging in the backbone. On cross-examination, Kermit Edwards asked Kwong to explain how the bullet entered at such a strange downward angle, considering that Clark stood over six feet tall and Washington was around five foot seven. That was a difficult question, Kwong responded, because the answer depended on the position of the victim and the location of the gun. If Clark was standing, the gun could have been higher, but perhaps Cowboy was bent over at a 45-degree angle. "A bullet can travel in all kinds of directions," Kwong added. "It's very hard to predict. It will not follow the same truth, as you would imagine."

THE NEXT WITNESS was Dr. Carl J. Rehling, director of the Alabama Department of Toxicology. Within days of Cowboy Clark's death, he received the pistol, bullet, and bloody shirt from Chief Barron. Rehling was one of the pioneers of toxicology in Alabama. In the early 1930s, as a twenty-seven-year-old instructor of analytical and organic chemistry at Alabama Polytechnic Institute (later Auburn University), he and Herbert W. Nixon developed the idea for a state crime lab. In the wake of the sensationalist and bungled Scottsboro Boys trials, the state legislature passed, and Governor Bibb Graves signed into law, a bill that created the state department of toxicology. In the depths of the Great Depression, Alabama appropriated a meager $8,500 per year (which included salaries) and mandated that the agency cooperate with coroners throughout the state to determine cause of death in cases involving "foul play" and provide scientific assistance to all law enforcement agencies.

In the Cowboy Clark case, Rehling's job was to determine whether the bullet removed from Clark's body was fired from the gun found inside Washington's paper sack. He conducted an extensive microscopic and chemical study. He weighed and measured the bullet and identified it as a Remington 156-grain Smith & Wesson. The bullet was flattened on one side; as an expert witness for the state, he explained that it struck and bounced off a hard, smooth surface at a slight angle. In the pathologist's opinion, something external, not internal, caused the flat place on the bullet.

Rehling also examined Clark's bloody shirt to determine the distance from which the gun was fired. "Based upon my findings, and experience, as well as studies with this particular weapon," he explained, the gunshot occurred twelve inches or more from the shirt. "How much more I cannot say."

Following the microscopic examination of the bullet and the shirt, he conducted a ballistics comparison by firing test bullets from the .38 Special into a cotton box—a long box packed with long-staple cotton, which stops, without marring or mutilating, the bullet. On the witness stand, he explained with didactic self-assurance that each bullet fired from that weapon exhibited a microscopic pattern of "lands and grooves" transferred from the barrel. "It is a sort of fingerprint of that individual barrel," he added. He concluded that the bullet retrieved during the autopsy had indeed been fired from Cowboy Clark's .38 Special.

THE GUNSHOT THAT killed Cowboy Clark was fired near John Adams's open bedroom window. Three months later, as the first day of testimony neared its end, Howard Sullinger called Adams as a state's witness and asked him to recount the events of that humid July evening. Adams told the jury about the two-tone Chevrolet that struck the chinaberry tree near his house and the police officer yelling, "Get out, boy." The prosecutor asked him to identify the individual who stepped out of the car. When Adams hesitated, Sullinger shouted, "Who was he? Who was the boy?"

From the witness stand, Adams looked to his right and pointed a wrinkled index finger at Caliph Washington. He recalled losing sight of Washington and Clark as they walked around the back of the patrol car. "I couldn't see nothing," he said. "I didn't see nothing." Adams explained that he heard the officer shout into his microphone, "Sergeant, I'm shot three times in the stomach."

Adams's common-law wife, Mary Davidson, occupied his bed that night. Even as a witness for the state, their "sinful" living arrangement shocked the straight-and-narrow prosecutor. "You just kind of wanted to see if you were going to like her and lived with her a while?" Sullinger asked. "No," replied Adams, "I been living with her about twelve [years]."

Mary Davidson testified that the "fuss from cars" made such a loud noise that she awoke from a deep sleep. She peered over Adams's prone body to gain a better view. She saw the glow from the headlights and the bright flashing light on top of Clark's patrol car. From her bed, she watched quietly as Clark ordered someone from the car. When Sullinger asked Davidson who emerged from the car, she pointed to the defendant and said, "Caliph. Caliph Washington." She also heard, but never saw, the shooting. "I just heard the gun fire," she added, "and that was all I knowed." Yet she had seen Washington standing near the car when a voice from the darkness called out to him, "Don't get in the car." Caliph ran away, Davidson added, and "I don't know where he went."

The final witness was Elijah Honeycutt. As Caliph Washington fled during the early morning hours of July 12, he stopped at Honeycutt's house and asked for a ride to Travellick. As a witness, Honeycutt testified that when Washington exited the car, he said he had just killed a policeman. Honeycutt thought he was joking. "Oh, no, you haven't did anything like that," he said. Caliph just laughed and walked away.

WHEN CALIPH WASHINGTON boarded the Memphis-bound bus in Amory two days later, one of the first things passenger Furman Jones noticed was the brown paper bag in his hand. Now three months later, Sullinger called Jones to the stand to identify the bag and testify on behalf of the state. When the prosecutor asked what the two men talked about on the bus, Jones said that after some small talk, Washington told him he killed a policeman in Alabama.

Did you ask the defendant how he killed him? Sullinger asked.

Jones responded, "He said he killed him with the policeman's pistol and he told me that the pistol was in his bag that he had."

Sullinger held up the bag and inquired, "Out of this bag?"

Jones said yes.

On cross-examination, K. C. Edwards probed Jones for inconsistencies in his story. But instead of discrediting Jones's testimony, Edwards
unwittingly strengthened the state's case, as the witness provided further
details on the conversation with Washington: "He told me that the polices
[*sic*] had been following him around, and he got out of the car there and
he said he kicked the polices and took his pistol and shot him."

The prosecutor immediately stood from his chair and asked court
reporter Sydney Eckstone to read back the testimony just given. The reporter
complied, and Sullinger looked at the jury. In a loud voice, he repeated the
line "Kicked the policeman and took his pistol and shot him."

A stunned Edwards turned to Jones and asked if Washington told
him about the police officer kicking or hitting him in any way.

"No, sir," he responded.

Edwards walked back to his chair and proclaimed in a frustrated
tone, "No further questions." Jones stepped down from the witness stand.

Following the brief testimonies of several material witnesses for the
prosecution, Judge Mathews closed the first day of the trial. He warned
the twelve men of the jury to speak to no one about the case, to allow no
one to speak to them about the proceedings, and to not discuss Caliph
Washington's trial among themselves until they heard all the evidence
and the charge of the court.

Bessemer's notorious lawman Lawton "Stud"
Grimes talks with Caliph Washington after his
arrest. Grimes later claimed that Washington
confessed to him about murdering Cowboy Clark.

6

"BECAUSE IT WAS SELF-DEFENSE"

ETECTIVE LAWTON "STUD" Grimes was the state's closing witness. For almost two decades, Jefferson County prosecutors in Bessemer used Stud to provide a colorful punctuation mark to the end of a case. His gruff manliness and ability to spin a story resonated with the white working-class men who filled the jury boxes—he was, after all, one of them. Whenever Stud investigated a crime or testified in a case, the news rumbled across Bessemer like an approaching thunderstorm.

At times, his police methods garnered national attention, including a 1955 case of a jealous wife who discovered a photograph of her fun-loving husband with a bikini-clad model. She demanded that Bessemer police arrest the woman for "alienation of affections and indecent exposure." Detective Grimes conducted an exhaustive search throughout the city, relying on the photo. A few days later, he arrested a sin-oozing brunette named Myrtle, placed her in the back of the car, transported her to the police station, and escorted her to an isolation cell. The red-faced detective brought Police Chief Charles Thomas Mullen to meet the scandalous woman—a life-size cardboard cutout used for a local beer promotion. "It's fantastic," Mullen said.

As the Washington trial resumed on Tuesday, October 8, prosecutor Sullinger called Stud Grimes to the stand. Grimes revealed that following Washington's arrest in Mississippi, the suspect made a voluntary oral statement about shooting James "Cowboy" Clark. Grimes said he had not mistreated or abused Washington or made any promise, inducement, or threat before the suspect made the statement. Grimes said he simply asked, "What happened?" Washington told him that he ran from the policeman because he had so much trouble with them over the years. When Cowboy arrested Caliph in Exeter Alley, he grabbed hold of the suspect's belt with his left hand and led him around the car. Clark then bent over to unlock the door with his right hand. Washington told Grimes, the detective testified, that he "just whirled in under him and grabbed his pistol and then stepped back and shot him two or three times."

When Grimes finished his testimony, Sullinger announced that the state rested.

Caught off guard by the prosecutor's sudden conclusion, Kermit Edwards was ill prepared to offer Washington's defense. "It's earlier than I expected," he told Judge Mathews. The attorney asked for five minutes to pull his case together, and the judge granted him ten.

The seemingly obvious legal strategy for Edwards was to portray Clark as a violent aggressor and Washington as a victim of police brutality. He could argue that the suspect acted in self-defense as Clark tried to pistol-whip him, and evidence would have supported at least part of this argument. The law of Alabama was clear that the killing of one human being by another was justifiable and without legal guilt when such a killing was in self-defense. "Neither divine nor human law," Judge Mathews once explained, "requires us to love our neighbor better than ourselves."

Edwards's task, then, was to convince the jury of three major points: first, that Washington had not provoked or encouraged the incident with

Clark; second, that the defendant had been in imminent danger of death or bodily harm from Clark; and third, that he had no reasonable hope of escape or retreat from the situation without putting his own life or safety in jeopardy.

But this was Bessemer, Alabama, in 1957. An all-white jury would find no sympathy for a black man who killed a white man, widowed his wife, and orphaned his children. Their emotional perceptions would be too much for Edwards to overcome. Washington had not even an ounce of hope of acquittal. When the trial reconvened, all Edwards could do was call a few witnesses for a limited and uninspired defense, sensing that a guilty verdict was inevitable.

Perhaps this explained why Edwards plodded through the testimony of defense witnesses—asking routine questions and failing to connect key pieces of evidence which might raise reasonable doubt in the minds of the jurors. When Lipscomb Police Chief Thurman P. Avery revealed that he had discovered a new dent on the right inside fender of patrol car number thirteen, the attorney never explored with the witness the possibility that the dent was caused by a ricocheting bullet—one that hit the fender and entered Cowboy Clark's body at an odd angle. "Something just dented it," Avery testified; "pierced it but didn't go through it; just glanced off. It happened that night." When he finished speaking, Edwards simply dismissed Avery from the stand.

As his last witness, he called Washington to testify on his own behalf, and to offer his own report of that fatal night for the jury to weigh alongside Grimes's convincing narrative. After the defendant settled in the oak chair on the witness stand, Edwards calmly led him through the events of July 11, 12, 13, and 14. For each question, Caliph Washington gave a short, precise answer. The car tailing him had no siren or flashing light. When the bullets whizzed by his window, he sped up. When the lights on the patrol car were turned on, he stopped right then. When Clark said, "Get out of that car, nigger. Put your hands up," Washington obeyed. When Clark asked about the whiskey, he told him that he had no liquor in his car.

According to Washington, Clark then led him around to the other side of the police car. He stopped, opened the door, and yelled: "Listen here, nigger, I want to know where that whiskey is at." You can search the car, Washington responded. He had nothing to hide. This only made Clark angrier. He bellowed, "You're going to be a smart nigger," and he drew the pistol from his holster. The lawman raised the gun to strike him, but Washington caught the officer's hands, and the pair "got to tussling" back and forth over the weapon. Clark tried to kick Washington's leg and push him back, while both of them held on to the gun. That was when the pistol fired three times. Washington never had control of the weapon, he claimed, and Clark's finger was on the trigger.

Following the third shot fired from the gun, Clark released the pistol into Washington's hands and fell against the car.

"What did you do?" Edwards asked.

"I run," the defendant said.

AS SULLINGER APPROACHED the witness stand to begin his cross-examination, Edwards noticed that prosecutor Sullinger was relying on several sheets of paper as a guide for questioning the defendant. Edwards petitioned Judge Mathews to allow him to review the pages, which appeared to be a statement, but the judge refused. Edwards then shouted a loud objection and demanded to see the papers.

Before Mathews could answer, the prosecutor interrupted, "What business is it of his what I am using to examine the witness with?"

Edwards jumped in and explained that Sullinger was using a statement made by Washington—which the defendant, and his attorney, had a right to review before it was used to impeach him. Although the law supported Edwards's argument, Judge Mathews overruled the objection.

Free to proceed, Sullinger began peppering Washington with a series of rapid-fire questions to draw out inconsistences between his testimony and the statement. Was Cowboy Clark standing close to you, the prosecutor asked, when you "grabbed the pistol and started to jerk it out of his hand?" The defendant answered, "No, sir." After you shot the officer, you said you laid him in the front seat of the car? He answered, "No, sir." Sullinger grumbled, "Didn't do anything for him, huh?" Washington answered, "No, sir."

For over ten minutes, Sullinger continued this unrelenting onslaught. The questioning took a toll on Washington, and he looked to Edwards for some relief. "Don't look at your lawyer," Sullinger yelled. "Look at me." Edwards objected, but Judge Mathews allowed the interrogation to continue.

Finally, an exasperated Edwards pleaded with the judge to stop the prosecutor's line of questioning and allow the defendant to review the statement that Sullinger was reading from. Mathews disagreed, and the questioning continued.

Emboldened by the free hand, Sullinger attempted to humiliate Washington. Holding Clark's pistol, he waved it in front of Washington's face and asked him if he ever held any part of the gun except the barrel.

Caliph Washington said no. As the prosecutor held the gun by the barrel, Washington showed how he had grabbed the barrel to keep the butt of the gun from coming down on his head. "I was just trying to hold it up," he explained.

Washington said he never had control of the pistol, and anyone who said he did was lying. Washington explained that the officer was already shot. "You mean while he had hold of this, he pulled the trigger . . . [and] shot himself? Is that how?" Sullinger enquired. "I don't know how it went off," the defendant answered. "It went off when we were tussling." Sullinger thought Washington's claim that Clark pulled the trigger and shot himself was ludicrous. The questions continued to pop fast:

SULLINGER: "You didn't have the gun in your hands then at all?"
WASHINGTON: "No."
SULLINGER: "You want to take that gun and show me how you backed off and shot that officer three times?"
WASHINGTON: "I didn't have it in my hands."
SULLINGER: "You heard Mr. Grimes's testimony, didn't you?"
WASHINGTON: "He lied."
SULLINGER: "Yes. Well, you heard the soldier boy off the bus, Jones?"

WASHINGTON: "He lied, too."

SULLINGER: "Lied, too?"

WASHINGTON: "I haven't talked to him in any ways."

SULLINGER: "That's right? And this boy, Honeycutt? He lied, too,
    didn't he?"

WASHINGTON: "Yes, sir."

SULLINGER: "And Adams lied? John Adams—the bald-headed
    Negro testified here yesterday? He lied, didn't he?"

WASHINGTON: "I guess he did."

SULLINGER: "Well, you heard him. Did he lie or didn't he lie?

WASHINGTON: "Yes, sir."

SULLINGER: "And Mary Davidson lied too, didn't she?"

WASHINGTON: "Sure did."

SULLINGER: "Then everybody here lied except you, haven't they?"

WASHINGTON: "Wasn't nobody there but me."

SULLINGER: "I see. Wasn't nobody there left but you, and you're
    testifying to suit yourself, is that it?"

WASHINGTON: "No, sir."

Sullinger suggested that Washington was the one lying. Since Cowboy Clark was dead and unable to testify, the prosecutor believed Caliph was making up his own version of the truth. Sullinger, barely pausing to catch his breath, asked: "Did you make up your mind that since the officer couldn't testify that you would come in here today and just tell the story that he tried to shoot you?"

Edwards jumped from his seat and yelled, "Don't answer that! We object." Judge Mathews agreed.

Sullinger stopped the questioning and dismissed Washington from the stand.

Following a short recess, to the surprise of the judge, K. C. Edwards rested the defendant's case.

FOR BOTH THE prosecution and defense, the admissibility of Caliph Washington's statement remained a serious issue. To support his use of the document, Sullinger called a rebuttal witness, deputy sheriff Walter C. Dean—the criminal investigator who wrote down Washington's words on July 14, the day he was captured. As Dean settled into the witness chair, Sullinger handed him a small stack of papers and asked if this was the statement signed by Washington. After he examined the papers and answered yes, the prosecutor submitted the statement as evidence.

Edwards offered his most spirited objection of the trial. This was inadmissible evidence, he insisted, because the statement was not presented during the state's main case against the defendant and was now being offered for the sole purpose of impeaching the defendant. The prosecutor simply wanted to catch Washington in a lie and thereby destroy his credibility.

For the next thirty minutes, Sullinger and Edwards argued over the document. Edwards pleaded with the judge to allow the defendant to read his own statement, but the prosecutor withdrew the evidence and began reading it into the court record. Edwards continued to object and pleaded with Judge Mathews to see the statement.

The judge finally relented, and Edwards read the statement carefully. As he finished, he looked up and again objected to the use of this evidence. The judge overruled.

FOLLOWING AN EIGHTY-MINUTE lunch recess, Judge Mathews resumed the trial and asked the attorneys to proceed with closing arguments. Although defense attorney K. C. Edwards meandered through the trial with no clear focus or direction, his closing attempted to connect the evidence to a cohesive argument in favor of acquittal. Caliph Washington sat behind a long oak table as Edwards walked over to the twelve white men who would determine his future. The bullet that killed Cowboy Clark, Edwards argued, was "the silent witness" in this trial. The silent witness could be heard if the jury would just look and listen. This was not a bullet fired with malice by Caliph Washington. This was a bullet fired accidentally by James Clark. The bullet spoke not in support of conviction but of acquittal. Washington and Clark struggled over the gun, and it fired; the bullet grazed the car door and ricocheted into the policeman's body. Edwards reminded the jury that the bullet was flat on one side, and there was also a new dent in the side of Clark's patrol car. For ninety minutes, Edwards did his best to convince the jury that this was a case not of murder committed in the heat of passion but of accident and self-defense.

At 3 p.m., it was Howard Sullinger's turn to present the state's closing arguments. He directed his impassioned appeal straight at the jury's sympathy, emotion, and prejudice. Caliph Washington had taken the life of a fine Christian man over nothing, he argued. "Jim Clark will never see the sun rise again," he pointed out. "He will never hear the birds sing again. He will never go back to his family again." Edwards objected to Sullinger's angry aspersions, but the prosecutor shot back, "Defendant doesn't like to be reminded that James Clark is dead."

Once again, Edwards objected, and Sullinger shouted, "James B. Clark is dead."

Mathews sustained the objection, but the prosecutor continued to stir drama: "I heard the pathologist say that he was dead!"

The judge instructed the jury to disregard the statements, and Sullinger continued the summation. Washington, he continued, was a "cold-blooded, ruthless killer" who had left an innocent man dying in the dirt. He had offered no assistance, just fled the scene, worried only about his own safety. "I don't believe a . . . killer like that boy would help anybody up out of the street. He shot him down in cold blood right there in the street."

In conclusion, Sullinger made a direct suggestion to the jury: "Get rid of this boy. I don't think he's needed in this community or any other community." James Clark was dead, and Washington lived, and "It ain't right."

WHEN HOWARD SULLINGER finished, Judge Mathews gave the jury his often-used, well-rehearsed oral charge in a capital murder trial. He reminded the twelve men of their solemn and grave responsibility in passing judgment on the life and liberty of a fellow citizen of Alabama. As jurors, they must use wisdom, patience, and courage to render a cold, dispassionate, and impartial decision. They must let neither prejudice nor sympathy influence the verdict. Every defendant, whether rich or poor, black or white, deserved a fair and impartial trial by a jury of his peers. "Our law knows neither creed nor color, condition nor nationality," Mathews explained.

This jury's sole objective, he said, was to ascertain the truth and render an honest, fair, and just verdict as a demonstration of complete justice between the state of Alabama and the defendant. Only the jurors could determine the facts in the trial, he noted, and "no mortal man can touch your judgment." The defendant entered the trial with the presumption of innocence, he reminded them, and it remained with him throughout the trial until "overthrown by evidence" that convinced the jury of his guilt beyond reasonable doubt. Reasonable doubt, the judge explained, was substantial doubt arising from the evidence and that remained after considering the testimony. In other words, the state was required to convince the jury of the defendant's guilt not beyond *all doubt* but beyond *all reasonable doubt*.

Judge Mathews finished reading the written charge. He looked up and said, "All right, gentlemen, you may retire." It was 4 p.m. The twelve white men stood and followed the bailiff from the jury box, as Caliph Washington feared for his life.

OUTSIDE THE COURTROOM where Washington was staring down his fate, a heightened fear of death and destruction worried many Americans that day. The Asian flu, a new strain, was spreading across the country, with a widespread outbreak in Alabama. The U.S. Public Health Service described it as the second biggest influenza epidemic of the century, behind the devastating flu crisis of 1918–19. Overhead, 560 miles out in space, the first artificial satellite, the Soviet Union–made *Sputnik*, was circling the globe every ninety-five minutes at speeds of more than eighteen thousand miles per hour. "This is a new day," an editorialist for the *Birmingham News* wrote of the beeping Communist satellite that was fired like a celestial bullet at the heart of American pride and democracy. The Associated Press reported that *Sputnik* was a "stunning blow" to the United States and a "smashing propaganda and psychological victory" for Russia. Communists now controlled the "high ground of space," and for many Americans this meant, as the *New York Times* reported, a "race for survival" and control of the world. Politicians branded the Soviet achievement the "technological Pearl Harbor" and a "great national emergency" that was an existential threat to the United States. The combined apocalyptic fear of foreign disease and foreign technology created a public frenzy and a sense of inevitable doom for many Americans.

That same day, the *Birmingham News* continued a four-part series on how Communists were directing racial events in the South. "We have moved unerringly along the path long ago planned for the South by Lenin, Stalin, and other Reds," journalist Edwin Strickland wrote. A few years later, the red-baiting Strickland would lead the Alabama Legislative Commission to Preserve the Peace—a state-appointed commission tasked with monitoring, investigating, and questioning "persons, groups and organizations who may be engaged in activities of an unlawful nature against the sovereignty of the state and against the peace and dignity of the state." Strickland reflected the views of many Americans that any organization or individuals expressing the same goals as the Communists must also be Communists. The platform of the Communist Party in America called for an end to racial discrimination, segregation, disenfranchisement, and lynching; guarantees for full political, social, and economic equality; and the "abolition of discriminatory practices" in jury selection and southern legal procedure. Since most civil rights organizations shared similar objectives, according to Strickland's logic, they must be Communist and their activities influenced by Marxist ideology. It seemed, in the minds of many Americans, that the foundations of freedom and democracy were crumbling. A writer from the *Birmingham News* summed up the intensity of the fear that day by declaring that the paper's contents would give readers "mental hiccups."

The banner front-page headline read: CRISIS, CRISIS, CRISIS, FLU, FLU, FLU, BEEP, BEEP, BEEP.

This culture of fear, tension, and paranoia served as the backdrop to the trial of Caliph Washington, which itself, ironically, revealed the unkept promises of American democracy. A little after 4:30 p.m. on Thursday, October 10, the jury announced it had reached a verdict. At 4:40 the jury reentered the courtroom. Washington watched as the men responsible for his life sat down in the hard oak chairs. "Will the defendant rise," Mathews said as he gestured to Washington. As the young man slowly stood, the judge looked over and asked the jury, "Gentlemen of the jury, have you reached a verdict?"

Jury foreman L. D. Watts answered, "We have, your honor."

Mathews instructed Watts to read the verdict.

"We, the jury, find the defendant guilty of murder in the first degree as charged in the indictment, and we fix his punishment at death."

Edwards asked Judge Mathews to poll the jury. Each of the twelve jurors was asked, "Is that your verdict?" Each answered in the affirmative. "All right, gentlemen, you may be excused," Mathews said.

As the jury left, Mathews called Washington to stand in front of the bench. "Caliph Washington," he said, "the jury fixes your punishment at death. Have you anything to say why you should not be sentenced, why sentence should not be pronounced upon you at this time?"

Washington trembled as he looked up and answered Mathews, "Yes, sir."

"All right, proceed," Mathews demanded.

"Because it was self-defense," Caliph pleaded.

"Well," the judge responded, "that is foreclosed by the verdict of the jury." He continued: "It is the judgment and sentence of the court that you be put to death by having a current of electricity caused to be coursed through your body, of sufficient intensity to produce death and that that course be continued until death is produced. May God have mercy on your soul." Mathews set the date of execution: December 13, 1957. At 12:01 a.m., Caliph Washington would die in the Alabama electric chair.

Washington hung his head and was escorted from the court by a uniformed sheriff's deputy and returned to the county jail, where he remained throughout the appeals process.

AFTER WASHINGTON RECEIVED the death penalty, state law required Judge Mathews to enter in the trial record, with or without the convicted man's consent, that the "defendant appeals from said judgment of conviction." With this automatic appeal came a suspension of the sentence until the Alabama Supreme Court heard the case, which could take months if not years.

Washington, however, was too poor to pay for the court costs and lawyer fees required for an appeal to the Alabama high court. By Thanksgiving 1957, he filed a statement of indigence. "My name is Caliph Washington," he wrote. "I am the indigent appellant entitled to an automatic appeal as provided by law, and I am without sufficient funds and have no reasonable way of securing the same to pay." By December, Judge Mathews appointed Kermit Edwards to prosecute the appeal for a fee not greater than $250.

In March 1958, Edwards, David Hood, and Orzell Billingsley filed a twenty-three-page brief with the Alabama Supreme Court arguing that the lower court's judgment should be reversed and a new trial granted before a fair and impartial jury. Most of the brief focused on Hood's initial concerns that the exclusion of blacks from the grand jury and the petit jury violated Caliph Washington's constitutional right to due process and equal protection under the Fourteenth Amendment. The attorneys summoned to court more than one hundred "bona fide Negro male citizens" of the Bessemer Cutoff to show that they had all the qualifications and none of the disqualifications to serve on a jury. The evidence showed beyond a doubt, the attorneys argued, that "there was an arbitrary, systematic, and intentional exclusion of Negroes from jury services solely because of their race, creed, or color, and in violation of the constitutional rights of this appellant."

The jury commissioners, the attorneys supposed, were skilled experts in excluding the majority of the population in the Cutoff from

jury rolls and boxes. In the Supreme Court's *Cassell v. Texas* decision
a few years back, they pointed out, Justice Felix Frankfurter affirmed
nondiscrimination in jury selection: "If one factor is uniform in a con-
tinuing series of events that are brought to pass through human intervention, the law would have to have the blindness of indifference rather
than the blindness of impartiality not to attribute the uniform factor to
man's purpose." Blacks summoned for jury duty, or serving on juries,
were a rarity in the Bessemer Cutoff, the brief continued, "and if they
were summoned and later served it was likely to be known all over the
community immediately." The exclusion of blacks from jury duty was
racial discrimination of the worst kind and prevented Washington from
receiving a fair trial.

The most serious error committed by the Bessemer court, the attorneys argued, was the use of the written statement to challenge Washington's credibility. During his cross-examination, the prosecutor used
the statement as a basis for questioning. Edwards asked Sullinger if he
was attempting to lay the foundation to impeach the defendant. If so,
Caliph and his counsel had the right to examine the statement before
testimony. At the time, Sullinger denied that he was laying a predicate.
Only after the defense rested its case did the prosecutor introduce the
statement as evidence. "It appeared to counsel," the attorneys argued,
"that there has never been, and could never be, a clearer violation, and,
in fact ignoring, of the rule which required that a proper predicate be
laid before an alleged prior contradictory statement of a witness may be
introduced." During the trial, the prosecutor never asked Washington
whether he made such a statement, nor was he ever allowed to read the
statement before answering questions. "The witness is entitled," the brief
continued, "where the statement is in writing, to read the same or have it
read to him before he can be required to answer whether or not he made
such statement."

The Alabama Supreme Court's 1928 ruling in *Manning v. State*, the
attorneys pointed out, held that a witness should be permitted to read
an entire written statement or deposition to "verify its authenticity and
contents." In addition, a statement of this kind was not admissible as evi-

dence in fact but could be used for the purpose of "testing recollection" of a witness or "for impeachment, which purpose or competency should be made plain to jury."

At trial, Sullinger complained that Edwards was attempting to read his mind to "determine and anticipate" if he intended to introduce the statement as evidence in fact. "It would appear that counsel did correctly read the solicitor's mind," the attorneys now argued, "because that is exactly what the solicitor did do." The introduction of the "prejudicial evidence" caused the jury to discount Washington's testimony and the physical facts that corroborated it "almost to a mathematical certainty": that during a struggle between Clark and Washington, the fatal shot was fired accidentally, struck the car, and deflected into the body of the deceased.

In conclusion, the appellant "earnestly insisted" that this verdict should be reversed and a new trial granted before a jury "properly and legally selected." K. C. Edwards, as the attorney of record for Washington, asked to "argue this cause orally before the court at some appropriate time."

In response, Attorney General John Patterson and Assistant Attorney General Edmon L. Rinehart filed the state's brief and argument on April 22, 1958. They contended there was "no error apparent" in the Bessemer court's conviction of Caliph Washington and asked the state's high court to affirm "in all respects" the verdict and judgment. The lack of blacks on the jury—or, as they emphasized, the "lack of proportional representation"—did not constitute discrimination, Patterson and Rinehart argued. "We contend," the brief continued, "that the evidence shows that the trial court properly ruled on the motion to quash the indictment and to quash the venire."

The attorneys also argued that admitting into trial evidence Washington's written statement was not a reversible error. Notwithstanding, they conceded that as a general rule and "proper practice," the witness should have been allowed to review the statement and either affirm or deny it. Regardless, they believed that since prosecutor Sullinger had referred to the statement during Washington's cross-examination, it was difficult to see how the defendant was misled or how the statement, "in any way, prejudiced the case." His testimony was consistent with the written statement, and the prosecution had already introduced self-incriminatory statements for which a predicate was laid, including "one in which the defendant admitted taking Clark's gun and shooting him." This "relatively trivial matter" did not influence the jury's verdict.

A *Birmingham News* photographer captures a heart-tugging
image of Florence Clark the day following her husband's death.

7

A VIOLENT
AND ACCIDENTAL DEATH

WHILE THE SIDES argued over Washington's appeal, Cowboy Clark's widow sought money from her husband's insurance policy. On June 24, 1957, less than three weeks prior to his death, Cowboy Clark had purchased a $1,000 accidental death policy from the United Security Life Insurance Company. If he died from drowning or bodily injury through "violent, external, and accidental means," it stated, then the company would pay the full amount to his wife and sole beneficiary, Florence Clark. The policy did not cover death caused by homicide, suicide, riot, insurrection, war, or airplane.

The week following Clark's death, Florence drove to the western Birmingham office of United Security Life to collect on the policy. Life's toll made the attractive dark-haired woman look older than her twenty-eight years: she now had an ex-husband, a dead husband, two small children, and no means of support. An employee of the insurance company explained to her that the company could not honor the claim, due to Washington's conviction. It would not pay her $1,000 but would give her a $2.40 refund on the premium. She accepted the check and drove back to her home in Lipscomb.

Within a few weeks, the widow Clark hired an attorney, W. E. Brobston of Bessemer, and in an effort to collect the $1,000, he filed a civil complaint against the insurance company and demanded a jury trial. In response, S. Palmer Keith, Jr., an attorney for United Security Life, filed a *demurrer*—accepting that although the facts in the case were true, they were still insufficient for the plaintiff to collect the money from the policy.

The suit came to a jury trial on June 4, 1958, in Judge Edward Lee Ball's municipal court in Bessemer. Just weeks before, the forty-six-year-old Ball was appointed to fill in for an ailing Freelin Mathews. A graduate of the University of Alabama, Edward Ball completed his legal studies at George Washington University in 1939. He practiced law in Bessemer until he joined the Army Air Corps during World War II, and as an officer in the 101st Airborne, he participated in the Normandy invasion. Following the war, he led the fight to end political corruption in Bessemer.

AS IN OTHER areas of the South, politics was a "major sport" in Bessemer, and local folks followed the crooked tomfoolery with fanatical interest. A local newspaper editorial writer believed corrupt government was the product of the "political thinking" of Bessemer's citizens. "If we enjoy the sensation of wallowing mentally in the gutter, our candidates for office can be counted upon to furnish the thrill." And they frequently did. Bribery, extortion, and payoffs were commonplace in Bessemer politics. "It's a hell-of-a-place," a citizen once noted, "whether you like it or hate it."

In Bessemer, "political shenanigans" were a constant, one writer believed, as was "the specter of corruption lurking in dark corners." Government leaders tried to disavow such notions with their first-rate abilities as popular entertainers. For over forty years, Jasper "Jap" Bryant, dubbed "Mr. Bessemer," was the city's most colorful and powerful political leader. Bryant, with a wad of white hair that resembled the top of an unraveled cotton swab, humored locals with his corncob civic boost-erism. The buttermilk-swigging Bryant served as a city alderman from 1913 until he became Bessemer's mayor in 1934—a position the popular bicycle shop owner held until his defeat in 1946.

Bryant's loss came at the hands of reform-minded World War II veter-ans who returned to Bessemer in 1945 and 1946 to wage war on the city's vice and corruption. In the war against Germany and Japan, American soldiers witnessed firsthand the devastating effects of a corrupt politi-cal order led by demagogues and filled with cronyism and extremism. Throughout the South, veterans came home to win, as historian Jennifer Brooks noted, "the homefront battle against . . . political incumbency, civic complacency, and electoral fraud." In Bessemer, attorneys Edward Ball and Edward Saunders, and the Veterans Committee for Better Besse-mer, fought to change the form of city government from mayor-alderman to a three-man city commission.

In their quest for reform, the committee campaigned against the city's political establishment, which they claimed misused federal funds, maintained excessive travel expenses, used prisoners as private laborers, and profited from various other underhanded deals. "These are but a few of the irregularities existing today in the management of your city," the veterans proclaimed. "If you believe that these con-ditions should be stamped out, help your own veterans restore good government to Bessemer." Over 90 percent of the city's electorate went to the polls in November 1946 to give the ex-servicemen a 190-vote victory over Jap Bryant and the old order. "What we did," Edward Ball said following the November 1946 election, "was in the interest of good government."

In that election, voters selected Ball as the new city attorney. When he took office in 1947, he began investigating political corrup-tion and illegal activities in the Cutoff. One commissioner, Joe F. Lewis, demanded a grand jury investigate the widespread professional gambling in the area and corruption in the Bessemer Police Department. Judge Gardner Goodwyn, Sr., appointed the grand jury, but the eighteen men found no organized gambling in Bessemer and concluded that the whole investigation was nothing more than a political witch hunt. In contrast to Commissioner Lewis's views of police corruption, the grand jurors described the city and county law enforcers in Bessemer as "vigilant, energetic, effective, and honest" in carrying out their duties. One citizen, however, proclaimed that the "public don't give a damn. They got the kind of law enforcement they want."

In 1950, weary of the political upheaval, Bessemer voters swept out Ed Ball and the other reformers and returned the old guard to office, including Mayor Bryant. Following his reelection in 1954, a grand jury indicted the mayor for "misconduct of a public officer" by profiting from the sale of property by the city and earning twice the money allowed by the Alabama Code. In April 1956, while awaiting trial on these charges of political corruption, Bryant died of a heart attack. He was succeeded in the mayor's office by Bessemer's next political kingpin, Jess Lanier, who would dominate city politics for the next eighteen years.

Following his failed reelection bid for city attorney in 1950, Ed Ball returned to private practice in Bessemer, and then assumed the circuit judgeship in 1958. A likable fellow who loved to tell stories and charm folks with his homespun humor, Ball was tall and bare-boned with dark wide-set eyes, a high forehead, and a receding hairline. From the bench, Ball exhibited a conscientious legal mind, and most of his decisions were careful, professional, and well grounded. "He was a good student of human nature," recalled one lawyer who argued cases before Ball. "He managed to become part of the establishment, but not offensive."

The question before Judge Ball's court on June 4, 1958, was whether Florence Clark should collect $1,000 from her husband's accidental death policy. The burden of proof in this civil case was much lower than in Caliph's criminal case. The Alabama Code established that the facts in a civil case must be established by a *preponderance of evidence*, whereas in a criminal case the evidence must prove guilt *beyond a reasonable doubt*. The paradox of the case was striking. Caliph Washington was convicted, beyond a reasonable doubt, of first-degree murder. But Florence Clark and her attorneys now needed to prove, based on a preponderance of the evidence, that James Clark's death was an accident.

Florence Clark's attorney Brobston played to the jury's sympathy and portrayed his client as a young, grieving widow mistreated by a heartless insurance company. The previous year, when officials at United Security Life refused her request, she hadn't known what to do. "I was in a state of shock at the time," she sobbed to the jury. "They told me to leave the policy and instead of them paying me off, I should come back to Lipscomb and sue the City of Lipscomb." She chose, instead, to sue the insurance company. She testified that company officials never explained why they refused to give her the $1,000. Regardless, she admitted in cross-examination that she knew all along that this was an accidental death policy.

Florence Clark's weepy testimony seemed to sway the all-male jury. Brobston anticipated that the insurance company's lawyer, S. Palmer Keith, would focus his case exclusively on the guilty verdict in the Caliph Washington criminal trial. So Brobston called to the witness stand deputy coroner James W. Thompson, who admitted that none of the forensic evidence proved that Clark died as a result of homicide—neither the autopsy, nor the death certificate, nor the coroner's report.

Brobston pressed the issue further: "You couldn't say that it was physically impossible for Mr. Clark to have been shot in a struggle over the gun, do you?"

Thompson conceded that he could not, which was the defense's contention in the criminal trial.

Brobston rested his case. Attorney Keith offered, as evidence to support the murder claim, the death certificate, coroner's report, criminal docket sheets, and a transcript of the Caliph Washington trial. Keith called no witnesses, and then rested his case.

Judge Ball now gave his oral charge to the jurors. The outcome of the trial, he instructed them, depended on their definition of the word *homicide*. If the jury decided that Caliph Washington intentionally killed Cowboy Clark, then Florence Clark had no right to collect the insurance money, but if they decided that he died as the result of an accident, she could receive the $1,000. The burden of proof, Ball explained, was upon Florence Clark and her lawyers. They had to prove to the jury's "reasonable satisfaction" that Cowboy Clark met his death through a violent accident in the natural course of human activities.

Despite claims of impartiality, Judge Ball appeared to be stacking the case in favor of the widow Clark. The jurors read the transcript of Washington's criminal trial, where a jury ruled that the homicide was first-degree murder; those twelve men were now being asked to decide that a homicide can be accidental. How could the insurance company win?

After less than twenty minutes, Edward E. Capps, the jury foreman, announced to the court, "We the jury, find for the plaintiff and against the defendant, $1,000." To help the young widow, they considered her husband's death an accident.

THE VERDICT BROUGHT no relief for Caliph Washington as he waited in the Jefferson County Jail in Bessemer for the Alabama Supreme Court to rule on his appeal. In 1958, seven justices sat on the court's bench: Thomas S. Lawson, Robert T. Simpson, Davis F. Stakely, John L. Goodwyn, Pelham J. Merrill, James S. Coleman, Jr., and Chief Justice James Edwin Livingston. All except Simpson were from counties in the Alabama Black Belt, that swath of rich soil ripe for growing cotton and uncompromising in tradition. Blacks constituted an overwhelming majority of the population in those counties, yet a handful of whites held the balance of power in politics there. As one keen Alabama observer noted, the black majority were seen as "good field hands and not much more." These justices espoused the values of this rural white society.

During the 1950s and 1960s, many of their rulings, or their lack of action, on racial issues reflected these values. They engaged in a judicial and procedural "massive resistance" to civil rights legal issues, including supporting the ban on NAACP activities in Alabama. "The furor of the times," authors Tony Freyer and Paul Pruitt wrote, "blinded many white lawyers and even more white office holders . . . to what they knew perfectly well, that too often Alabama courts were inadequate to conduct even routine business."

For years, critics blasted the provincial nature of Alabama's judicial practices and its antiquated procedural system, which remained mostly unchanged since 1852. As Pruitt and Freyer discovered, the high court justices received so many appeals that they were unable to make "coherent use of their own procedures." The court's business was to interpret the law and offer rulings on lower court errors.

But because of the heavy docket load, the justices considered cases in four-member divisions, as authorized by Alabama law: the court might "sit, hear, consider, and determine cases and exercise all its powers and jurisdiction, in sections of four judges." The chief justice served as the fourth member in each of the two divisions. Four members of the court constituted a majority, and if all agreed on a case, their judgment would become the opinion of the court. If any member of the division deciding the case disagreed with the judgment, the case would go before the entire court for consideration. For that reason alone, judges rarely wrote dissenting opinions, to allow cases to move more quickly through the system.

As Pruitt and Freyer showed, most cases heard before the Alabama Supreme Court were "one-man decisions" made by a justice who wrote the opinion before the court issued its final ruling. Cases submitted were assigned to a particular judge on a rotating basis, beginning with the court's junior member and then moving "up the ladder" to the senior. Caliph Washington's case went to senior associate justice Thomas Seay "Buster" Lawson, the head of the Lawson Division, which also included justices Davis Fonville Stakely and Pelham J. Merrill.

Kind, benevolent, and paternalistic, Thomas Lawson was an old school Black Belt judge with conservative racial views in line with others of his generation. Born 1906 in the Hale County hamlet of Greensboro, he grew up in an elite Bourbon-class home. His father was president of the People's Bank of Greensboro and served seven terms as the city's mayor. His mother, Amy Seay, was the daughter of the two-term Alabama governor Thomas Seay. The younger Lawson graduated from the University of Alabama with a bachelor of laws in 1929 and practiced in Selma and Greensboro before becoming a state assistant attorney general in January 1931 under Greensboro native Thomas E. Knight, Jr., one of the key players during the Scottsboro Boys trials. Under Knight and his successor, Albert Carmichael, Lawson labored as one of the state's prosecutors in the cases against the nine boys accused of raping two white women. In 1937, Lawson helped end the trial phase by abandoning the cases against the four remaining defendants.

In November 1938, voters elected the thirty-two-year-old Lawson to be Alabama's attorney general, a position he held almost four years. On October 1, 1942, Governor Frank Dixon appointed him to the Alabama Supreme Court to fill the seat vacated by the death of Thomas E. Knight, Sr., the father of his former mentor and the author of the majority opinion upholding the verdicts and death sentences in the initial Scottsboro Boys trials. In November 1942, voters elected Lawson to the Alabama Supreme Court.

A pious Methodist, Lawson was the self-appointed guardian of the morals of the court, often scolding his fellow justices for their lapses with alcohol and women. When a rumor circulated that one of the justices was carrying on a torrid love affair with the sister of Alabama governor James "Big Jim" Folsom, the crusading Lawson decided to confront his colleague. Lawson arrived at the man's home, as the story was told, and discovered every light in the house burning bright, but no one was willing to answer his repeated knocks on the front door. Walking around to the back of the house, he peered through a window to find his fellow judge sitting disrobed on a large Persian rug eating turnip greens and cornbread with five-foot-ten-and-a-half-inch naked Big Ruby Folsom.

The puritanical Lawson looked and acted the part of the omniscient and distinguished jurist: he had a long, pleasant face, an uncomplicated smile, and deep-set probing eyes under close-cropped slate-colored hair. He was shrewd, listened carefully, and responded in judiciously chosen words. "He understood the power of words," an acquaintance recalled, "and liked that power."

IN THE CALIPH Washington case, Lawson followed the usual procedure for a criminal appeal. He studied the briefs filed by the two sides and composed a memorandum for the other members of the division who would hear the oral argument. "In this way," as one justice described the process, "each member of the panel is fairly well informed of what the case is all about prior to the argument, thus saving consider-able time."

For oral arguments, the state was divided into eight geographic divi-sions, also referred to as the "call of the divisions" procedure—each divi-sion having one week set aside to hear oral arguments. Beginning on the fourth Monday of November, the court heard oral arguments from the nine counties of the sixth division: Blount, Walker, Winston, Cullman, Fayette, Lamar, Marion, Tuscaloosa, and Jefferson (including the Cut-off). By the mid-twentieth century, most of the justices found the system an "anachronistic and defective" leftover from the nineteenth century, when communication was slow and getting to Montgomery from some parts of the state took days.

During the 1950s, the Alabama Supreme Court rarely heard oral arguments. Most appellate lawyers submitted their appeals on briefs to speed up the slow process. Some justices on the court, like Pelham Merrill, found oral arguments a waste of time. "Generally to argue," he once said, "means delay." One court observer agreed that a request for an oral argument reflected a "conscious delaying tactic to give time." Other justices considered oral arguments a welcome relief from the cold and cloistered task of reviewing trial transcripts and briefs. "Were it not for cases argued orally," Justice John Goodwyn once said, "our work would be wholly confined to the written word."

Caliph Washington's attorneys hoped delay would keep their client out of the electric chair for the unforeseeable future. Justices Livingston, Lawson, Merrill, and Stakely heard the oral arguments in Washington's case on Friday morning, November 28, 1958, in the colorless courtroom in the old Judicial Department Building on Dexter Avenue in Montgom-ery. The four black-robed justices entered the courtroom from the two dark, six-paneled doors behind the long wooden bench, and everyone in the room rose to their feet. The marshal of the court announced, "The Alabama Supreme Court is now in session." The appellant and the appel-lee had thirty minutes each to argue their cases.

During the weeks after the oral arguments, Justice Lawson prepared an opinion to take into conference with Livingston, Stakely, and Merrill. The four justices gathered around the long, narrow table in the Supreme

Court conference room—a spacious, high-ceilinged room, with comfortable leather chairs and plenty of bound law books—to discuss several cases, including Caliph Washington's appeal. In order of seniority, Livingston sat at the head of the table, with Lawson to his right, Stakely to his left, and Merrill to the right of Lawson. No one was allowed in as the justices discussed the cases. "It is a sacred rule," one justice said at the time, "that anything taking place there, anything said or done concerning a case, remains there."

They discussed cases according to seniority, so Chief Justice Livingston's cases were first. "Often there are heated words of disagreement as to the law," a justice recalled, "but it goes no further than that. Each justice respects the right of the others to disagree." When Livingston finished, Lawson led the discussion on the Caliph Washington case. After the justices' thorough give-and-take, Lawson read the opinion he authored.

His colleagues interrupted him frequently to ask questions and discuss further. After he concluded, the group voted in reverse order of seniority: Merrill, Stakely, Lawson, and Livingston. This way, in theory, junior members would not be "unduly influenced by the vote of the seniors." All four justices voted in favor of Lawson's opinion on the Washington case.

On Thursday, February 12, 1959, Justice Lawson handed down the supreme court's decision in *Caliph Washington v. State of Alabama*. In point after point, he refused to find fault with the lower court's actions. The bloody shirt, the pearl-handled pistol, and the brown paper sack were all correctly admitted as evidence. The bullet taken from James Clark's body "was properly identified and accounted for" and admitted without error.

On the other hand, Lawson noted that the flattened surface of the bullet, along with the testimony of the state toxicologist, was "advantageous to the defendant" and supported Washington's testimony that he did not grab the gun, step back, and shoot Clark. "In other words," Lawson added, "this evidence was in some way supportive of the theory that the pistol was accidentally discharged during the tussle which ensued after the deceased raised his arm to strike the defendant."

Justice Lawson provided a bewildering review of the constitutional issues raised in the defendant's brief on whether juries that excluded blacks denied a defendant equal protection under the Fourteenth Amendment. Lawson argued that the burden of proof was on the defendant to prove the alleged racial discrimination, and the facts proved otherwise. The grand jury that indicted the defendant included a black. In addition, four members of Washington's "own race" were in the jury pool. The defendant's lawyers never charged "fraud or irregular practice" in the method of selecting the grand jury. "The fact, if it be a fact," Lawson wrote, "that Negroes were excluded from prior jury rolls and boxes because of their race can only serve to shed light on the conduct of the members of the Jury Board in making up the jury box of August, 1957." This was not sufficient to show systematic exclusion in the indictment of Caliph Washington.

Regardless, Lawson conceded that "few, if any," blacks served on Bessemer Cutoff juries. This was a federal question, he added, and the U.S. Supreme Court "should determine whether or not the lower court denied Washington's federal rights." At every turn, Lawson circumvented constitutional issues. In short, he and the rest of the Alabama Supreme Court did what most southern courts were doing: sidestepping the race issue and finding other reasons to overturn a lower court decision and avoid a constitutional showdown.

Lawson reviewed the damaging evidence against Caliph Washington: the witnesses that placed him at the scene of the shooting, the "voluntary" oral confession he gave to Lawton Grimes, and the testimony of Furman Jones and Elijah Honeycutt that Washington admitted killing a policeman. From the witness stand, Washington denied making statements to Grimes, Jones, and Honeycutt.

During the defendant's cross-examination, Justice Lawson pointed out in his opinion, the lower court allowed the prosecuting attorney to question him from a written statement. The defendant, however, was never allowed to see the document in order to "refresh his memory or to explain any inconsistency, although his counsel requested that he be permitted to do so." According to Lawson, the rule of law was clear: a witness was not bound to answer questions about a writing produced by him unless he first had the opportunity to read the document. In *Parker v. State*, the Alabama high court had ruled that if a statement was to be introduced as evidence to impeach a witness, the "statement must be first shown to the witness in order to allow the witness to refresh his memory and to explain any inconsistency."

In the Washington case, however, attorneys for the state of Alabama never argued that the prosecutor admitted the statement correctly into evidence. The error was "harmless to the defendant," they believed, and should not compel the high court to reverse the lower court's ruling. Lawson admitted that the written statement contained much of the same account that Washington related from the witness stand. Regardless, the document contained "numerous statements which were apparently in contradiction of other aspects of the defendant's testimony on cross-examination." This placed Caliph Washington in the position of having told the jury "untruths either on the stand or in the making" of the written statement.

In addition, the state used the "oral confession" given to Stud Grimes in the same way. Particularly damaging was the statement attributed by Grimes to Washington that "I just whirled in under him and grabbed his pistol and then stepped back and shot him two or three times." The defendant countered with testimony that provided an "entirely different situation, which if believed by the jury might well have resulted in a different verdict." The prosecutor, Lawson believed, used Grimes's testimony improperly, and it too "reflected upon the defendant's veracity." The state had no basis in arguing that this was of no injury to the defendant. "We do not feel," Lawson added, "that the rule of error without injury should be applied to this case where a man's life is at stake."

To the contrary, for this error, Lawson concluded, the "judgment of the trial court is reversed and the cause is remanded." Caliph Washington would stand trial again for the murder of Cowboy Clark. He would get another chance, not because of discrimination in the jury pool, but because of procedure related to evidence—an incremental stop, at best, toward civil rights and equal treatment.

For now, he returned to his Bessemer jail cell. Many residents of the city's black community grieved at Caliph Washington's plight. "The Washington family were very heavy laden," a neighbor later recalled, "as were the rest of the black citizens of Bessemer. To be accused of killing a policeman stirred everyone up." Yet most blacks felt powerless to force city officials to exert justice, fairness, and equality in the case. It was as if, one resident recalled, that the entire civil rights movement was bypassing Bessemer.

Asbury Howard (*third from left*) with leaders of the International
Union of Mine, Mill and Smelter Workers in 1954.

8

"THERE ARE LOTS OF
WAYS TO FIGHT"

T HE QUEST FOR justice and civil rights was deeply engrained in
the culture of Bessemer's black community. By the late 1950s, the
civil rights movement in Birmingham had a foundation in the churches,
where Christ's followers sought justice through nonviolent direct action.
Influenced by Martin Luther King, Jr.'s, words and deeds in Montgomery, many black preachers in Birmingham, especially Fred Shuttlesworth,
encouraged their church members to shine the light of truth on the injustices of segregation with love and nonviolence.

In marked contrast, Bessemer's most recognizable civil rights leader,
Asbury Howard, embraced violence as a necessary means for achieving
racial equality. "Armed resistance paid off more than a peaceful approach,"
he said. Blacks in Bessemer would fight back with guns instead of nonviolent actions and words because the "majority . . . understood that type
of talk." Since the early 1930s, Howard was an outspoken agitator and
one of Alabama's most controversial radicals. He embraced unionism,
avowed Communism, and proclaimed Christianity—an ideal antagonist

for the fascist-like white power structure in Bessemer. A longtime friend described Howard as "cagey and smart" with above-average intelligence who exerted "considerable influence" over other black miners.

Born in Autaugaville, Alabama, on January 18, 1907, Howard moved to Bessemer as a youth. In 1924, he was hired by Tennessee Coal and Iron's (TCI's) Muscoda red-ore mines as a mucker—a backbreaking job, shoveling iron ore into mine cars deep underground in ten- or twelve-hour shifts. During the early years of the Great Depression, Howard, like many other blacks in Bessemer and Birmingham, embraced unionism and soon became imbued with Communist ideals. At weekly meetings, he was exposed to literature including Karl Marx and Friedrich Engels's *The Communist Manifesto*, Vladimir Lenin's *What Is to Be Done*, and perhaps most important for Howard, James S. Allen's 1938 *Negro Liberation*. Allen argued that blacks must embrace Communism to achieve self-determination, destroy Jim Crow, and gain the "right to be treated on a plane of equality with the whites; in political life, the right to vote, to hold office, etc." Only then would the "Negro toilers and the white masses" be united in the struggle against capitalism.

In June 1933, restoring capitalism was on President Franklin Roosevelt's mind as he signed the National Industrial Recovery Act (NIRA), which recognized the workers' right to organize unions and obligated employers to bargain collectively with workers (but not with unions). The passage of the NIRA led to a boom in unionization throughout the county, including Bessemer. And when white Bessemer attorney Jim Lipscomb initiated an organizing drive for the radical, left-wing International Union of Mine, Mill and Smelter Workers (IUMMSW), Asbury Howard joined the effort. Large groups of black miners (and a few whites) flocked to sign up, giving the organizing drive, as one historian observed, "an air of civil rights activism."

In addition, as historian Robin Kelley has shown, these gatherings seemed more like spirit-filled revival services than union meetings. In Bessemer, one participant at a Mine and Mill meeting observed that "if you substitute "God" for "union," "devil" for "employer," and "hell" for "unorganized," you would have a "rousing sermon." The stories the speakers told, minus their vulgar language, "might well have been used to show the power and goodness of God instead of the union. And his 'why not join' was so much in the church tone, I was afraid he was going to have us sing the hymn of invitation."

In May 1934, with membership booming, union leaders called a strike in the mines operated by the Bessemer district's largest iron and steel companies: TCI, Sloss-Sheffield, Woodward, and Republic. After eight thousand men walked off the job, a wave of violence swept through the mining camps and Bessemer. When the companies ignored the workers' demands for union recognition, a seven-hour workday, and a wage increase, union officials went to war. For several weeks in May and June, firebombings, dynamite explosions, and gun battles with company lawmen were frequent. Even after Governor Benjamin Miller ordered in the Alabama National Guard, dozens of fistfights continued throughout Bessemer, including a large street melee that guardsmen had to halt.

In response, industry leaders, local politicians, and vigilante groups resorted to strong-arm tactics to keep the unions and the Communists out of Bessemer. The Ku Klux Klan experienced a revival of membership and began terrorizing suspected union leaders and Communists. Party leader Saul Davis was kidnapped from his Bessemer home, stripped, and flogged for several hours. Blaming the violence on the failure of local law enforcement, TCI officials hired "special deputies" to protect the life and property of the company from union activists and Communist radicals like Asbury Howard.

Following an investigation, FBI agents concluded that Howard was the primary instigator of the violence at Muscoda and was responsible for the plan to shoot any employee who crossed the picket lines. Miners adopted the slogan "No Union Minor Move—All Scabs Off Red Mountain." When the bloody strikes ended on June 27, 1934, two strikebreakers were dead, several company employees were wounded, and the IUMMSW remained unrecognized and weakened. Nonetheless, police intimidation and vigilante violence continued for months.

In 1935, after the Supreme Court declared the National Industrial Recovery Act unconstitutional, Senator Robert Wagner (D-NY) introduced the more comprehensive National Labor Relations Act. Approved by Congress and signed into law by President Roosevelt, the Wagner

Act, as it was soon called, restored workers' rights to join unions, outlawed unfair labor practices by employers, and forced businesses to bargain collectively with labor unions. The act also created the powerful National Labor Relations Board (NLRB) to resolve labor disputes and intervene if employers retaliated against workers who organized, joined, or led unions.

In Bessemer, tensions reached another boiling point on May 31, 1936, when miners in the IUMMSW (now affiliated with the new CIO—Congress of Industrial Organizations) organized another strike. Once again, FBI agents maintained, labor agitator Asbury Howard planned all the strikers' "dirty work" in open meetings on TCI property. The FBI held Howard responsible for the acts of violence committed by blacks in Bessemer because his radical rhetoric "inspired" his people to fight for their rights. "He was imbued with Communist ideology," one agent wrote, "and would do anything for the present Communist leadership in the IUMMSW at Bessemer." According to informants, Howard used the union office to mimeograph and produce Communist literature for distribution among the black population in Bessemer.

Bessemer police officers apprehended several suspects (most likely including Howard) under the 1934 seditious literature law (similar to an earlier ordinance in Birmingham), which banned any publication "advocating the overthrow of organized government by force or any unlawful means." In 1936, when Bessemer police arrested black IUMMSW member and Communist organizer Bart Logan (he used the alias Jack Barton) for possession of these unlawful materials, he was taken to the city jail where a TCI employment manager "abusively" questioned him. "He wanted to know all the [names of] Communist leaders of the country," Logan said, and specifically asked him about First Lady Eleanor Roosevelt. When Logan was brought before Bessemer municipal judge W. Frank Ball (Judge Ed Ball's uncle), Ball refused to read the literature before announcing a guilty verdict, ordering a $100 fine, and sentencing him to 180 days of hard labor. "It is all Communist stuff and you cannot have it in Bessemer," he said.

Horrified by the suspect's treatment, white Alabama native Joseph Gelders, head of the southern branch of the National Committee for the Defense of Political Prisoners, arrived in Bessemer to arrange legal counsel and bond for Logan, though he was ultimately unable to secure either. On his return to Birmingham, as he stepped off the bus near his home, several men grabbed him and shoved him onto the floor of a car. While the vigilantes stomped and kicked him, they read literature found in the victim's briefcase and laughed sadistically. Several hours later the men stopped in an isolated area, dragged Gelders from the car, tore off his clothes, and lashed him with a leather strap until he was unconscious. When Gelders later identified his attackers, one of them turned out to be a "special investigator" for TCI.

In the end, the IUMMSW lacked financial support to sustain the walkout, and in a few weeks the strike ended. TCI retaliated by firing Asbury Howard and more than 150 other workers in Bessemer. Howard appealed to the NLRB for relief. Following a lengthy hearing in Birmingham, the board ordered the company to reinstate all the fired miners and provide them with back pay. Howard received $1,004. The NLRB's decision paved the way for union recognition.

In 1937, after the last skull was cracked, the last house bombed or shot up, and the last radical meeting disrupted, organized labor won bloody recognition from U.S. Steel's Tennessee Coal and Iron division. "Every year we hammered away to change life some more," Asbury Howard later recalled. "We fought and gave of our blood . . . and we did change it." Although the fight was over, Bessemer's boilersuit culture of violence was so deep-rooted that night riders, roaming gangs, and other vigilantes continued to commit acts of terror, especially against those challenging the social or economic order. Many in Bessemer's political establishment endorsed this "ridiculous and arousing" violence and intimidation. "Such invasion of fundamental human and civil liberties," one newspaper writer complained, "cannot be dismissed with a light touch." But few citizens demanded an end to such practices. "The amazing thing," one Birmingham journalist noted in 1940, "is that unless the power of public protest and pressure is brought to bear to check the further development of these stupid and intolerable excesses, they apparently may go on. That simply must not be!"

In this milieu, Asbury Howard solidified his reputation as Bessemer's most fearless civil rights leader. "I and my union stand for racial equality," he said, "and through trade unionism, Jim Crowism will eventually be broken in the South." These words were not hollow. For Howard, the fight for union recognition was the beginning of a broader plan to achieve racial equality through voting rights for the disenfranchised black majority. He organized and taught schools for blacks in Bessemer on how to become registered voters and to persuade them, once they received the franchise, to cast their votes for Franklin Roosevelt. When Bessemer's Democratic Party executive committee decided to bar blacks from the polls, Howard organized a delegation to march on city hall in protest. When word reached the committee about the planned march, they rescinded the order.

During World War II, Howard took leave from his mining job to work full time for the union. Considering the IUMMSW leader a security threat, the FBI stepped up its investigations and described him as a mainstay of the Communist machine and a person who was "very necessary to the Communists who controlled the union because of his large following." Howard continued to duplicate and distribute Communist literature in Bessemer and was a member of such Communist front organizations as the Good Neighbor Club and the Alabama People's Education Association. When FBI agents examined his mail, they discovered that he received both the Communist newspaper, the *Daily Worker*, and literature from the Baptist Sunday School Board. Howard had somehow reconciled his Christian beliefs with his Communist ideals.

Following the war, during the Red Scare, the IUMMSW lost significant membership. One observer emphasized that the union survived only by "appearing to champion" the cause of equal rights for blacks. Howard continued his IUMMSW work, but the Cold War's anti-Communist fervor compelled him to hide his beliefs and activities. Informants explained to FBI agents that Howard now "avoided open espousal" of party rhetoric and anything that would arouse suspicion. He was quite clever to give no indication of Communist connections, which made it difficult for investigators to "pinpoint" his Red activities. "We've all got to be lily white right now," Howard said at the time. "They are just waiting to catch us with literature or anything that can be connected with the Communist Party.

There are lots of ways to fight," including at the ballot box. The FBI, however, concluded that he continued to pay his Communist Party dues to a union office in Denver.

In 1947, the Republican-controlled Congress passed the Taft-Hartley Labor Management Relations Act, which placed restrictions on unions' ability to strike, gave employers more flexibility, and required all union officials to sign an annual sworn statement that they were not a member of, or affiliated with, the Communist Party or any organization that advocates the overthrow of the U.S. government by "force or by any illegal or unconstitutional means." In 1949, the CIO expelled all individuals and unions suspected of membership in the Communist Party, which included the entire IUMMSW and Asbury Howard. The mostly white United Steel Workers of America seized the opportunity and won the right to represent the mine workers in Muscoda, but only, as one historian noted, "after resorting to racist and anti-Communist propaganda, KKK-style intimidation, and physical assault," which were the norm in Bessemer. The battle between the rival unions would continue for the next decade with frequent violent clashes.

February 22, 1952, was the eve of an election called by the NLRB to determine which union—CIO United Steel Workers or the IUMMSW—would represent employees at Republic Steel's Spalding and Edwards iron ore mines. Throughout the Bessemer area, representatives from both unions engaged in fierce campaigns to win the votes of workers. Asbury Howard and other IUMMSW leaders drove around spouting union propaganda from a big loudspeaker mounted atop a panel van. An interracial group of rank-and-file members followed close behind in an automobile caravan. When Howard's parade reached the Jonesboro section of Bessemer, a car filled with white CIO representatives zoomed in front, slammed on the brakes, and blocked the road. A few seconds later, seven more carloads of steelworkers arrived. The IUMMSW group was surrounded and vastly outnumbered. Someone, presumably Asbury Howard, spoke through the loudspeaker and warned the steelworkers not to attack. "We will defend ourselves," the voice announced. "You steel people go about your business." A man from the CIO fired a shotgun at the side of the van. In an instant, men from both unions were out of their vehicles and engaged in what observers described as a "pitched gun battle." Almost a hundred men were shooting pistols, shotguns, and rifles at each other from behind cars, trees, and dirt mounds.

Bessemer police officer W. J. Moore arrived on the scene a few minutes later and witnessed no shots fired, just a hundred or more union workers "milling around the area" and scores of spent shell casings littering the ground. The air smelled of gunpowder. As Moore and at least a dozen city police and county deputies tried to restore the peace, they discovered that the only injury was to John Harper of the steelworkers, who received a non-life-threatening shotgun blast to the seat of his britches. Asbury Howard later claimed that he was "shooting for the engine but hit the caboose."

Bessemer police officers arrested twelve workers from both unions, including Howard, who was charged with disorderly conduct, discharging of firearms, and assault with intent to murder. Howard quickly posted bond and within weeks was on a nationwide speaking tour to raise money for the defense fund supporting those IUMMSW members who were jailed following the "Battle of Jonesboro." FBI agents followed his every move—watching, listening, and reporting—as he spoke to unions and Communist organizations. He told an audience in Spokane, Washington, that blacks were fighting for equal rights and equal pay and against Jim Crow and discrimination. "Negroes are getting tired of Jim Crow and the Ku Klux Klan," he said, "and we have decided to defend our rights by taking matters into our own hands."

He told those listening to avoid coming into the South and stirring up trouble. "Outside workers have gone into the South to organize," he added, "but they were run out. The only ones who can do this job are the people who live there." He asked them to simply provide "financial and moral support" in the civil rights struggle. Union workers in Bessemer, he explained, were standing firm in their fight against the United Steel Workers and the Ku Klux Klan, who were often one and the same. Black and white workers in the IUMMSW, he added, were fighting together against "Jim Crowism" in the South and setting into motion forces of "peace and real democracy" throughout the region. An informant told FBI agents that Howard was raising not only money but also getting the

"Communist Party line regarding discrimination and civil rights before the rank and file members of the union."

BACK IN BESSEMER, Asbury Howard continued his push for voting rights for the disenfranchised black majority. While some members of the black community registered and voted during the 1920s and 1930s, that number dwindled to a scant few in the 1940s. Howard organized and served as president of the Bessemer Voters' League, a group dedicated to increasing voter registration, not just for union members but for blacks throughout Bessemer. "Discrimination is everywhere against the Negro in the South," he complained, especially for those wanting to vote. An informant told FBI agents that the league was a loose organization of black laborers who were primarily members of the IUMMSW. Asbury Howard served as the "guiding spirit," the informant added, and the purpose of the organization was to "control votes in union as well as in general elections."

Howard and other local black leaders, including Caliph Washington's attorney David Hood, coached league members on how to pass the tortuous "understanding test" that the Bessemer Cutoff Board of Registrars used for black applicants seeking the franchise. "White registrants," one newspaper editor noted at the time, "were assumed to know all the answers without any quiz" or were given a question such as "Who was the first President of the United States?" The "choice questions," the editor explained, "were saved for the Negroes." The Bessemer registrar asked as many as thirty-five questions about constitutional issues, legal statutes, and governmental structures. In addition, black registrants were expected to know the correct answer to questions about specific politicians, judges, civil servants, and lawmen:

> Who are the Circuit Judges of Bessemer? Who is the Civil and Criminal Judge? Who is Solicitor in the Bessemer Cut-Off? What form of government does Bessemer have? Name the Commissioners, their titles, and their terms of office. Who is the City Recorder? Who is the City Attorney? What form of Government

does Birmingham have? Name the Commissioners and their titles. Who is Chief of Police? Name the Circuit County Judges sitting in Birmingham. Who is the Judge of Misdemeanors and Felonies?

Eight years later, voter registration among blacks in Bessemer increased from seventy-five to two thousand—much to the dismay of local white officials—and the Bessemer Voters' League emerged as the city's dominant civil rights organization.

By 1956, with the ongoing Montgomery Bus Boycott garnering widespread attention, fear of black activism in Bessemer increased the anxiety among white residents. Throughout an entire week in February of that year, rumors of an "impending racial clash" sent white citizens into a frenzied panic. As the great terror spread, hardware and sporting goods stores sold out of weapons and ammunition. No protests, however, materialized. "Police were at a loss," observed a newspaper reporter, "to explain how the rumors began and whether they were circulated maliciously."

The following year, a few weeks before Caliph Washington's confrontation with Cowboy Clark, dynamite exploded at the Bessemer home of Asbury Howard and at the nearby Allen Temple AME Church. Luellen White was sitting on the front porch of her house when a late-model gray sedan, filled with unrobed white men, stopped near the church. A man in the front seat lit an object and threw it toward the church building. "I then saw a flash of light," White added, "and heard a loud noise. The next thing I knew I was sitting on the floor with glass being thrown all around me." In the church, the Alabama Association for the Advancement of Human Rights was holding a mass meeting and a Sunday evening church service when the blast shattered the stained glass window over the choir loft. A handful of people ran from the building, but most sat still while the twelve-year-old keynote speaker, evangelist George Hawkins, led the group in prayer. When he finished, Hawkins preached a sermon on "Abiding in God."

A few minutes after the Allen Temple bombing, an explosion occurred outside Asbury Howard's home. Neighbors reported that a carload of white men stopped near Howard's residence and tossed something near the house. The explosion broke windows and left a large hole in the ground—neither Howard nor his family were home at the time. Police Chief George Barron assigned detectives Lawton "Stud" Grimes and Andy Eubanks to investigate. Barron seemed surprised at the incident, because Bessemer had no racial trouble. "We actually don't know," he added, "the cause of the bombings."

The blasts were presumed to be racial bombings, but an unnamed FBI informant from Bessemer told investigators that the explosions were only made to look like the work of segregationist vigilantes. The Allen Temple blast was only a distraction from the real target, Asbury Howard. The bombings were the work of an official with the United Steel Workers of America and his "henchmen" who targeted Howard because of his standing as an "influential member of a rival labor organization" and his popularity among black working-class citizens in Bessemer. "This situation is a disgrace to our nation," one union leader proclaimed, "and lowers our moral standing in world affairs."

While Howard's Communist activities alienated some blacks in the Marvel City, for many, his work with the Bessemer Voters' League overshadowed his Marxist philosophy. As more and more black residents passed the intricate examination and voted, white Bessemer officials increased their efforts to intimidate Howard. In January 1959, police arrested the leader on charges of violating the Bessemer City Code, Section 27.72, which prohibited anyone from printing, publishing, circulating, selling, offering to sale, giving away, delivering, or exposing to view, within the Bessemer city limits, "any newspaper, publication or handbill of an obscene, licentious, lewd, indecent, libelous, or scurrilous nature . . . or any abusive or intemperate matter tending to provoke a breach of peace, or any matter prejudicial to good morals."

A few weeks before his arrest, Howard saw a political cartoon captioned "Hands That Can Still Pray," drawn by a white Southern Baptist artist named Jack Hamm from Baylor University in Waco, Texas. Hamm's stark black and white drawing depicted a handcuffed, kneeling black man, hands clasped in prayer. A card attached to the cuffs read: "You Can't Enter Here; You Can't Ride Here; You Can't Work Here; You Can't Play Here; You Can't Study Here; You Can't Eat Here; You Can't Drink

Here; You Can't Walk Here; You Can't Worship Here." The praying man, his eyes in a heavenly gaze, pleaded, "Lord, help all Americans to see that you intended human beings everywhere to have the same rights."

Asbury Howard was so moved by the image that he asked a white Bessemer sign painter, Albert McAllister, to reproduce the cartoon on a yard and a half of square canvas and add the words "Vote Today for a Better Tomorrow." Howard planned to place the banner on the walls of the Bessemer Voters' League meeting hall to encourage more blacks to register to vote. He never had the chance. A "confidential source" tipped Chief Barron that Howard commissioned "a sign painter of Caucasian descent" to paint a poster depicting "a Negro bound with chains with slogans encouraging Negro political activity." On January 21, 1959, Barron confiscated the unfinished artwork and arrested Howard and McAllister for violating the city code because he felt that "probable violence . . . might result from [the] appearance of such a sign before the public."

At police headquarters in Bessemer City Hall, the local black radical and the befuddled white printer were booked and released on bond. "I wasn't informed of the charge against me or what law I had violated until the next day," Howard said at the time. Prior to the January 24 trial, Chief Barron received "indications that groups of agitators" might disrupt the legal proceedings. He stationed most of his police force on duty that day along the second-floor corridor, to screen everyone going into or coming out of James Hammonds's courtroom.

After the judge gaveled his court into session, both Asbury Howard and Albert McAllister pleaded not guilty before a room of mostly empty chairs. From the witness stand, Chief Barron explained in detail how Howard and McAllister had violated the city code. Bessemer's prosecuting attorney summarized the case against the two men with the simple phrase, "It is my opinion that showing a man in chains is prejudicial to good order." David Hood, the defendants' attorney, told the judge, "If an attempt to induce or cause people to register to vote is an offense, then the Fourteenth and Fifteenth Amendments to the United States Constitution are void."

Nonetheless Judge Hammonds convicted the pair of provoking a "breach of peace" and undermining public morality in Bessemer. He fined each defendant $105 and sentenced them to six months in jail. Both men appealed their convictions and posted bonds as they awaited the outcome of their appeal across the street in the Jefferson County Circuit Court.

As Asbury Howard left the courtroom and walked down the stairway to the first floor of the city hall, he noticed forty to fifty white men lining the walls of the small lobby. As he cleared the last step, he was struck in the back of the head with such force that it slammed him to the floor. A few days later he recounted:

> The crowd of men around the wall rushed towards me. They closed in and pounced upon me. They lashed out with their feet in an effort to stomp and mutilate my face, head, and body. I struggled the best I knew how even though my back was on the floor. I finally managed to reach a corner.

His thirty-year-old son, Asbury Jr., punched, kicked, and gouged his way through the white crowd in a fruitless effort to reach his father. "My son put up a furious battle against unequal odds," the elder Howard recollected.

The mob, most likely Bessemer Klansmen and union thugs, pushed the lone city police officer on the first floor—identified only as a tubercular runt with thick eyeglasses—into a corner. The officer later told Chief Barron that he "could not observe any activity" in the lobby because someone knocked his glasses to the floor. Apparently, the policemen on duty outside the courtroom either ignored the noise from the fracas or returned to police headquarters at the rear of the building. Barron later claimed that he heard a "rumbling sound" and then someone shouted, "There's a fight," and he ran immediately with a group of Bessemer police to the lobby. Howard estimated that some fifteen minutes passed before Barron and his officers arrived, just as the white assaulters exited through the front doors and scattered.

"I was badly shaken up, bruised, and bleeding badly," the elder Howard recalled. Weak from loss of blood, he staggered through the front doors of the city hall and waited for someone to treat his injuries. He claimed that a city police officer told him to "get away from here," or he would be arrested for vagrancy. Chief Barron later told FBI investigators that he asked Howard repeatedly for the identity of the persons who attacked him, but Howard only asked to "see a photographer."

Two of Howard's friends drove him to Bessemer General Hospital, where he needed ten stitches to close the gaping wound in his head. Barron later recalled that Howard never identified any of the assailants, provided any information, made a statement, or filed a complaint concerning the attack.

But Howard did contact the ACLU in New York, and the incident received national publicity. Citizens from all over the country and prominent leaders such as Martin Luther King, Jr., Senator Hubert H. Humphrey (D-MN), Eleanor Roosevelt, and Reinhold Niebuhr urged the U.S. Justice Department to intervene in the Howard case. Even the usually aseptic *Birmingham News* complained that the incident gave the community an "additional black eye" and scolded the Bessemer police for not upholding "law and order." Investigators from the FBI office in Birmingham argued (based on the "best available information") that the Bessemer officers "did not stand by idly and allow the beating of the Howards to take place."

Clarence Kelley, the special agent in charge of the Birmingham FBI office, suggested in a report to FBI director J. Edgar Hoover, that the arrest of Howard was justifiable because a "large portion of the white population of Bessemer was composed of coal miners and steel workers who may well have caused serious trouble had a poster of the type purchased by Howard been displayed there." Kelley, who sixteen years later would become FBI director, emphasized that the Bessemer Police Department failed to conduct a complete, thorough, and exhaustive investigation to identify and arrest the assailants. "No proof has been brought out that the Bessemer police department condoned the activities of the attackers," Kelley wrote. "However, a reasonable implication might be inferred that such was case."

The only arrest police did make that day was of Asbury Howard, Jr., charged with disorderly conduct and resisting arrest. "I didn't believe in the nonviolent philosophy," the younger Howard said many years later. "We didn't know if we could practice nonviolence," especially in a town like Bessemer. "I think maybe some look down on us for that, for not really being people that were nonviolent. I just couldn't handle that. I had to retaliate, whether it meant life or death."

Ultimately, both Howards (and the printer) served several months on a Bessemer chain gang—with the elder Howard digging ditches dressed in a coat, tie, and dress slacks. On the way to and from the city jail each day, black convicts were chained to each other in a caged truck and driven through black sections of Bessemer for "educational purposes." In other words, chain gangs served as a reminder to all black citizens to avoid challenging the racial status quo and to stay in their place on the bottom rung of the social ladder.

Those black citizens who dared speak out did so anonymously for fear of retaliation. "We've got so little," a mother explained, "they might take that from us too, if they knew what we said." Most of the city's black population lived in areas with no streetlights, no sewage, running water that seldom flowed, streets made of dirt, and dilapidated houses. "Look at this place," said a tenant living in a crumbling shotgun shack. "These houses are killing people." Some whites recognized how bad the living conditions were for blacks in Bessemer. "If I were you," one white woman advised a black woman, "I'd move out of here, even if it's no farther than Birmingham. Bessemer is a terrible place for a Negro."

In the second trial, Caliph Washington
claimed that Mississippi state troopers
tried to hang and shoot him.

9

"I JUST SAY I AM INNOCENT"

LIKE MANY WHITE elites, Judge Gardner Foster Goodwyn, Jr., had a provincial and Pollyannaish view of Bessemer. He was "made of good material," one acquaintance wrote in 1937, but had the odd notion that Bessemer was a city of "exemplary morals" and gracious living. "He has indeed," the writer continued, "lived a very sheltered life." Born 1914 in Bessemer to Judge Gardner Goodwyn, Sr., and his wife Lora, he earned a law degree from the University of Alabama in 1938 and practiced law in Bessemer for several years before serving on the legal staff in the Alabama Attorney General's Office from 1945 to 1950. In 1950, voters in the Bessemer Cutoff elected him a circuit judge.

On November 19, 1959, Caliph Washington appeared in a Bessemer courtroom for a pretrial hearing under the watchful eye of Goodwyn, a slow-talking, erudite, and personable jurist whose court decisions reflected his straight-laced moralism.

During the pretrial hearing, Goodwyn appeared confused about Washington's legal representation. It was no wonder, as Orzell Billingsley and David Hood moved in and out of the courtroom like two busy travelers in a railway station. "Who is the counsel of record?" Goodwyn asked.

The courtroom remained silent. The judge scanned the faces, looking for someone to step forward to offer a defense for a young man fighting for his life.

"If the man's got counsel," prosecutor Howard Sullinger proclaimed, "then let it be known who's going to represent the man." No one said a word.

Goodwyn then asked Washington if he had hired a defense attorney. He answered no.

The judge turned to Caliph's mother, Aslee Washington, and asked if she had retained a lawyer.

She said no. "I haven't been able to get nothing," she added. "I can't hardly get me something to eat."

Kermit Edwards stood and asked to withdraw as Caliph's attorney because of the "great imposition" of having to defend the case again. "I would like to be relieved of it as of now," he asked the judge.

Goodwyn asked Orzell Billingsley if he would accept the appointment as counsel for Caliph Washington. Billingsley declined. The judge inquired why David Hood had not appeared in court that morning. "I believe I will issue a warrant of arrest for him," he told the deputy sheriff, "and let you find him and bring him in."

Following a recess, Deputy Sheriff Clyde Morris brought David Hood into the courtroom, and Goodwyn scolded the lawyer: "Well, you have inconvenienced everyone . . . and you have delayed us unduly." He asked Hood if he would accept a court appointment as counsel for the defendant.

The Washingtons had no money to hire counsel, Hood emphasized, and he needed cash to provide a quality defense.

Goodwyn overruled Edwards's motion to withdraw from the case. The judge then asked Washington and his mother if it was agreeable for Edwards to remain as defense attorney. They approved.

Initial chaos resolved, the trial began at 9 a.m. on a cold, blustery

Monday, December 7, 1959—the eighteenth anniversary of Japan's bombing of Pearl Harbor.

For Howard Sullinger and K. C. Edwards, the first order of business was the striking of the jury. Of the forty-seven men in the jury pool, several admitted that they believed Washington was guilty of murdering Cowboy Clark. Edwards challenged these jurors for cause, and Goodwyn dismissed them. Others expressed opposition to capital punishment. On Sullinger's challenges, the judge excused them. The final twelve selected for the jury were all white, blue-collar residents of the Bessemer Cutoff: Reuben Edward Aaron (section foreman), John C. Bousack (butcher), James Kenneth Davis (millwright), I. W. Elliott (tractor operator), Cleon S. Glover (well driller), William Frank Kelley (machinist), John Calvin Knowles (heavy equipment operator), Curtis Robert McGinis, Jr. (crane operator), James Thomas Rasco (weighman), William H. Russell (electrician), Jewell Stacey (blacksmith), and Melvin J. Vines (steelworker).

Once the clerk swore in the witnesses, his honor declared that all witnesses were to stay out of the courtroom and not discuss the case until called to testify. Most of the witnesses from the previous trial were subpoenaed to give testimony. All appeared at the courthouse except two. Birdie Robinson had a mental breakdown soon after the first trial and was confined to Searcy Hospital (formally known as Mount Vernon Asylum for the Colored Insane) near Mobile. Also missing was one of the state's key witnesses, Furman Jones, whose whereabouts were unknown.

Following a lunch break, the trial resumed at 2 p.m., and Howard Sullinger offered a brief opening statement. "May it please the court and gentlemen of the jury," he said in a loud voice, "this is a prosecution by the people of the state of Alabama against the defendant, Caliph Washington." Sullinger then read the original indictment that charged Washington with the first-degree murder of James B. Clark. Edwards, in his opening statement, explained that Caliph Washington, in response to the indictment's charge, contended that he was not guilty by reason of self-defense.

Throughout the 1957 trial, Howard Sullinger suffered from a severe head and chest cold that left him plodding through the testimony and evidence. At the new trial, however, he moved swiftly. His first witness, James Thompson, deputy coroner for Jefferson County, answered Sullinger's rapid questions eagerly, with full details. He described the condition of Cowboy Clark's body. He provided photographs he snapped of the corpse. The prosecutor showed them to the jury. Edwards objected and accused Sullinger of horrifying the jury and inflaming their minds against the defendant. The judge overruled, and the question-and-answer session continued. Thompson discussed the path the deadly bullet traveled through the vital organs. While speaking, he drew a small white envelope from his pocket and handed it to Sullinger. The prosecutor pulled out the bullet and showed it to the jury, while Thompson explained how he and Dr. Kwong removed it from the officer's spine.

Next, Thompson described the interrogation of Caliph Washington on Sunday night, July 14, 1957. He sat quietly in the room as Deputy Sheriff Walter Dean elicited Washington's statement. Now almost two and a half years later, prosecutor Sullinger had him identify the written statement, and then offered the document as the key piece of evidence in the state's case. Edwards objected to the statement and argued that the prosecutor had not shown the document to be voluntary or to contain the words of the defendant. Judge Goodwyn overruled him, and Sullinger read the statement to the jury. "My name is Caliph Washington," he began, and some ten minutes later he concluded, "I believe that's all."

Edwards believed the statement provided detailed descriptions of all the events of July 12, 13, and 14, except for the Clark shooting. On cross-examination, he asked Thompson to explain why, after dwelling on so many close, precise details, all that was recorded about the actual shooting was "he was pretty close to me and I started to jerk the pistol out of his hand and we fumbled around and the pistol went off two or three times." Thompson replied, "It's how he told it." No one in the room asked Washington to provide any more information. By the time Thompson left the witness stand some ninety minutes later, Sullinger introduced most of the state's evidence against Washington: autopsy photographs, the bullet, the gun, and the statement.

Next, Carl Rehling returned to talk about the ballistics report and microscopic examination of Cowboy Clark's bloody blue shirt. The shirt, however, was lost during the first verdict's appeal to the Alabama Supreme Court, and Sullinger offered a certificate from the court as evidence in its place. "This is the first time this has happened in thirty years," he told the judge. "I have no idea what happened and all I know is that we sent it to them and when they shipped the exhibits back, it wasn't there." Perhaps the supreme court did lose the shirt, but the circuit solicitor's office in Bessemer had a poor record of maintaining and storing exhibits through the years, so county officials might have accidently misplaced or purposely discarded the evidence. Nonetheless, Edwards accepted the certificate, and with that the first day of the trial concluded at 4:30 p.m. Bailiff James Vines announced that the "court will be in recess until nine o'clock."

The next morning Edwards cross-examined Rehling and theorized how the bullet might have gone astray as Clark and Washington struggled. Edwards took the pistol, raised it over his head, aimed the barrel to the floor, and asked: If one person was on one side of a car door and the other person on the other, and the gun fired, and the bullet struck the car, would it enter the victim's body at a severe angle in a downward trajectory? Yes, Rehling answered.

Throughout the day, other witnesses from the 1957 trial took the stand for the state and offered no new revelations. M. H. Karr recalled selling the gun to Cowboy Clark. Officer A. J. Wood remembered the night he found Clark dying in the dirt. John Adams and Mary Davidson told what they witnessed from their bedroom window after the car hit the chinaberry tree. Elijah Honeycutt thought back to the night he drove Caliph to Travellick.

Washington sat in the courtroom as if he were on a train taking a trip for the second time, making the same stops, but what destination awaited remained in question. His defense failed to slow the speeding train, and Edwards's efforts to undermine the credibility of each witness during cross-examination seemed petty and even nitpicky.

The state, however, called several new witnesses to strengthen its case against Washington. Robert Shields described in a low trembling voice the double date with the Robinson sisters on July 11. "You don't have to be afraid to speak out," Judge Goodwyn told Shields in a soothing tone, "because you won't offend anyone." The witness nodded and explained how that night he and Caliph drank two beers each and sipped on a half-pint of gin with their dates at the Blue Gardenia nightclub—this in contrast to teetotaling claims by Washington and the Robinson sisters at the 1957 trial. Shields recalled how Washington dropped him off at his home on Park Avenue around midnight, and then returned early the next morning and pleaded for help. "I asked him what the trouble was," Shields explained, and Caliph said, "I killed a polices [sic]."

When the judge asked Edwards if he had any questions, he simply said, "I have nothing," and the witness stepped down. Why Edwards refused to cross-examine the witness is a mystery. Perhaps Shields's testimony revealed a side to Washington's character that he could not defend.

Nevertheless, the state next called Tommy Lee Silmon, Shields's stepfather. Silmon walked down the aisle toward the witness chair, dragging his lame left leg behind him like a heavy cotton sack. He suffered permanent damage from the shotgun wound inflicted by the Bessemer officer during the Washington manhunt. Silmon testified that the first time he saw Caliph Washington at his house, he spoke of being in trouble with the law. "He told me he had outrun the police. [They] had got in behind him up there in a car and he had to out run them." When he saw Caliph sometime later, the story had changed— he told Silmon he had killed a police officer. "You what?" he recalled shouting at the young man. Silmon then recounted the story of riding with Caliph and the unknown driver to Earnest Cross's house in Adamsville.

On cross-examination, Edwards asked Silmon if he could identify the driver. "No, sir," he responded. "I couldn't testify on who it was or nothing. I didn't even know." The defense attorney asked if Silmon had been drinking that day. "That's right," Silmon replied, "sure were." Edwards then lowered his voice and accused the witness of being drunk. "It wouldn't taken much more to make me drunk," Silmon said comically, and several of the spectators in the small courtroom laughed. "Let's have quiet," a stone-faced Goodwyn warned the audience. Edwards then asked if Silmon drove to Earnest Cross's house and forgot in his drunken stupor. Silmon shook his head and said no.

Earnest Cross, however, testified that he only saw one man in the car. "I don't know the fellow's name," he said. "I know him if I sees him." Sullinger asked if it was the "little, short, scrawny-looking fellow" with the bad leg who just testified. Cross answered yes. Then Cross explained that Caliph told him about tussling with the police officer before the gun fired.

This revelation surprised and angered prosecutor Sullinger. Cross had never revealed the story until that moment. "You never told me that, have you?" Sullinger sneered. "Didn't nobody ask me," Cross replied. The witness went on to explain how he, Zack Graham, and Grover Pearson drove Caliph to Amory to catch the Greyhound bus.

The next witness, State Trooper J. W. Warren, told of taking Washington off the Memphis-bound bus in Byhalia, arresting the suspect, and driving him to trooper headquarters in New Albany. Warren, who testified in the previous trial, also offered a new revelation: during their hour-long drive on U.S. 78, Caliph made a voluntary statement about the Cowboy Clark shooting. Sullinger asked Warren if he or his partner, Pete Connell, threatened or abused the suspect or offered him any inducements to make the statement. No sir, the witness answered, the statement was voluntary.

According to Warren, Washington said that he and "another negro named Johnny Walker, whom he later changed to Johnny Taylor," were riding around in Washington's father's car when a policeman "got after them." When the officer pulled them over to the side of the road, Caliph got out of the car and stood with his hands over his head, while the "other negro run around the car and shot the policeman with a pistol that shot small bullets." Warren then recollected asking the suspect how he ended up with the officer's gun. He claimed Washington answered: "Johnny called me back and gave me the gun and some ammunition, and I took it and run."

During a brief cross-examination, Edwards did not ask why Trooper Warren failed to recount this statement in the first trial. Caliph's attorney was apparently either incompetent, uninterested in the case, or convinced of a guilty verdict.

The state's key witness from the first trial, Furman Jones, Washington's seatmate on the Memphis-bound bus, failed to answer his subpoena for the 1959 trial. To offset this loss, prosecutor Sullinger asked Judge Goodwyn if he could introduce Jones's testimony from 1957 as state's evidence. Edwards, however, objected. Jones's testimony was the "most damaging that appears anywhere in this record," he argued, and the case was too important to deprive a defendant with court-appointed counsel the right to cross-examine (even though Edwards neglected to cross-examine earlier witnesses). Edwards said Judge Mathews appointed him Washington's defender only two weeks before the trial began, and he was ill prepared to question Jones. "I did not know of the existence of Furman Jones or know anything about him," he explained, and the use of his previous testimony in the current trial was a hardship. "Since that time, certain information which I am not at liberty to disclose has come to my attention which might conceivably enable me to take an entirely different tack in my cross-examination if I had that opportunity again of this particular witness."

Judge Goodwyn offered Edwards a hollow victory: he would allow into the court record the prosecutor's direct and redirect examinations, but not the defense's cross- and recross-examinations.

At the beginning of the trial's third day, prosecutor Sullinger instructed court reporter Sydney Eckstone to read aloud the transcript of Furman Jones's 1957 testimony. The jury heard Jones recall the defendant saying that "he had done killed a police over in Alabama" and was "trying to get away." When Eckstone finished reading, Sullinger announced that the state rested its case.

K. C. Edwards chose to call Caliph Washington as the only witness for the defense. Much as he had in 1957, Washington recounted the date with the Robinson sisters ("I do not drink"), the incident with the officer ("Me and this police officer got to tussling over a gun and the gun went off and shot him"), and his capture in Mississippi ("They came on the bus. They told me and the soldier to stand up. We did."). He denied making a statement to State Trooper Warren about riding around Bessemer with Johnny Thomas or Johnny Walker.

Then Washington made a new revelation about the Mississippi trooper. On the trip from Byhalia to New Albany, he claimed, Warren threatened him. "He tried to shoot me," Caliph said, "[and] hang me." He recalled that at some point during the drive back to trooper headquarters, Pete Connell pulled the patrol car over into the woods. Warren took the handcuffs off Washington's wrists, opened the car door, and told the suspect to run. Presumably, if the suspect ran, the officers could shoot him and then claim they shot him while he tried to escape. But before this could happen, Caliph claimed, a white man walked by and told the officers to leave him alone and take him to jail. They complied and took the suspect to New Albany.

A few minutes later, Howard Sullinger asked why Caliph had not testified in the first trial that Warren had threatened to shoot, hang, and kill him. "You didn't ask me," he responded.

Attorney Edwards led Caliph through the questioning he received from Bessemer officers following his return from Mississippi on Sunday evening, July 14. Caliph claimed the officers questioned him extensively before Deputy Sheriff Walter Dean began writing anything down on paper. The statement, Edwards pointed out, omitted the key point about how Caliph and Clark tussled over the gun—details that the defendant claimed he provided to the law enforcement officials that evening.

On cross-examination, Sullinger asked Caliph if he read the paper after it was completed.

He had looked the document over but couldn't understand it. "I can only read and write a little," he added.

Sullinger spent most of his cross-examination bombarding Washington with questions about the Clark incident. "Isn't it a fact that you snatched this officer's gun," he shouted, "and backed toward the rear of that patrol car, and as the officer came at you started firing that gun?" Before Caliph could answer, Sullinger walked in front of the jury box, raised his arms in the air, and claimed that Clark had his arms up ("just like this") and you shot at him three times and hit him once. "Isn't that correct?" Sullinger barked.

"No, sir," Caliph answered.

When Caliph finished his testimony, he walked back to the defense table. Edwards stood and rested his case.

In his closing argument, Edwards told the jury that Caliph acted in self-defense when Cowboy Clark struck him with the pistol. While Clark and Washington struggled, the pistol fired accidentally, and the bullet ricocheted off the side of the car and killed Clark. These were key points that Edwards struggled to connect clearly during the 1957 trial.

Sullinger, however, portrayed Caliph Washington as a trained killer, willing and able to take someone's life with no remorse. "I suppose they teach them that in the service," he continued, "but to teach a character like that, tricks like that and then put him back here with civilian life, is about the biggest mistake that the armed forces have made."

When Sullinger finished, Judge Goodwyn gave the routine oral instructions before retiring the jury to consider a verdict. He praised the twelve men's dedication, patience, and citizenship; he explained the four degrees of homicide, types of punishment, reasonable doubt, self-defense, and verdict forms. He reminded them that Caliph Washington entered the trial with a presumption of innocence. "It is a fact which is to be considered as evidence," he continued, "and should not be disregarded." When his honor finished at 5:45 p.m., the twelve men moved to the jury room with copies of the original indictment and the verdict forms.

Nearly three hours later, at 8:35 p.m., the jury announced they had reached a verdict. Caliph stood expressionless as the jury foreman, William F. Kelly, read, "We, the jury, find the defendant guilty of murder in the first degree as charged in the indictment and we fix his punishment at death."

Bailiff Vines handed Judge Goodwyn the verdict, and he examined the slip of paper. His honor looked up, focused on Caliph Washington, restated the verdict and punishment, and asked, "Do you have anything to say as to why the judgment of the court in the sentence of the law should not now be pronounced upon you?"

Caliph answered yes, and Judge Goodwyn told him to speak.

"I just say I am innocent," Caliph responded. "It is self-defense. I'd like to have an appeal."

Goodwyn listened intently. When Washington stopped speaking, the judge coldly told the defendant he was guilty as charged and that his punishment was fixed at death by electrocution at Kilby Prison in Montgomery on February 18, 1960.

The appeal process would begin anew.

Alabama's Kilby Prison in Montgomery, where
Caliph Washington waited on death row.

10

"YOU BELONG TO
THE STATE OF ALABAMA"

A FEW DAYS FOLLOWING Caliph Washington's second conviction, a state prison transfer truck arrived at the county jail in Bessemer. Sheriff's deputies handcuffed Washington and led him from his cell into the slow-moving elevator for the ride to the basement of the courthouse. In the narrow alley behind the building awaited state prison guards. The guards pushed Washington into the back of a converted truck, a vehicle inmates and officials alike referred to as the "long chain" because of the method used to secure the convicts. The prisoners sat on long benches facing each other—knees and shoulders nearly touching—bound together by the long chain and a single destination: the big house in Montgomery.

The engine roared as the bus traveled the narrow road east from Bessemer until they reached U.S. 31, the key artery to the state capital in this pre-freeway era. Along this lost highway, they passed through sleepy villages like Saginaw, Varnons, Minooka, Verbena, and Pine Level. Within two hours, the truck arrived at the classification and receiving center at Kilby Prison, some four miles northeast of the capital. The prisoners were "tense and scared," one observer noted, although they would never admit the fear to anyone but themselves. For all male prisoners entering Alabama's penal system, this was the first stop.

The center, just outside the gleaming white walls of Kilby Prison, was a two-story E-shaped building made of red brick. Guards pulled Washington from the "long chain" and escorted him into the building. They removed his handcuffs and then his clothes. Guard Joseph E. Bonnett noted on Caliph Washington's classification card that the prisoner had no money, billfold, social security card, keys, pen, identification papers, jewelry, or pictures. Bonnett then took the naked prisoner and placed him in a tiny stall, where he sprayed him with the insecticide DDT to kill any potential parasites. Caliph was hosed off and given a "septic bath" so that the filth and grime from the county jail were not transferred to the state prison. Cleansing process complete, Bonnett carefully fingerprinted the naked Washington: right thumb, forefinger, middle finger, ring finger, little finger; then up the left hand from thumb to pinky; and finally both full hands. According to classification records, Caliph Washington stood sixty-seven inches tall and weighed 175 pounds.

As Caliph wiped the black ink from his fingers and hands, Bonnett handed the young man a large white coverall and a pair of white canvas slippers. "Less than 10 minutes of prison life," a reporter once observed, taught any prisoner arriving at the classification and receiving center "that he would be told what to do and when to do it." Washington didn't have to wait long for the next order. Once attired, the guard yelled, "Over here," and opened a heavy iron door that led to a dark, narrow staircase. Caliph walked up the stairs, where a door swung open and another guard escorted him into a quarantine dormitory cell.

For the next few days, he waited. He could receive no visitors or mail, nor could he write a letter to his parents. Aslee and Doug Washington, however, did receive a letter from the classification center informing them that their son had been received.

Prisoners entering the quarantine dormitory completed a battery of tests, including a complete physical and dental examination, as well as extensive psychiatric and general intelligence tests. Prisoners also went through a series of interviews to determine personal, or "social," history, including family life, previous employment, sexual orientation, and drug use. All test results, interview transcripts, FBI arrest records, and findings from the presentence investigations were placed in the prisoner's file and presented to the classification board. The final step of the classification process was the prisoner's interview with the classification board. Interviews lasted five to fifteen minutes, and at the end, the board assigned a status to the prisoner—minimum, medium, or maximum security—and a prison.

A death row inmate, Washington was automatically classified as a maximum-security prisoner. Following his physical examination, he was photographed: one shot staring into the camera, the other a profile view. He received standard-issue prison clothes—again all white—with his number etched on the inside. Caliph's prison number was Z276: all death row inmates received a Z designation, the last letter of the alphabet and symbolic of the prisoner's final stop. "You belong to the State of Alabama now," one prison official liked to tell a newly classified inmate. "You're nothing but a number."

The classification board assigned Washington to the special detention unit at Atmore Prison, some hundred miles south of Montgomery, near the Florida border. At times, blacks lived on death row at Kilby, but at other times state officials kept the unit strictly segregated. While whites remained on Kilby's death row, black men were routinely transported back and forth on the "long chain" from Kilby to Atmore and back again for clemency hearings, appeals, and executions.

Quietly situated sixty miles northeast of Mobile, Atmore Prison encompassed 8,360 acres of fertile Alabama soil. At this overgrown road camp, most of Atmore's residents worked twelve-hour days of hard labor in the scorching Alabama sun—digging ditches, building railroads, picking cotton, clearing roads, and raising sugarcane, cabbage, cotton, collards, corn, and kudzu (which was shipped around the state for erosion control). When Caliph Washington arrived at this "hell-hole of hell-holes," as one inmate described it, he undoubtedly saw the careworn prisoners working the fields under the watchful eyes of guards on horseback with loaded shotguns lying across their legs. The warden believed that spending all their time working made prisoners too tired to cause any trouble.

As the prison transfer truck pulled to a stop near the octagon-shaped guard tower, guards unloaded Caliph and the other prisoners and led them through the double set of iron doors. Once prison officials examined his papers, guards took him down a long, dark hallway to one of sixteen cells in the segregation unit, a special facility built to separate the hardest criminals—the "incorrigibles and the agitators"—from the rest of the prison population. The eight-by-ten cell was nothing more than a damp, airless hole with few furnishings: a double bunk bed, a washbasin, and an opening in the floor for a toilet. At the end of the hallway was the shower unit. Federal regulations mandated a shower no less than twice a week, but the guards rarely complied. Death row inmates were allowed to exercise weekly, but separately from the general prison population.

When Caliph Washington arrived at Atmore, the prison was relatively new, having been constructed in 1955 at the cost of $850,000. Six years before, at the old prison facility at the site, a fire began in the loft of one of Atmore's long wooden cellblocks, a matchstick-framed structure over twenty years old. At the time, Atmore housed 870 convicts, over six hundred of whom were black. No one was injured in the blaze, and local fire officials concluded that "defective wiring" probably started it. Prison officials, however, later admitted that inmates caused the fire.

Soon afterward, convict laborers began rebuilding the facility. During construction, the hardest criminals were sent off to Kilby, while the remaining souls lived in makeshift tents at the construction site. The project moved at a slow pace, taking over six years to complete, due to poor state funding, inadequate building materials, and low worker morale. A heavily reinforced concrete structure took the place of the flimsy wooden construction of the old facility. Inmates and prison reformers hoped that the fire cleansed the prison of its iniquities, but no amount of reinforced concrete could keep graft, corruption, and negligence from the dark hallways of Atmore.

FOR OVER FIFTY years, starting in 1875, Alabama had no large prison facilities to shelter a criminal population. Instead, released from any obligation of taking care of inmates, budget-strapped state and county governments leased convicts as a significant source of revenue. Businesses housed and fed the prisoners, 90 to 95 percent of whom were black, in return for a captive workforce that could be exploited in lumberyards and mines and on farms and railroads. Most male convicts worked in horrific conditions in coalmines near Birmingham, where contractors whipped them for disobedience, attempted escape, and to enforce company rules. Many critics, as historian Mary Ellen Curtin wrote, called convict lease a "new form of slavery."

In 1911, a massive explosion at Banner Mine in northwestern Jefferson County killed 125 convicts and resulted in a public outcry over the use of prisoners in such an unjust and unsafe manner. The following year, executives at TCI decided that their workforce would be made up of only free men and no prisoners, but other companies continued the practice. The abolition of convict lease was long talked about in the Alabama legislature, but many politicians only saw the economic benefit of the system, which generated over $3 million in income for the state in 1919. So prisoners continued to work in the mines and the calls for abolition continued. "The evil and the danger" of convict lease, Governor Thomas Kilby wrote in 1923, "lies in subjecting the convict to the greed, cupidity and brutality of the man who works him and over works him for profit." That same year the new Kilby Prison opened, and the state began purchasing additional property for correctional facilities in preparation for the death of convict lease. That came in 1928, when the Alabama legislature made it illegal for "any person to lease or let for hire any state convict to any person, firm, or corporation." Alabama was the last state in the nation to abolish the practice.

Most former convict lease prisoners found their new home on a state-purchased 3,600-acre farm in Escambia County near Atmore. Dubbed the Moffett State Farm in 1928, the facility received the "final movement of convicts from the mines" on June 30 of that year. The state later purchased four thousand additional acres and added additional cell houses, a cold storage plant, a canning plant, and a forty-two-mile railroad. The facility consisted of a series of wood-frame barracks with concrete foundations, each containing showers and toilet facilities.

Just as under the convict-lease system, Alabama officials had little interest in the inmates' well-being after they arrived at Atmore or other state prisons. As author James Goodman wrote, life at Atmore during the 1930s and 1940s was brutal. Prisoners lived in constant fear that every other inmate was a menace. At any time during the day or night, whether at dinner, work, or sleep, a convict faced the threat of a bare-fisted or knife-wielding ambush from another prisoner. Guards ignored most of the violence while participating in their own form of sadistic concentration-camp savagery by ordering prisoners to come closer for a chat, then shooting them for attempted assault or telling them to walk away, then sending a barrage of bullets into their back for attempted escape.

The prison seemed just as inhospitable in the late 1950s. At times, those working in the fields would dig up the remains of long-forgotten prisoners from decades before, when guards would beat a prisoner to death and force other convicts to bury the corpse in the fields where they worked. Escapes were rarely successful. The prison farm at Atmore was so large and so isolated that a prisoner who got beyond the fence could run all day and still not leave state lands. "They (prisoners) just wouldn't run," one warden recalled, "because you could see them too far." The thirty-five man-hunting dogs in the prison kennel also deterred potential escapees.

Guards paid close attention to the prisoners. Heads were counted at the beginning and end of each day. "We'd call them out and line them up," one guard said, "and we had a platform that was at the foot of the bed for them to sit on . . . and they'd be sitting on that platform and they'd be so tired that they'd lay back on the floor. We could count them by laying there." At other times, work crews met in a designated corner of the wire-enclosed prison yard. Prisoners were beaten or put in solitary confinement if they were late for these open-air head counts. After checking each inmate, the guards escorted them out of the yard, marching them in two single-file lines—"just like in the movies."

Until the 1950s, if a prisoner caused trouble or defied authority, guards and wardens used an eighteen-inch-long tapered razor strap to whip him with as many as twenty-one lashes on the buttocks. The restrictions rarely stopped guards from using the strap whenever it pleased them. On February 1, 1951, Alabama governor Gordon Persons put an end to the practice and to what he saw as the "last relic of brute force and barbarism" in the Alabama prison system. In a vivid public display, he burned thirty straps outside the capital building. "There'll be no more whipping of prisoners in Alabama," he announced. "Whipping is a sign of weakness on the part of those in authority. It is inhuman and will not be tolerated."

Regardless of this reform, the prison culture that Caliph Washington entered just a few years later remained a violent, inhumane place. Atmore had a reputation as not only the "murderers' home," the residence of the state's most incorrigible prisoners, but also as the home of Alabama's most aggressive homosexual prisoners (or "tush hogs" in inmate lingo). Much of the prison violence among inmates was over sex. When a new inmate arrived at the prison, the "wolves," the hardened longtime prisoners, intimidated the young convicts as part of a courtship ritual. Some "gal-boys" remained attached to one inmate, but others acted like prostitutes, selling themselves to the highest bidder. Most of the wolves did not tolerate other inmates coveting their human slaves and often murdered anyone who tried to steal away their prize gal. Guards often ignored the sexual subculture at Atmore, believing that a prisoner with a "wife," "gal boy," or "tush hog" worked harder and fought less.

Entrance salaries for guards at Atmore during the late 1950s were approximately $258 a month, "substantially below acceptable standards." The bad pay and violent work made hiring and keeping guards difficult. One year, the turnover rate was over 70 percent; most years it averaged 40. Those hired for work at Atmore were poor and at times just as hungry and tormented as the prisoners and only one rung up the socioeconomic hierarchy. As an inmate concluded, the only two questions asked of potential guards during the interview process were "Do you hate niggers?" and "Can you shoot a gun?" Low pay and poor working conditions drove many guards to graft and corruption.

In a lengthy letter to the Alabama governor, one desperate Atmore resident complained about the widespread negligence, misconduct, corruption, and graft at the facility. "The whole prison is a Big Joke on society," he wrote. The anonymous prisoner ("For my own safety I must remain unknown") described the lucrative black market in operation at Atmore, where inmates with enough scratch could purchase additional clothes, soap, food, and medical care. The right amount of money could buy a prisoner out of solitary confinement or off a harsh work detail. In addition, the inmate believed much of the prison's farm produce and livestock were being sold under the table. "There is a lot of pigs being transported away from here at night on private trucks . . . over to Mississippi to a private plantation." Many prisoners considered the entire system corrupt, and complained that they were cogs in the biggest "racket" in the state. One inmate said:

> We convicts slaved year round on seven or eight thousand acres of soil. . . Did we wear clothes from the cotton we grew? We were half naked most of the time. Did we eat from the square miles of Irish potatoes we grew? We ate what they called seconds, rotten potatoes or poor potatoes. Who got the quality potatoes? Who got paid? . . . Somebody got a make on all that stuff we raised. How much of the money taken in went to run our prison? How much went into the pockets of the prison heads?

Caliph Washington had little time to witness the alleged corruption at Atmore. Within weeks of his arrival, and for reasons only known to prison officials, the state transferred him back to the city of steel and stone: Kilby Prison.

When it first opened in 1923, the facility was hailed as one of the country's most modern prisons. Named for Alabama's reform-minded governor Thomas Erby Kilby, the twenty-seven-acre complex was enclosed by a twenty-foot-high white concrete wall topped by a fatally shocking 2,400-volt electrified barbed wire. Constructed in thirty-foot sections and then pieced together, the wall was twenty inches thick at the base and tapered to a width of twelve inches at the top, which discouraged any prisoner from digging through the wall.

The final cost of constructing Kilby was $2.5 million, almost three times the original estimate of $728,864. The facility was built on the site of Camp Sheridan, some four miles northeast of the state capital, at the intersection of the Seaboard Air Line Railway and the upper Wetumpka Road. During World War I, Camp Sheridan served as a training facility for infantrymen, including F. Scott Fitzgerald, who, while stationed there, fell in love with a local girl, Zelda Sayre.

The vast prison complex was a gloomy and symmetrical series of uniform buildings surrounded by a vast grassy yard, enclosed by a colossal white wall, and guarded by a squat red-brick administration building.

High above the gate was a circular terra-cotta display of the great seal of Alabama and the boldly lettered words KILBY PRISON etched in stone. Inside, a short concrete corridor connected the administration building with the first of the two identical main cell houses covered in a uniform red shale brick veneer.

The main cellblocks were monolithic structures with five tiers of cells—an archetypal "big house" as in 1930s prison movies—with an open well from the bottom of the cell house to the top. The first-floor cells were seven-foot-wide singles. The second- through fifth-floor cells were eight feet long, ten feet wide, and six feet high. Guards could stand on the ground floor and gaze upward to the cement walkways and light-green iron railings on each floor. The few plastered walls were painted a bland cream color, and all the ironwork in the prison was painted light green. Most cells had barred windows and a giant locking iron door for entry. Six-inch concrete divisions separated each cell. By the 1950s, this type of prison construction was outdated because of the cell positioning that required large numbers of guards to maintain security. In addition to the personnel problems, Kilby suffered from inadequate maintenance, which left water pipes rusting, walls crumbling, and foundations decaying all over the prison complex.

All but the death row inmates lived in the two large cell houses. All prisoners wore white, nonstriped, lightweight cotton uniforms—barely sufficient covering during Alabama's winter months. Their daily routine began at 4:30 a.m., when the first breakfast bell rang. The cell doors clanged open, and almost a thousand prisoners made their way to the mess hall. They had until 6 a.m. to eat, dress, and "straighten their cell." Once completed, the inmates reported for work in the large prison yard, where guards escorted groups to their respective workplaces. Prison officials assigned each prisoner a specific job: some worked in the cotton mill, others in the tag plant; some helped out in the hospital; many farmed the Kilby lands, and others served as day laborers outside the prison walls.

The cotton mill and tag plant were the only industries inside the walls of Kilby. The cotton mill was the prison's most profitable and self-sufficient industrial venture, producing all textile products for the other prisons in the state and turning a $1.6 million annual profit. Working conditions, however, were poor. "I don't really know what to think of the work in the cotton mill," a visitor once concluded, "but I believe that hell looks something like it and has something of its temperature." Nearby, more than two hundred inmates worked in the tag plant, producing all of Alabama's automobile license plates and road signs. Other, smaller industries existed at Kilby, such as a woodwork shop, a blacksmith shop, and a leather goods shop, in which many of the inmates worked during their "off hours."

Each day, prisoners worked until 11:30 a.m., when they were escorted back to the mess hall for their noon meal prepared by the convict kitchen staff. Much of the food came from the two-thousand-acre farms worked by medium-security convicts. The farm not only grew staple crops like corn, soybeans, and wheat, but it also produced over fifteen thousand gallons of syrup, extracted every year from its sugarcane crop by the workers in the syrup mill. The Kilby complex also included a large canning plant that preserved the foodstuffs grown on the farm. The state's food allowance, however, was the lowest in the nation, as prisoners received sixty cents each for a day's food. This allotment remained unchanged from the 1940s through the 1960s, even though consumer prices rose some 28 percent. The typical lunch menu was plain and filling: Monday, creamed potatoes, butter beans with cured meat, and corn muffins; Tuesday, frankfurters and beans; Wednesday, macaroni and cheese, and black-eyed peas with seasoned meat; Thursday, ham hock with cabbage; Friday, fish. All meals were served on metal trays with separators.

Once lunch was completed, inmates worked another shift until 5 p.m. Following the evening meal, prisoners reported to their cells for lockdown and the daily count. After the completed count, and provided no one was missing, prisoners had free time until lights out at 10 p.m. Inmates often gathered in the main recreation room, where they played pool, dominoes, chess, checkers, bridge, pinochle—even poker. Gambling was "legal" only under the supervision of guards within the recreation room, and prisoners could use only poker chips in the games, redeemable for "jugaloos"—plastic disks worth five, ten, twenty-five, and fifty-cent pieces. By the late 1950s, prisoners purchased television sets from their welfare funds—money obtained from the sale of handmade items produced during the inmates' free time. Prisoners also purchased athletic equipment for baseball, football, softball, tennis, basketball, handball, and boxing in the prison yard.

WHERE CALIPH WASHINGTON lived, however, the busy hum of prison life at Kilby was never heard. Just beyond the main cell houses, down a narrow concrete corridor, was the heavy iron door entrance to the detention and punitive cell house. Here was "Little Alcatraz," where the incorrigibles and the death row inmates were separated from the rest of the prison population. Here the sounds of prison life were replaced by the oppressive silence of those awaiting death. Here the sun never shined. It was a world of gray steel, one newspaperman wrote in the late 1950s, where the days and nights were no different. "There are no windows in death row," he added, "only time, and the everlasting glow of electric lights."

Unlike the main cellblocks, the detention center was only two tiers high. Death row contained four to twenty men at any given time, and their lives differed drastically from those of the regular prisoners. During their daily routines, they remained entirely apart from the main prison population. Their cells were essentially the same as those in the main prison, but each prisoner had his own cell, depending on the size of the death row population at the time. The inmates were fed only twice a day, at 7 a.m. and 3 p.m., inside their cells—they were never allowed to eat in the mess hall. Prison officials allowed them to order special food twice a week, such as peanut butter, bread, candy bars, or milk.

Death row inmates received visitors every Saturday, whereas general inmates saw visitors every other Sunday. Death row inmates could not see more than eight visitors at a time, and only three could be adults. Of the eight, only one could be listed as a "friend"—the rest had to be close relatives. To guard against further conflict among prisoners, married inmates could not receive female "friends"; only single or divorced inmates had that privilege. Before an inmate received visitors, he filled out a request form with the visitors' full names, addresses, and relation. Caliph's list included thirty-two potential visitors: his mother and father, four aunts, four uncles, two cousins, five friends, eight sisters, six brothers, and one grandmother, Pearl Walker. A guard approved the list, and then sent copies of the form to the warden, deputy warden, and commanding shift warden, as well as the information tower and the office for filing.

Death row inmates never worked. They waited in a small cell where every moment seemed like a day. "You had to find work for yourself," one of Caliph's fellow inmates said. "There was no air, no sight of the sky, no exercise. You were let out only once a week to walk six or eight feet away, handcuffed, to get a quick shower. Then you walked back to your cell." They spent most of their time reading, sleeping, and talking to other inmates; a few wrote poetry or songs. Ideally they had two hours of "exercise" every day. "Exercise" consisted of walks inside a small wire enclosure, another measure to keep the condemned men away from the rest of the prison population. Those on death row could not join the sports teams or visit the recreation rooms, nor could they watch television. They just sat and waited for death. While the guards turned out the lights at 10 p.m. for the general population, the death row inmates usually went to bed anywhere from 8 p.m. to 10 p.m., depending on the guard. This small group of men awoke later than the rest of the inmates and went to bed earlier—there was nothing else for them to do but sleep.

Adjoining death row were the punitive cells for solitary confinement. A prisoner was put into solitary confinement for any number of crimes: fighting, encouraging a fight, being found with a weapon, disrespecting a guard or other authority, engaging in illegal exchanges of possessions (drugs, weapons, or simply personal possessions), possessing paper money, engaging in aggressive homosexual behavior, refusing to work, or even criticizing the rules. The maximum time that an inmate could spend in solitary was twenty-one days. Prisoners had various nicknames for the punitive cell: snake pit, doghouse, and the hole. Whatever they called it, this was an unusually small cell, reportedly anywhere from five by eight feet to eight by ten feet. The walls were not plastered, so the concrete remained bare and uninviting. There were no windows, and the only light seeped in through the inches between the ground and the bottom of the steel door. There was no lavatory or toilet, no bed, no mattress. Some cells were equipped with a hole in the ground as a toilet; others simply had a slop bucket. Most had a handcuff bar attached to the wall for prisoners who needed restraint. Those in solitary confinement were given bread and water three times a day, and every third day a full meal—all through the gap between the floor and the door. A doctor checked the conditions of the prisoners daily, but the prisoners were allowed only twenty minutes of "exercise" in the same wire enclosure as the death row inmates. If the weather was bad, they never left the cell and never saw anyone.

The abuse from the guards was worse in the segregation unit. One prisoner compared Atmore's guards to those in the Kilby segregation unit:

> Atmore had the reputation of being a murderer's home, and it was. But the guards and prison officials at Atmore were kind compared with these at Kilby. Atmore set way back in the country . . . and it was uncivilized. In a way uncivilized things can be better than the civilized. Kilby was near Montgomery. Kilby was modern. Kilby went at its inmates like a machine. The punishment and the beatings rolled off the guards there like the cotton off the machines.

Caliph and the other condemned black inmates found little time to adjust to life on Kilby's death row. In a few weeks prison officials handcuffed each of the convicts, led them to the long train prison transfer truck, and took them back to Atmore. A few weeks later, they returned to Kilby. Back and forth they went for almost three years. Most of the reasons for placing the black prisoners on this circuit-riding death row were unclear. Nevertheless, many of their return trips to Kilby coincided with the scheduled execution of one of their numbers. Perhaps state prison officials believed that all the black prisoners should witness the violent death of one of their own. Another death row prisoner remembered the nights someone died in the chair: "If I live to be a hundred I will never forget that day because the juice was turned on in the death chamber. When they turned on the juice . . . we could hear the z-z-z-z-z-z of the electric current outside in death row." After the "juice was squeezed into him," a guard came out and told the other death row inmates that the prisoner had "died hard" and they "stuck a needle through his head" just to make certain he was dead. "I sweated my clothes wet," the inmate recalled. Caliph Washington undoubtedly sat nearby and sweated too.

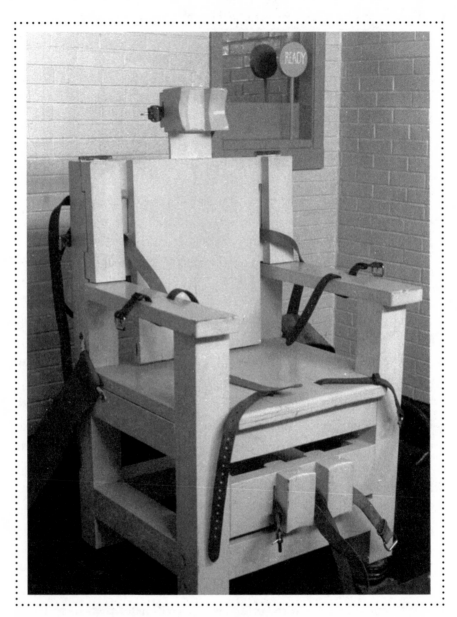
Alabama's electric chair, dubbed "Big Yellow Mama."

11

"PLEASE SPARE MY LIFE"

I N LOUISIANA, THEY called it "Gruesome Gertie." Tennessee officials named theirs "Old Smokey." Several states, including Georgia
and Florida, used the moniker "Old Sparky." Other states dubbed the
electric chair "Sizzlin' Sally." After Alabama prison officials painted
theirs with five gallons of shocking, reflective-yellow, center-stripe road
paint, someone said, "That's one big yellow mama." The name stuck.
Since it was first used on convicted murderer Horace DeVaughn in April
1927, some 144 inmates—121 black, 24 white—had died in "Big Yellow
Mama" by the time Caliph Washington arrived on death row in the late
1950s. Alabama law was clear on the matter: a convict sentenced to
death would be killed by electricity of "sufficient intensity."

First introduced in New York in 1890, the electric chair was seen
as a humane and modern alternative to hanging in an era driven by
new technologies and a progressive impulse to reform. Over thirty-five
years later, when Alabama changed from hangings to electrocutions as

the favored method of state-performed executions, Kilby warden T. J. Shirley promised Ed Mason furlough or perhaps a parole if he built the state's electric chair. A native of London, England, the forty-two-year-old Mason was serving a lengthy sentence for burglarizing six homes in Mobile to pay off his gambling debts. "I had lost a large sum on the races in New Orleans," he told a reporter in 1927. "It was a sort of gambling fever that had me, I guess, but I never harmed anyone bodily and never intended doing anyone bodily harm." A master carpenter, Mason arrived at Kilby soon after the prison opened its doors in 1923 and spent his days building cabinets, desks, cradles, and caskets. In November 1926 he selected several giant pieces of wood from a maple tree and set about crafting the state's instrument of death in the prison's woodworking shop. As he worked, he gave the chair little thought. "Every stroke of the saw meant liberty to me," he later said, "and the fact that it would aid in bringing death to others just didn't occur to me." But those working in the shop with Mason understood the purpose of the big maple chair. "I've called on each one to help me," he said at the time, "and each one refused to touch the chair."

But as Mason completed his task, an overwhelming sense of hopelessness enveloped him. "This is my first electric chair," he lamented, "and if I were called upon to make another I'd flatly refuse and pay the penalty. Whatever it might be, it could be no worse than a troubled conscience." The squat, stiff-backed electric chair stood four feet, five inches tall and weighed 150 pounds. It had smooth flat armrests, a sliding back, and an adjustable headrest—like a barber chair for a man the size of Jack's giant. The master carpenter also fitted the chair with heavy leather straps for securing the doomed inmate. Mason finished the project in six weeks and named the unadorned smooth-sanded chair "Plain Bill," after Alabama's sawed-off, five-foot-one governor, W. W. "Plain Bill" Brandon—a man of quiet generosity who handed out paroles like Bible tracts. Everyone deserved a second chance, he believed, and to blunt criticism of his leniency, he often quoted the motto of the Salvation Army: "A man may be down, but he is never out." Nevertheless, when Brandon left office in early 1927, Mason found himself still in, and not out. "Plain Bill" forgot to grant Mason's free time. In response, the irritated prisoner changed the name of his chair to "Plain Bull." When he finally received his furlough from Governor Bibb Graves, Mason left the state and was never heard from again, despite efforts to locate him.

Mason completed only the woodwork on the chair—the job of wiring fell to state engineer Harry C. Norman. Norman, having never tackled a project of this sort, traveled to neighboring states to see how other electric chairs were designed and wired. The architect of Florida's chair told Norman to keep it simple: "The desired process of electrocution requires that a sufficient voltage be applied to cause instant death with the least burning." Alabama's engineer drew up plans for the chair with semiautomatic controls; once the switch was thrown, a prisoner would get a first fist-clinching jolt of power; the current would then reduce and automatically build back up to 2,250 volts for a second shot of electricity.

On April 8, 1927, Horace DeVaughn, convicted of murdering two lovers on a lonely road near Birmingham, would be the first to test Mason's and Norman's handiwork. Engineer Norman knew so much about the workings of his device that prison officials tapped him to apply the electrodes to the condemned prisoner. After the prisoner sat in the chair and guards secured him with the leather straps, Norman was to take a sponge, which had soaked for almost two days in a saltwater solution, and fit it inside a band he made of screen wire and a few strips of brass. He would then place this atop the condemned person's head and strap it around the chin. This flexible but snug-fitting crown would prevent the flesh from burning and allow for good conduction. Norman would repeat the same process on a smaller band that would attach to the lower left leg. He would then connect the electrodes and create an electrical current between the head and leg. Norman, however, quit the job just days before DeVaughn's date with the chair. "A few nightmares persuaded me," Norman later recalled, "to quit the prison post" because he didn't like the "idea of electricity shooting through a man." DeVaughn didn't like it much either when novice prison officials turned the juice on over and over again, four shots in all, to get the inmate well done and well dead.

The history of electrocution in the United States was character-
ized by, as Supreme Court Justice William Brennan wrote years later,
"repeated failures" to kill the prisoner on the first try. It was "difficult
to imagine how such procedures constitute anything less than 'death by
installments'—a form of torture [that] would rival that of burning at the
stake." Evidence suggested, Brennan argued, that death by electrocution
was a violent, inhumane, and painful indignity "far beyond the mere
extinguishment of life." When the switch was thrown, eyewitnesses
reported, the doomed criminal would lurch, cringe, leap, or "fight the
straps with amazing strength." At times the blazing electrical current
would pop a prisoner's eyeballs out of their sockets like a cork from a
champagne bottle; their stomach, bladder, and bowels would empty all
contents; their body would contort and twist as their skin turned red,
swelled, and stretched "to the point of breaking"; the sizzling sounds
and pungent smells of bacon frying in a cast-iron skillet filled the room
of death as the condemned convict's body would boil on the inside and
fry on the outside.

By the 1930s and 1940s, electrocutions in Alabama soon became
so routine, as one Kilby warden recalled, that it was just part of a "good
day's work" to pull the switch and send a lightning strike into a prisoner's body. With "neatness and dispatch," a trained crew of prison officials
administered Alabama justice with quick efficiency. "A five-year-
old child could pull the switch," a Kilby official believed. The switch
started a generator, which built up power until it sent the two shocks—
ninety seconds apart—into the condemned man. "Unconsciousness
comes in the flicker of an eye," warden Frank Boswell said, "and death
in a flash."

State law mandated that the Kilby warden (or his appointed representative) turn on the electrical current at exactly 12:01 a.m. on Fri-
days. On February 9, 1934, Boswell and his crew electrocuted five black
men—Bennie Foster, John Thompson, Harie White, Ernest Waller, and
Solomon Roper—all within thirty minutes. In 1936, the chair saw its
most yearly activity, with seventeen individuals meeting death. Kilby's
warden, wrote one newspaper reporter, "has known sorrow, pity, regret,

horror, spent wakeful nights over his job, but through it all has felt that it was a good job well done and that justice has been carried out for the good of humanity."

Year after year, men, and a few women, took the final thirteen steps from the holding cell (what prison officials called the Bible Room), through a small green door, and into a cramped gray room where the electric chair waited. The tiny death parade—the "ghostly train," as one writer described it—moved slowly along the narrow corridor with the prisoner flanked by the prison chaplain and often a Salvation Army captain. Arm in arm, the three repeated the Twenty-third Psalm ("Though I walk through the valley of the shadow of death, I will fear no evil") as they inched closer to the green door. When the door to the "room of no return" opened, most prisoners closed their eyes to avoid gazing upon the instrument of their death. "I've never seen one who didn't," remembered a Kilby guard. The guards inside the chamber led the prisoner into the arms of the death chair.

Most accepted the inevitability of the end and remained calm and composed. "It's amazing how well the majority of the condemned people take it," one warden said. "Most of them want to go braver than the one before him." When the guards stepped clear, the room grew quiet. The chaplain often repeated Psalm 23. Many times, the prisoner repeated the words or moved his lips in silent recitation. As the guards began attaching the electrodes, sometimes either the prisoner, the chaplain, or both, said a brief prayer.

During the 1930s and 1940s, warden Frank Boswell trusted no one but himself to handle the sponges—if they were too dry, then not enough current passed through the body; too wet, and the current burned the muscles. "So I stay in front, dampen my own sponges, and carefully superintend the strapping of the condemned in the chair," Boswell once said.

With the sponge work and the wiring completed, the warden then asked if the condemned prisoner had any last words. Most did not. A few gave final statements. "I believe the Lord hath forgiven all of my sins," declared Clarence Hardy before his death in 1942. "I ask all the people to forgive me. I am satisfied of going to heaven and hope that all of you people will meet me there." Some condemned men were never repentant. Elbert J. Burns, who was strapped in the chair four years after Hardy, told all present that he hoped "everyone who had anything to do with executing me goes to hell." With his last words, a black hood was draped over his head. One newspaper reporter remembered that, when the guards covered the prisoner's face, he seemed to no longer be a human being: "He looked like an animal with that thing over his head." With everything connected, a prison official then picked up a wooden paddle with "Ready" carved on one side and held it up to the small glass window between the death chamber and the control room. Unless a last-second reprieve from the governor or a higher court arrived to spare the prisoner's life, all options had run out. Someone threw the switch.

IN NOVEMBER 1959, Caliph Washington and the rest of Alabama's black, circuit-riding death row inmates returned to Kilby Prison for the December 4 execution of one of their little group, Ernest Cornell Walker. Walker, convicted of raping a white woman in Homewood, Alabama, pleaded for his life in front of Governor John Patterson on December 2. "I know now that I did wrong and I'm sorry," he told the governor. Patterson showed no mercy, even though attorneys contended that Walker was mentally incompetent and had the intelligence of a child. Throughout much of the next day, he sat on the edge of the bed in the Bible Room and wept inconsolably. That evening he refused his last supper and spent his last few hours reading a Bible and visiting with Kilby chaplain R. S. Watson—he soon professed his faith in Jesus Christ to the soft-spoken minister. Just before the solemn hour of midnight, Walker showed no emotion as he walked the final steps to the death chamber to "ride the lightning." As guards strapped him in the chair, he told Watson, "Thanks, Reverend." He then spoke his last words: "Jesus has saved me." For a moment, the entire prison seemed quiet. Nearby, Caliph Washington and the other death row inmates watched, listened, and waited.

When the executioner threw the switch, the dull sound of the generator began building, and the horrific noise of death echoed throughout the cellblock. The generator was separate from the prison's main power system, so when the current built to its climax, the lights in the building continued to burn bright. The dimming of the lights during an execution was what was on "television and in the movies," one guard said, and it was not the reality in Kilby. Nonetheless, at 12:14 a.m., two physicians pronounced Walker dead.

One week later, a white inmate, Edwin Ray Dockery, went to the chair still proclaiming his innocence. "Look, I never for one minute denied that I killed a man," Dockery explained. "I got a bum rap on this deal. I claim it was self-defense, but the jury convicted me of murder. There was nobody there but the two of us. I'm alive and he is dead. Nobody believes me." But unlike Caliph Washington, who also pleaded self-defense, Dockery had a long record of crime and violent behavior before his conviction in the murder of Willie T. Heatherly in 1958. "I've been in trouble since I was fourteen and I guess this more or less evens things up. I lived as a burglar. I have robbed people. Twice I escaped from prison. Sooner or later things catch up with you, and that's why I'm here in Kilby now."

Kilby prison officials allowed condemned inmates an opportunity to order a final meal of their choosing. Most refused. Dockery, however, ordered a dozen oysters, a dozen shrimp, two veal cutlets, a salad, six buttered rolls, half a banana pie, ice cream, and expensive cigars. Once he finished his last supper, he lit a cigar and visited with Father William Wiggins, a Roman Catholic priest, and Reverend Tilford Junkins, one of Alabama's most prominent Southern Baptist evangelists. After listening to the salvation plan from both theological perspectives, the inmate converted to Catholicism—most likely to the chagrin of the Baptist preacher. Just before midnight, Dockery walked to the death chamber, flanked by Wiggins and Junkins. He smiled as he sat in the chair and told the onlookers "I am not guilty of first degree murder." By 12:10 a.m., he was dead. As the warden removed the black hood, Dockery still wore a smile.

Columbus Boggs was on Alabama's death row for murder. During the summer of 1957, Boggs escaped the Etowah County Jail in east Alabama, where he was being held on charges of assault and attempted robbery. He stole a truck and went on a statewide crime spree—heisting cars, robbing businesses, and stealing weapons. While crisscrossing Alabama, Boggs stopped in Uniontown, near Selma, and robbed a small grocery store and murdered the elderly owner for $80. An all-white jury in Dallas County deliberated sixty minutes before declaring him guilty, and the judge sentenced him to death. Four months after Dockery's electrocution on April 29, 1961, Columbus Boggs died in the electric chair.

UNLESS THE ALABAMA Supreme Court overturned his conviction, Caliph Washington would someday meet the same fate. He waited for the high court's decision as days turned into weeks, weeks into months, and months into years. No word came. He passed his time like many other death row inmates: sleeping, reading, praying, thinking, and fighting. By the early 1960s, Alabama prison officials stopped moving the black inmates back and forth from Atmore and packed in as many as four prisoners per cell on Kilby's death row.

In September 1961, Caliph Washington was sharing cell space with three black men, Willie Seals, Jr., Drewey Aaron, and Charles Hamilton. Seals and Aaron earned spots on Alabama's death row for raping white women, and Hamilton for burglary with the "intent to ravish." One afternoon, as guard B. G. Weldon walked along the corridor just outside the death row cells, he noticed blood covering Hamilton's shirt. Following an investigation, Lieutenant W. L. Trawick learned that Seals and Aaron beat Hamilton over the head repeatedly with their fists, while Washington cheered them on. "The subject was shouting," Trawick wrote in a report to the disciplinary board, "and encouraging other inmates to attack Hamilton." Caliph Washington, he added, "was one of the main instigators of the fracas," although he never hit anyone. The Kilby disciplinary board, which included warden Martin J. Wiman, assistant warden William C. Holman, and classification officer Marlin

C. Barton, reviewed the report and ordered Washington and the others to spend twenty-one days in one of the airless solitary confinement cells. Guards ordered Washington to strip down to his shorts and nothing more for his stay in the hole.

On September 9, 1961, they led the inmate down the stairs to cell number five, opened the door, handed him a slop bucket, and pushed him inside. For days, Caliph Washington sat on the stone cold floor with no mattress, cot, or blanket. The only time he left the cell was to empty his slop bucket in a nearby toilet. "His is a life without sunrise or sunset," one reporter noted, "and things like rain or blue sky matter not at all because it is always black in his four walls of steel; and chilly and uncomfortable, too, because there's nothing in there with him but a small container for a latrine." His only visitor was the guard who stopped by three times a day to feed him a "non-palatable" diet of bread and water and listen to his complaints. Caliph liked to talk, and this was his chance each day to communicate with another human being. Otherwise he sat in the silent darkness. After only a week, prison officials let Caliph out of the hole and returned him to his cell on death row.

A few weeks later, on November 24, 1961—the day after Thanksgiving—another black death row inmate, Joe Henry Johnson, became the first person executed in the state's electric chair since Boggs's death some seventeen months before. In January 1960, an all-white jury in northern Alabama convicted Johnson of the savage beating deaths of two women in Atmore, near the Tennessee border. According to trial testimony, Dicie Boyd caught seventeen-year-old Joe Henry in her barn engaged in sexual activity with her milking cow. To hide his bestial sin, Johnson raped and murdered the sixty-two-year-old Miss Dicie, and then bludgeoned to death her eighty-nine-year-old mother, Rowena Boyd. "May God have mercy on me and be with me" were Johnson's last words.

By Christmas 1961, Caliph had waited two full years for some word from the Alabama Supreme Court. None came. He slipped deeper into a dark, quiet despair. In February 1962 he earned a fresh trip to the hole for "exchanging personal possessions and papers" with other inmates and "publicly criticizing rules and regulations of the holding unit." The disciplinary board also punished Thomas Stain, Roosevelt Howard, Drewey Aaron, Willie Seals, William Bowen, and Wilmon Gosa. In August of that year, Gosa, who was convicted of murdering his five-year-old daughter with a butcher's knife, made no final statement before he was strapped in the chair and put to death.

As 1962 was nearing an end, Caliph Washington awaited word on his appeal. The case was being heard by the Simpson division of the Alabama Supreme Court, led by the fifty-nine-year-old associate justice, Robert Tennent Simpson. A native of the northern Alabama hamlet of Florence, Simpson earned his law degree from the University of Alabama in 1917—just as America was entering the Great War. Simpson soon joined the army and saw action in France during the Meuse-Argonne offensive, where he earned a Silver Star for bravery. After the war, he practiced law, served as a circuit solicitor, and sat on the bench of the court of appeals. Alabama voters elected him to the state supreme court in 1944.

In 1962, the other members of the Simpson division included John Lancaster Goodwyn, a Montgomery native who served on the bench since 1951, and James Samuel Coleman, Jr., of Eutaw, who was elected to the court in 1957. During the discussion of Washington's appeal, the justices divided over the decision, making it necessary for the entire court to hear the case in general conference. Chief Justice Ed Livingston prepared the majority opinion. Born in 1892 in the Black Belt community of Notasulga, Alabama, Livingston earned his law degree at the University of Alabama in 1918. His homespun humor and storytelling ability served him well during his twenty years as a practicing attorney in Tuscaloosa and as a part-time law school instructor. He drove a rusty, oil-burning, ramshackle Ford around town with a host of missing parts, including the license plate. Once while rambling through Bessemer, a motorcycle policeman pulled him over for driving without an automobile tag. When the officer asked why, Livingston said, "Mr. Officer, I could tell you a cock and bull story which you probably would not believe, so I will tell you the truth. I am a teacher in the law school in Tuscaloosa, and one of my students is the license inspector, and I am riding the hell out of the situation."

In 1940, he rode his popularity to election as an associate justice of the Alabama Supreme Court. In 1951, Governor Gordon Persons appointed "Judge Ed" as chief justice, where he reminded young attorneys that the practice of law was a privilege and not a right. Still, his deep respect for the law and his keen legal mind never transcended his Black Belt racial views. When the U.S. Supreme Court handed down the *Brown* decision, Livingston attacked it for attempting to take over local governments by writing opinions, not laws. "I have nothing but reverence for the Supreme Court as an institution," he said, "but that's as far as it goes." By the late 1950s, like many white southerners, Livingston became more reactionary in his support of segregated schools. "I would close every school from the highest to the lowest before I would go to school with colored people," he emphasized. "I'm for segregation in every phase of life, and I don't care who knows." The justice was "riding the hell" out of the racial situation.

Still, in the Caliph Washington case, Furman Jones's testimony, and not race, was the key issue. On October 4, 1962, Alabama's high court handed down its decision in *Caliph Washington v. State of Alabama*. The focus of the appeal was based on the admissibility of Furman Jones's testimony from the first trial. "It is a well-settled rule in Alabama," Livingston argued, "that when a witness is a nonresident, or has removed from the state permanently or for an indefinite time, his sworn testimony taken on any previous trial for the same offense may be offered in a subsequent trial if a proper predicate is laid." If the proper foundation (predicate) was never provided, then prior testimony of the witness was inadmissible.

Livingston, however, argued that circuit solicitor Howard Sullinger provided the background necessary for offering Jones's testimony. The prosecution proved, through evidence and testimony, that Furman Jones's address was Box 465, Jonesville, South Carolina, and that a deputy sheriff sent a subpoena to the address. The chief justice added: "The sufficiency of a predicate for the introduction of testimony given by a witness on a former trial is addressed to the trial court's sound discretion." In conclusion, Livingston emphasized that the evidence in the Caliph Washington case was clear and sufficient to "justify the verdict reached by the jury. . . . The Court has carefully examined the record, as is our duty under the automatic appeal statute, supra, and find no error to reverse." Justices Simpson, Goodwyn, Merrill, and Harwood concurred with Livingston's opinion.

Justice Coleman, however, dissented. He argued that the prosecution failed to provide a proper predicate for the admission of Furman Jones's testimony from the first trial. "I am of the opinion," he wrote, "that the court erred in allowing his testimony to be admitted. . . . As I understand the opinion of the majority, they hold that Jones' former testimony laid its own proper predicate. I, therefore, respectfully dissent."

With the conviction confirmed, Caliph Washington's execution date was set for Friday, December 7, 1962. His attorneys, however, filed an application for rehearing on October 19, and the court once again stayed the date of execution pending the ruling. On January 17, the Alabama Supreme Court denied the application and set the execution date of Friday, March 29, 1963.

ATTORNEYS KERMIT EDWARDS, David Hood, and Orzell Billingsley all left the case following the high court's decision. They were replaced by two white Birmingham lawyers, Robert Morel Montgomery and Fred Blanton, Jr. Dashing, patrician, flamboyant, and supremely self-confident, Morel Montgomery was a specialist in criminal defense and one of the city's best trial lawyers. By 1964, he had practiced law for forty years and never had a client executed. "He tried hundreds of capital cases," his son once said, "and never lost anyone to the electric chair. That was some accomplishment."

But for Morel, these cases were less about saving a life than about boosting his ego and receiving more notoriety. He thrived on high-profile capital murder cases like Caliph Washington's and once boasted, "If you want to change things in this world, keep your name in the news-

(*Right*) James B. "Cowboy" Clark and stepdaughter June Orr.

(*Below*) Two Alabama state troopers and a Jefferson County sheriff's deputy examine Cowboy Clark's blood on Exeter Alley.

(*Above*) Lipscomb mayor Bill Olvey (*left*), police chief Thurman Avery (*behind car door*), and an unidentified policeman at the scene of Cowboy Clark's death.

(*Left*) Caliph Washington surrounded by white lawmen in Mississippi.

Bessemer police officer Lawton "Stud" Grimes talking with Bessemer Commissioner of Public Safety, Herman Thompson, and Jefferson County sheriff's deputies Arvel Doss and Charlie Stamps.

Kermit Charles Edwards was the attorney of record for the Caliph Washington trials in 1957 and 1959.

With the courage of a lion, Orzell Billingsley, Jr., was one of Alabama's most fearless black attorneys.

The Alabama Supreme Court in 1958. Front row, left to right: Thomas S. Lawson, J. Ed Livingston, Robert T. Simpson. Back row, left to right: Pelham J. Merrill, Davis F. Stakely, John L. Goodwyn, and James S. Coleman.

HANDS THAT CAN STILL PRAY

Asbury Howard hoped to display Jack Hamm's cartoon in Bessemer,
but instead he found himself arrested, tried, and beaten.

Alabama governor George C. Wallace granted Caliph
Washington thirteen stays of execution in 1963.

The power of prayer sustained Caliph Washington during years of prison isolation and, once he was a free man, throughout his ministry. Here Washington offers a prayer at a wedding during the 1990s.

Caliph and Christine Washington and their six children.

paper, be the news good or bad." Morel Montgomery's name was frequently in the local papers for both his brilliant legal victories and his unseemly underworld clientele. He provided legal representation for a southeastern liquor syndicate controlled by Chicago mobster Al Capone and was once indicted for "violating or conspiring to violate" internal revenue laws governing illegal whiskey. Montgomery also received a two-year suspension by the Alabama Bar Association following a bribery charge.

In contrast, the handsome cigar-smoking Fred Blanton championed the lost causes of underdogs in appellate cases. "I always want to do my duty for indigent defendants who need representation," Blanton once wrote, "and I welcome assistance from whatever source available."

Even with the hardworking and compassionate duo of Montgomery and Blanton on his case, Caliph Washington was running out of options. As his clemency hearing approached, he found himself sinking deeper into the darkness of despair. Most condemned men expected nothing good to come from the hearing, and Caliph was losing all hope. One day as he sat on his bunk, a preacher walked by and asked him what he was "crawled up in a hull about?" Washington glared at the minister and snapped, "How would you feel if you were fixing to die in a couple of weeks?" The minister could see the depression and desperation on Caliph's face. "The impact of having to die doesn't sink in until . . . before your clemency hearing," Washington continued. "It's pretty hard to pretend that you're going to live on when down in your heart you know that you will have to die. That you will be executed."

Two weeks prior to the clemency hearing, on March 5, a tornado roared through Bessemer like a runaway freight train, destroying or damaging more than one hundred homes and businesses. "It is fantastic," Mayor Jess Lanier said, "that no one was killed." That same day, down the road in Kilby Prison, Caliph Washington's hopelessness turned to storming rage, and he lashed out at inmate Robert Swain, a twenty-two-year-old black man who was on death row for raping a white woman in Talladega. The bloody fistfight with Swain earned Washington another twenty-one-day trip to the hole. In this dark room he would wait for his clemency hearing.

Unknown to Washington, a lone glimmer of hope emerged from a most unlikely source: Alabama's new governor, George Wallace. Following his stinging defeat to the race-baiting John Patterson in 1958, the politically opportunistic Wallace vowed to supporters that "no other son-of-a-bitch will out nigger me again." He returned to his work as a circuit judge for Barbour and Bullock Counties and forced a confrontation with the U.S. Civil Rights Commission over voting records from his circuit.

When he refused to hand over the materials, Federal Judge Frank Johnson held Wallace in contempt for defying the commission. Rather than face jail time, the manipulative Wallace quietly turned over the records to a grand jury and they passed them to the commission, allowing Wallace to brag about defying the federal government. "This empty but symbolic gesture," historian Glenn Eskew wrote, "appealed to many Alabama voters, who saw meaning in the resistance to federal encroachment." Keeping true to his pledge, Wallace resorted to racial demagoguery throughout his 1962 campaign, blasted the federal government for encroaching on states' rights, and vowed to "stand in the schoolhouse door" to stop integration. "He is a fighter," Wallace supporter and Bessemer mayor Jess Lanier proclaimed, "and our state loves a fighter." He won in a landslide.

In January 1963, Wallace took the oath of office for his first term as the state's chief executive and promised in his inaugural speech to maintain segregation in Alabama now, tomorrow, and forever. If Wallace was willing to compromise most of his core principles for political expediency, he also remained, however, morally opposed to the death penalty. "I, like many other governors before me," he said in 1963, "wish this cup would pass from me." He loathed the "terrible burden" of this "solemn and awesome" power to choose life or death for another human. "Any governor would dread this duty and responsibility," he wrote. "But it's something the governor has got to face under the law." This was one of the most serious obligations of his office, he emphasized. "No decision is made without much time, effort and study devoted to the decision. . . . You may be sure that this matter causes me to lose much sleep and I have given prayerful consideration to every case involved."

Those who worked closely with Wallace during these years believed the governor had, at the least, serious reservations about the use of the death penalty. Albert Brewer, a key Wallace supporter in the Alabama House of Representatives, recalled that the issue caused the governor great consternation. "He simply did not want someone executed at the hands of the state," Brewer emphasized. Wallace's personal lawyer, Maury Smith, was more direct. "I believe he was opposed to the death penalty," Smith said. "He was a very sensitive man and easy to appeal to. . . . That really was his nature." State legal adviser Hugh Maddox agreed: "Most people would be quite surprised at Wallace's true feelings on the death penalty."

Each previous Alabama governor sent a long line of prisoners to their death in the state's electric chair. Between 1927 and 1963, on average, Alabama governors allowed almost seventeen executions per four-year term. The highest number of electrocutions, thirty-two, occurred during the term of Frank Dixon between 1939 and 1942. The lowest number was four during James Folsom's second term from 1955 to 1959. John Patterson, George Wallace's predecessor, approved five executions between 1959 and 1962.

While wrestling with the moral dilemma of capital punishment, Wallace decided to postpone all Alabama executions. For Caliph Washington, and the seven others waiting for death, having George Wallace occupying the governor's office saved their lives. Beginning on March 22, 1963, just one week prior to the scheduled execution, Wallace issued a reprieve for Washington. The formal citation bore the state's seal and began with the antiquated salutation: "In the Name and by the Authority of the State of Alabama, I, George C. Wallace, Governor of the State of Alabama; To all Sheriffs, Keepers of Prisoners, Civil Magistrates and others to whom these presents shall come—GREETINGS." The document reviewed Washington's conviction of first-degree murder and his sentence of death, to be carried out on March 29, 1963. "And Whereas," it continued, "for divers good and sufficient reasons it appears to me that the said Caliph Washington should be granted a reprieve. Now, Therefore, I George C. Wallace, Governor of the State of Alabama, by virtue of the power and authority in me vested by the Constitution and laws of the State of Alabama, do by these present, order that reprieve be and it is hereby granted to Caliph Washington until Friday, June 7, 1963, at which time, unless otherwise ordered, let the sentence of death be executed."

On May 29, Wallace granted Washington another reprieve until August 9. On July 19, 1963, the governor postponed the execution until November 29; on September 19, he delayed it until December 6. A reporter for the *Birmingham News* branded Wallace a "softie when it comes to staying the execution of Kilby Prison Death Row inmates." Washington and seven other inmates were all scheduled to die on December 6. "If the governor does not again deal out mercy and all eight are executed," the reporter added, "it will be an all-time record for the more than 30 years the state has been executing condemned men in the Kilby electric chair." Joining Caliph for the December 6 date were Drewey Aaron, William F. Bowen, Roosevelt Howard, James Cobern, Johnnie Coleman, Robert Swain, and Leroy Taylor. "Governor Wallace has said little about how he feels," the *News* reported, "but judging from the past, most guesses here are that more reprieves will be granted."

The journalist was correct. On December 3, Wallace granted Washington another reprieve and pushed the date of execution back to February 28, 1964. At the time, one Alabama newspaper editor complained that although Wallace had a reputation as a "wicked despot and race-hater," he was proving "to be the most soft-hearted of all Alabama governors" on the death penalty. The delays continued. On February 25, Wallace gave Washington until April 10; on April 6, he gave him until June 26; on June 16, he gave him until September 11.

While Caliph waited and prayed, the Civil Rights Act of 1964—outlawing public segregation—took effect on July 2. Five days later in Bessemer, a group of black teens decided to test the act's public accommodation provision at McLellan's store, located in the business district on Second Avenue and Nineteenth Street. Inspired by the civil rights campaign in Birmingham a year before, classmates Edward Harris, Albert Shade, Tommy White, Willie Duff, Herman Williams, Herbert Pigrom, and three others decided to eat at the store's segregated lunch counter on Tuesday, July 7. A nervous waitress asked, "What do y'all want?" The teens ordered cherry Cokes and she responded, "You know y'all not supposed to be over here." From the front window, the manager spotted a group of white men walking towards the store carrying child-size baseball bats. He tried to lock the doors before they entered, but they forced their way inside, ran to the lunch counter, and began beating the teens. Without training in nonviolent direct action, the boys fought back as they dashed for the exit. "It wasn't like we were going to sit there and take a beating," Pigrom recalled.

By the time they made it out the front door, the store was in shambles and blood stained the floor. Police Chief George Barron said none of the white assailants could be identified, and no charges were filed. "We were naïve enough to think the law was the law," one of the teens later said, "and things were going to change."

In the nearby Jefferson County Courthouse, a grand jury urged the governor to allow Caliph Washington's sentence to be carried out and demanded that no clemency be considered "for such a cold-blooded murder and the taking of human life." During Wallace's first eighteen months in office, he gave Washington seven reprieves and scores of others to the rest of the death row inmates.

While no prisoner died in Big Yellow Mama during those months, this changed in the fall of 1964. James Cobern, a white thirty-eight-year-old itinerant farm worker from Chilton County, had been on death row since being convicted of the 1959 murder of his ex-girlfriend, Mamie Belle Walker. Walker's mutilated body was found near the café she owned in December 1959, and Cobern was sentenced to death the following year. After granting eleven stays of execution, Wallace allowed the sentence to proceed upon the twelfth request. Hundreds of letters poured into the governor's office asking that Cobern's life be spared, but the governor held fast. The evening of September 3, Cobern ate his last meal: chicken, french fries, rolls, milk, coffee, and coconut cream pie. Cobern smiled and shook hands with guards, ministers, and onlookers as he went to the electric chair. His last words were "Everything is all right." He died at 12:14 a.m. on September 4.

For Caliph Washington, Cobern's death cast a foreboding shadow on his scheduled execution a week later. Would Wallace deny Washington's request? Would he be the next person to die in the Alabama electric chair? On September 8 at the clemency hearing, Washington begged Wallace, "Please spare my life." Wallace told Washington that he "agonized over such matters, but it is a decision the governor must make."

Two days later, on Thursday, September 10, Caliph Washington had still received no word from the governor. He took up residence in the Bible Room and spent his time praying. Just hours before he was due to sit in the chair, Wallace issued another reprieve and reset the execution for September 25.

Time, which was once Caliph Washington's only friend in prison, now became his most feared enemy. With each reprieve from Wallace, the next execution date was set closer. In the next six weeks, Caliph would have five more clemency hearings, and Wallace would test his solemn responsibility. On September 24, the governor issued another stay just a few hours before Washington's scheduled death. The new date was set for October 9, but Wallace issued yet another late reprieve to spare his life. He delayed the October 30 execution on the evening of the 29th. The next date was set for November 20, but he stopped the proceedings on November 19. The state rescheduled the electrocution for December 4, 1964.

Wallace's thirteen stays of execution prevented Caliph Washington from taking those final thirteen steps into the broad maple arms of Big Yellow Mama. The governor received several letters urging him to give Washington more time. "There seems to be a reasonable doubt of his guilt," Birmingham resident Eileen Walbert wrote on December 1. "It would be a terrible thing if an innocent man were to die. I beg of you to spare his life. At this season of the year it would be a wonderful gift for us all." On December 2, Wallace again heard Caliph's plea for clemency. Following the hearing, he retired to his office to consider a fourteenth reprieve.

Early the next morning he issued an executive order. "After oral hearing and careful consideration of the facts," he wrote, Caliph Washington should not receive executive clemency. "Therefore, let the sentence of the court be executed as provided by law." The final decision came over seven years since the incident with Cowboy Clark, five years since the last conviction, and twenty-three months since the appeal was denied. It followed thirteen reprieves from George Wallace.

Federal judge Frank M. Johnson ordered Caliph Washington
released from Kilby Prison in July 1965.

12

CALLED BY LIGHTNING

CALIPH WASHINGTON KNEW the state was about to make an end to him. Once again, he took up residency in the tiny Bible Room. Guards shaved his head to prepare him to wear the death crown. "They took me in there," Caliph said, ". . . and left me to pray. It felt pretty bad." In just a few short hours, he would be clamped, capped, hooded, and electrocuted in the Alabama electric chair.

It was December 3, 1964, when Caliph Washington received word of Wallace's decision, and by that afternoon, family and friends gathered at the prison as Kilby officials made their final preparations. For spiritual support, Washington turned to Reverend Lucius C. Walker, a Baptist minister from Bessemer, and Sister Helen Cooley, his one-time Sunday school teacher. Cooley was an ordained leader in her Baptist church and a vigorous and unsung civil rights activist who worked closely with Asbury Howard. When the Washington family first moved to Bessemer in the 1940s, Sister Cooley and her husband James lived next door. An active member of New Hope Missionary Baptist Church, which the Washington children attended, she taught Bible lessons to Caliph and played a key role in the youngster's spiritual formation. She encouraged Caliph as he responded to a revival preacher's call for "sinners to repent" and walked the aisle to accept Jesus as his savior. When Caliph went to prison in 1957, she visited him often and offered spiritual guidance. "I never talked to him about what happened" with the police officer, Cooley said. "It didn't matter. I told him to pray, and ask the Lord to take charge; I prayed with him and asked the Lord to be merciful."

But during those seven long years in prison, Caliph struggled with bitterness, anger, and depression. For a time, he believed, God had forgotten him, but the faith of those who surrounded him, and especially the devotion of Caliph's mother, Aslee, never faded. As time slipped away that hollow December day, she expected another miracle. "I wait it out with Jesus," she said. "God is able. He has been dated [for death] so many times. But God ain't ready. When God ain't ready, it ain't gonna happen . . . Yes, Lord."

ATTORNEY FRED BLANTON was Caliph Washington's last hope. On Thursday, December 3, 1964, while Caliph waited in the Bible Room, Blanton began a whirlwind of legal activity trying to prevent Washington's execution. Thinking that he had exhausted all possible legal avenues at the state level, Blanton sought relief from the U.S. District Court for the Middle District of Alabama, Northern Division, and Judge Frank M. Johnson, Jr. A law school classmate and onetime friend of George Wallace, Johnson was a Republican from the piney hills of Winston County in northwestern Alabama. Up in these isolated hills, farmers tilled their own soil and remained fiercely independent. On the eve of the Civil War, Winston residents rejected Alabama's call for secession, declared neutrality in the coming war, and proclaimed themselves the "Free State of Winston," although they remained under Alabama control and faced reprisals. After the war, Winston County became a Republican island in the sea of Alabama Democrats.

Unlike those judges from the Black Belt counties who struggled with the contradictions of judicial principles and racial traditions, Frank Johnson was unwavering. "I didn't have any ingrained racial prejudices that I had to cope with," he once recalled. "That was one of the problems I didn't have." When asked what shaped his racial attitudes, Johnson simply and drily answered, "The law."

As a federal judge, the focused and serious-minded Johnson followed the letter of the law precisely and stared down lawyers in his courtroom as if he were "aiming down a rifle barrel." He was never a crusading judge interested in social change, but his rulings on voting rights, prisons, desegregation, and education resulted in just that throughout Alabama.

Early on the morning of December 3, Blanton filed petitions for a stay of execution and a writ of habeas corpus on behalf of Caliph Washington in Frank Johnson's court. One of the cornerstones of personal liberty in the United States, habeas corpus, the Latin phrase for "that you have the body," has its roots in English law as a way of providing relief from unlawful imprisonment of citizens. In his petition, Blanton argued that Caliph's conviction, imprisonment, and death sentence were all violations of his constitutional rights.

Judge Johnson, however, denied the petitions because Washington had not satisfied "all remedies" under Title 28 § 2254 of the U.S. Code. Judge Johnson issued his decision at 11:25 a.m., just over twelve hours prior to Washington's 12:01 a.m. execution. The judge wrote that Caliph Washington's petition failed to specify if he had exhausted all remedies at the state level. "The right of habeas corpus through the State courts is his proper remedy," Johnson argued. In addition, the judge also added that the question of whether Caliph knowingly waived the assistance of counsel, when he was constitutionally guaranteed the right to such, could not be answered by the record and therefore should be presented through a petition for a writ of *error coram nobis* (writ of error, where a court reviews its own judgment where there are errors of fact). Such a petition, said Judge Johnson, must be filed with the Alabama Supreme Court in order to exhaust the remedies available to him.

The state should be given the opportunity to inquire into such conten-
tions if they had merit and to correct the problem prior to intervention
of federal courts.

Johnson noted, however, that Washington could file another writ
of habeas corpus in *forma pauperis* if he could again show that all state
remedies were exhausted. Giving Washington the right to file in *forma
pauperis*—a Latin phrase meaning "in the manner of a pauper"—meant
the court would waive all filing fees and court costs for the indigent
appellee.

Blanton hurriedly filed a petition for a writ of *error coram nobis*
with the Alabama Supreme Court, and by midafternoon, the state's
high court rejected the petition. Within minutes, he was back in Frank
Johnson's court filing another petition for writ of habeas corpus and
a stay of execution. In his hastily composed petition, he argued that
the state of Alabama violated Caliph Washington's constitutional
rights because of (1) the cruel and unusual punishment of granting
Washington so many unsolicited reprieves, (2) inappropriately allowing testimony from a previous trial to be read in a later trial, (3) the
admissibility of Washington's purported confession, and (4) how "certain confessions and admissions against his interest were admitted on
the trial of this case [and] were obtained by police officers when he was
not . . . represented by counsel and at a time when he did not knowingly
waive the assistance of counsel."

At 4:57 p.m., Judge Johnson stayed Caliph Washington's execution "pending a determination by this court of the issues presented."
The judge ordered Kilby Prison's warden, William C. Holman, to
appear in court and tell Johnson why he should not grant the defendant's petition.

In his order staying Washington's execution, Judge Johnson ruled
that the Alabama Supreme Court erred in denying Washington's application to file a petition for a writ of *error coram nobis*, citing a Supreme
Court decision in the case *Chessman v. Teets*. According to his interpretation, the decision required the courts to adjudicate "all conten-
tions of a substantial nature that involved the constitutionality of a

conviction no matter how guilty the accused may be found to be." In this case, Washington's right to appeal flowed from the right of due process, and Judge Johnson stated that Washington should and would receive every opportunity to show that the court erred in some way in ordering his death.

AS SOON AS the warden received word of Judge Johnson's decision, Kilby guards led Caliph Washington from the Bible Room and returned him to a cell with the other death row inmates. "If it is His [God's] will for me to die," Washington told a reporter, "I will; if it is not His will, I won't. I just try to have faith in God." Nearby, family and friends rejoiced. Aslee Washington had her miracle. For Caliph, the closeness of death transformed his life. "Facing death," he later said, "and then being reprieved at the last minute . . . sure brought me a strong faith in God" and a calling to become a minister. "I look to him now," he added, "because I know my help comes from Him . . . something I didn't know a while ago." It was as if God had called him by lightning.

Even though Caliph Washington found spiritual freedom, physically he was still very much in Kilby Prison. On January 8, the Alabama Attorney General's Office filed an answer to Blanton's arguments and asked Johnson to dismiss the appeal. The state's attorneys argued that the Alabama Supreme Court committed no reversible error in any of its previous rulings, and that Caliph Washington waived his right to claim the denial of due process by failing to object to the use of the confessions at earlier trials. In addition, Washington never requested a lawyer be present at his interrogation by police. "In the absence of request for counsel at interrogation," the state argued, "there was no violation of [Washington's] constitutional rights where resulting confession was obtained which was shown to be voluntarily given." The state ignored the issue of cruel and unusual punishment that Blanton raised in his petition.

Johnson was not swayed by the state's responses. On February 9, 1965, at a pretrial conference in his chambers, he denied the motion to dismiss and ruled that Washington was "entitled to a hearing in this Court on the merits of his case." Attorneys for both sides agreed that the case required no oral testimony and that both parties would write and submit briefs to the court. Judge Johnson ordered both sides to address all four constitutional issues raised by Blanton in his December 3, 1964 petition: (1) cruel and unusual punishment in the granting of thirteen reprieves, (2) lack of counsel at Washington's apparent confessions, (3) the right of submitting testimony from a previous trial without cross-examination, and (4) violation of due process by the use of involuntary confessions. With the procedural issues agreed upon by both parties, Washington's lawyer, Fred Blanton, began researching and writing an extensive brief in accordance with Johnson's pretrial order.

Judge Johnson asked for Blanton to file the brief by April 5, 1965. For weeks, and with no hope of recompense, Blanton worked long hours reading legal texts, case law, scientific research, the Bible, and other sources to support his arguments. His first argument would be the most challenging. How could Caliph Washington's thirteen reprieves from death be considered cruel and unusual punishment? Blanton discovered that his argument had "little consideration in either the fields of medicine or law" and that he made creative use of sources to support his proposition "in a general bibliographical sense rather than in a specific legal sense."

Blanton's frustration over sources compelled the attorney to offer a "caveat" at the beginning of his brief and explain, in humble, apologetic tones, how he found no case law to support his argument. But following this meek start, Blanton cast his argument in clear moral tones:

A human being who has been sentenced to death and who has been granted 13 reprieves by the governor, 11 not at his request, and of which 5 reprieves were granted approximately 24 to 36 hours prior to the time of execution, has been subjected to "cruel and unusual punishment" within the meaning of the 8th Amendment to the Constitution of the United States as the same is made applicable to the State of Alabama by the due process clause of the 14th Amendment to the Constitution of the United States.

The thirteen reprieves granted by Governor George Wallace were not gifts of mercy, Blanton supposed, but instruments of torture—a mental torture just as cruel and unusual as any form of physical torture.

Wallace's reprieves, Blanton continued, placed Caliph Washington under "extreme acute emotional stress" because Washington was aware of his "impending death" at the hands of the state. This stress was not manifested as a "result of an accident, not as a result of his own conduct, but as a sole result of a power residing in, and exercised alone, by the Governor of the state of Alabama, acting for, and on behalf of, the state." Blanton believed that the severe emotional stress and anguish of preparing for execution on the "brink of eternity" created a "traumatic neurosis" in Caliph Washington—similar to those seen in soldiers preparing for combat.

Blanton's evidence in support of this argument was thin, and most of the cases he cited had no substantial relevance to Caliph Washington's dilemma. The one exception was the strong dissenting opinion in the U.S. Supreme Court's *Francis v. Resweber* case. On May 3, 1946, Louisiana prison officials failed in their attempt to execute Willie Francis in the state's electric chair, Gruesome Gertie. Francis claimed that when the executioner threw the switch, an electrical current reached his body but failed to kill him. Prison officials, however, believed that no amount of electricity reached Francis and ordered a second execution. Willie Francis appealed to the high court and argued that a second execution constituted cruel and unusual punishment. In a five-to-four decision, the Supreme Court sided with the state and allowed the execution to proceed. In dissent, four justices argued "death by installments" was indeed cruel and unusual punishment.

Fred Blanton saw the parallels. The only major difference between the two cases was that for Willie Francis the mental torture of the near-execution was strictly accidental. In Washington's case, Blanton believed, the thirteen reprieves granted by Wallace were intentionally cruel and provided the same level of mental anguish as one execution gone wrong.

Next, lawyer Blanton argued that the taking and using of a confession when Caliph was without counsel, was offered no counsel, was not informed he could have counsel, and never waived the assistance of counsel, was a violation of the Sixth Amendment and the due process clause of the Fourteenth Amendment. From his arrest in Mississippi to his interrogation in Alabama, Washington provided several "voluntary confessions" that formed the heart of the defense's prosecution of the case. "Once the individual is seized," Blanton proclaimed, "he feels the pincers of the state and his ordeal has begun."

Blanton was pointing to the standard practice of the time: to obtain a confession from a suspect at all costs and then build a case around it—which the prosecution in Caliph Washington's case did. Even a lawyer of such limited abilities as Kermit Edwards, the defendant's court-appointed attorney in 1957 and 1959, objected to the use of the confession:

> We object to it as not being shown to be voluntary, not shown to be in the words of the defendant, not shown that he was advised he could have had or should have had a counsel present at the time that the statement was made; he was not given the benefit of counsel and advice of counsel before requiring him to answer the questions and to make the statement made on that occasion.

To support his argument, Blanton relied heavily on the 1964 U.S. Supreme Court decision in *Escobedo v. Illinois*. Escobedo was a Mexican worker arrested in Illinois as a murder suspect. While under interrogation, police denied his request to speak with his attorney and refused to allow his attorney the right to see his client. Following several hours of intense questioning, and with no counsel present, the suspect provided enough of a confession for the state to build a solid case against him. The state convicted Escobedo, and following a serious of appeals, his case ended up at the U.S. Supreme Court.

In a narrow five-to-four decision, the justices on the high court ruled in favor of Escobedo and concluded: "No system worth preserving should have to fear that if an accused is permitted to consult with a lawyer, he will become aware of, and exercise, [his] rights." The justices ruled that a confession given by a suspect during law enforcement questioning was invalid unless the suspect had the opportunity to speak to, or refuse, counsel. The opinion increased the burden on police to demonstrate that a confession met these requirements, where previously the burden rested on the accused to show that the confession was involuntary.

Caliph Washington's situation differed from *Escobedo*. Escobedo retained an attorney prior to giving his confession, while Washington had no attorney (although David Hood represented him in 1955), nor had he requested to speak with one. To bolster his argument, Blanton pointed to a California Supreme Court application of *Escobedo* in *People v. Dorado*. Judges on the California high court argued that a suspect had a constitutional right to counsel that "cannot be lost because he did not request or retain counsel" and that the use of an "involuntary confession" led to the "denial of due process and requires reversal regardless of other evidence of guilt." The facts in Caliph Washington's case, Blanton added, led to the obvious conclusion that the "defendant's confession could not be properly introduced into evidence, because the police investigation was no "general inquiry into an unsolved crime" but a focused search for one key suspect (Washington).

Caliph was also in the custody of Bessemer police officers and Jefferson County sheriff's deputies, who "carried out a process of interrogation that lent itself to incriminating statements." Pointing directly to the rules of confession in *Escobedo*, Blanton emphasized that Alabama officials never informed the defendant of his right to counsel, or of his absolute right to remain silent, and that "no evidence established that he had waived these rights." Finally, the attorney anticipated that the state would object to the application of *Escobedo* since Washington was convicted five years before the decision. "If right to counsel be one of the fundamental rights essential to a fair trial," Blanton emphasized, "then that trial denying right to counsel is not fair whether it occurred before or after *Escobedo*."

In the third point, Blanton argued that Furman Jones's testimony from the first trial (in 1957) should not have been admitted into evidence in the second trial (in 1959) because no proper predicate was laid for Jones's absence. This, the attorney added, denied Washington the right to confront and cross-examine the witness against him. Quoting from Acts 25:16, Blanton emphasized that it was the Roman custom to allow any man about to die the opportunity to face his accusers and have the right to "answer for himself concerning the crime laid against him." The Apostle Paul was "confronted by his accusers in Rome as related in Acts," he continued, just as Caliph Washington "should be confronted by his accusers in Bessemer as related in the Constitution." This was a precious and absolute right, Blanton emphasized, guaranteed by the citizens of the United States in the Sixth Amendment of the U.S. Constitution and by residents of Alabama in Article I, Section 6 of the Alabama Constitution.

In Washington's first trial in 1957, Furman Jones testified that Washington admitted to killing a police officer. In 1959, Bessemer authorities mailed a subpoena to Jones's last-known address in South Carolina. Jones failed to answer the summons, and in lieu of his absence, the prosecution moved to read the transcript of his testimony from the first trial. Attorney Kermit Edwards objected. He was anxious to question the witness again because in 1957, he only had a few days to prepare for Washington's trial. In 1959, he had new evidence he wanted to use to confront Jones. But Howard Sullinger, the circuit solicitor at the time, argued that they could not force Furman Jones to appear at trial, but that they had reasonably tried to locate him. Judge Gardner Goodwyn overruled Edwards's objection and allowed the reading of the transcript before the jury. Edwards's exception to Goodwyn's ruling was part of the court's transcript.

The standard for admitting witnesses' testimony from prior trials appears in the ruling from Caliph Washington's second appeal before the Alabama Supreme Court. The Alabama Supreme Court provided the standard for admitting testimony from a previous trial in its ruling on Caliph Washington's second appeal. The court ruled that a "sworn testimony taken on any previous trial for the same offense may be offered in a subsequent trial if a proper predicate is laid." The court agreed that the trial court established the predicate for reading Jones's testimony. Blanton disagreed and blasted the Supreme Court's circular reasoning, quoting Justice Coleman's short dissenting opinion in the second *Washington v. State*: "As I understand the opinion of the majority, they hold that Jones's former testimony laid its own proper predicate. I, therefore, respectfully dissent."

In Blanton's final point, he argued that the introduction into evidence of Washington's involuntary confessions violated the due process clause of the Fourteenth Amendment. The attorney pointed out that the prosecution used nine supposed confessions made by Caliph Washington to J. W. Thompson, Elijah Honeycutt, Robert Shields, Tommy Silmon, Earnest Cross, J. W. Warren, Lawton Grimes, Furman Jones, and Walter C. Dean (who wrote down the written statement). In only two of these nine confessions did the defendant's attorney raise any objections, which served as the basis for Blanton's contention that Judge Gardner Goodwyn violated the established rules for determining whether a confession was voluntary. The attorney pointed to the U.S. Supreme Court decision in *Jackson v. Denno*, which established the rule that a judge must hold a hearing outside the presence of a jury in order to determine if a confession is involuntary. The trial court in the *Jackson* case instructed the jury to determine both whether a confession was voluntary and the weight that that confession should receive as evidence. The Supreme Court decision changed the rule so that a judge could no longer submit confessions to the jury if an objection was raised to its possible involuntariness. Blanton pointed to a subsequent high court decision in *Boles v. Stevenson*, where the justices ruled that, even if the defense attorney raised no objection to a confession at trial, the judge still had to determine whether the defendant gave that confession voluntarily. If the judge failed to do so, the defendant could request a new trial on appeal. Blanton argued that Washington was entitled to protection under *Jackson* and *Boles*, even though both decisions were handed down in 1964—five years after Caliph's last trial.

Fred Blanton submitted the forty-seven-page brief to Judge Johnson on April 1, 1965—arguing that Caliph Washington's constitutional rights, as guaranteed in the Sixth, Eighth, and Fourteenth Amendments, were violated and his petition for writ of habeas corpus must be granted. Blanton's brief was compelling, well reasoned, and persuasive.

Alabama's assistant attorney general David Clark prepared the fact-based, dispassionate response to Blanton's brief. For Clark, the case was clear. The petition for a writ of habeas corpus should be dismissed because, as the attorney wrote, Caliph Washington was given all of the constitutional rights granted in both the U.S. and Alabama Constitutions. To support this central argument, Clark chose to begin his brief by refuting Blanton's assertions on the right to counsel and his interpretations of *Escobedo*.

The *Escobedo* decision, the assistant attorney general argued, was so different from Washington's situation that it had no real relevance. Police arrested Escobedo without a warrant, and he was interrogated but made no statement and was released the same day after his attorney received a writ of habeas corpus. Eleven days later, police arrested Escobedo again and took him to the police station, where he refused to make any statement without his attorney present. When his attorney arrived, police officers denied him access to his client. During Escobedo's second interrogation, the suspect was made to stand handcuffed for a lengthy period of time. He repeatedly asked to speak to his lawyer but was told that his lawyer did not want to see him. One police officer told Escobedo if he made certain admissions, he would be released.

"None of these facts are present," Clark argued, in the current case. Furthermore, he added, the Supreme Court emphasized in its decision that its findings related only to the case before them. "The United States Supreme Court has not specifically held that [the] accused has a constitutional right to be informed that he has the right to counsel when he is interrogated and which interrogation culminates in a confession," he added. Clark revealed the inherent weakness in the *Escobedo* decision and anticipated the *Miranda* decision the following year, which would provide law enforcement with clear guidelines on how to ensure due process. Clark added that Washington was advised of his rights and that his confession should not be ruled inadmissible solely by the fact that it was made in the custody of police officers.

Next, Clark moved systematically through Blanton's third point on the use of Furman Jones's testimony from the first trial. Clark argued that the state had indeed laid the predicate, and he quoted at length from the second Washington trial—trying to emphasize the wisdom in the Alabama Supreme Court's original ruling. He chose, however, to ignore Judge Coleman's dissent.

On Blanton's fourth point, Clark offered a lengthy rebuttal to the notion that Caliph Washington's confessions violated the due process clause of the Fourteenth Amendment. In supporting this argument, Blanton relied heavily on the *Jackson* decision, which Clark retorted "was of no help to him." The Supreme Court intended for *Jackson* to apply only to the procedure in New York, the assistant attorney general argued, which differed greatly from procedure in Alabama. New York juries consider the voluntariness of a confession along with a defendant's guilt or innocence. Alabama, he explained, followed the Wigmore or "Orthodox" rule where a judge listens to "all the evidence and then rules on voluntariness for the purpose of admissibility of the confession." The jury then considers voluntariness as it affects the confession's "weight or credibility." Clark pointed to the Alabama Supreme Court decision in *Phillips v. State*, where the court outlined proper procedure for confessions.

Before the trial court permitted the introduction of any confession as evidence, the state was "required to account for the treatment accorded" the defendant from the moment he was apprehended by law enforcement. Any confession made without threat, physical mistreatment, hope of reward, or an "inducement of any kind" was voluntary according to the *Phillips* definition. Clark argued that the state laid the proper predicate by presenting testimony to show that Caliph Washington's confessions were made without threat, mistreatment, or inducement. "A predicate was properly laid to each admission of a statement of a witness about the petitioner [Washington] confessing about the killing of James

Clark," the assistant attorney general added. Washington's lawyer made no request to question the admissibility of these confessions without the jury present. "He thereby," Clark continued, "waived such right."

Attorney David Clark chose to deal with Blanton's cruel and unusual argument last. The number of reprieves an Alabama governor grants had never been determined by the courts. Limiting the number would establish a "dangerous precedent" and diminish the power of the governor. "It must be assumed," Clark continued, "that the governor used discretion in granting such a reprieve or reprieves." An abuse of that power would merit strong consideration, but such abuse was not shown. In fact, the attorney argued, since death was the "maximum punishment" in Alabama, "something less than electrocution (a reprieve) could not be considered cruel and unusual punishment." Blanton, however, argued that Caliph Washington's punishment was less severe, but more cruel and unusual.

If Judge Johnson ruled on this contentious point, he needed justification under the law, not through Blanton's moral musings and Clark's political fears. "I approach . . . [a case] strictly from a legal standpoint," Johnson once said. "My interests are restricted to the law suit that's presented." His main concern was whether a case was presented with legal issues and how he would decide those legal issues. "There is no way to construe the Constitution of United States literally at this time," Johnson explained, "and make it a document that has any viability. And if that's called judicial activism, then I submit that it's something necessary in our form of government."

On July 6, 1965, Judge Johnson issued his "opinion and order" in *Washington v. Holman*. Following a review of the history of the case, Johnson listed the four points of consideration before his court. He concluded, however, that the only issues "necessary and appropriate" to discuss in disposing of the case were points two and three—which dealt with the admissibility of the confessions obtained when Caliph Washington had no counsel and whether the use of testimony from the first trial was a "denial of Washington's right to be confronted by the witness against him and his right of cross-examination." He never mentioned the other two points anywhere else in the document.

Courts had long been interested, Johnson continued, in how law enforcement officials obtain confessions that serve the basis of convictions. A basic tenet in American law was that all courts and law enforcement agencies must comply with the due process clause of the Fourteenth Amendment. The U.S. Supreme Court recently expanded this concept in the *Gideon v. Wainwright* decision, which concluded that the due process clause required states to "make counsel available" to indigents accused in state criminal prosecutions. "The philosophy of Gideon," Johnson continued, "has raised other serious constitutional questions" in the Caliph Washington case, "namely, at what stage of the proceedings is a defendant entitled to the assistance of counsel."

Johnson emphasized the unique and "crude historical facts" and context surrounding Washington's confession and argued that case law verified that the admission into evidence of a confession depends upon the "totality of the circumstances." The judge believed that the *Escobedo* case was "very close in point" to Caliph Washington's case and "this court feels it is controlling." Caliph was interrogated in Bessemer without a lawyer present, and their method of questioning elicited an "incriminating statement." In addition, police never warned him of his right to remain silent.

Johnson then drew the parallels between Escobedo and Washington. Escobedo was twenty-two and Mexican; Washington was seventeen and black. No one advised Escobedo of his constitutional rights; the only advice given Washington was contained in the statement written by the officers that he signed: "I have not been mistreated in any way since I was arrested, nor promised any help or reward to make this statement, and I know it may be used in court at my trial for killing a policeman." There was no question, Johnson concluded, that Washington had no legal representation. He was never offered counsel. He was never informed that he could have counsel, and he never "knowingly waived" his right to counsel. In the *Escobedo* case, Escobedo "had become the accused," and the police were interrogating him to build a case against him.

In Washington's case, there was no "unsolved crime," because from the beginning, the investigation focused solely on him. Although he never requested counsel before making a confession, Washington still maintained his "constitutional right" to have one. "The constitutional right to counsel does not arise from the request for counsel," Johnson wrote, "but comes into being by reasons of the circumstances of the particular case." The judge was not suggesting that all incriminating statements and confessions made by an "uncounseled accused" were inadmissible, but each circumstance had to be considered, and in Washington's case, Johnson concluded that the admission of the written confession, made without the right of legal counsel, was a denial of Caliph Washington's Sixth and Fourteenth Amendment rights.

Judge Johnson then turned his attention to the question of Furman Jones's testimony. Johnson reviewed Alabama's rules of "admissibility of prior testimony" and concluded that they were "well settled" by the Alabama Supreme Court. When a witness was a nonresident or had moved to another state, testimony taken from any previous trial for the same offense might be "offered and admitted in a subsequent trial provided a proper predicate is laid." The rule, however, was "equally clear" that without a proper predicate, prior testimony was inadmissible. "State Supreme Court Justice Coleman in his dissent was correct," Johnson affirmed, "in concluding that no proper predicate was laid for the admission of the former testimony of Furman Jones." The right of confrontation and cross-examination was a fundamental constitutional right, the judge continued, guaranteed under the U.S. and Alabama Constitutions. The exception, as in the Washington case, "must be used only in such a manner as to guarantee due process by the laying of a proper predicate to show that the witness was, in fact, unavailable." In Caliph Washington's trial, the predicate was "insufficient," and the use of Jones's testimony from the previous trial was a denial of the defendant's constitutional rights guaranteed by the Sixth and Fourteenth Amendments.

As Judge Johnson began offering his opinion earlier in the brief, he promised to explain his "reasons hereinafter appearing" as to why he chose not to address the other two points. Perhaps he deemed them unnecessary and inappropriate to the disposing of the case.

Nonetheless, Johnson left no ambiguity in his final disposition of the Caliph Washington case. The judge declared "void and invalid" the guilty verdict of the November 9, 1959, trial and ordered that the conviction and sentence be "hereby set aside."

Johnson also ordered Caliph Washington discharged from the custody of the state and of William Holman of Kilby Prison "to the extent that such custody is or may be pursuant to the conviction and judgment" of the circuit court in Bessemer. "It is ORDERED that Caliph Washington's discharge from said custody be no later than 10 a.m., July 9, 1965."

While charming and charismatic, district attorney James D.
Hammonds had a dark side that included quid pro quo schemes
and violence against political and personal opponents.

13

A THUNDEROUS ARRIVAL

May all the world forget you ever stood.
And may all the world regret you did no good.

—JOHNNY CASH

O N JULY 8, 1965, Caliph Washington was returning to Bessemer, nevermore to be confined in the decaying Kilby Prison. In
less than five years, the state would close the facility. Inmates, prison
officials, and politicians complained about the nearly fifty-year-old,
outdated, run-down penitentiary. "It's a waste of money to operate it,"
prison commissioner Frank Lee said at the time. "It's not the kind of
situation you would want any of your relatives or next door neighbors
confined in."

In 1967, the Alabama legislature authorized the construction of
a new maximum-security prison at Atmore on the 8,700-acre prison
farm. When the new facility, Holman Prison, was opened, the state
closed Kilby and looked to sell the 2,000 acres of prime Montgomery
real estate for redevelopment. On January 21, 1970, the last prisoners
left the crumbling facility, and the state contracted with a Hollywood
film company to blow apart Kilby's massive stone walls as part of the

finale of Metro-Goldwyn-Mayer's film *The Traveling Executioner,* a black comedy about a man (played by Stacy Keach) who traveled around the South, charging $100 to execute criminals in the electric chair that he kept in the back of his truck. But the filming of the scene did not go as planned. After the dust and smoke cleared from the powerful explosions, the walls stood undisturbed as the last remnants of Alabama's most brutal prison and as a monument to the 153 men and women who died at the hands of an Alabama executioner.

When Caliph Washington exited Kilby in 1965, he left behind sixteen men awaiting death at the hands of the state of Alabama. These included five white men: convicted murderers Harold Leon Edwards, John Lokos, Gerald Eaton, Clarence Cecil, and child molester and killer James Milford Duncan. Of the eleven black men who remained on death row, three were convicted of raping white women in separate incidents: Drewey Aaron, Frank Lee Rudolph, and Robert Swain—a death penalty crime that fell disproportionally on black men. Between 1927 and 1965, twenty-six of the twenty-eight men (93 percent) who died in the Alabama electric chair for the crime of rape were black. Nonetheless, the remaining seven on death row in 1965 were convicted murderers: Roosevelt Howard, Leroy Taylor, Billy Boulden, Johnnie Coleman, Riley Sanders, Ben Mathis, James E. Hinton, and Johnnie Daniel Beecher.

None of Caliph Washington's death mates would depart this life in Alabama's electric chair, and Big Yellow Mama went unused for eighteen more years. William Bowen's death in January 15, 1965, was the last execution in the South until John Spenkelink died in Florida's chair on May 25, 1979, and the last in Alabama until John Lewis Evans's death in 1983. In 1962, forty-six individuals were put to death in the United States. By 1965, that number dropped to six, including the hanging of Perry Smith and Dick Hickock, famous for the Clutter family killings described in Truman Capote's *In Cold Blood.* In 1966, only one prisoner was executed in the United States, and in 1967 the number was two.

A number of factors played into this sudden and dramatic decline in capital punishment in Alabama and beyond. Various individual legal appeals by prisoners, especially the challenging of race-based jury exclusion, helped keep the electric chair quiet in Alabama. The state placed a "sort of moratorium" on the death penalty, as did other states, while the U.S. Supreme Court wrestled with the constitutionality of capital punishment. Nonetheless, these legal activities failed to dissuade Alabama juries from handing out more death verdicts. By 1971, with the chair at its new home at Holman Prison in Atmore, twenty-eight men occupied death row. The lawyers for one of those inmates convinced Judge Aubrey M. Cates, Jr., of the state court of criminal appeals to rule that the death sentence could not be carried out in Holman because state law mandated executions take place "inside the walls of Kilby Prison"—even though it was torn down. "To change the Alabama law," one authority contended, "would mean that any executions carried out involving those already under sentence would be inflicting the death penalty under a law passed after the culprit was convicted."

While Alabama's courts were arguing semantics, the U.S. Supreme Court began considering whether capital punishment violated the Eighth Amendment ban on cruel and unusual punishment. In the 1972 *Furman v. Georgia* decision, the court struck down state laws that gave juries "broad discretion" in imposing the death penalty. "These death sentences are cruel and unusual in the same way that being struck by lightning is cruel and unusual," Justice Potter Stewart wrote. "I simply conclude that the Eighth and Fourteenth Amendments cannot tolerate the infliction of a sentence of death under legal systems that permit this unique penalty to be so wantonly and so freakishly imposed." But none of these glacial changes meant that Caliph Washington was a free man.

ON JULY 8, 1965, Caliph Washington must have felt like he had once again been struck by lightning. For the last time, he exited the death row cellblock at Kilby and walked to the prison's gatehouse. Waiting at the gate were not the familiar faces of his mama and his papa, but the blank expressions of two Jefferson County sheriff's deputies, Charlie Stamps and J. C. Williams. Washington was getting a free ride back to Bessemer—handcuffed in the back of the sheriff's automobile. His "home" would be in a cell in the Jefferson County Jail in Bessemer, where he started his jail time almost exactly eight years before. This bewildering twist to his ordeal came from the pen of Judge Frank Johnson, who overturned his conviction and ordered his release. At the end of "Opinion and Order," Johnson wrote: "This court does not enjoin the State of Alabama authorities, if they see fit to do so, from reprosecuting and, if appropriate, punishing Washington in such a manner that complies with the constitutional requirements." In response, the district attorney in Bessemer vowed to see justice done in the Cowboy Clark case.

As Caliph Washington returned to Bessemer that July, the skies were angry. A violent storm hit Bessemer and pounded the city with forty-five-mile-per-hour winds, large hailstones, torrential rain, and violent lightning and thunder. Caliph Washington's thunderous arrival coincided with front-page headlines announcing that a federal judge enjoined the Bessemer Board of Education from "requiring segregation of the races in any school under its supervision." Bessemer officials were now required to submit a plan for integrating all of the city's schools. Once again, the white community was on edge. A few months later, one Bessemer leader would proclaim that "the white race is supreme in this world by the mandate of God Almighty." Integrating a white-controlled school system with a predominantly black student population would be challenging, both socially and politically, in the corrupt and hostile Bessemer environment.

Bessemer changed little in the intervening eight years. The county made some improvements in the Jefferson County Courthouse, including air conditioning and automatic cell doors, but the atmosphere was still hostile for Caliph Washington, the "police killer." Circuit solicitor Howard Sullinger, who was so dogged in his prosecution of Caliph in 1957 and 1959, died suddenly in December 1962, just weeks following his election to a fifth term. "His love for Bessemer and for western sections of Jefferson County was pronounced," a newspaper writer proclaimed. "He was a quiet man but with great reserves of energy . . . well liked, studious, and a true servant of the law."

Soon after Sullinger's death, Alabama governor John Patterson appointed James Hammonds the new circuit solicitor. A law school class-mate at the University of Alabama, Hammonds worked on Patterson's successful 1958 gubernatorial campaign and received the new position as a political payback. He would serve two years of Sullinger's term of office and then face election in 1964—which he won. While charming and charismatic, Hammonds had a dark side, with several previous ethical lapses. In 1960, while serving as a municipal judge in Bessemer, he ran afoul of the Internal Revenue Service for failing to report $14,000 in legal fees paid to him by liquor interests in 1956. Hammonds, who was later cleared of tax evasion charges, claimed that he was hiding the "tainted" money from his wife, who frowned upon his work with such sinful clients. The next year, he was forced to resign as a municipal judge when Bessemer officials discovered Hammonds's involvement in a bond-splitting scheme. A neighbor once described him as likable and a "good actor," with the ability to turn his emotions "on and off" at will. "He wants to please everybody," he added, "and he has a good personality. He has good everything, but judgment."

A native of the tiny southern Alabama town of Chapman, James Daniel Hammonds was born in September 1919, attended public schools in Butler and Lowndes Counties, and served in World War II. After completing his law degree in 1949, he moved to Bessemer to set up a general legal practice specializing in, ironically, income tax law. Hammonds said at the time that he found the practice of law "interesting, challenging, and the most satisfying work I can follow." He believed his profession would "better equip me to take an active and intelligent part in the affairs of my community, state, and nation."

By July 1965, as Caliph Washington settled once again into the county jail, Hammonds had emerged as Bessemer's most powerful king-pin. With Hammonds overseeing Washington's case, hopes dimmed for a speedy trial. The prosecutor had other priorities. As the deputy district attorney (a state amendment changed the name from circuit solicitor in 1965) on the public payroll, Hammonds found the low salary a financial burden compared to the income he generated through representing wealthy clients. He complained to friends that he had high expenses and the new job "just wasn't paying . . . enough money to take care of them." Hammonds decided to supplement his income by tapping into Bessemer's underworld and organized crime. By using his office and position as cover, he maintained the appearance of an energetic crusader who challenged vice and corruption in Bessemer. To stay above the illegal fray, he hired a gunsel—an ex-con named Jonah Ray "Fat Boy" Smith—who would orchestrate a host of nefarious schemes. Hammonds gave Smith a "special investigator" badge, a .45-caliber, nickel-plated, bone-handled pistol, and the authority to "do what he wanted to do at any time, and against anybody." And that's just what Fat Boy Smith did. Working from his small Bessemer Pak-a-Sak grocery store, Smith directed Hammonds's illegal machinations, which included bribery, extortion, intimidation, and attempted murder. The inner life of Bessemer politics continued much as it was in the 1890s.

At first, Smith's and Hammonds's efforts appeared to be a series of quid pro quo schemes. When one woman complained about her ex-husband's chronic harassment, she paid Smith $250 to have him committed to the state mental hospital in Tuscaloosa. When the man's new wife complained about his institutionalization, she paid Smith and Hammonds to have him released. On another occasion, when one of Hammonds's friends ended up in jail for failing to pay child support, he gave the district attorney $850 to make certain his ex-wife would drop the charges. Fat Boy Smith later claimed that he drove to the woman's house and told her to stop asking for child support. When she refused, Hammonds indicted her father on a trumped-up arson and insurance fraud scheme.

This was a small monetary return compared to the large sums of illegal money that flowed through Bessemer. Most of the unlawful activities (gambling, prostitution, moonshine) took place along the Bessemer Super Highway between Bessemer and Birmingham. Illegal establishments boomed along the road following the early 1950s effort to clean up Phenix City, Alabama, located along the Chattahoochee River near Fort Benning and the Georgia border. The 1954 cold-blooded murder of Alabama attorney general nominee Albert Patterson in the small town focused state and national attention on what some described as the most "wicked city in America." During the clampdown on the sin-makers in

Phenix City, some of the gamblers, pimps, prostitutes, and mobsters simply packed up and moved across the state to Bessemer, where they operated free from legal restraint. In the years to follow, when Bessemer police arrested a prostitute, they asked the woman to pull down her lower lip in search of an identifying mark. "If the inside of her lip was tattooed with the letter B," a local resident once observed, it was "perfect evidence" that she was controlled by the former Phenix City Mafia. As Bessemer policeman Lawton Grimes, Jr., concluded, "Phenix City never saw the day when it was as corrupt as Bessemer."

BY THE MID-1960S, the Bessemer Super Highway, as one journalist noted, was a "seamy strip of joints, cheap motels, and honky tonks" filled with "free-swinging, swashbuckling law violations." The Bessemer Cut-off's district attorney, James Hammonds, stood to profit mightily if he could offer protection to these establishments for a cut of the earnings. "I have nothing against gambling," Hammonds reportedly said, "and you have nothing to worry about from this office." Hammonds predicted that when his friend John Patterson became governor again in 1967, gambling would be legalized throughout the state, and those who "paid and played" would be able to pick prime locations and receive more political favors.

But Patterson finished a distant seventh in the primary elections held on May 3, 1966. In that same election, however, Hammonds defeated Bessemer attorney Robert E. Paden 11,166 to 8,323 and later won the November general election without opposition. Once again reaffirmed by the voters, Hammonds continued to spread his protection, control, and intimidation. When the sheriff's office or a local police office planned to raid a gambling house, Hammonds would call and say to an owner in good standing with the district attorney, "Let's go fishing"— the signal to close up and get out of the building. For those who refused to pay, Hammonds had the establishments raided and closed by either sheriff's deputies or Fat Boy Smith—the latter whom Hammonds gave a free hand to enter any club, confiscate cash, and in general "do what he wanted."

Political and legal opponents were also a target of Hammonds's wrath. When he clashed with Bessemer police chief George Barron, Fat Boy Smith came up with a plan to disgrace Barron and prevent him from interfering with their business transactions. "We can't move him out," Smith said at the time, "but if we can get something on him, we can get him in our hands and everything will be all right." Smith hired a couple of local hoods, Alton Batson and Willard Slayton, to plant moonshine in a car owned by Barron's son, a law student at the University of Alabama, and then have police arrest the young man for transporting illegal shine.

As soon as Batson and Slayton finished that job, Smith paid the men $200 to "beat the devil" out of a local accountant who publically criticized Hammonds and was causing trouble for the district attorney. "You can kill him if necessary but take him and just beat him unmercifully," Smith told the men. "He has messed the big man up." Batson telephoned Hammonds and pledged his loyalty: "We will get them . . . and tear Bessemer up for you if you want us to because we're tired of people picking on you."

But for Batson and Slayton, this was all a ruse. Batson was working undercover as an informer for the Jefferson County Sheriff's Office, and Slayton was a special investigator with the Alcohol and Tobacco Tax Unit of the U.S. Treasury Department. "I was working for the sheriff's office on various occasions about gambling," Batson said at the time, "and . . . trying to apprehend the fact about what was disgracing the Cutoff." Unbeknownst to Hammonds, two disgruntled gamblers, convinced that he set up their clubs for raids, contacted Jefferson County sheriff Mel Bailey and told "a shocking story of a gambling and protection racket in the Cutoff, and of how money could buy a person out of almost any kind of trouble." They pleaded with Bailey to keep their conversation a secret because the "boss" had "ways of dealing with those who got out of line." Bailey long suspected that the widespread lawlessness in the Bessemer area existed at the pleasure of Boss Hammonds and Fat Boy Smith, whom he called the "enforcer." Bailey worked closely with the recently appointed assistant deputy (informally the "major") in charge of the sheriff's office in Bessemer, David Orange.

Orange, who a decade before began his law enforcement career with the Caliph Washington manhunt, arranged for the accountant to "disappear for a couple of days." Bailey and Orange released a fake story to the local television stations that the accountant was abducted and beaten by unknown assailants. Hammonds was pleased and told Batson that the job was "beautiful."

Hammonds's methods were extreme even by Bessemer's standards. With rumors of widespread corruption in the district attorney's office, Judge Gardner Goodwyn, Jr. (the judge in Caliph Washington's second trial) empaneled a special grand jury to "investigate charges of gambling and a protection racket" in the Bessemer Cutoff. "If you find such a poisonous plant exists," Goodwyn instructed the jurors, "gentlemen, do not limit your duties to pruning the limbs but pull the roots out regardless in whose yard you find them." Ironically, Hammonds, as district attorney, would supervise the work of a grand jury. For two weeks, the district attorney presided over deliberations and questioned witnesses, and several "key witnesses" took impromptu "vacations to Florida" to avoid the probe.

But on September 22, that all changed when Mel Bailey arrived at the courthouse to testify. History does not record what Bailey told the grand jury about Hammonds, who most likely questioned the witness, but it must have been damning. Following Bailey's behind-closed-door testimony, Hammonds recused himself. "No explanation was offered in open court," the *Birmingham News* reported, "for the DA's action."

In response, Goodwyn appointed two attorneys, Clewis Trucks and Powell Lipscomb, as special prosecutors to continue the grand jury's work. On October 7, the grand jurors concluded that the Bessemer gaming establishments were operating in "complete disregard and defiance of the law" and had become a "disgrace to our community." Ironically, the grand jury report directed its toughest criticism at the sheriff's department and the circuit judges for their "lackadaisical law enforcement practices." Orange was flabbergasted. "When they finished," he said, "they had turned and focused on us more than the bootlegging and gambling activities." The report added that there was insufficient evidence to "bring indictments" on Bailey's charges of a "protection ring and organized gambling" in Bessemer. Regardless, the grand jurors indicted several individuals involved in local gaming.

Many of those indicted were under Hammonds's protection at one time, including Escelle "Touey" Headrick (another of the district attorney's "special investigators") who ran the gaming tables at various clubs in and around Bessemer. When Headrick's case came before Gardner Goodwyn in May 1967, the judge threw it out and freed Headrick on the grounds of being a victim of entrapment. "The court finds that the keeping of the gaming table, which is the subject of this prosecution," Goodwyn proclaimed, "was approved and protected by the deputy district attorney, Mr. James Hammonds, which continued until it was terminated by Sheriff Mel Bailey's raid on the club where the table was kept."

In public, Hammonds called Goodwyn's accusations part of a witch hunt by political enemies unsuccessful in defeating him at the ballot box. Behind the scenes, Hammonds and Smith targeted the judge. "We were constantly trying to figure out some way to shoot the man a curve, to belittle the man, to discredit him in some way," Smith said at the time, "and we were bitterly opposed to the things that the judge stood for." Evidence suggests, however, that Hammonds wanted to go far beyond just ruining Goodwyn's reputation.

Hammonds told a friend that he was going to "get that damn judge off my ass" and had a way to stop him. "I knew he meant violence of some kind," the neighbor later told a jury. "He is prone to do this, and this is not the first occasion he ever mentioned violence. . . . I mean physical violence to the point of extermination."

Soon afterward Hammonds informed Fat Boy Smith to expect a visit from a man from New York. "This is a fellow that will get LBJ [President Lyndon B. Johnson] if you want him got," Hammonds explained. On May 24, a late-model yellow Cadillac convertible with New York license plates pulled up outside Smith's Pak-a-Sak. Out stepped Rodolpho "Rudy" Pipolo, a forty-year-old, dark-haired Sicilian from the Bronx, who weighed close to three hundred pounds. Pipolo entered the store and introduced himself to Smith, saying that he was there to help James Hammonds. Smith listened as Pipolo explained that he was a restaurant owner who was affiliated with New York gambling interests and that there was great concern that "some people down here [presumably Gardner Goodwyn] were interfering" with gaming activities in the Bessemer Cutoff. Smith later recalled that Pipolo peppered him with questions: If something happened to Judge Goodwyn, "would there be anybody else in power that would interfere?" Where did he park his car? What route did he take to work? How far was it to the river? Where could he hire a good "wheel man" who knew the route to the river? Pipolo explained that he needed $25,000 to complete the job—a $10,000 retainer and $15,000 when the "job is done." He never used a high-powered rifle from a distance, preferring instead a handgun with a silencer at close range so he could "see the expression" on his face. He would then take the body down to the river, handcuff it to weights, and dump it in the water. "They could never put no case against anybody unless they find the corpse," he added.

For reasons unclear (perhaps Pipolo unnerved Smith), Fat Boy began talking to sheriff's deputies in Bessemer about the assassination plot. Immediately, David Orange contacted the FBI and received a detailed report on Rudy Pipolo. Born December 5, 1926, in New York to immigrant parents, Pipolo was a chef and a part owner of the Sea Hunt Super Club in the Bronx. According to the FBI, the restaurant served as a front for his underworld activities as a Mafia soldier and an alleged hit man in the powerful Gambino crime family of New York. The "capo" or captain he reported to was the Gambino family's *consigliere* (counselor) Joseph N. Gallo. Born in Bessemer in 1912, Gallo was described in FBI reports as a "high echelon" Mafia figure who profited mightily from gambling, race-fixing, and labor racketeering. He was the heir apparent to the head of the family, "The Don" Carlo Gambino. According to FBI informants, Rudy Pipolo became a mobster in the late 1950s when he allegedly fulfilled part of a murder contract on mobster Frank Scalice, who was shot down by two gunmen (one presumably Pipolo) in a vegetable market in the Bronx on June 17, 1957. "As a result of the contract being well handled," an FBI agent reported, Gambino leaders invited Pipolo to join the family—or, in mafia terminology, he became a "made man."

By 1967, the FBI believed Pipolo was involved in a number of illegal activities, including "shylocking" (high-interest rate loans backed by
violence), dealing "swag" (the acquisition and selling of stolen goods),
and running illegal card and crap games. Agents warned David Orange
that Judge Gardner Goodwyn was in grave danger if Hammonds had
hired Pipolo—not even the man who made the contract could break the
contract. Orange assigned a deputy to stay with Goodwyn twenty-four
hours a day. "In fact," Orange said at the time, "this man [the deputy] is
even staying in his home. . . . We consider it that serious."

A few days later, Earl Morgan, the Jefferson County district attorney in Birmingham, took over the Bessemer DA's office. Morgan's action
marked the first major breach in the "invisible dam" that separated the
Cutoff from the rest of Jefferson County since solicitor Hugo Black's
efforts in 1915, and it ended the fifty-two-year-old hands-off policy
of the Birmingham district attorney's office toward operation of the
DA's office at Bessemer. The forty-three-year-old Earl Morgan was an
energetic yet soft-spoken attorney with deep roots in Alabama politics. As a lad, he served as a page in the U.S. House of Representatives
from 1937 to 1943 while Luther Patrick was the congressman from
Jefferson County and the Speaker of the House was Alabamian William Bankhead. Following service in the Eighth Air Force during World
War II, he graduated from law school at the University of Alabama in
December 1950 (six months behind James Hammonds) and entered
private practice in Birmingham. In 1963, George Wallace hired him
as the governor's executive secretary—a position he held until Wallace
appointed him Jefferson County's circuit solicitor in December 1964,
following the death of Emmett Perry. By 1966, an editorial writer for
one Birmingham paper praised Morgan. "He is an able public official,"
he wrote, "and we should count ourselves fortunate to have him as District Attorney."

James Hammonds was no doubt surprised when Morgan and a small
cadre of underlings appeared at the county courthouse in Bessemer and
relieved him of his duties. Morgan possessed no legal authority to fire
Hammonds, so he reassigned him to review and summarize "all the
cases that have been handled under his administration." Within days,

sheriff's deputies were fanning out across the Cutoff serving subpoenas to appear before a new grand jury empaneled by Judge Gardner Goodwyn. Major Orange took special precautions to prevent witnesses from taking any new "vacations" to avoid testimony.

Morgan took personal charge of the grand jury, while his handpicked assistants, Ken Moore and Harry Pickens, began working through the judicial backlog, which included Caliph Washington's case. The testimony was emotionally charged as witness after witness stepped forward to tell of Hammonds's activities. "I was scared," one witness said, "and still am . . . so many rumors and what you read in the newspapers and it's hard to know what to believe and who to believe." Before his testimony, the witness asked Morgan, "Could you keep me from being bumped off?"

By the end of the summer of 1967, Hammonds was indicted on six counts of bribery and two counts of conspiracy to commit murder. He was arrested and placed in a cell in Bessemer's Jefferson County Jail, not far from Caliph Washington. Hammonds quickly posted $10,000 bond and was released. Rudy Pipolo received an indictment on one count of conspiracy to commit murder. He quietly surrendered to authorities and was later acquitted by a Bessemer jury that found little convincing evidence that he was involved in this plot to murder the judge. Soon afterward, Pipolo filed a $400,000 libel suit against the *Birmingham News* for publishing a story that identified Pipolo as a Mafia figure involved in a murder plot. Pipolo said the accusations left him embarrassed, humiliated, and suffering from poor health and severe financial losses. At the trial, FBI agents testified about their "personal knowledge" of Rudy Pipolo, which, as one lawyer later explained, enabled the jury to "draw the correct inference as to . . . the truth" and reject the libel suit. Pipolo returned to New York, where the FBI continued to monitor his activities until his death in 1983.

In response to the indictment, Hammonds charged that the grand jury proceedings were being orchestrated by his "political enemies" and that he had "discharged the duties of his office without fear or favor to anyone." He predicted that he would be cleared of all charges "when the light of truth finally exposes my accusers." Hammonds sued Morgan and Alabama attorney general MacDonald Gallion in an effort to regain the duties of his office that went with the title he still held, deputy district attorney for the Bessemer Division of Jefferson County. He also fought efforts by the Alabama State Bar to censor him for the "alleged misconduct."

Hammonds received some measure of exoneration the next year when juries dropped seven of the eight charges against him. In March 1968, he was found guilty on one charge of bribery. "I was wrongfully convicted," he later told an official with the Alabama State Bar, and "although I am innocent of that charge, I have elected not to appeal the same." Hammonds cited finances as his reason to not file an appeal.

In May 1968, on the eve of his sentencing, Hammonds also gave up the fight to remain district attorney and resigned. "The affairs of this elective office had been in a state of uncertainty," he added, "and I felt it in the public interest to terminate litigation over this office . . . out of a regard for the people who elected me." Hammonds was sentenced to two years imprisonment but was placed on probation and never served any jail time.

Hammonds also surrendered his law license, rather than facing disciplinary action by the Alabama Bar. "It is . . . my desire to surrender my privilege to practice law," he wrote, "until such time as the controversy over my conduct has been resolved." Hammonds never practiced law again.

The week following Hammonds's resignation, Alabama governor Albert Brewer appointed Harry E. Pickens as the new district attorney for the Bessemer Cutoff. He was a short, wiry, long-faced man of fifty, with generous ears, deep-set eyes, and the un-southern habit of talking too fast in the courtroom. "These jurors might have trouble hearing you," a judge once scolded him. "You talk like a machine gun." Pickens was a native of the Bessemer area and earned a law degree from the University of Alabama. Earl Morgan called the decision a splendid choice: "I think the people of the Cutoff area are extremely fortunate to have the services of a man of Mr. Pickens's high character and with twelve years of experience."

Pickens's appointment closed another chapter in Bessemer's tumultuous history, but Caliph Washington still waited for his closure behind a cell door in the Jefferson County Jail in Bessemer—almost three years since Judge Frank Johnson ordered him released. He made a note in his diary: "Bessemer Attorney Harry Picken [*sic*] enter office May 15 or 16, Thursday noon 1968, after Hammond [*sic*] resigning." While James Hammonds fought for money and power in Bessemer, Caliph Washington sat in his cell and prayed for freedom.

In a bitter irony, ACLU attorney Charles "Chuck" Morgan used
Caliph Washington to integrate Alabama's prisons, but he
did little to help Washington gain his release.

14

WHEREABOUTS UNKNOWN

A SLEE WASHINGTON, CALIPH'S mother, could not understand why her son was still in jail. She believed that God worked a miracle through Judge Frank Johnson, and she wanted to thank him and ask him why Caliph remained behind bars. Aslee, who never learned to read or write, asked a friend to write Johnson and request an audience with him. "She would like very much to thank you personally for ordering his release," the friend wrote, "and would also like to see your order." In July 1965, Washington's family and friends believed that Johnson's decree would result in Caliph's immediate release from prison. "There are so many things about his release and re-arrest that are puzzling," the family friend wrote Johnson.

In response, the judge wrote Aslee Washington that her request for a private meeting was inappropriate and unnecessary. "This Court's order was based strictly upon the applicable and controlling laws as I understood it," he explained. "Nothing else entered into the matter; therefore, no expression of appreciation is appropriate." Johnson explained that

Caliph Washington was represented in his court by "competent counsel," and that any questions should be directed to that attorney, Fred Blanton.

Blanton, however, would not represent Caliph Washington during the appeal of Johnson's ruling. "I would have liked very much to have supported your decision in the Court of Appeals for the Fifth Circuit," Blanton wrote Johnson. "I had hoped the court in New Orleans would have appointed me, but such was not the case." He complained that the Washington family talked with attorneys for the ACLU and the Legal Defense Fund of the NAACP and that he had been "frozen out of the picture." He wanted to help "indigent defendants," like Caliph Washington, receive quality legal advice, but "to be upstaged, especially after that hectic day in Montgomery last December, is hard to take."

What Blanton did not realize was that the Washington family had no patience to gamble on another court-appointed attorney. They needed some certainty after the last public defendant, Kermit Edwards, mounted defenses that twice resulted in the death penalty for his client. Within days of the state's appeal to the Fifth Circuit, the Washington family formally retained Orzell Billingsley, Jr., and David Hood, Jr., to represent Caliph in all state and federal courts. Part of that agreement "authorized and empowered" them to "employ any and all other attorneys" that they deemed necessary to "represent us in this matter." Since the Washingtons had no money to pay attorneys, Billingsley looked for funding sources (and legal assistance) elsewhere—namely from the NAACP and the ACLU.

Orzell Billingsley asked for assistance from his close friend and long-time drinking partner, Charles "Chuck" Morgan, Jr., who opened the ACLU's southern regional office in Atlanta in 1964. The thirty-four-year-old Morgan earned a law degree from the University of Alabama and maintained a lucrative private law practice in Birmingham until he became involved in several high-profile civil rights cases during the 1950s and 1960s. This brought Morgan and Billingsley into the same legal circles and highlighted their mutual passion for equal justice, unbridled notoriety, high legal fees, and smooth bourbon. "We did our drinking 'across the tracks,'" Morgan remembered, "usually at Orzell's house, which stood beside the railroad tracks, so near to them that it literally shook when trains approached. In Birmingham the lines were so clearly drawn that it was against the law even to fish or to play checkers with blacks, let alone to 'socialize' or plot with them. But plot we did."

In 1963, the flamboyant and outspoken Morgan left Birmingham following the bombing of the Sixteenth Street Baptist Church and a highly publicized rant in which he placed the blame on the white community. "Every person in this community who has in any way contributed during the past several years to the popularity of hatred is at least as guilty, or more so, than the demented fool who threw that bomb," Morgan wrote. Following a brief stint with the NAACP Legal Defense Fund, he went to work for the ACLU in Atlanta, but the plotting and drinking with Orzell continued—even if the communication took place by telephone and the whiskey flowed from separate bottles.

Late afternoons for these two lawyers, as Morgan later recalled, were a "thigh slapping, tornadic event." Morgan pulled a bottle of bourbon from his bottom desk drawer, as one writer later observed, began drinking heavily, and called Billingsley or one of his "Alabama cronies" to "dream up schemes" saturated with "whiskey soaked optimism." Perhaps on one of those long-distance binges, Billingsley and Morgan agreed to help Washington to simultaneously gain his freedom and to make a legal challenge to racial segregation in Alabama's prisons and jails.

On September 2, 1965, Morgan wrote a letter informing Edward W. Wadsworth, the clerk for Fifth Circuit Court of Appeals, that he would appear at the court on behalf of lawyers Billingsley and Hood and appellant Caliph Washington. In reality, however, Morgan decided to focus almost exclusively on the jail segregation case and turn over the appeal to Erskine Smith, a leader in the Alabama ACLU, and a partner in the progressive-minded firm of Berkowitz, Lefkovits, Vann, Patrick & Smith. The thirty-one-year-old reform-minded Smith moved with his family from Los Angeles to Birmingham in 1947 and, like many new residents, found the racial tensions perplexing. After graduating high school, he moved to Washington, D.C., and worked as an administrative assistant to Alabama congressman Laurie Battle to provide enough money to pay for college at George Washington University. He later received his law degree at the University of Alabama and returned to Birmingham to practice law. In the early 1960s, Smith was among other young Birmingham attorneys who successfully fought to change the city's form of government, which ultimately ended the political career of Eugene "Bull" Connor—Birmingham's longtime city commissioner who ordered the use of police dogs and fire hoses on civil rights demonstrators in May 1963. Two years later, in 1965, the Caliph Washington case intrigued Smith. "I have offered to assist in the defense of this case without compensation," he wrote, "but I will not be able to devote sufficient time, without assistance." Smith and Morgan would bring the power and prestige (and Billingsley hoped the money) of the ACLU to Washington's defense team.

Orzell Billingsley also solicited legal assistance from the NAACP, which just a few months before reopened its Alabama chapter headquarters for the first time since the state barred the organization from operating in the state in 1956. On June 1, 1964, the U.S. Supreme Court ruled that Alabama had no constitutional basis to prohibit the NAACP from operating in the state. Billingsley was one of the lawyers that fought the case for eight years through fourteen state and federal court appeals and four Supreme Court appeals.

For Caliph Washington's case, Billingsley contacted the new Alabama field director, Julian Hall, told him Washington's story, and urged the organization to get involved in "just about the best case . . . at this time in Alabama." In turn, Hall contacted attorney Robert Carter, senior counsel with the NAACP Legal Defense Fund in New York, and asked for support "not only for the benefit of the defendant, but because of the publicity to be derived." Although Hall was no lawyer and professed ignorance as to the "legal ramifications of this case," Billingsley assured him that a favorable outcome was not in doubt because of Washington's strong legal position. Come see for yourself, Hall wrote Carter, and "investigate the merits of this case."

In response, Barbara Morris, an associate counsel with the defense fund, explained to Hall that Bessemer was a long way from New York City and that the local field directors had to investigate civil rights cases and provide research materials so the office could evaluate its merits. "I would suggest this course of action to you," she wrote Hall.

Orzell Billingsley, in turn, sent scraps of information on Caliph Washington to the defense fund, which brought another response from Barbara Morris. "Inasmuch as you have not sent a letter," she wrote, "I am at a loss to know what you desire me to do." She wondered if Billingsley was seeking financial and legal assistance from her office. "If that is a fact," she continued, "we would be pleased to know who Caliph Washington is, why he is in jail, or on what grounds he bases his plea to be released from jail (since I have a notion that would be his desire) and any other facts which would enable me to know what on earth you are talking about."

Billingsley never responded to Morris's letter—most likely because he had already surreptitiously added Robert Carter of the NAACP as an attorney of record to documents filed with the Fifth Circuit Court. When the NAACP sent no monetary or legal support for Caliph Washington's appeal, Erskine Smith wrote Robert Carter and asked him to employ Billingsley and Hood on behalf of the NAACP. The Birmingham lawyer described the Washington case as "meritorious" and one that might become "landmark" in its impact. "I believe that your organization would gain a great deal of respect by undertaking the defense," he emphasized.

NAACP representatives noted that "our name was entered in the case without our knowledge" and expressed doubt that the organization would "undertake financial responsibility" for Washington's legal expenses—especially since Orzell Billingsley "had quoted some exorbitant fee" for his legal services. Barbara Morris complained to Erskine Smith that Billingsley had never responded to previous requests for additional materials related to the Caliph Washington case "so that we can intelligently evaluate our ability to participate in the litigation." Billingsley, however, still offered no response but continued to submit court documents bearing the name of the NAACP.

The Alabama chapter of NAACP and Julian Hall were nonetheless eager to participate in Washington's defense, but they had no money to finance the case. This was the first local civil rights organization to show substantial interest in Caliph Washington—over eight years after his arrest. Through the years Caliph's mother, Aslee, asked for assistance at a few mass meetings of the Alabama Christian Movement for Human Rights (ACMHR, an affiliate of the Southern Christian Leadership Conference (SCLC) and the driving force behind the civil rights protests in Birmingham). At times, the group took up a special "love offering" for Washington and provided prayers for the imprisoned man but little else. "We could have done more," recalled Reverend Abraham Woods, an ACMHR leader, "and we should have done more, but we were fighting for voting rights and the hiring of black police officers. We had to focus on the big picture. It was tragic to leave him behind, but that was the reality."

Reverend C. Herbert Oliver, executive secretary of the Inter-Citizens Committee (Birmingham), a group that publicized cases of alleged police brutality and unjust crimes committed against blacks, said that Caliph Washington's was "not one of the cases we highlighted." Nonetheless, just before he left Birmingham for a position in New York in 1965, Oliver researched and wrote a lengthy "synopsis" of the case and criticized state courts for giving Washington the death penalty while awarding the widow insurance money for an accidental death. "When the death certificate, the coroner's certificate, and the whole Alabama Court system concur in the judgment of homicide and award death," Oliver wrote, "how can this whole system turn around and award money on grounds that it was accidental? We have no objection to the widow receiving money by some means, but why should Washington receive death? Should a man be put to death for first degree murder when the Alabama Court system says in effect it was not murder but accidental?"

Oliver's synopsis of the case was widely circulated locally and attracted the attention of the Concerned White Citizens of Alabama (CWCA). The organization had its origins in early 1965, when seventy-two white Alabamians traveled to Selma and marched to the Dallas County Courthouse to proclaim that there were "white people in Alabama who . . . speak out against" police brutality, voter registration intimidation, the absence of public civility, and suppression of dissent. On March 6, 1965, Reverend Joseph Ellwanger, a Lutheran minister of a predominately black congregation in Birmingham, proclaimed from the Dallas County Courthouse steps, "We are sickened by the totalitarian atmosphere of intimidation and fear." The next day, state and local police fought several hundred civil rights marchers at the Edmund Pettus Bridge on "Bloody Sunday" in Selma.

During the weeks following the march, the CWCA drafted bylaws, elected officers, and approved a mission statement:

The purpose of this organization shall be to promote by non-violent and non-partisan action, the spirit and the letter of the Constitution of the United States of America, The Bill of Rights and the constitution of the state of Alabama. Violations of these principles shall be brought to the attention of the public and of elected officials. It shall be our concern that life, liberty, and the pursuit of happiness be shared equally by all persons in Alabama.

The officers included Reverend Joseph Ellwanger (president), Congregationalist minister Al Henry (vice president), Helen Morin (treasurer), and Eileen Walbert (secretary).

Eileen Kelley Walbert was one of Birmingham's most outspoken critics of the racial status quo. In the years following World War II, she moved to Birmingham from New York with her musician husband Jim and grew to abhor the city's racial climate. "The fact that we couldn't associate with anybody we wanted to was just wrong," she later recalled. "Our husbands and friends had just returned from Europe fighting against fascists and here we were living in a fascist state. It was not democratic. We were not living by the Constitution." Eileen joined the Birmingham Council on Human Relations and worked for racial equality and many other causes, including her passionate opposition to capital punishment.

For years, participants in the monthly meetings of Birmingham Council on Human Relations listened to speakers encourage the group to do more than just write letters and make pious statements. During the civil rights era, as Walbert described it, several black leaders were urging them to become "active and overt" agents of change. In 1965, at the beginning of the Selma voting rights campaign, Hosea Williams of the SCLC spoke to the group and urged them to "take some warm bodies" down to Selma and "show that you care." When he finished speaking, Walbert said, "How would it be if some white people went to Selma to let the world know that those people who are trying to prevent American citizens the right and privilege to register and vote did not speak for all the white people in Alabama?" The boldness of her pronouncement thrilled Williams, but not everyone in the group supported the idea, and the Birmingham Council formed the CWCA.

From its beginnings, Walbert and the other members were deeply concerned with the struggles of Caliph Washington. Walbert, with her deep opposition to the death penalty, learned of his case months before and wrote Governor George Wallace pleading for the condemned man's life. In 1965, she brought the case to the CWCA's attention. At a meeting on July 10, 1965, members took note of Washington's move from Kilby Prison to the Jefferson County Jail in Bessemer. "We will investigate," one person said. By the fall, the group was circulating materials on behalf of Caliph Washington. "We need your help!" Eileen Walbert wrote. In the "interest of justice," the group reviewed the case and raised a small amount of money, which they sent to Orzell Billingsley and David Hood as defense lawyers, "whom we consider interested, just, and trustworthy." CWCA members believed that having a legal defense fund "at our disposal" was imperative in handling immediate and future legal expenses in the Washington case. For CWCA members, the most urgent goal was to see Caliph released on bond while awaiting the Fifth Circuit's decision in the state's appeal. Billingsley explained that it would cost at least $1,000 for the bail application, and defending Washington in a future criminal trial would cost over $5,000. Walbert and the others, however, remained undaunted. By November, the group raised $406 for Washington's legal defense, which they sent to Billingsley and Hood with the mandate to "get Caliph out of jail" while he awaited a new trial in Bessemer.

The lawyers, however, saw no hope in getting Washington released on bail pending a new trial, but they did believe the Fifth Circuit Court of Appeals might provide some relief while that court considered the state's appeal. On December 3, 1965, exactly a year after Judge Johnson stayed Washington's execution, Billingsley filed an application for bail pending review to the Fifth Circuit. He argued that Caliph's imprisonment, without bond, was a violation of the Eighth Amendment, the equal protection and due process clauses of the Fourteenth Amendment, and the Federal Rules of Criminal Procedure. "Appellee [Washington] moves the court," Billingsley wrote, "for an order admitting him to bail pending final determination" of the state's appeal of Judge Johnson's order.

Court clerk Edward Wadsworth informed Billingsley and the other lawyers that judges Elbert P. Tuttle, Joseph C. Hutcheson, and Walter P. Gewin would review Washington's bail application "without oral argument on or about" December 16, 1965. "This is only the date on which it is now expected that the matter will be forwarded for ruling," Wadsworth explained, "and does not mean that this office will be able to advise counsel of the court's action by then." With the holidays fast approaching, it was doubtful the court ruling would come until early 1966—leaving Caliph to spend his ninth Christmas in jail.

Nonetheless, Washington's small band of supporters remained steadfast and continued to press forward. On December 13, 1965, the group held a benefit and fundraiser for him at the home of Dr. Abraham Siegel, a pathologist at the Medical College of Alabama (later the University of Alabama School of Medicine) in Birmingham and a civil rights advocate. Two years earlier, following the racially motivated bombing of the Sixteenth Street Baptist Church and the death of four little girls, Siegel ripped down a whites' only sign near his office. "In view of recent events in our city which took the lives of innocent children," he wrote at the time, "signs such as these constantly remind me of the effect of my failure as a citizen, and the failure of this institution of higher learning, to exert a constructive influence in our community."

At the Caliph Washington fundraiser, Reverend Joseph Ellwanger of the CWCA and Julian Hall of the NAACP made passionate appeals for monetary support from the small gathering. "I made it clear," Hall wrote the next day, the "financial situation" and the "significance of this case" in the arena of civil rights law. "What is needed now is as much exposure in Birmingham before as many friends . . . of the NAACP as possible. There is no doubt that the Alabama State Conference of the NAACP is making itself heard" through the Washington case.

With this fundraiser, Washington's supporters raised $1,500 for his legal defense. For the first time, Caliph, the indigent defendant, had some money to gain better representation to the state and federal court systems. On December 27, Erskine Smith wrote Orzell Billingsley to make certain that the names of all the lawyers in the federal appeals case were entered in circuit court in Bessemer "for the possible trial of the case on reprosecution." Smith, who recognized that Billingsley would "carry the bulk of the defense" of Washington, wanted to determine under what order and authority Caliph was being held: Was it under the original indictment, a new indictment, or a warrant? When would the tentative trial take place? Who would be the judge? Smith hoped to get a head start on the legal paperwork in order to make a quick application for bond or file another writ of habeas corpus in circuit court in Bessemer. Smith seemed to hold out little hope that Caliph would be granted bail from the federal appeals court.

AS 1965 CLOSED, Caliph, his family, and his friends had mixed emotions. A federal judge spared his life and later ordered his release from Kilby Prison, but he was rearrested and returned to Bessemer—back to where it all began in 1957. The Civil Rights Act of 1964 put an end to racial segregation in public places, but not behind the jailhouse doors, where Washington remained in the Jefferson County Jail—still operating under the old racial order, just like all the other prisons and jails in the South. Outside his cell, poor but proud southern black folks, just like Caliph, moved at lightning speed toward achieving racial equality. These were the key players in the *movement*—taking strides toward freedom, marching in the streets for justice, and pressing on toward the prize of civil rights. "Those people keep a moving," a prison song writer once wrote, "and that's what tortures me." It was the fierce, evangelistic "urgency of now" that motivated blacks to keep moving, Martin Luther King, Jr., explained in *Why We Can't Wait*. Caliph Washington, however, had no choice but to sit, wait, pray, and hope.

The new year brought disappointing news. Caliph Washington received notice that the Fifth Circuit judges had denied his application for bail, without any clear explanation. After reading the ruling, a frustrated Orzell Billingsley wrote, "We have not decided our next step at this time." Washington's lawyers seemed convinced that Bessemer was holding Caliph illegally. The three-judge panel, however, ordered that the appeal of Frank Johnson's habeas corpus ruling be expedited and placed on the calendar for "hearing at the earliest practicable date." Nonetheless, few things moved fast in the overworked Fifth Circuit, and Washington's accelerated case would be heard on Monday, April 18, 1966, in New Orleans before judges Warren L. Jones (Florida), Walter P. Gewin (Alabama), and Edwin F. Hunter (Louisiana).

Individually, these three, like other judges in the Fifth Circuit, were increasingly sympathetic to the rights of blacks. "These judges were a mixed bag," one observer concluded, "No obvious common factor accounted for their support for equal rights." Edwin Hunter saw himself as a "conscientious jurist with a sense of fair play" and respect for the Supreme Court's decisions. In 1962 he was the first federal judge to use the Civil Rights Act of 1960 to break through a "pattern of discrimination" by registering black voters himself. Court watchers considered Warren Jones an enigmatic figure who managed to bridge the liberal and conservative factions in the Fifth Circuit. "Neither an avowed segregationist nor a result-oriented activist," one writer noted, he believed in the effectiveness of the judicial process and the importance of abiding by the doctrine of *stare decisis* ("to stand by things decided)." In 1963 he quipped that the Fifth Circuit was spending most of its time "putting Negroes in schools and governors in jail."

The lone Alabamian and the only Democrat on the panel, fifty-eight-year-old Walter Pettus Gewin, was appointed to the Fifth Circuit by President John Kennedy in 1961. At the beginning of his judicial career, he was often described as one of "Kennedy's segregationist appointees," but by 1966, his views were changing. "Gewin was no racist," a keen observer of the Fifth Circuit wrote, "but it took time for him to develop a sensitivity to the injustice of racial discrimination." Chuck Morgan, Erskine Smith, and the other attorneys seemed pleased with the makeup of the three-judge panel.

Erskine Smith agreed to argue on behalf of Caliph Washington and in support of Frank Johnson's ruling, while assistant attorney general David Clark would represent Holman and the state of Alabama in opposing his decision. In a broad constitutional sense, the appeals court would consider only two issues from Frank Johnson's habeas corpus ruling: the prosecution's use of Washington's apparent "confessions" obtained without the presence of an attorney, and the use of Furman Jones's testimony from a previous trial without laying the proper predicate.

David Clark argued that Johnson erred in finding the conviction unconstitutional because the use of Washington's confessions made without counsel did not violate his right to obtain the assistance of an attorney. The assistant attorney general added that Johnson was wrong in his retroactive application of the *Escobedo* decision to a case tried five years before. In addition, Clark contended that prosecutors laid the proper predicate for the admission into evidence of Furman Jones's testimony from the previous trial. "Therefore," he added, "petitioner's constitutional right to confrontation and cross-examination of the witness against him was not violated."

In response, Smith criticized Clark for providing an incomplete record to the court in the state's brief, which should disqualify the appellant from "arguing his first speculation of error." Clark was intentional in his effort to omit any reference to the facts from the original trial transcript that proved that police violated Washington's constitutional rights. The record showed that the arrest warrant for Caliph Washington was issued on July 15, 1957; the defendant was arrested on July 14, and counsel was appointed on September 23. "Therefore, the defendant was without counsel of any sort," Smith continued, "for a period exceeding two months during which time the alleged confession was made."

As Fred Blanton contended months before, Smith argued that the *Escobedo* case was "remarkably similar to the facts" in the Caliph Washington case except that the uneducated defendant was just seventeen years old and "sufficiently uninformed of his rights" to request counsel. Danny Escobedo was twenty-two and retained counsel prior to questioning and asked for his attorney during interrogation. The entire process violated Washington's rights as outlined in the Fifth and Sixth Amendments, Smith added; his client was an "ignorant and poor" individual who was forced to give an involuntary confession. The attorney also argued that even the law enforcement officers in Bessemer, who arrested and questioned Washington, received "formal and practical training in the methods and techniques of interrogation" and should have known to have a lawyer present. In private, Smith speculated that the only reason the state appealed Johnson's decision to the Fifth Circuit was to "clarify the *Escobedo* doctrine," which the U.S. Supreme Court was expected to do soon.

Next, Smith turned his attention to the testimony of Furman Jones. The basic constitutional right of a defendant to confront and cross-examine an accuser in criminal cases was guaranteed to all citizens of the United States. Caliph Washington's prosecutors, Smith argued, made no real effort to locate Jones and had no justification for his absence from the second trial. If the state was allowed to introduce testimony from a previous trial, he added, then "prosecution becomes a lazy occupation" that deprives cross-examination and the opportunity to observe the witness's demeanor and attitude. Depriving a defendant of this basic right could cost him his freedom and life. "Therefore," Smith continued, "the prosecution should be held to the highest degree of compliance with laying a proper predicate of an adequate reason for the absence of the witness that would permit the introduction of testimony on the previous trial."

In his summary conclusion, Erskine Smith emphasized that Judge Johnson's granting of the writ of habeas corpus was proper because Caliph Washington was being "unlawfully held" based on a flawed conviction in which the Bessemer prosecutor used an involuntary confession (obtained while the defendant was without counsel) and the testimony of a witness from the previous trial (without first laying the proper predicate). Now it was up to the judges to agree with Johnson's ruling or overturn his decision and send Caliph Washington back to death row.

Erskine Smith returned to Birmingham to await the judge's decision. Upon reflection, the attorney believed that the three judges were sympathetic to the argument that no proper predicate was laid for introducing Furman Jones's testimony. In addition, Smith thought the judges were of the opinion that Caliph Washington, because of his age and race, "fit neatly" into the Escobedo decision. "I certainly have been encouraged that we will receive a favorable result in this case," Smith wrote Chuck Morgan on April 20, 1966.

But nothing ever seemed to come swiftly, clearly, or favorably in Caliph Washington's legal trials. The three judges released their decision on August 8, 1966—over three months after the oral arguments. Judge Walter Gewin wrote the opinion of the court. Following a brief review of the facts of the case, Gewin turned his attention to the confession in the context of the Escobedo decision. Since Frank Johnson's ruling and

Erskine Smith's oral arguments, the U.S. Supreme Court clarified and reaffirmed *Escobedo* (and what Gewin called the "problem of self-incrimination") in the *Miranda v. Arizona* decision of June 13, 1966. Writing the majority opinion, Chief Justice Earl Warren outlined principles for police to follow during a "custodial interrogation" of a person. The decision required that prior to any questioning, the suspect must be advised by law enforcement officials that he or she had the right to remain silent and that anything the person said might be used against him or her; the suspect had a right to an attorney, either hired or appointed. The individual could also waive these rights "voluntarily, knowingly, and intelligently." At any point during the questioning, however, the suspect could halt the process and ask for an attorney. Answering some questions or volunteering a few statements never deprived the suspect the right to "refrain from answering any further inquiries" until he or she consulted with an attorney. In addition, if he or she was alone and expressed an unwillingness to answer questions, the police had no right to question the individual.

As applied to Caliph Washington's case, Judge Gewin concluded that *Miranda* and *Escobedo* supported Johnson's conclusion that the confession was inadmissible, but the principles in those cases were "limited in their application." Gewin pointed to the Supreme Court's *Johnson v. New Jersey* decision of June 20, 1966, which prohibited "us from applying the principles of *Escobedo* and *Miranda* in judging" whether Washington's confession was admissible. The high court held that the two cases were applicable, particularly on this issue, only to subsequent court decisions and could not be retroactively applied to earlier cases. "We must reverse the finding of the District Court that the confession was inadmissible under the standards of *Escobedo*," Gewin concluded.

Nonetheless, in a curious turn, Gewin touched upon the "voluntary nature" of Caliph Washington's confession. Eighteen months before, at the February 8, 1965, pretrial hearing for *Washington v. Holman*, both sides agreed to allow Judge Johnson to "inquire into petitioner's allegedly unconstitutional detention" by examining four points: (1) cruel and unusual punishment in the granting of thirteen reprieves, (2) lack of counsel at Washington's apparent confessions, (3) the right of submitting testimony from a previous trial without cross-examination, and (4) violation of due process by the use of involuntary confessions. Johnson ruled on the constitutional issues in points two and three but ignored points one and four. Now, on appeal, Judge Gewin opined that Johnson's decision did not prevent Washington from "invoking the safeguards" in *Escobedo* as part of an "involuntariness claim" as a violation of due process.

The argument was even stronger now that the Supreme Court provided guidance on "what due process required." But that was as far as Gewin dared to go on this issue. "We make no decision regarding issue number four," he added. "That question has not been presented to us for determination." Yet Gewin emphasized that the record showed that the jury was present during the trial judge's evidence hearing on the admissibility of the confession. "In light of *Jackson v. Demo*," the judge added, "in which the Court held that voluntariness must be determined in a proceeding separate and apart from the jury, the petitioner's claim may have merit." Fred Blanton emphasized this point in his brief submitted to Judge Johnson on April 1, 1965, but it was too late to help Caliph Washington before the Fifth Circuit Court of Appeals.

The other question the judges considered was whether a proper predicate was laid before the state introduced the transcript of Furman Jones's testimony, "which was admitted into evidence by the trial court upon the contention by the State that the witness was a nonresident of Alabama and not subject to compulsory process." In other words, what proof did the prosecutors use to prove Jones's whereabouts? The only proof, Gewin noted, was the testimony of Jack Brown, a deputy sheriff in Jefferson County, South Carolina, who admitted mailing a subpoena to Jones at his last known address. In the trial, Judge Gardner Goodwyn ruled that Brown's testimony "constituted proper proof" that the witness resided outside the court's jurisdiction and was unavailable to testify. Gewin called the evidence "insufficient" and "most inadequate." The state fell short of exercising due diligence in its search for the witness, the judges believed, and simply indicated the remote possibility that Jones was somewhere "beyond the borders" of Alabama.

The constitutional guarantees to confront and cross-examine a witness, Gewin emphasized, "cannot be side-stepped because it happens to be convenient for one of the parties." The U.S. Constitution, the Alabama Constitution, and the case law all provided safeguards for the protection of this fundamental right. In Washington's case, prior testimony can be admitted as evidence only when it complies with the safeguards and "does no violence" to protected constitutional rights. "The constitutional right of confrontation," Gewin continued, "could never have any greater meaning than when a person is on trial for his life. . . . In this case the likelihood that such a penalty would be imposed was not remote or highly speculative in view of the fact that Washington had been given the death sentence on his first trial."

Judges Gewin, Jones, and Hunter affirmed Frank Johnson's conclusion that prosecutors never laid a proper predicate before Furman Jones's testimony from the previous trial was admitted as evidence. "Thus, petitioner [Caliph Washington] was convicted in violation of the Sixth and Fourteenth Amendments," they concluded. The judges had both overturned and upheld parts of Johnson's legal reasoning, but in the end, the writ of habeas corpus remained intact, and the verdict in Washington's second trial was still overturned. The decision of the Fifth Circuit made little difference to Caliph Washington. He would not return to Kilby Prison, but he remained confined to the county jail in Bessemer, awaiting a third trial.

The court's "favorable decision" pleased Erskine Smith. He hoped, however, that the state might decide against an appeal to the U.S. Supreme Court so that he could provide Caliph Washington with legal assistance in Jefferson County courts. To that end, he asked Chuck Morgan to contact "our mutual friend," Alabama attorney general Richmond Flowers. "I really do not see any reason for the attorney general to seek a further appeal in this case," Smith wrote. "Perhaps you can convince him of this." Flowers, a lame duck by the fall of 1966, finished a distant second to George Wallace's wife, Lurleen, in the Democratic primary for governor. As a gubernatorial candidate, he actively courted the black vote and was labeled as "soft on the race question." The *New York Times* reported that Flowers was the "first major white candidate in modern times to campaign directly among Negroes in the Deep South." A frequent target of the most rabid segregationists, the tall, red-headed Flowers was spat upon while on the campaign trail and endured threats, a beating, and alienation from friends and family.

Regardless of whether Morgan influenced Flowers, the attorney general chose not to file an appeal. With this round of legal fighting concluded, Erskine Smith told Orzell Billingsley that he planned to convince Bessemer district attorney James Hammonds to abandon the prosecution of Caliph Washington or, in legal terms, to have the case *nolle prossed*. "I understand . . . that all witnesses have disappeared or died," Smith wrote, "including the other police officer, who I understand has now died. Apparently the only witness who could present damaging evidence against Caliph Washington is one Furman Jones whose whereabouts were unknown at the last trial and apparently remain unknown."

But for Caliph Washington, nothing came of Smith's efforts. Bessemer neither abandoned nor tried the case. James Hammonds was so embroiled in scandal that most cases in the Bessemer district attorney's office were delayed. On the other side, Washington's lawyers were distracted. They remained much too busy fighting a highly publicized court battle with the state over integrating all prison cells in Alabama to worry about one man, in one cell, in one jail, in one town. So Caliph Washington waited and his anxious mother fretted. Soon, following the decision of the Fifth Circuit, Aslee Washington sent a letter to the U.S. Department of Justice and pleaded for help. She explained that after Judge Johnson ordered her son's release from Kilby Prison, deputies from Bessemer "picked my son up" and placed him in the county jail. Now the Fifth Circuit upheld Johnson's decision, yet Caliph Washington remained in jail. She failed to understand. "I am still unable to effect his release," Eileen Walbert wrote on behalf of Mrs. Washington, "and am writing you for aid and advice in effecting his release for I feel that his civil rights are now and have been continually violated."

"IT'S ANOTHER SHOWDOWN BETWEEN ALABAMA AND THE FEDERAL GOVERNMENT"

This *Birmingham News* editorial cartoon depicts the state of Alabama making another stand against integration—this time in the prison system.

15

SINNERS TO CONVERT

OCCUPYING A CELL near Caliph Washington in the Jefferson County Jail in Bessemer was Gary Gurley, a hard-nosed white man with a fiery temper that belied his last name. Washington and Gurley shared much in common. They grew up near each other in Bessemer, but the laws and customs of segregation kept them worlds apart. In 1957 both were poorly educated seventeen-year-old males accused of violent crimes—Washington for the murder of Cowboy Clark, and Gurley for the robbery of $107.30 from Ralph Keef, the assistant manager at Track Side Service Station in Bessemer. Ironically, they both ended up on the circuit court docket the same day in October 1957—Gurley's armed robbery case came first, and then Caliph Washington's for murder. Local juries convicted both men, with Washington sentenced to death and Gurley to over ten years. Both rode the long train to Kilby Prison in Montgomery, where they were housed in segregated cellblocks. Now years later, on a humid summer night in the Jefferson County Jail, the men, who led parallel lives, would meet.

It was nearing 10 p.m. Four other prisoners, part of a cleanup crew, were returning to their cells. Unbeknownst to guards and other prisoners, the four were planning to break out that night, having spent weeks secretly fashioning and sharpening cell-house knives. Their jailbreak plan was simple. As one journalist later reported, "They'd grab a guard and use him as a hostage in forcing their way to freedom." The time came, and with lightning quickness one took hold of a guard and held a knife to his throat, as the other men relieved him of his ring of keys. They quickly unlocked all the cell doors. "Let's go," another one told the rest of the prisoners. "Everybody that wants to. . . . Let's go." Gary Gurley jumped from his bunk and hurried toward freedom.

He had taken only a few steps, however, when someone with a vise-like grip grabbed his arm and spun him around. Caliph Washington glared at Gurley and asked, "Where you going?"

Gurley responded, "I'm going with them," as he pointed to the men holding the guard with the knives.

"You're not going anywhere, man," Washington said.

"Who's gonna stop me?" Gary asked.

"Me," Caliph said as he pushed Gurley back into the cell and slammed him against the metal bunk. At six-foot-one and a solid 190 pounds, Gurley was no featherweight, but Caliph had gained almost sixty pounds since his arrest in 1957, weighing in at over 230 pounds on his five-foot-eight frame. Despite Gurley's desperate attempts to break free, Washington could not be moved. The others had no choice but to leave Gary Gurley behind.

The escapees pushed forward with their hostage. When they reached the locked steel door of the cellblock, one of the prisoners yelled to the warden just outside, "Let us out or we'll kill this man," as he pulled the knife tighter against the hostage's throat.

The warden, who was sitting at a desk, finishing paperwork, looked up and said, "Go ahead and kill him," and continued his work.

His bluff paid off. The prisoners were unwilling to add a murder charge to their rap sheet, especially the killing of a police officer, which could likely result in the death sentence. In the end, the would-be jailbreakers surrendered.

Back in the cellblock, Caliph Washington looked at Gary Gurley and said, "I told you." All Gary could do was nod his head in thanks.

In the succeeding months, Washington and Gurley developed a deep cross-racial friendship, perhaps the first for both men, spending hours talking. Washington shared his faith in God, and Gurley had a jail cell conversion. When Gurley received probation, Caliph Washington stayed behind, but Gurley was a changed man. "He's a neat dresser, handsome, and an accomplished speaker," one observer later noted. He took a job as an upholsterer and spent his free time talking to young people about his experiences in the hope of keeping them from following his path. "He'll do anything he can," a journalist wrote, "to keep it from happening to other youngsters." Whenever he shared his faith and experiences, he always told about Caliph Washington. "He's the reason I'm on the outside now," Gurley said a few years later, "and I want to help all the people I can. He saved my life."

Washington's impact on Gurley almost did not happen; it was just providence that allowed their close proximity. Even as late as 1966 and 1967, state laws mandated racial separation of prisoners in Alabama and most other southern states. It was Jim Crow's last legally enforced stronghold. The ACLU's Chuck Morgan wanted to change that with the unwitting help of Caliph Washington. The state of Alabama, as it had throughout the civil rights era, would fight the change and make one last stand to preserve the final place where it remained legal to segregate by race and the last place almost no one cared about integrating.

For decades, Morgan spoke of his hatred for all prisons and jails, but in the Deep South, he believed, they were worse. Morgan loathed the "clanging of metal doors, the jangle of five-inch-long door keys, the grating sound of scraping metal chairs and cups and trays, the filtered voices over speaker systems through slits in metal doors, and the clanging of the bells." So Morgan and Orzell Billingsley began drinking whiskey and plotting a legal assault on racial segregation in jails and prisons. Billingsley knew the perfect client to lead a class action suit: Caliph Washington.

Billingsley also suggested another black client for the lawsuit, Johnnie ("Big Time") Coleman, who was also awaiting a new trial after an all-white jury sentenced him to death for the murder of a white mechanic, John D. "Screwdriver" Johnson. On appeal, Billingsley argued before the Alabama Supreme Court that Coleman's conviction should be overturned and the defendant granted a new trial because of the systematic exclusion of blacks on the grand and petit juries in Greene County. The judges, however, disagreed. "No sufficient proof having been produced at the hearing on the motion for a new trial," wrote Judge Robert Simpson, "or at any other state of the proceedings, it is clear appellant may not now complain. Therefore, we are left under no doubt that appellant's point on systematic exclusion of Negroes from the jury rolls in Greene County is not well taken." Nonetheless, Billingsley appealed the case to the Supreme Court, and the justices ruled unanimously that Coleman was "entitled to have his day in court on his allegations of systematic exclusion of Negroes from the grand and petit juries sitting in his case."

While "Big Time" Coleman and Caliph Washington awaited new trials, they joined the prison-integration lawsuit, along with two staffers from the SCLC, Hosea Williams and Thomas Houck, Jr. In January 1966, Birmingham police arrested Williams (black) and Houck (white) for leading voting rights demonstrations in the city streets. At the time, Orzell Billingsley was skeptical of an attempt to replicate the highly successful 1963 marches and pronounced that a "campaign to get blacks to apply to register would be far more likely to produce the desired results than marches in the streets." But now the duo served a useful purpose, allowing Billingsley and Morgan to add two plaintiffs who were confined in segregated cells in arguably the country's most famous lockup, the Birmingham Jail—where Jimmie Tarlton wrote his famous folk ballad and Martin Luther King began composing the most important written document of the era, the "Letter from Birmingham Jail." To round out the suit, Morgan also included two minors as plaintiffs, Cecil McCargo, Jr., and Willie Allen.

Crafting a class action lawsuit that made clever use of the arrangement of the plaintiffs' and defendants' names thrilled Chuck Morgan and ensured that the case would be long remembered. The lead plaintiff would be Caliph Washington, and the first defendant listed would be A. Frank Lee, commissioner of corrections for Alabama. The prison integration suit, much to Morgan's delight, would be styled *Washington v. Lee.*

The other defendants in the suit would include all members of Alabama's board of corrections: John F. Britton, Charlie Cashion, Herschell Luttrell, Max McLaughlin, and William Mitch; Mel Bailey, sheriff of Jefferson County; Robert Austin, warden of the Birmingham Jail; and "all other wardens and jailers of city and town jails of Alabama, jointly and severally, who are similarly situated."

The principal defendant was commissioner Abiel Frank Lee, a fifty-eight-year-old, blunt-talking former lawman from Alabama's Black Belt. The lightning-charged demands of his job kept Lee busy seven days a week—relaxation, vacation, and sleep were rare, but his addiction to sturdy black coffee kept him working, moving, and talking. "He likes conversation," an acquaintance explained, "and seldom runs out of suggestions and questions on any subject." Born in Eutaw on February 21, 1909, Lee served twenty years as sheriff of 81 percent black Greene County, a position he inherited from his father, James Frank Lee. "The Lees prided themselves on not needing guns," one tongue-in-cheek observer wrote. "When they sent word to the wanted, the guilty parties stumbled over each other in the race to run themselves in." When the younger Lee went to work as a deputy commissioner for the Alabama Department of Corrections in 1954, his brother "Big Bill," took over the family law enforcement business. "There were lots of grown men with families," Frank later recalled, "who never knew anybody but a Lee as sheriff." In Montgomery, Frank Lee and his wife Rosalind lived at 1810 Federal Drive, directly across the street from Kilby Prison—the facility he called unfit for "human habitation." When he became prison commissioner in 1960, he fought to replace the ancient facility and to modernize the Alabama prison system. "I've spent all the time and effort at my command," he said, "to revamp and renovate the Alabama prison system and abolish the antiquity." The system was now "on the move," Lee believed, and this unnecessary lawsuit would hinder that progress.

On February 18, 1966, Chuck Morgan and Orzell Billingsley filed the official civil action complaint in the U.S. District Court in Montgomery. In legal terms, the complaint was concise and straightforward. They based their argument on "common questions of law and fact" that affected the civil rights of blacks "to be not segregated, classified, designated or otherwise subjected to racial distinctions in confinement" in prisons and jails in Alabama. "Utilizing, enforcing, and maintaining" the "policy, custom, practice, scheme or usage" of racially segregating prisoners violated the due process and equal protection clauses of the Eighth and Fourteenth Amendments. Caliph Washington, Willie Allen, Cecil McCargo, Jr., Thomas E. Houck, Jr., Hosea Williams, and Johnnie Coleman would represent the interests of all of Alabama's black population, white civil rights workers, and prison inmates, who were "so numerous as to make it impracticable" to bring them before the court. Morgan and Billingsley asked the court to provide "common relief" and issue an order that declared unconstitutional the practice of segregating blacks "or otherwise treating them on a basis different from whites."

Specifically, Morgan and Billingsley were attacking fourteen sections of Title 45 of the Alabama Code of 1940 as recompiled in 1958. The three most relevant sections of the code (121, 122, and 123) mandated that before conviction, male and female, white and black prisoners must be kept "separate and apart." The state considered the mixing of races and sexes (except married couples) to be unlawful; jailers or other law officers who violated these prohibitions would be fined $50 to $100. The only exception to the law was if the jail facility had an insufficient "number of apartments" to house prisoners separately. The complaint also highlighted other sections of the code that made racial distinctions: the commissioner's annual report contained the racial designation of convicts (Section 19); the board of commissioners recorded the "complexion" of each convict (Section 30); sheriffs, chiefs of police, and town marshals made monthly reports highlighting each prisoners' race (Section 177); each county jail or town prison provided "separate compartments" and bath facilities for whites and blacks (Section 183); and white and black prisoners on work crews were never "to be chained together" or allowed to sleep together (Section 52). Whenever practical, in the judgment of the governor and the director, the code specified, "arrangements shall be made for keeping white and colored convicts at separate prisons and they shall not be allowed to be kept at the same place," a provision that Caliph Washington knew all too well when the state transported black death row inmates back and forth between Kilby and Atmore.

In the end, the plaintiffs "respectfully prayed" that the court would take the case, appoint a special three-judge court, and issue a temporary restraining order or a preliminary injunction (to be made permanent later) to stop state, county, and local officials from segregating black prisoners and excluding blacks from employment in law enforcement. Morgan and Billingsley asked the court to put the case on the docket quickly and order speedy proceedings. In the complaint, they justified their request in the legalese of personal injury attorneys: "The plaintiffs and others similarly situated and affected on whose behalf this suit is brought are suffering irreparable injury and are threatened with irreparable injury in the future by reason of the acts herein complained of." After reading the complaint, Judge Frank Johnson notified Elbert P. Tuttle, chief judge of the Fifth Circuit, that the civil action was one required by a congressional act to be "heard and determined by a district court of three judges. On March 21, 1966, Judge Tuttle designated three Alabamians, Richard T. Rives, Seybourn H. Lynne, and Frank Johnson, as the three judges who would "constitute the said court to hear and determine the action."

The senior circuit judge on the panel was seventy-one-year-old Richard Taylor Rives. Decades before, in 1912, Dick Rives made his livelihood pressing pants at a small self-owned business on Dexter Avenue in Montgomery. One customer, attorney Wiley Hill (an uncle to future Alabama senator Lister Hill), sent him a note that read, "If you would like to study law, I'll show you which books to read." Rives never considered a legal career, but he jumped at the opportunity to read the law with Hill. At the time, young Dick Rives never suspected that his father visited Hill and asked the attorney to take the boy under his tutelage. Almost two years later, on March 13, 1914, nineteen-year-old Dick Rives passed the Alabama bar examination and joined Hill's practice. Thirty years later, Rives was one of Alabama's most prominent and well-paid trial lawyers, whom friends described as a neopopulist political activist with liberal leanings. During the presidential election of 1948, he remained loyal to Harry Truman while most Alabama Democrats bolted the party in favor of the Dixiecrat candidate Strom Thurmond. That same year, while Truman was losing white southern voters by advocating civil rights, Rives fought an unsuccessful personal battle to defeat a state amendment to further restrict black voting rights. "When we use arbitrary law as the basis for white supremacy," he proclaimed at the time, "we are building on quicksand." In paternalistic tones common to his generation, he added:

> But when we assert the white man's leadership in terms of intelligence, character and sense of justice we are building upon a solid foundation. The chains we forge to shackle qualified Negroes can be used to keep white voters of Alabama from walking in the polls. These chains would not only breed resistance in the Negro, but for worse, would rub a moral cancer on the character of the white man.

In 1951, Alabama's two U.S. senators, Lister Hill and John Sparkman, convinced President Truman to nominate "loyal Dick Rives" to succeed Leon McCord as a judge on the Fifth Circuit.

Throughout the 1950s and 1960s, Rives's civil rights rulings stirred the "wrath and embitterment" of white citizens in Alabama. One journalist believed that these rulings left Rives a pariah in his hometown of Montgomery, where he "suffered indignity and brutality" at the hands of radical segregationists. "For all we ever saw," a Montgomery paper reported in 1966, "Judge Rives bore his cross sorrowfully, but without flinching."

A decade before the *Washington v. Lee* case, Rives, Frank Johnson, and Seybourn Lynne sat on another three-judge panel that struck down segregated seating on municipal buses in Montgomery. The *Browder v. Gayle* decision was a significant and long-awaited legal victory for civil rights activists during the Montgomery Bus Boycott—although the boycott continued several more months while the city appealed the ruling to the U.S. Supreme Court, which ultimately upheld the decision. Nonetheless, the three-judge ruling was not unanimous. Seybourn Lynne cast the dissenting vote and proclaimed that "only a profound, philosophical disagreement . . . that the separate but equal doctrine can no longer be safely followed as . . . the law would prompt this, my first dissent."

Unlike Richard Rives, Seybourn Harris Lynne decided at an early age to become a lawyer—no doubt influenced by the fact that his father, grandfather, uncles, and several cousins were all attorneys. "It never occurred to me to be anything but a lawyer," Lynne said. Born on July 25, 1907, in the Tennessee River city of Decatur, Lynne earned his law degree from the University of Alabama in 1930 and won a 1934 election to a judgeship in his native Morgan County. During World War II, he earned a Bronze Star and achieved the rank of lieutenant colonel in his handling of a wide variety of legal matters for the judge advocate general. Following the war, President Truman appointed him to the federal bench on January 9, 1946, succeeding the late T. A. M. Murphree.

Lynne's first case was a lengthy thirty-defendant white lightning moonshine trial that, as one observer noted, provided the new judge an "intensive workout the first week of his return to the civilian bench." By 1953, he became the chief judge of the Northern District of Alabama, and his rulings during the civil rights era would define his career. During the 1950s and 1960s, one critic noted, Lynne, who ironically opposed judicial activism, designated himself as the "great deterrent to desegregation," and his rulings time and again helped preserve the "southern way of life." Nonetheless, in 1963, Lynne prohibited Governor George Wallace from barring two black students (Vivian Malone and James Hood) from attending the University of Alabama. "The governor of a sovereign state has no authority to obstruct or prevent the execution of lawful orders of a court of the United States," he wrote. From the bench, Lynne preferred to deal with tax cases because they were explicit, leaving little room for interpretation. He preferred the absolute rather than cases that compelled him to ponder the intricacies of the law. "A trial judge is . . . engaged in the business of moving cases along," he once said.

Making an informed ruling in *Washington v. Lee* would not be so easy or straightforward for Seybourn Lynne or the other judges. The case would be lengthy and complex and require voluminous paper-work, much to the chagrin of Lynne. Chuck Morgan described Lynne as "bright, competent, and consistently wrong." On the other hand, Morgan believed the prison integration case would find sympathetic jurists in Frank Johnson and Richard Rives. "Unlike many—perhaps most—judges, south and north," Morgan wrote, Johnson and Rives "really believed in the Constitution."

Judge Johnson ordered the plaintiffs and the defendants to submit briefs to the court on the legal and constitutional questions involved by November 1, 1966. Seven lawyers would be representing various defendants. Sheriff Mel Bailey used the legal services of Birmingham attorneys Frank Dominick and Walter Fletcher. Warden Bob Austin used J. M. Breckenridge and Earl McBee of the City of Birmingham's law department. Commissioner Frank Lee and the five members of the board of corrections would be defended by Richmond Flowers and assistant attorney general Gordon Madison, who would handle most of the workload. Madison, whom Flowers described as a "brilliant, experienced lawyer," headed the federal section in the attorney general's office. "He was constantly negotiating," Flowers recalled. "He trusted me, and I trusted him."

The affable sixty-six-year-old James Gordon Madison served under five Alabama attorney generals since his appointment by Si Garrett in 1952. A native of the simple crossroads village of Denbigh, Virginia, Gordon Madison descended from an illustrious family of Virginia lawyers, who included President James Madison and a great-grandfather who studied law with Thomas Jefferson. In 1917, Gordon Madison moved to Perry County in the Alabama Black Belt. Following his graduation in 1921, he went on to earn a law degree from the University of Alabama in 1925 and began his law practice in Tuscaloosa with the firm of Foster, Rice, Madison & Rosenfeld. White Tuscaloosa voters elected him to the Alabama Senate in 1942, and he quickly gained a reputation as a hard-working and efficient leader. His efforts gained the attention of Senator Lister Hill, who tapped Madison to run his 1944 reelection bid. It would become a bruising referendum on the senator's support of Franklin Roosevelt's New Deal. Hill's challenger was James Simpson, a cheerless Birmingham corporate lawyer who used white supremacy as his battle cry and, as *Time* magazine reported, "lambasted Lister Hill as a traitor to southern ideals, a tool of Washington's 'radical Yankee' administration, a 'rubber stamp' for 'C.I.O. bosses,' [and] a typical New Dealer." Hill, however, remained confident of victory, especially with the "clear and able" Madison running his campaign. Hill defeated Simpson by 25,000 votes. Almost immediately, speculation emerged that Madison would receive a nomination to the federal judgeship in Birmingham, but the nod went to Seybourn Lynne.

Although he remained loyal to Hill and the Democratic Party during the political upheavals of the Dixiecrat era, Madison was no supporter of civil rights. As the head of the federal section in the attorney general's office, he would lead Alabama's legal opposition to civil rights throughout the 1950s and 1960s. "The people of Alabama are never going to send white children to nigra schools," he once told a federal judge in Montgomery, "and the sooner these Justice Department people understood that, the sooner we can give a quality education to everyone." Nonetheless, the assistant attorney general believed in compliance with final court rulings. As an individual and as a citizen of Alabama, Madison said, he opposed integration, "but as a lawyer, I can't say that." Defying integration was like playing bridge, he supposed. "You play each hand so you lose as few hands as possible."

By the late 1960s, Gordon Madison was weary of defending the state in a storm of civil rights suits. His brief in *Washington v. Lee* reflected this fatigue and disillusionment. It began with the monotone announcement that the case was yet "another desegregation suit," but this time it focused on prisons and jails. Black prisoners did not want to be segregated, Madison continued, and made note of a recent court decision that "made it unmistakably clear" that racial discrimination by government representatives would not be tolerated. Judicial intervention stopped racial discrimination in schools, housing, recreational facilities, and employment, the court emphasized in the *Edwards v. Sard* decision, but prisons were different. Madison jumped on this point: "Unless perhaps in extreme cases the courts should not interfere with the conduct of a prison or its discipline." He also highlighted the *Tally v. Stephens* case, where the court specified that prison officials must have "wide latitude and discretion" in managing and operating a prison. "The Courts cannot take over the management of prisons," the decision noted, "and they cannot undertake to review every complaint made by a convict about his treatment while in prison."

Next, Madison reviewed the fourteen sections of Title 45 of the Alabama Code referred to in the complaint, and he concluded that half of the sections made no reference to separating prisoners according to race and needed no consideration by the court. However, the other seven sections dealt with racial separation and "should be considered by the court in light of the cases cited in the brief," especially the *Edwards* and *Tally* decisions. In other words, the state was inviting the court to rule on the Fourteenth Amendment issues of due process and equal protection.

Madison, however, strongly disagreed with the plaintiffs' conclusion that racial segregation of prisoners was a violation of the cruel and unusual punishment clause of the Eighth Amendment. "This contention is plainly without merit," he wrote. Before the 1954 *Brown* decision, racial separation was legal throughout American society and upheld by some of the greatest jurists in the country. "If the Constitution is to be considered in the light of developing civilization," Madison added, "a good long look should be taken of present day events in this country before any new or novel constitutional pronouncements are made by this court."

In response, Chuck Morgan submitted his twenty-one-page brief on October 31. In it, he argued that Alabama's prison segregation statutes violated the cruel and unusual punishment clause of the Eighth Amendment and the due process and equal protection clauses of the Fourteenth Amendment. "The underlying legal principles seem not contested," he added, because states could no longer constitutionally mandate segregation in the public sphere. The principle within the *Brown* decision extended to all state institutions. The central issue before the three judges was whether there was any reason to exclude jails and prisons from the "broad proscriptions" of the law. "There are none," Morgan wrote, and the "compelling need" in the case was a "speedy and effective" integration of the state's correctional facilities.

Morgan rejected the defendants' notion that prison officials maintained racial segregation for prison security and discipline. This was not a case that involved a fight between inmates or disciplinary action taken by prison officials. "Plaintiffs have broken no prison rules of any kind," he added. This case was about "statutory segregation" in prisons and jails in Alabama, and race-based separation was unconstitutional in any form. Justifying racial segregation as a way to avoid violence was a well-worn position of whites who opposed integration. The prophets of segregation predicted "blood flowing in the streets" if public schools were integrated, but there were few violent incidents. They argued that the integration of lunch counters and restaurants would bring "thorough-going" racial violence because community standards were too deeply entrenched "to be touched by a mere external act of the government." But after integration, Morgan wrote, southerners discovered that the real problem was "the fear and distrust that the old custom of separation had created and preserved." In fact, the attorney supposed, segregationists predicted that every public meeting between whites and blacks would bring violence and discord, but these "prophecies proved empty" too. "Violence is not the child of integration," Morgan argued, but "the child of distrust and fear."

Therefore the "threat of violence and disorder is not pertinent," Morgan wrote. "Even if desegregation of Alabama's penal institutions were to inevitably occasion some racial disturbance, no grounds exist to deny Negroes their constitutional right to be free from racial segregation." Maintaining separation by race did nothing to prepare inmates for life outside the walls of prison in an integrated society. The former white prisoner was unprepared to face this reality because he came from a world where he learned that blacks and whites could never live together because the differences were too pronounced. "This is sinister and even cruel preparation for men who must learn to live in a society struggling to solve racial problems," Morgan emphasized. Black inmates in Alabama prisons and jails received a reverse education, he argued, and learned only disrespect for the rule of law and resentment over the unfairness created by unjust laws—especially Jim Crow laws that forced a prisoner "to live in segregated quarters, eat in a segregated dining room, sleep in a segregated cell block, exercise in a segregated prison yard, work on a segregated work detail and worship in a segregated prison chapel." By maintaining segregated prison facilities, the state of Alabama denied the "elemental concepts of decency," depreciated the "dignity of man," and violated the cruel and unusual punishment clause of the Eighth Amendment. "The history of civil rights legislation and the decisions of the courts," Morgan emphasized, "makes it too plain for argument that the practice of racial discrimination is a violation of the fundamental concepts of American democracy and the commitment of that democracy to the belief in the dignity and sanctity of each citizen."

In the end, Morgan believed the court should declare unconstitutional the sections of the code that required segregation and order the state to take affirmative steps to integrate.

On November 29, 1966, Chuck Morgan and Gordon Madison presented oral arguments before judges Johnson, Rives, and Lynne in Montgomery. Morgan's key expert witness was John O. Boone, who worked for fourteen years at the Atlanta Federal Penitentiary and conducted a lengthy study of prisons in the Deep South for the Southern Regional Council. On cross-examination, Madison asked Boone to discuss the integration process at the federal level. "How long did it take?" he asked.

"Overnight," Boone answered. He testified that when the process of integrating a prison was handled well, racial tensions and violence decreased.

The assistant attorney general then tried to get Boone to agree that federal prisoners and state prisoners were completely different types of criminals.

"I have met some of your ex-inmates," Boone said. "In fact, I have encountered hundreds and hundreds of them in federal prisons."

"Are not the type of prisoners usually found in federal penal institutions different?" Madison continued.

Boone said no.

"[Different] than those in state [prisons]?" Madison asked.

"No, sir," the witness said, "they are the same men." Boone showed, much to Madison's dismay, that former Alabama inmates were serving time in desegregated federal prison without any of the prophesized bloodshed.

Attorney Madison had no better luck questioning the state's witnesses. Birmingham Jail warden Robert Austin testified that in his experience integration "created no problems" with respect to trusties, work gangs, farm crews, and maintenance crews. He added that he did not "foresee much problem" in integrating the Birmingham Jail, except in the drunk tanks.

Jefferson County sheriff Mel Bailey, whom Morgan described as "too wholesome to be real and too outsized to argue with," echoed similar themes. At over six-foot-five, Bailey's country-boy innocence masked an intelligent and unflappable lawman. The sheriff was up for reelection in 1966 and courting black voters, so he provided only limited answers to Madison's questions. But when Judge Johnson asked, "Is there any instance in your experience where it is necessary to classify solely because of race . . . in order to maintain and operate your prison properly?" Bailey said, "I would have to say no." The state's witness admitted that segregation was unnecessary for maintaining safety and order in an Alabama jail.

This was a key point of emphasis when Johnson, Rives, and Lynne handed down their unanimous ruling on December 12, 1966. In writing the opinion, Judge Johnson pointed out that this notion of maintaining "routine prison security and discipline" was the state's only defense in refuting that the prison segregation statutes violated the equal protection clause of the Fourteenth Amendment. "We disagree," he wrote. Prisoners forfeited many privileges and rights upon being incarcerated. However, the judges emphasized, due process and equal protection "follow them into prison and protect them from unconstitutional action on the part of prison authorities carried out under color of state law." Johnson gave as an example the drunk tank in the Birmingham Jail, which might get so crowded on Saturday nights that the warden might need to separate the races. The recognition of these special situations did nothing to justify those sections in the Alabama Code and the general practice of separating the races arbitrarily. "Such statutes and practices must be declared unconstitutional," Johnson stressed.

The three judges, however, rejected the plaintiffs' argument that the racial separation of prisoners violated the cruel and unusual punishment clause of the Eighth Amendment. "[It] is without merit," Johnson wrote. That clause was adopted to prevent "inhuman, barbarous or torturous punishment[,] . . . and segregation of individuals, while incarcerated, solely by reason of their race does not, in the opinion of this court, constitute cruel and unusual punishment."

Johnson, Rives, and Lynne recognized that the operation of a statewide prison or a local jail was a specialized endeavor that required the "sober judgment" of experienced individuals such as Frank Lee and Mel Bailey. (Bob Austin was not mentioned.) These were dangerous jobs with intense pressures. "In light of this recognition," Johnson underscored, "this court will not at this time require an immediate and total desegregation of state, county and city penal facilities in the state of Alabama." The judges mandated that Kilby, Atmore, and other maximum-security prisons integrate in one year. Minimum- and medium-security institutions—Draper and Julia Tutwiler Prisons—had six months to complete desegregation. The honor farms, educational facilities, the youth center, and the hospital must be integrated immediately.

Most likely, the judges used Frank Lee's testimony during oral arguments as a basis for this timetable for integration. When asked by the court how long he would need to integrate, Lee answered, "I would hate to think that we would have to do it in less than a year's time—even though if we get such an order, we would start tomorrow." The court also ordered Lee to supervise the desegregation not only of state prisons but also of city and county jails. Every three months, Lee had to report to the court the progress of integration. Finally, the court declared unconstitutional seven state statutes of the Alabama Code that mandated racial segregation in Alabama's prisons and jails.

With the legal victory in *Washington v. Lee*, Chuck Morgan and Orzell Billingsley conquered the last stronghold of state-mandated segregation in Alabama. Perhaps most surprising to Morgan was seeing Seybourn

Lynne, who had so bitterly opposed Rives and Johnson a decade earlier, joining his fellow jurists in a unanimous decision. Avant-garde civil rights and civil liberties lawyers like Morgan could never afford to "write off" old-school segregationist judges. There were just too many. "Besides, it is not the nature of southern Protestants to write off people," Morgan later wrote. "Without 'sinners' there would be no one to convert."

Civil rights demonstrators sing during a protest at the Jefferson County Jail in Bessemer in 1967. Standing on the first step are Fred Shuttlesworth (*left*) and Asbury Howard (*right*).

16

SEGREGATION'S LAST STAND

I N THE ALABAMA Attorney General's Office, Richmond Flowers took the news of another loss in Frank Johnson's courtroom in stride. "I tried a world of lawsuits before Frank Johnson," Flowers later recalled, "because we had a lot of civil rights suits. I lost them all. . . . You couldn't defend what I was obligated by my position to defend." When Governor George Wallace criticized the attorney general for not fighting hard enough, Flowers responded, "The fight's over. We've lost the fight. Now we've got to live with the beast."

For Flowers, an appeal of the *Washington v. Lee* decision would be "the beast" for the new attorney general, MacDonald "Mac" Gallion. Flowers returned to private law practice in Montgomery in January 1967 with hopes of running for governor again in 1970. Instead he found himself indicted, tried, convicted, disbarred, and imprisoned for a complicated stock issuance and sale in an insurance company and a scheme to extort funds from several companies through threats of investigations and closure suits. After sixteen months in jail, Flowers received a parole in 1973 and a full pardon from President Jimmy Carter in 1978. This provided the former attorney general, as many Alabama political observers believed, personal vindication over "trumped up" charges by the "Wallace machine."

Flowers's successor, fifty-four-year-old Mac Gallion, was also his predecessor. Elected in 1958, Gallion's first term was marked by his "resistance within the framework of the law" to federal authority in civil rights matters and by his hostility to any efforts by blacks to end segregation or gain voting rights. Gallion, like many other red-baiting whites of his generation, saw civil rights activists as nothing more than Communist conspirators who were endangering the peace and security of America. In 1961, he told a White Citizens' Council rally in Montgomery that the Freedom Riders were a "foolish group of meddlers, bleeding hearts, publicity seekers, and assorted misfits" who were not promoting freedom, democracy, religion, and America, but just the opposite. "It is a cold, calculated, deliberate attack upon America itself," Gallion proclaimed, "upon the vital organs of our form of government, upon American prestige in the world and upon the very existence of America as the last bulwark across the path of atheist communism in the world." Alabama was in grave peril, he added, and the citizens of Alabama had front-row seats to watch the American Communist front in action. Gallion emphasized:

> We particularly in the South, have had set-back after set-back in our fight in this cause. I am firmly convinced that the South stands today as the last great bulwark of strength—the last bastion of defense—across this dangerous march to the left . . . this is no time to stop fighting; this is no time to become discouraged; it is no time to bow our head in abject defeat. On the contrary, it is the time to fight within the bounds of the law with all the determination and with all the heart and wisdom that we can muster at our command.

Gallion fought the federal government at every opportunity. When the U.S. Civil Rights Commission condemned "abuses of police power" in Alabama and recommended an investigation of police brutality and the misconduct of some court officials, Gallion called the charges unproven "gossip, old wives tales, and rumor."

George MacDonald Gallion was born in Montgomery in 1913 and raised in Birmingham. He earned a law degree from the University of Alabama in 1937 and practiced law in Birmingham until joining the Marines at the beginning of World War II. While fighting in the South Pacific, he was wounded in Saipan and received the Purple Heart. Following the war, he moved to Montgomery, where he maintained a private practice and at times worked as an assistant attorney general for the state.

Following the Phenix City assassination of Alabama attorney general-elect Albert Patterson in 1954, Governor Gordon Persons appointed Gallion as a special counsel, and he participated in the murder investigation and the cleanup of Alabama's "sin city." From 1955 to 1959, he went on to work as the chief assistant attorney general for Albert's son, John Patterson, who was elected in his father's place. In 1958, Alabama voters elected Gallion attorney general in the same election that sent John Patterson to the governor's office. The duo would emerge as symbols of white Alabama's massive resistance to civil rights.

In 1962, Gallion finished fourth in the governor's race that saw George Wallace elected to his first term. Four years later, following the tenure of the more moderate Richmond Flowers, voters returned segregationist MacDonald Gallion to the Alabama Attorney General's Office by a two-to-one margin. This was disappointing news to blacks and liberal-minded whites in the state. "He's the worst racist we have," one hyperbolic Alabamian wrote. Soon after the election, a newspaper reporter observed that blacks now faced dealing with Wallace without the support of Flowers, who often fought the governor and his hardcore supporters.

Soon after taking office, Gallion received a memo, presumably from Gordon Madison, that outlined reasons not to appeal the *Washington v. Lee* case to the U.S. Supreme Court. Losing the appeal could result in prohibitive injunctions and sharply curtail the "wide range of discretion" the three judges had left to prison and jail officials. The Supreme Court could find error in allowing Frank Lee to supervise the desegregation of jails and order the work done under "some federal official appointed by the court." If the high court affirmed the decision, then *Washington v. Lee* mandates would be binding precedent on all states, not just Alabama, and those states would "not be so free to handle their own cases when and if they arise." Most important, the author of the memo concluded, "legal study and consideration does not reveal any substantial grounds for reversal."

Frank Lee and the board of corrections had other ideas. On February 3, 1967, Lee informed MacDonald Gallion that the board wanted the *Washington v. Lee* decision appealed to the U.S. Supreme Court. "I will appreciate your cooperation in seeing that this action is taken," Lee wrote, "and followed through." Gallion complied, and the state of Alabama would once again fight to hold on to the last bastion of legally sanctioned segregation.

Three days later, on February 6, Gordon Madison submitted a "Notice of Appeal to the Supreme Court of the United States" in the federal district court in Montgomery. Madison raised five questions for appeal: (1) Do state statutes that require racial separation of black and white prisoners in state penal institutions and county and city jails violate the provisions of the Fourteenth Amendment? (2) Does a prisoner serving a penitentiary sentence have the constitutional right to question the validity of state laws that require racial separation of prisoners? (3) Does the federal district court have the "jurisdiction and authority" to compel Frank Lee to supervise the integration of all state prisons, including cities under ten thousand residents? (4) Do the sections of Title 45 of the Alabama Code violate the Fourteenth Amendment by requiring racial segregation in Alabama prisons and jails? (5) Does the federal district court have the authority to order Frank Lee to make reports to the court on the progress made to end segregation in prisons and jails in Alabama?

In addition, on February 13, 1967, Madison submitted to Judge Frank Johnson a motion for a stay in implementing the desegregation order until the Supreme Court ruled on the appeal. Two days later, Johnson, with the consent of judges Rives and Lynne, denied the stay but granted them twenty days to present a motion for a stay pending appeal before the U.S. Supreme Court. To handle the legal work for the state of

Alabama before the nation's high court, Gallion hired Nicholas Hare as a special assistant attorney general.

Born in Monroeville, Alabama, in 1911, Nicholas Stallworth "Nick" Hare was a member of one of the most respected legal families in the state. His father, Judge Francis Hare, was a long-serving circuit judge for the Twenty-first Judicial Circuit, comprised of the southern Alabama counties of Conecuh, Escambia, and Monroe. In 1914, the elder Hare took in his orphaned nephew, also named Francis, who would later become one of the state's most celebrated personal injury attorneys and trial practitioners. The Hares were close friends with another family of attorneys who included A. C. Lee and his daughter Alice Finch Lee (who was the same age as Nick). The youngest daughter, Nelle Harper Lee, who for a time pursued a law degree, would later turn to writing and use her father as the model for lawyer Atticus Finch and a case tried in Judge Hare's courtroom as the basis for her novel *To Kill a Mockingbird*.

Nick Hare earned his law degree at the University of Alabama in 1935 and practiced in Birmingham until 1950, when he returned to Monroeville. During the early civil rights era, he became one of the state's leading defenders of segregation. In 1955, he sponsored several segregationist bills in the statehouse, including the "freedom of choice" act (future Birmingham mayor Albert Boutwell was the author and sponsor in the senate), which allowed parents to choose whether or not to send their children to segregated or integrated schools—this and other legislation allowed Alabama to effectively avoid compliance with the *Brown* decision for the next fifteen years. At the 1956 Democratic National Convention, Hare drafted, and the Alabama delegation adopted, the "Southern Declaration of Principle," which expressed the state's defiant position on segregation in words and emotions reminiscent of similar statements issued by southern Democrats at the 1948 convention, and one entitled "The Southern Manifesto" signed by eighty-two southern representatives and nineteen senators. Opposing lawyer Chuck Morgan described Hare as a "bespectacled, reasonable gentleman with the amorphously nice manners which typify Black Belt upbringing."

In February 1967, Nick Hare's first priority was to submit an application for a stay pending appeal to Justice Hugo Black, the supervising judge of the Fifth Circuit. The application included an affidavit from Frank Lee, who pleaded for the stay. "We must have more time," he said, to accomplish orderly desegregation "without unduly upsetting or impairing prison discipline or security" and preventing a "serious and dangerous situation." Lee emphasized that the existing prisons in the state were built for racial segregation, and the state needed more time to build new facilities. In addition, inmates needed time to adjust to integration, so "violent and incorrigible" prisoners would not use the change in prison routine as an opportunity to riot, escape, or conduct a violent blood feud. Prison guards also needed time to be trained, prepared, and oriented to integrated facilities. "After all," Lee added, "our prison personnel are poorly paid and largely uneducated." Other states had psychiatrists, psychologists, and counselors to help with this period of adjustment, but Alabama had none. "I am fearful," Lee added, "that immediate integration will disrupt the relative calm of the Alabama prison system." Lee suggested the gradual approach: take a few steps toward integration, then wait, evaluate, and take a few more steps.

On March 1, 1967, Nicholas Hare traveled to Washington, D.C., and hand-delivered the application to Justice Hugo Black, who two days before celebrated his eighty-first birthday. Black was the anchor of the court's liberal wing and a tireless advocate of individual rights. Over fifty years earlier, Black served as Jefferson County's circuit solicitor and gained a reputation as a crusading prosecutor who fought to end rampant police brutality in Bessemer and restore the "fundamental rights and constitutional privileges of its citizens." On March 4, 1967, Justice Black issued an order that stayed the ruling of the three-judge panel, but ultimately the application would have to be considered by the full court. Black made special note that counsel for the appellee filed "no opposition."

In response, Chuck Morgan filed a hastily written opposition brief. Morgan argued that the state's request was just another ruse to preserve racial segregation, which, in turn, would further injure Caliph Washington and the other appellees. "The threat of racial violence," he wrote, "cannot justify the denial of constitutional rights." Nonetheless, the full Supreme Court granted the stay while the justices heard the appeal.

On September 12, 1967, the state filed its appellant's brief to the high court. It reiterated its central argument from the Fifth Circuit brief, that maintaining segregation in Alabama's prisons and jails was a matter of "prison discipline and internal security." This was the first case to come before the U.S. Supreme Court, Nicholas Hare argued, that dealt with the authority of federal courts to "direct particulars of prison management." Hare believed that the justices' decision in the appealed *Lee v. Washington* turned on whether the Fourteenth Amendment favored the opinions of federal judges over the opinions of prison administrators on how best to maintain prison discipline and security. The attorney emphasized that even if the justices affirmed the unconstitutionality of the Alabama statutes mandating prison segregation, they should not follow the mandate of the district court, which would "inflexibly force the racial integration of every state prison, county jail, city jail and small town calaboose in the State of Alabama . . . without regard to . . . other valid considerations."

In short, Hare asked the Supreme Court justices to consider three points: (1) Bob Austin, warden of the Birmingham Jail, was not representative of all other wardens and jailers in the state, and this suit should not be considered a true class action suit; (2) state statutes requiring the separation of prisoners by race in state, county, city and town jails in the state of Alabama did not violate the Fourteenth Amendment; and (3) the single most important issue in the case was giving prison administrators the flexibility to maintain discipline and security without being hampered by "inflexible judicial orders" even if that flexible discretion included racial segregation. After reading the brief, Hugh Maddox, legal adviser to the governor, wrote Hare and proclaimed, "I believe that we ought to win this case hands down."

A month after Hare submitted his brief to the high court, Chuck Morgan presented his on behalf of Caliph Washington and the other appellees, carefully and factually restating the arguments from his brief submitted to the district court months before. He asked the Supreme Court justices to affirm the decision and questioned the justification and merit of the state's appeal. He argued that the three-judge panel accommodated the wishes of the state. The lower court did not require Frank

Lee and jailers throughout the state to submit a desegregation plan, nor did it mandate immediate integration of all penal facilities in Alabama. "The district court allowed them literally every concession they requested," Morgan added, and Frank Lee and Robert Austin were given such flexibility that they essentially wrote their own desegregation order. When Birmingham Jail warden Austin saw no problems with integration other than the drunk tank, the judges "specifically excepted" from its decree "in very exceptional instances" the drunk tanks or bullpens about which appellant expressed some concern. "The decree of the court is thus an effectuation of appellants' own judgment," Morgan concluded. "Plainly, the argument that the courts have usurped the discretion of prison officials is without merit."

In response, Nick Hare wrote and submitted a reply brief to the Supreme Court. He saw the brief as a vehicle to highlight the dangerous situation that would be created if the court upset the "honored, judicially recognized, principle" of allowing prison administrators wide discretion in dealing with safety and security. Taking that flexibility away through an "inflexible fiat" in an effort to stop "one alleged invidious practice," the attorney supposed, would make racial separation under any circumstance impossible. The three-judge panel moved "too far and too fast," and the state needed more time. With a nod to the second *Brown* decision, Hare emphasized that even schools were integrated with "deliberate speed." However, the legal theory behind the original *Brown* decision, that separate facilities were unequal, could not be applied to prisons, the attorney argued. Separate cells for prisoners were not inherently unequal, and racial separation was not always discriminatory. "Prison officials still need reasonable discretion," he wrote, "not because the prisoners are white or black, but because they are dangerous." These were not schoolchildren but men who were "vicious, violent, rebellious and deadly." To emphasize this point, he submitted several newspaper accounts of race-based prison riots in the fall of 1967.

The nine justices of the U.S. Supreme Court heard the oral arguments in the appeal on Tuesday, November 7, 1967, in the daunting marble-laden court chamber with forty-one-foot-high ceilings. Sitting behind the raised mahogany bench were Chief Justice Earl Warren and the associate justices: Hugo Black, William O. Douglas, John M. Harlan, William Brennan, Potter Stewart, Byron White, Abe Fortas, and Thurgood Marshall (the high court's first black member and newest justice). Nicholas Hare would argue the case on behalf of the state of Alabama, and Chuck Morgan would represent Caliph Washington and the other prisoners.

Hare addressed the court first. As he spoke, his voice revealed a refined and unhurried Alabama Black Belt drawl that seemed to glide, not echo, throughout the chamber. Following a brief review of the history of the case, he explained to the justices that even if they held the Alabama statutes as unconstitutional, the case required modification. "It is too rigid," he said. "It destroys unnecessarily reasonable administrative discretion on the part of prison officials." This decision in the Caliph Washington case was of overriding importance and would set the pattern for prison administration throughout the country.

Following a straight-shot introduction, Hare's words poured forth like a politician's filibuster as he wandered aimlessly through his key arguments like a lost hunter who keeps covering his same tracks again and again. Through the haze of his remarks, he emphasized a few key points. Robert Austin was not representative of all jail wardens because the Birmingham City Jail was modern and the size of a small prison. Alabama was a rural state, and most of the jails in its sixty-seven counties were nothing more than a "one-cell calaboose." The order of the federal judges in Alabama could not be binding on those jailers. "They ought to have their day in court," he added. "It is just elemental justice. It is a matter of due process."

Hare refused to concede that the Alabama statutes requiring racial separation in the state's prisons and jails were unconstitutional. "I make no point of it," he said. On the other hand, the court's efforts to force integration went too far. "They destroyed," he argued in a raised voice, "reasonable, sensible, common sense discretion on the part of prison officials." With the fervor of a rural Baptist minister, he added that these were dangerous criminals who were looking to make more trouble. "The weight of my argument to you gentlemen is this," he said, "It's not law; it is common sense." Prison officials must have the flexibility to segregate prisoners by race for safety. "This court must revise the lower court's opinion," he said, "so that it is in line with the great body of law which allows reasonable, sensible discretion in prison officials." This was not discrimination, he supposed, but pragmatism.

Justice Byron White interrupted and said he understood the thrust of Hare's appeal but found it deeply troubling. White believed Hare was telling the justices that the state of Alabama, regardless of the ruling in the particular case, would not apply the will of the court—as it had in so many other cases. (Hare helped the state avoid compliance with the *Brown* decision.) The attorney rejected this interpretation: "No Sir. No Sir." (With Hare's accent, it sounded like *No Suh. No Suh.*) The state would "attempt to comply" with the decision of the court.

Again, Hare asked the justices for more time because the state was revamping the prison system. Alabama's prisons were overcrowded and outdated, but the state was closing down and destroying Kilby Prison and building a new facility at Atmore. By July 1969, he predicted, the state would have a new prison system where there would be no distinction based upon race. These new prisons were equipped to handle integration and would be fully integrated.

Justice Marshall interrupted and asked, "So Alabama is going to abolish all segregation in these prisons?"

Hare told the justice, "yes sir," but insisted that the lower court's decision needed to be revised so that "reasonable discretion" to maintain discipline and security would be left to prison officials without the fear of violating a court order. "You can't wait until trouble happens," Hare said. The way the order stood, he added, if there was a race riot, the warden's hands would be tied, and if he tried to separate prisoners based on race, he would be in trouble with the court. But the lower court, in the opinion of one of the justices, already provided for exceptions and given one example, the drunk tanks. The three judges did not limit prison officials from segregating; they just used an instance to show that racial separation might be necessary. Marshall asked, "How much more assurance do you want than that?" Hare said the courts needed to "spell this out more positively" so that prison officials could anticipate problems and stop them before they occurred.

By the time he stopped talking, Nicholas Hare stood before the justices for just over thirty-seven minutes. Chuck Morgan, by contrast, spoke with quick, precise, and powerful words that asked for speedy implementation of the court order. He reminded the nine justices that the prison segregation statute was just one in a long line of century-old discriminatory laws of the state of Alabama. The *Lee v. Washington* case must be understood in that context, he added, because it was another legal struggle to abolish the "dual system of justice" in Alabama, the South, and the nation. Morgan added: "This is the end of the system of justice for those who live, instead of die, in Alabama's desegregated instrumentality of justice, which is its electric chair."

Morgan skillfully rebutted each of the state's key arguments. He pointed out that judges Johnson, Rives, and Lynne were flexible and accommodating, made "appropriate use of judicial power," and granted the state every concession imaginable in crafting the order. When the state asked for no injunction, the court issued no injunction. When Robert Austin expressed concern about the drunk tank, the court made an exception. Frank Lee asked for a year to desegregate, and the judges gave him a year. "The court went down the line and established a pattern and timetable for desegregation," Morgan added. He believed that if the state went back to the three-judge panel and explained the difficulties they were having in implementing the order, the judges would say, "We will work it out." But Frank Lee and the state had not done so. "This case was tried in 1966," Morgan said, "and some of the problems that didn't exist then are on the record now and I don't know where they came from."

The state contended that the central problem was prison riots, but Morgan said that Alabama and the rest of the United States had more problems with disorder outside prisons than inside. One reason, he supposed, was because blacks did not feel that they could take their struggle out of the streets and into the courts. They felt this way because the "courthouse in the Deep South has always represented to them an instrumentality of oppression." Jails and prisons were also oppressing and discriminating against blacks through segregating them by race. Morgan said he had no doubt that the conclusion in the *Brown* decision that separate facilities were "inherently unequal" applied in a "constantly greater degree" in prisons and jails. "It is high-nigh time," he added, "that the state of Alabama provided a prison system that is no longer packed and overcrowded, and provided one that is fair."

For Morgan, it seemed inconceivable that small-town jails in Alabama had the space to keep prisoners segregated by race. Laws mandating segregation in these facilities were exacerbating racial tensions, not quieting them. Walker County, a coal-mining county northwest of Birmingham, had no municipal jails with more than one room—it included the towns of Carbon Hill, Cordova, Dora, Nauvoo, Oakman, Parish, and Sipsey.

Justice Hugo Black looked down and asked Morgan how the policemen in charge of these "calabooses" enforced segregation when they arrested black and white lawbreakers at the same time.

Morgan quipped that he reckoned that the two races never got drunk on the same night. This answer brought forth an echoing laughter from those in the chamber. Years later, Morgan wrote that he and Justice Black both understood that poverty, ignorance, and segregation were the primary causes of racial tension and disorder. "We both knew," he wrote, "that when we got the instruments of power straightened out and poor blacks and whites got an equal start, and a fair shake, they would get along all right, even in Walker County, even in a calaboose, even on Saturday night."

In his conclusion, Chuck Morgan explained that he made no contention that prison officials should be denied discretion to protect prisoners. He used civil rights leader Martin Luther King, Jr., as an example. The week before the oral arguments in the *Lee v. Washington* case, on October 30, 1967, King was incarcerated in the Jefferson County Jail in Bessemer, in a cell just a few feet away from Caliph Washington. Ironically, King's imprisonment was the result of the June 12, 1967, ruling by the Supreme Court in *Walker v. Birmingham* that upheld his conviction for violating a lower court order and proceeding with a march in Birmingham four years earlier on April 12, 1963. To thwart any unwarranted publicity and civil unrest, Jefferson County officials decided to force King to serve his jail time in Bessemer, not in Birmingham. Chuck Morgan explained to the justices that there was no question that the jail in Bessemer contained "certain kinds of prisoners that you wouldn't want Dr. King to be confined with" and that the federal court order before them that day did nothing to prevent Bessemer officials from using "responsible discretion . . . in a non-discriminatory manner" to protect the civil rights leader. Morgan emphasized this point because, as he told the court, he believed Justice Black was more familiar with the explosive nature of Bessemer's culture of violence than "any man, at least historically." In the end, he simply asked the justices to strike down racial discrimination in American prisons by affirming the lower court ruling. The oral arguments lasted almost fifty-five minutes.

On November 8, 1967, James Free of the *Birmingham News* described the *Lee v. Washington* case as another in a long series of "last-ditch legal battles" between elected officials in Alabama and federal courts over integration. Free believed that George Wallace established this pattern of resisting federal authority and maintaining segregation through as many "legal maneuvers" as possible, although John Patterson and MacDonald Gallion embraced the same strategy before Wallace. Alabama officials fought legal battles to maintain segregation in elementary and secondary schools, colleges and universities, hospitals, public facilities, and welfare programs, and now jails and prisons. Free suggested that Gallion filed the appeal of this "rather weak case" only to garner support of segregationists in an apparent challenge to Alabama senator Lister Hill in the elections of 1968. (Ultimately Hill chose not to run for reelection, but Gallion did not run for the open seat.) "Once again," Free wrote, "Alabama is pictured to the remainder of the country as the last bastion of segregation—as the state that will be the very last if possible in complying" with civil rights laws.

On November 15, 1967, Nicholas Hare filed a supplemental brief to "clarify certain matters" that arose during oral argument, primarily Chuck Morgan's implication that Commissioner Frank Lee and the Alabama Board of Corrections served at the "pleasure of the governor" and were under such pressure that they could not use independent judgment; therefore a court order was needed to force compliance. Hare argued that Lee served as commissioner of "one of the most independent prison boards" in the country, with five members serving ten-year terms. The governor filled vacancies (with senate approval) from a list compiled by the chief justice of the Alabama Supreme Court, the presiding judge of the court of appeals, and the lieutenant governor.

Chuck Morgan disagreed. In a reply to the supplemental brief, he wrote that his conclusions about the board of corrections were based in a clear understanding of fact, not some misunderstanding of the law, as Hare contended. He pointed to the board of trustees at his alma mater, the University of Alabama, as a supposed independent body that was immune from political manipulation. Nonetheless, that did not dissuade Governor George Wallace from standing in the schoolhouse door in 1963. That stand, Morgan wrote, symbolized the "reluctance or inability" of an independent board to stand in opposition to the governor. George and Lurleen Wallace dominated Alabama politics, he added, and a "stand-in-the-jailhouse door" might never happen. "But that the striking down of statutory racial bars in Alabama would result in voluntary state action taxes credulity." Alabama would never integrate prisons unless forced to by the courts. "Thus Alabama's recent, if not total history, clearly demonstrates that . . . a court order is not merely a legal means to a constitutional end; almost as importantly it sometimes serves as a mantle necessarily worn by state officials conscientiously attempting to comply with the requirements of law in a racially changing society."

On March 11, 1968, the nine justices issued a terse, unsigned three-sentence opinion affirming the ruling of the three-judge panel. The court rejected Alabama's claim that *Lee v. Washington* was not a real class action suit and found nothing in the lower court ruling that prohibited segregation for prison security and discipline. They wrote, in the stilted language of the high court: "We do not so read the 'Order, Judgment and Decree' of the district court, which when read as a whole we find unexceptionable." Justices Black, Harlan, and Stewart offered a concurring opinion to "make explicit something that is left to be gathered" through implication from the opinion of the court as a whole:

> This is that prison authorities have the right, acting in good faith and in particularized circumstances, to take into account racial tensions in maintaining security, discipline, and good order in prisons and jails. We are unwilling to assume that state or local

prison authorities might mistakenly regard such an explicit pronouncement as evincing any dilution of this Court's firm commitment to the Fourteenth Amendment's prohibition of racial discrimination.

With a sense of resignation, Nicholas Hare informed Frank Lee of the Supreme Court's decision. "We are closing our file on the matter," he wrote. "In spite of the disappointing outcome . . . I know that we fought a good fight and no apologies are due anyone."

The ACLU considered *Washington v. Lee* one of the top one-hundred legal victories ("greatest hits") in the history of the organization, alongside such landmark cases as *Brown v. Board* (outlawing segregation), *Engel v. Vitale* (school prayer), *Gideon v. Wainwright* (right to an attorney), *Reynolds v. Sims* (one man, one vote), and *Miranda v. Arizona* (police must inform suspects of their rights). On a personal level, Chuck Morgan saw this victory as another validation of his own self-described greatness—a sense of self that would eclipse many of his legal causes. For Caliph Washington, there was the bitter irony of helping desegregate the jails and prisons of Alabama, just so he could continue to sit in one for years to come.

Bessemer native Edward L. Ball served as the judge in the Clark
insurance trial, heard Caliph Washington's habeas corpus proceedings,
and served as trial judge in Caliph Washington's third trial.

17

"SOJOURN IN THE
SHADOW OF DEATH"

L IKE CALIPH WASHINGTON, Johnnie "Big Time" Coleman was
waiting for a new trial. Coleman, Caliph's fellow death row inmate
and plaintiff in the *Washington v. Lee* case, saw his murder conviction
overturned because of the systematic exclusion of blacks from the grand
jury that indicted him. In 1962, an all-white jury sentenced him to death
for the murder of a white mechanic, John D. "Screwdriver" Johnson.
Prosecutors claimed that Coleman stole a shotgun, shells, and clothes
from a store in Eutaw, Alabama, and used them that night to murder
and rob Johnson. At best, the prosecution had circumstantial evidence
to tie the suspect to the crimes, including a button found near the store
that the state argued came from Coleman's shirt and specks on the shotguns shells that matched particles in the defendant's pocket. During the
appeal, the threads of Coleman's story echoed Caliph Washington's in
several ways. After having Coleman's murder conviction overturned by a
higher court, Judge Frank Johnson ordered Coleman's release from Kilby
in January 1968, but Coleman was immediately rearrested by Greene

County sheriff William "Big Bill" Lee (brother of Frank Lee) and placed in the county jail to await a new trial. Unlike Caliph Washington, however, Coleman waited just a few short weeks for the trial to begin.

In early April 1968, Coleman stood trial in the same Eutaw courtroom alongside the same lawyer, Orzell Billingsley, before the same judge, and listened to the same prosecutor question the same witnesses. But unlike his trial six years before, when Coleman faced an all-white jury, this time his guilt or innocence would be determined by an all-black jury. Following two days of testimony and summations, the jury retired to consider the evidence and emerged in just two hours to declare "Big Time" Coleman not guilty of murder. The verdict brought forth shouts of jubilation from the black spectators in the courtroom; at the first trial, just six years before, local blacks were too intimidated to attend. At a mass community meeting that followed the trial, a local pastor proclaimed that this was just the beginning of "what can happen when black folks stick together." A teary-eyed Coleman agreed. "A change is going to come about," he said. "And I'm a symbol of it."

While Coleman celebrated freedom, eighty miles north of Eutaw in Bessemer, Caliph Washington waited for his opportunity for justice. Frustrated by years of delays, he felt abandoned by the band of lawyers who used his name to set legal precedent in *Washington v. Lee* but did little or nothing to help him gain his freedom. Chuck Morgan, the iconic civil libertarian, refused to take Caliph's case, having already moved on to his next high-profile battle. During April 1968, Washington complained to a friend that not one of his attorneys—Billingsley, Hood, or Smith—had come to see him in "many, many months," and he prayed for legal guidance.

When no help arrived, Washington read up on criminal procedure and composed a handwritten application for designation as *in forma pauperis*—in the hope of getting a court-appointed attorney. "Come now Caliph Washington," he wrote,

who is under oath, states:

1. He is a citizen of the United States of legal age.

2. He is a pauper without funds to pay the cost of this action.

3. He seeks the relief petition in good faith.

4. He feels he is entitled to the relief entitled under the guarantees of the Constitution of the United States and proceeds with his case without prepayment of cost.

Washington's notes suggest that he mailed a copy of this application to various court officials in Bessemer; if he did so, the application was never acted upon.

As time permitted, and without Caliph's knowledge, Orzell Billingsley and Erskine Smith continued their pro bono work. In January 1968, while awaiting the Supreme Court's decision in *Lee v. Washington*, Billingsley wrote another writ of habeas corpus and mailed a draft to Erskine Smith. In response, Smith wrote that he still did not understand "what writ or warrant" Caliph was being held under and whether he was reindicted. "Although we believe a speedy trial has been denied the defendant, we may have a lengthy series of independent litigation on this through the state and federal courts and the petition may precipitate an early trial in the case," Smith wrote, and Caliph needed to understand the "possible consequences of filing this petition." But Smith believed that now was the time to file the petition after they "gathered the necessary information as to the present status" of the case. For whatever reason (perhaps due to the upheaval in the district attorney's office in Bessemer), Billingsley delayed filing the writ and was still contemplating the legal maneuver in May 1968, when Chuck Morgan told him to "go ahead and file and see what happens." But Billingsley did not heed Morgan's advice.

In the meantime, the individuals supporting the imprisoned man organized a new group, the Caliph Washington Defense Committee, to keep the pressure on Caliph's lawyers and public officials—the type of support that rallied around Johnnie Coleman in Greene County. The defense committee included Reverend Larry Morkert and Eilleen Walbert of the Concerned White Citizens of Alabama; union activist and Bessemer civil rights leader Asbury Howard; Caliph's mother, Aslee; and Reverend Ralph Galt of the Birmingham Council on Human Relations.

A newcomer to the area, Ralph Galt was a recent faculty hire at Miles

College, a traditionally black institution in Fairfield, the second largest city in the Bessemer Cutoff. As a white Congregationalist minister on a Colored Methodist Episcopal (CME) campus, Galt saw his work as a prophetic calling of God. "I do not consider myself an outsider in the community," he once wrote, "but rather a messenger, preacher, or missionary sent by God." Gray-haired and bookish, Galt's quiet appearance masked his raging evangelistic fervor for God and justice. Born in Baoding, China (southwest of Beijing) on September 6, 1915, Ralph was the son of Congregationalist missionaries. His father, Elmer, was a bike-riding evangelist who spent thirty-one years ministering to the spiritual and social needs in Hebei province. His mother, Altie Cumings, was a teacher in the mission schools. Young Ralph inherited his parents' love of China and their hunger for knowledge. He became fluent in Mandarin Chinese and was so completely acculturated that he thought of himself as more Chinese than American. Yet he chose the faith of his father rather than the Buddhism that surrounded him. "They do not pray to a Christian God," Galt once wrote, "but to an all-powerful creative spirit. My father always believed, and I believe, that you must leave all other religions behind to become a Christian."

Ralph also shared his father's pacifist views on war. "For as far back as I can remember," Galt wrote later, "our family, my father, and I, were pacifist although this was not a tradition in our church." These antiwar and antiviolence perspectives drew young Galt to the writings and teachings of Gandhi, Toyohiko Kagawa, and E. Stanley Jones. From Gandhi, he learned the philosophy of nonviolence and direct action that would be used so effectively by Martin Luther King, Jr. Jones's teachings deepened Galt's opposition to war, and Kagawa's writings influenced his views on Christianity, socialism, and economic cooperatives.

In the mid-1930s, Ralph Galt came to America and entered tiny Grinnell College in Iowa, where he quickly organized a chapter of the pacifist organization Fellowship of Reconciliation (FOR) and invited Toyohiko Kagawa to speak on campus. Following his graduation from Grinnell, Galt began studies at Union Theological Seminary in New York City, where he worked with poor people through the FOR. "I felt like I had two cultural homes," Galt said, "and I was like a bridge. I was never unhappy about that but considered it a privilege."

By 1940, Galt married, graduated from seminary, and returned to China, where he served the rural poor near his father's mission. Following the bombing of Pearl Harbor on December 7, 1941, Japanese forces that occupied the area designated the Galts as "enemy aliens" and placed them under house arrest. After six months, they allowed the Galts to return to the United States in exchange for some prisoners of war, but before releasing them, the Japanese staged a propaganda interview before the media. When Japanese officials tried to get the Galts to publicly blame the United States for the war, Ralph said that "all who engage in war are sinning against man and God and . . . Japan sinned by invading China. We should have peace together, not war."

When the family returned to the United States in 1942, they found an America solidly behind the war effort. Ralph Galt, however, went on a speaking tour of conscientious objector camps on behalf of the Fellowship of Reconciliation. When the government required him to register for the wartime draft, Galt refused. "I am not trying to shirk my social responsibility," he wrote in September 1942, "and I try to obey all just and equitable laws," but the Selective Service Act was an unjust law because war was a "great evil" and a horrible sin in the eyes of God. Like an Old Testament prophet, Galt warned that if America continued to participate in a sinful war, God's judgment would soon follow. "God does not want men," Galt proclaimed, "his creatures, to kill and hate each other in war.

Federal officials responded swiftly and arrested Galt. He was tried in federal court and sentenced to serve five years in the federal prison in Ashland, Kentucky, where he served alongside bootleggers, conscientious objectors, and others who refused to register for the draft. According to Galt, he convinced prison officials to permit racial integration in dining halls and recreation rooms at the prison, where he met the black pacifist Bayard Rustin. Over a decade later, Rustin served as a key adviser to Martin Luther King during the Montgomery Bus Boycott and provided King with a deeper understanding of the philosophy and tactics of nonviolent direct action.

After twenty-one months in prison (one-third of the sentence), Galt received parole, moved to Oklahoma, and began a ministry on a Shawnee

Indian reservation in 1944. Galt established several social ministries to the Shawnees, including a series of co-ops, which compelled outsiders to brand the minister a Communist. Galt rejected the notion. "My faith includes social action," he said, "in the name of, and because of, my faith in Jesus Christ." Co-ops, he added, were neither capitalist nor Communist but simply cooperative.

For the next twenty years, he served as a pastor in small churches in the upper South and the Midwest, before moving to Birmingham in 1966, where he believed he could act as a peacemaker in the wake of violent upheavals in the state. Galt and his wife Louise quickly joined civil and human rights organizations, assisted students in registering as conscientious objectors, started cooperatives, registered new black voters, and established a prison ministry. The last brought him into contact with Caliph Washington.

On April 28, 1968, Galt visited Washington, who had been transferred to the Jefferson County Jail in Birmingham, most likely because of space issues in Bessemer—although Galt later claimed that county officials moved Caliph from jail to jail and at times isolated him as punishment for the *Washington v. Lee* case. Washington told Reverend Galt that he would stand trial sometime in May 1968. "I did not understand exactly how he learned this," Galt wrote after the meeting, but "he feels that he could expect no justice in such a trial." Washington pleaded with Galt to send at least one of his attorneys to visit him in jail immediately. Following the meeting, Galt wrote to each of the lawyers and relayed Caliph's request for "closer direct contact" with the men who supposedly represented him. Washington was frustrated and wanted the attorneys to seek his release through a writ of habeas corpus, filed on the grounds that the state violated his constitutional right to a speedy trial. "He has already served in jail more time than a minimum required for a life sentence," Galt added, and none of Caliph's prison time would count as time served if another white Bessemer jury convicted him a third time.

In early May, sheriff's deputies moved Caliph back to the county jail in Bessemer, presumably to stand trial, but nothing happened: no lawyers came to visit, he saw no judge, and he had no trial. Throughout May and June, members of his defense committee kept the pressure on the individual attorneys, the ACLU, and the NAACP Legal Defense Fund to take some action on Washington's behalf. None came. In July, a frustrated Washington wrote to the one man who helped him in the past, Judge Frank Johnson. He explained that after Johnson ordered his release in July 1965, he had been incarcerated in Bessemer or Birmingham without benefit of counsel. "I haven't even been inside a courtroom since I have been here," he wrote, "and no one ever has informed me of no court date." Caliph understood that Judge Johnson's order required Bessemer officials to retry the case or release him from custody. "Three years have fully passed and still I sit here not knowing anything," he wrote. Caliph asked the judge to order the state to release him or appoint a lawyer to represent him in Johnson's court on a new writ of habeas corpus. "Sir, I will appreciate this greatly," he added, "because I have been denied my right to a speedy trial." He added:

> On July 14th this year I have be [sic] in confinement eleven years. Never has I been allowed bond at no time, even though I don't have money to make one anyway. Sir, I hope that my writing this letter, wont [sic] be bothersome to you, because it is about all I can do, for I have prayed for things to be righted. But, some people just don't seem to care for anything but money. And the only reason I writing to you is that I've been reading about how honorable you are. And I believe that you are about the most just man there is where the law are concern. [sic] I take it that you are a Christian at heart, and I pray for you and your family each day. Because you, really has done a great deed for me and my family. If there are anything more you can spare towards us, it will be so much appreciated.

Judge Frank Johnson, however, could offer Caliph no advice or assistance in his predicament.

In August, Bessemer district attorney Harry Pickens wrote a letter to Caliph's mother, Aslee, and requested that she come see him at his office in the Jefferson County Courthouse in Bessemer. She brought several witnesses with her to listen to Pickens explain that Caliph had no lawyers on record to defend him. "You must get a defense lawyer for him," he said, and submit his name as the attorney of record for him. If she failed to do so, the court would appoint a lawyer for him. Aslee was stunned and "quite agitated." Ralph Galt tried to soothe her with the promise of hiring a "real good active lawyer" before the deadline, but she had no money to pay for one—the age-old problem of poor people lacking access to quality legal representation. But where were all those other attorneys who had provided Caliph legal assistance for over eleven years? What happened to Fred Blanton and Robert Morel Montgomery? Where were Erskine Smith, Chuck Morgan, and Robert Carter? And what had become of K. C. Edwards, David Hood, and Orzell Billingsley?

Caliph also wondered what happened to Orzell. "I am quite disappointed in your service of my case," he wrote Billingsley, and it seems "to me that you are no longer interested in this case of mines [sic]." Washington heard on several different occasions that Billingsley repeatedly denied being Caliph's attorney. "So now I ask that you let me know how you stand on this case," he wrote, "so, I'll know what to do for myself. If you are my attorney, then I do expect to hear from you personally."

Orzell Billingsley must have responded immediately, because within days of Caliph's letter, on October 8, 1968, he filed the long-hoped-for writ of habeas corpus in the Jefferson County Court in Bessemer. The writ would require the sheriff of Jefferson County or any authorized deputy sheriff to bring Caliph Washington before the county court in Bessemer and show cause, if there be any, of his detention.

Ten days later, on October 18, Special Circuit Judge Robert W. Gwin granted the writ and "ordered, adjudged and decreed" that the sheriff "produce the body of Caliph Washington before this court" on November 11 at 10 a.m. If Harry Pickens could not justify the ongoing incarceration of Washington, then a circuit judge could set the captive free. At least the case was finally moving forward after years of waiting.

The news thrilled Erskine Smith, and he wrote Orzell Billingsley that he was "most anxious to be of assistance" in helping Caliph Washington. Smith sent Billingsley a copy of the *Needel v. Scafati* decision— a Massachusetts case that Smith believed applied directly and clearly to Washington's situation. The case involved a man held under warrant without indictment or arraignment who was indigent, ignorant, without counsel, and in no position to claim his right. "Caliph seems to fit in all of these categories," Smith wrote, "but we must be aware of the fact that the district attorney will contend, because of our appearance in the Fifth Circuit, that he continuously had a lawyer since we entered the case." Erskine Smith said he told Harry Pickens that although David Hood and Orzell Billingsley appeared on the brief submitted to the Fifth Circuit, they were never paid, nor were they ever entered as the attorneys of record. Smith wanted to establish before the court that Caliph Washington was without representation since the Fifth's ruling and had no lawyer to advise him that there was a "lack of a speedy trial." Erskine advised Orzell to tell Harry Pickens and the judge in the habeas proceedings that he was recently engaged to represent Caliph Washington in filing the writ. "I think this would be accurate," Smith added, "since Caliph Washington has continually and insistently asked some, almost any, lawyer, to file a petition for habeas corpus on his behalf."

Caliph's habeas corpus proceedings began at just after 11 a.m. on November 11, 1968, in the courtroom of Judge Edward L. Ball, the same judge who presided over the jury that awarded James "Cowboy" Clark's widow the money from the accidental death insurance policy a decade earlier. Orzell Billingsley stood before the judge on behalf of Caliph Washington. Harry Pickens represented the state and spoke first, reviewing the history of the case and explaining why Washington was still in custody. Billingsley argued that Caliph's confinement without bond was a violation of the cruel and unusual provision of the Eighth Amendment, the due process clause of the Fourteenth Amendment, and the Alabama Constitution. Not to mention, Billingsley quickly made note for the record, "he was tried by a jury in this court and the jury consisted of all white male citizens."

Since courts set aside the convictions of 1957 and 1959, Judge Ball believed the proceedings should focus on why Caliph Washington was still imprisoned after the 1965 order of Judge Frank Johnson and its subsequent affirmation by the Fifth Circuit in 1966. "As I read Judge Johnson's order," he said, "—just my thinking on it—he did not enjoin the state from rearresting him or reprosecuting . . . , but it looks like we're down to whether or not he has been denied a fair and speedy trial. I believe that's the guts of your petition." Billingsley agreed.

Harry Pickens argued that his office had made a good faith effort to bring Caliph Washington to trial. He first learned of the case in November 1967 following "certain changes" in the personnel in the district attorney's office (the removal of James Hammonds) and immediately began searching for witnesses. "It's been a long time since 1959," he added, but he eventually located Furman Jones, who was missing from the last trial but was willing now to come testify. Pickens discovered that a few of the witnesses died during the last decade, but he located enough of the others to set a trial date of Monday, June 17, 1968. Nonetheless, he could find no attorney representing Caliph Washington.

To support his claims, Pickens relied on the testimony of the lone witness called before the court, Elmore McAdory, the circuit clerk in Bessemer. McAdory, who served as the clerk of Cutoff since 1952, told Judge Ball that no attorney representing Caliph Washington visited his office from the time Caliph was released from Kilby Prison in July 1965 until Orzell Billingsley filed the writ in October 1968. The defendant had no attorney of record, and no attorney, other than Harry Pickens, had requested a trial between 1965 and 1968. "Since I've been down here I have made an effort," Pickens explained to Judge Ball, "and have had conversations with members of the family . . . attempting to find out who the attorney was in this case." He could find none until Billingsley came with the October writ.

Orzell Billingsley, however, argued that Washington was indigent and that the court failed in its efforts to guarantee his constitutional right to a speedy trial by not appointing an attorney to defend him. "We contend that the defendant has been confined in jail for over eleven years," Billingsley said, "and even if he is convicted again, he will not get credit for the time he's served. Eleven years without bond is cruel punishment, and we contend he should be released." To support his argument, Billingsley cited the *Needel* decision furnished by Erskine Smith. Pickens, however, disagreed and argued that *Needel* presented nowhere "near the almost insurmountable problems" that Caliph Washington's case presented. The *Needel* case covered a period of four years, while Washington's wait covered about eighteen months (not eleven years) from the Fifth Circuit decision of August 8, 1966, to the scheduled trial of June 17, 1968. He asked Judge Ball to "compartmentalize the time" being discussed before the court because there was a distinct difference between someone in jail awaiting trial and someone under a death sentence. "The court will, I'm sure," Pickens added, "take into consideration the appreciable distance of time from the event itself and of the court ramifications." The district attorney said he was "ready, willing, and able" to take Caliph Washington to trial in December 1968 or January 1969. Therefore the writ was unnecessary and should be denied. Billingsley simply responded, "You can't do that."

From the bench, Judge Ball appeared sympathetic to Washington's plight and said he was interested only in the question of a fair and speedy trial. He told Pickens and Billingsley that they need not call any other witnesses because he wanted to make a quick decision. "Let's not delay it," he said as he closed the proceedings.

Eight days later, Judge Ball handed down his ruling. When he examined the record, he saw that in 1965 Caliph Washington was represented by Robert Morel Montgomery and Fred Blanton. The judge looked further and saw Orzell Billingsley, Erskine Smith, and Charles Morgan representing Caliph in 1966 and 1967—although much of that legal work was on the *Washington v. Lee* case, which was never about getting Caliph out of jail. Ironically, Morgan's and Billingsley's scheme to use Washington's name to integrate the prisons and jails did more to hurt his case than to help it. Nonetheless, Ball ruled:

It is, therefore, the opinion of the court that the petitioner has not been indigent since the original proceedings in the United States District Court. . . . That even though the petitioner has had all of the aforementioned counsel available to him [since that time], it appears without dispute that the petitioner has made no effort and has made no formal request or motion for an earlier setting of his case. The case was set for trial . . . and the district attorney made several efforts to secure the identity of any attorney or attorneys who represented the defendant and was successful in getting that information from the family of the defendant. THEREFORE WRIT DENIED, November 18, 1968.

Within weeks, Billingsley was preparing an appeal of Ball's ruling to the Alabama Supreme Court—most likely because Washington believed a favorable ruling from the higher court would bring immediate freedom, whereas another trial in Bessemer could send him back to death row (even with the unstated moratorium on capital punishment in the state). Ralph Galt wrote Billingsley, "We certainly would like to have an encouraging word to give to our friend Caliph Washington if possible." It was a risky strategy. If the appeal failed, the trial, which Harry Pickens promised would take place in December 1968 or January 1969, would be delayed months, if not years.

A few weeks after Billingsley appealed Ball's denial of the writ to the Alabama Supreme Court, Galt told him that the defense committee was happy with the filing but unhappy about the delays. The committee hoped to have a favorable ruling within two weeks, but they had now waited forty days in the wilderness with no news. "If the court has not yet acted," Galt wrote, "can you in any way stimulate it to act soon? We certainly hope that the case can be brought to a speedy and happy conclusion as soon as possible."

Attorneys filed briefs to the Alabama Supreme Court in March 1969. Bessemer officials simply argued that the writ should be denied so that Caliph Washington could be "remanded to the lawful custody" of the district court to await a pending trial. On the other side, Billingsley argued that Caliph Washington was sitting in jail, indigent, denied due process, denied his right to speedy trial, denied assistance of counsel, and enduring cruel and unusual punishment. He was unaware of his right to a speedy trial, he wrote, "and the state offered no reason, explanation, or excuse for the protracted delay other than difficulty finding witnesses." For years, the case was "languishing unnoticed" and neglected in the Bessemer district attorney's office because of the upheaval there, which was "perhaps understandable, but not thereby constitutionally permissible." Washington should not be blamed for the delay, Billingsley argued. It was the duty of the prosecutor to proceed promptly and not allow so much time to lapse that an incarcerated indigent must now face the impossible task of reconstructing a defense: "The fact cannot be overlooked that each passing day renders investigation of his case more difficult."

Billingsley pointed to the precedent established in the *Hamilton* decision (Charles Hamilton was another of Caliph's death row cellmates) that when a criminal defendant was without counsel at any critical stage, a subsequent conviction could not stand.

In addition, Billingsley argued that Washington spent years of cruel and unusual punishment on Alabama's death row. "The time has come," he continued, to set free a man who has endured such pain and suffering awaiting death in Alabama's electric chair. No one, the attorney wrote, was in favor of this type of prolonged punishment. As one journalist noted, capital punishment was the "great unfinished piece of business in this country," and no solution to it was "worse than the existing solution, which was to leave several hundred men imprisoned in the nation's death houses in state of permanent insecurity on the question whether they will live or die violently." Billingsley added that in Washington's case, the solution was self-evident in light of the "unanimity of agreement" on the death penalty. "In this particular case," he added, "where the sojourn in the shadow of death was so protracted and the state was in part chargeable with the delay . . . the writ should granted."

Despite Billingsley's emotional appeal, the case languished for months in judicial limbo among the growing backlog of cases in the appellate courts. Ralph Galt kept up the pressure on Billingsley through constant phone calls and a barrage of letters—even though he rarely responded. He urged the attorney "as soon and fast as possible" to do any and everything in his power to convince the Alabama Supreme Court to speed up Washington's release. Galt suggested that Billingsley go to Montgomery and speak to one of the justices to "get Caliph's case moving" again. "Even if you can press the Alabama Supreme Court so hard that it reacts and makes a negative decision," he wrote, "that might still speed up his ultimate release because the case could then be appealed to a higher court." Galt sensed that Caliph Washington needed to be freed before he became "mentally institutionalized" and unable to ever deal with the problems in the outside world.

While no word came from the high court in Montgomery, in late August, Billingsley informed Galt that he was putting forth "every effort to get an immediate decision." Galt told him that those were wonderful words of encouragement, but "now we wonder if you have had time or opportunity to do specific things about it yet. If so, what actions did you take?"

By September 1969, Caliph's appeal was removed from the Alabama Supreme Court docket, most likely due to the backlog of cases, and reassigned to the newly created Alabama Court of Criminal Appeals, where it would be considered, without oral arguments, by presiding Judge Anna Lola Price. For almost twenty years, Price was the only female judge in Alabama, serving first on the old state court of appeals and now on the new criminal court. She began her legal career as a stenographer at a small firm of Griffith & Brown in Cullman, where she studied law in order to better understand the clerical work she was being asked to do. On a whim, she decided to "come down to Montgomery to see what the [bar] exam was like," passed, became a member of the bar, and was soon hired as an associate at her firm. In 1947, she moved to Montgomery to serve as a legal adviser to Alabama governor James "Big Jim" Folsom, who later appointed her to the court.

On October 6, 1969, the Committee for Caliph Washington, composed of members of the CWCA, the "defense committee," and other interested people, asked Judge Price to take action. "For more than four years," they wrote, "this man has been held in jail or prison without benefit of bond, and we would like to know if steps can be taken legally to obtain bond. We realize that your court has a heavy back-log of cases, but this one has been in the hands of various courts for so many years, we would like to appeal to you to move as quickly as possible on the habeas corpus hearing."

In the Jefferson County Jail in Bessemer, Washington continued to wait impatiently. For unclear reasons, the jail warden placed him in solitary confinement for what Ralph Galt described as another "long unjust stay." Galt later said that Washington was being punished by Bessemer officials as retribution for "acting like Martin Luther King" and keeping things "stirred up" in the county jail. Once he was released from solitary, the warden refused to allow him to meet privately with that "radical social activist" white preacher Ralph Galt. Yet Galt still came every week to visit and pray with Washington as jail officials listened. Washington continued to complain to Galt about Billingsley. Washington criticized

Billingsley for his lack of effort in his case and suggested that if he did not have enough time, he should hire another attorney to help or just turn the entire case over to someone else. Following the meeting, Galt wrote Billingsley: "Please try to get him out on bond. He believes that you promised to do this when you first took the case, but he has the impression that you did not definitely try."

On November 4, 1969, the ruling finally came from the Alabama Court of Criminal Appeals. Judge Price wrote the decision of the court and reviewed the history of the case and the decision of Judge Ball emphasizing that neither Washington nor his lawyers made a request for a trial. As a precedent, Price pointed to the opinion in the 1967 *Hampton v. State of Oklahoma*, which held that the failure of a defendant to demand an earlier trial was "fatal to his request for discharge under habeas corpus" because in the "absence of such effort," he waived his right to a speedy trial under the Constitution. "Mere passage of time," Price wrote, "does not establish an unconstitutional denial of a speedy trial or due process . . . nor can a defendant sit by without effort to obtain an earlier trial or himself contribute to the delay and thereafter be heard to complain." The only question for Caliph Washington, she added, was whether the state denied him a speedy trial, but neither he nor anyone on his behalf made such a request, so Judge Ball was correct in ruling that the defendant was not entitled to discharge on habeas corpus.

Two days later, Harry Pickens stopped Aslee Washington while she was on her way to visit her son and told her that he was "getting ready to try Caliph in a new trial very soon." Washington still did not believe he could receive a fair trial in "racist Bessemer" and preferred to quickly appeal the habeas ruling in the Alabama Supreme Court and in federal district courts before Pickens scheduled a new trial. Ralph Galt told Orzell Billingsley that the situation was "extremely dangerous and urgent" and that he needed to move quickly. Billingsley was looking at broader constitutional issues beyond Washington's lone case. "I am of the opinion that several actions can be taken on behalf of the defendant Mr. Caliph Washington," he wrote Galt in a brief reply, "including further attacks on the jury system in the Bessemer Cutoff."

In April 1970, Caliph Washington leaves prison for the first time in thirteen years. He is greeted by Orzell Billingsley.

18

"IN A WASTED LAND OF NO WANT"

CALIPH WASHINGTON LONGED for freedom as he entered his thirteenth year of imprisonment. Although he found encouragement through his faith, family, and friends, at times he grew discouraged through all the pain and suffering of waiting. He was tired and weary when he wrote a friend, "I shall soon be an old man in a wasted land of no want." Ralph Galt, however, refused to allow him to sit and rot in jail. His relentless efforts to spread the news about Washington's plight were finally creating more publicity in early 1970. At Miles College, where Galt taught, a writer for a student publication called on all students to show their concern by making the name Caliph Washington a "conversation piece" among friends, neighbors, and church members. For thirteen years, the writer argued, Washington never received the publicity needed to compel Americans to "look under its rug to see the dust of racism." If they looked, they would see a man wrongly convicted, which was a "sin against God and an abomination of humanity." The writer encouraged students to make certain that Washington was not "judged under the modern day Black Code laws, but rather under a fair, impartial law (if there is such a thing for a black man)."

The Caliph Washington Defense Committee recruited new supporters through an emotional appeal to help free the unjustly imprisoned and forgotten man. "Is it possible for people in our city to secure justice for a man in prison?" they asked. "Justice starts with us!" The committee organized a Caliph Washington Benefit Buffet Supper, where supporters brought covered dishes and discussed the case. "Mr. Washington is a black man," read the invitation to the event, "strong, sensitive, and still young! The deals of his case are known and need to be heard." Attendees at the Thurgood Memorial CME Church in Birmingham on Friday, March 6, 1970, ate homemade dishes prepared by blacks and whites from throughout the area and listened to pleas for help from Aslee Washington, Ralph Galt, Larry Morkert, and others. In the end, the benefit raised several hundred dollars for Caliph Washington's defense.

The following Monday, March 9, while Caliph's lawyers were still preparing a habeas writ for filing in federal court, Harry Pickens informed Orzell Billingsley that the date was set for a new trial to begin on Monday, April 6, 1970. Within days, Erskine Smith withdrew from the case because of his heavy workload and other commitments in capital cases. "I will be in no position to prepare or try the captioned case on April 6, 1970, nor anytime in the foreseeable future," he wrote Billingsley. He expressed deep concern about Washington's plight but could offer no more help. The acerbic Chuck Morgan also wrote Billingsley and pulled out of the case, even though he had never been a part of it. "Since I don't believe that an appearance was ever entered in the above case in my name," he wrote, "and I don't have time to handle the case, I just want to let you know that I won't. Now that I've gone through all this and volunteered not to volunteer I'm sure you're appreciative of the wonderful assistance we've rendered to you in this matter."

At the arraignment on Friday, March 13, with Orzell Billingsley at his side, Caliph Washington pleaded not guilty in the 1957 murder of James "Cowboy" Clark. Billingsley remained the attorney of record, but his heavy drinking was taking a devastating toll on his personal and professional life. Fortunately, he received much-needed support from Russell Jackson "Jack" Drake, a twenty-four-year-old wild-eyed white graduate of the University of Alabama Law School, who led antiwar protests on campus, advocated civil rights, and frequently clashed with university administrators over free speech issues. After receiving his law degree in 1969, Drake went to work as the staff attorney with the Selma Inter-Religious Project, an ecumenical social and religious ministry that supported civil rights causes in Alabama's Black Belt. Through his legal work, Drake became friends with Billingsley, who in turn invited the young lawyer to help with the Caliph Washington case.

Drake found Billingsley a brilliant attorney with tremendous court-room skills. An approachable and generous man, Orzell could never say no to anyone in the black community who needed his help—most of whom, like Caliph Washington, had no money. This left him flittering from client to client and gave Billingsley the reputation of an overworked, disorganized, unfocused, and undependable lawyer. "This was not necessarily a shortcoming on his part," Drake later recalled, "but a reflection of the demands of the time." Orzell's passion for justice and compassion for individuals kept him overextended. He increasingly turned to alcohol for comfort. "People just used him up," Drake added, "and in a sense, he got destroyed by the people he wanted to help." In 1970, he had Drake to help carry the load in the burdensome and time-consuming Caliph Washington case.

Drake drafted documents and made frequent trips to the Jefferson County Jail to meet with Washington. He described Washington as a "very gentle person," who was "genuine, likeable, bright, and well-read" and was always willing to share his faith. He enjoyed the visits, but he feared each trip to Bessemer because of the hostile atmosphere in what he described as a "mean, rough-ass" city; he found the attitudes of many of the older police officers especially disturbing, and he later described them as "some of the worst you could find in Jefferson County." But they ignored the baby-faced, thin-as-a-broom-straw Jack Drake. "They never saw me as a threat to the status quo," he later recalled. "They were unconcerned about my activities."

Attorney David Hood was often deemed a threat to the Bessemer white establishment, but he remained undeterred and determined to help Caliph Washington. He too would represent Caliph, some fifteen years after he first served as the lad's attorney in the public exposure case in 1955. Also joining the defense team was another native of the Bessemer Cutoff, U. W. Clemon. This was Clemon's first criminal law case since graduating from Columbia School of Law in 1968, where he studied under a scholarship provided by the NAACP Legal Defense and Educational Fund. Upon completion of his degree, Clemon received an Earl Warren Fellowship to concentrate on civil rights legal work under the tutelage of Constance Baker Motley and Jack Greenberg of the NAACP. By 1970, the twenty-six-year-old Clemon was working on civil rights cases in Alabama, and the Caliph Washington case was one he knew about since his teenage years in the Westfield community near Bessemer. "I thought that a gross miscarriage of justice had occurred," Clemon later recalled. "I was very impressed with his sincerity." The case also touched a personal chord with the attorney. In the late 1950s, about the same time as Caliph's incident with Cowboy Clark, U. W. Clemon witnessed one of his friends being abused by two white police officers from nearby Fairfield. "I was indignant," Clemon later recalled, "and at age thirteen, from that point on, I pretty much wanted to do civil rights law."

The Washington case also helped solidify Clemon's opposition to capital punishment. "The Caliph Washington experience, to me, was another exhibit to the insanity of that approach to justice," Clemon once said. "The death penalty if carried out is unmerited. You don't have a chance to correct mistakes, and sometimes mistakes can only be corrected after long periods of time. But in my judgment, the Lord intervenes in appropriate cases." Caliph's life had been spared, and now Clemon was optimistic that he could help the defendant clear his name and win his freedom.

To that end, Clemon and the other attorneys filed a motion to quash the indictment and refill the jury box—once again challenging the systemic exclusion of blacks from the original grand jury that returned

Caliph Washington's indictment in September 1957. Orzell Billingsley asked the court clerk to summon, as witnesses on behalf of the motion, a cross section of current and former Bessemer officials and black residents of the Cutoff, including James Hammonds, Elmore McAdory (the clerk), Judge Edward Ball, and Judge Gardner Goodwyn. The record is silent as to whether Goodwyn and Hammonds were sitting in Judge Ball's court on March 27, 1970, when Ball convened a hearing to consider the motion to quash.

Before taking any testimony, District Attorney Harry Pickens moved to dismiss the motion because Billingsley filed practically the same document in 1957, which the court ruled on then. Clemon argued that Washington was entitled to a grand jury made up of a "representative cross section of the community" to listen to the evidence, "which was not the case in 1957." Judge Ball, however, pointed out that this question was settled: the county court denied the motion years before; the majority of the judges on the Alabama Supreme Court affirmed the conviction (Judge James Coleman's dissent focused on the use testimony from the previous trial and not on the racial makeup of the grand jury); and Judge Frank Johnson granted a writ of habeas corpus, but not on the grounds that blacks were excluded from the original grand jury. Judge Ball wished that Johnson had ruled on that question: "He either refused it or overlooked it, or it wasn't raised." He looked at Billingsley and said, "You know more about it than I do, because you were there." In fact, Fred Blanton never raised the issue.

Nonetheless, Ball ruled that Washington's attorneys had the right to raise issues related to the constitutionality of the petit jury but not the grand jury. Billingsley countered that it was "never too late to raise these issues" and pointed to the Johnnie Coleman case from 1968 as an example of revisiting the racial makeup of a grand jury. "He is the D.A.," the attorney said, "but that doesn't mean he shouldn't join in to aid the defendant [and] protect his constitutional rights." In response, Harry Pickens argued that his duty was to prosecute Caliph Washington. Billingsley, Drake, Clemon, and Hood had the responsibility to defend him. "My duty obligates me," Pickens continued, "to see that that man

[Washington] gets a fair and impartial trial, and I'm sure his lawyers will see that I perform my duty properly."

Judge Ball granted Pickens's request and denied the motion to quash the indictment. Billingsley, Clemon, and Drake then turned to the racial makeup of the petit jury for Washington's trial, scheduled to begin on April 6. County officials compiled the jury rolls in August 1969, and Billingsley requested an opportunity to examine those rolls to determine how many blacks would be potential jurors in the case. Judge Ball quickly agreed and then asked, "Are there any other matters you wish to bring up?" Billingsley made a motion that the court grant Caliph Washington bond until the trial began. "He's been in jail for thirteen years," Billingsley said, "and is entitled to bond." Harry Pickens responded, "I'm going to oppose that." But without hesitation Judge Ball said, "I'll set the bond at $10,000," then immediately closed the proceedings. Afterward, Ball told a newspaper reporter covering the hearing that he had no special reason for granting the bond. "He had been tried twice, sentenced to the electric chair twice, and spent some time in jail," Ball said. "His attorneys asked for a bond, and I gave it to him. That's all."

If Caliph Washington made bail, this would be his opportunity to take his first free steps in over twelve years. "Caliph's health is good," Orzell Billingsley said after the hearing. "He couldn't be in good spirits being in jail [over] twelve years, but I imagine he has new hope after getting approved for bail." Raising the money to make bail was another matter, but members of the defense committee began seeking funding. "We are pretty hopeful that he will be released," Reverend Larry Morkert said, but Caliph remained in the Jefferson County Jail over the weekend as the group struggled to find the money. Late in the afternoon on Tuesday, April 1, 1970, committee members raised enough money and collateral to convince the O.K. Bond Company in Bessemer to put up the money.

With bond made, Caliph changed from his jail clothes into a rumpled pair of dress slacks, a white shirt, and a light-colored cardigan sweater. As he walked through the door from the jail, he carried a large paper sack filled with his meager belongings from thirteen years behind bars. The first person to greet him was Orzell Billingsley. Family members picked up a smiling Caliph Washington and drove him home. He had one week to enjoy freedom, surrounded by his family and friends, before the new trial started.

Washington's release brought unprecedented publicity in the local and national media. Emory Jackson, editor of the *Birmingham World*, opined that his thirteen years in prison waiting was a "form of punishment within itself." Alabama's legal system was "working poorly" in the Washington case, he added, and "he was and is entitled to a speedy trial. Five years of waiting for trial is both a reflection on Alabama's trial system and the rights of man in a democracy."

Garnering most national attention was a public statement issued by four ministers, including Larry Morkert of St. Paul's Lutheran, Ralph Galt of Miles College, Eugene Farrell of Our Lady of Fatima Catholic Church, and Jesse Douglas of Thurgood Memorial CME Church. The statement, entitled "Forgotten Man Imprisoned 13 Years for a Death Declared Accidental by the Alabama Supreme Court," appealed to Christians throughout the country to "care a little more and work a lot harder for the cause of justice" by helping Caliph Washington. In the statement, they traced the history of Washington's long "nightmare" from the death of James "Cowboy" Clark through his trials and mistrials, reprieves and stays, and the long wait in jail for justice. They told of how Caliph became a minister and wanted nothing more than to be free to serve others. "This man needs the concern and help of a great many people today," they wrote. "Not tomorrow or next week; otherwise we risk letting time run out and condemning Caliph Washington to the 'wasted land of no want.'"

The four ministers encouraged those interested in helping Washington to attend a public demonstration and prayer vigil on Saturday, April 4, 1970—the second anniversary of the assassination of Martin Luther King, Jr. The ministers pledged to take the "march of justice" begun by King in 1963 into the 1970s. "We will beg God to send his justice into this city of so many injustices of man to another," they wrote. "His truth and his justice is marching on."

The vigil would begin at noon on the courthouse steps in Bessemer—
an appropriate spot, the ministers thought, because it was where Caliph
Washington was denied justice. On the morning of Saturday, April 4,
more than two hundred people gathered in Birmingham's Kelly Ingram
Park—the site of battles between civil rights demonstrators and city
police in 1963—and began a fifty-two-car caravan to Bessemer.

The group was met at the city limits by a large contingent of Bessemer
police officers, who escorted them to a staging area near Third Avenue
North and Sixteenth Street in downtown Bessemer. There they joined
five hundred or so other people and marched just over two blocks up
Third Avenue to the courthouse steps. Police reported that the group
sang hymns and songs of peace in an orderly fashion. Among the many
speakers were the organizers, Ralph Galt, Larry Morkert, Eugene Farrell,
Jesse Douglas, and Bessemer civil rights leader Asbury Howard. Each
gave a short talk on the work of Martin Luther King and the injustice
of holding Caliph Washington in jail for over a dozen years. "Prayers
were offered up by some of the ministers," a police report noted, "all for
the release of Washington from the Bessemer county jail." Police chief
George Barron noted, "There was no disturbance or trouble of any kind,"
and following the ninety-minute vigil, police escorted the caravan back
to Birmingham without difficulty.

Two days later, on Monday April 6, 1970, the third trial of Caliph
Washington began: nearly thirteen years after the incident with Cowboy Clark, over a decade since his last trial, and almost five years since
he left death row. In the intervening years, memories faded, witnesses
died, lawyers resigned, judges retired, and politicians and policemen
came and went. Wrecking crews razed the crime scene to make room for
government-subsidized housing. "This brings paradox and irony," one
newspaperman noted, "into a case already full of weird incidents and
baffling circumstances." Yet Caliph would once again sit in the same
courtroom, one that changed little in the intervening years, before a jury
with his fate in their hands.

Judge Edward L. Ball would preside, just as he had over the jury that
awarded Cowboy Clark's widow the insurance settlement on a policy that

stipulated that it would not be payable in the event of a homicide. Much of the widespread pretrial publicity focused on this apparent inconsistency in justice by two courts in the same district: one court ruled the death a homicide and sentenced the convicted "killer" to the electric chair, while the other ruled the death an accident and granted the grieving widow an insurance payout. Ball explained to reporters that his judgment in that case had nothing to do with whether Clark's death was accidental. "It is a longtime common law that one jury can find one way, another jury another way, on the same set of facts," he said the day Caliph's third trial began. Nonetheless, Ball maintained the strong belief that not paying the widow in the case was "repugnant to the insuring clause."

Judge Ball gaveled the court into session at 9 a.m. on April 6 for the third round of *State of Alabama v. Caliph Washington*. The courtroom was packed with spectators—mostly Caliph's family and friends. In the long hallway just outside, two hundred more people lined the walls of the corridor. Sitting quiet and alone in the courtroom was Florence Talley Clark Rutledge Long, Cowboy Clark's widow, who was recently divorced from her fourth husband, Lannie Long. (Later she changed her mind and remarried him in August 1970.) Several Jefferson County sheriff's deputies stood near the doors to prevent any disorder. Caliph Washington, relaxed and sporting a new dark preacher's suit, sat at the defense table with his Bible open in front of him; sitting with him were Orzell Billingsley, David Hood, U. W. Clemon, and Jack Drake. "I was scared to death when we walked into that courtroom," Drake later recalled. "The tensions were so high." Across the aisle from Drake and the other defense lawyers was the workman-like prosecutor, Harry Pickens, and his assistant Dawson Britton.

The attorneys from both sides spent most of the morning striking the jury from a venire of sixty-six mostly working-class folks living in the Cutoff. They included welders, electricians, boilermakers, mechanics, truck drivers, crane operators, maids, housewives, and beauticians. Unlike thirteen years earlier, when the entire jury pool was all white men, thirty of those summoned for jury duty on April 6, 1970, were women and nineteen were black—a change brought about in no small part by a

1965 federal lawsuit filed by Orzell Billingsley and Charles Morgan. On February 7, 1966, a three-judge panel composed of Frank Johnson, Richard Rives, and Clarence Allgood handed down the *White v. Crook* decision, which ordered the inclusion of blacks on jury rolls and also struck down Alabama's law excluding women from jury service. When women first began appearing on jury rolls, Jefferson County district attorney Earl Morgan announced that he "deplored the fact that our southern women will be exposed to some of the sordid details of . . . the cases."

Perhaps this was what Morgan had in mind when attorneys finished striking the jury in the Caliph Washington case and were left with eight white women, three black men, and one black woman to listen to the graphic testimony of Cowboy Clark's death. The jury makeup in the Washington case reflected the revolutionary changes in Alabama's criminal justice system that occurred since the late 1950s, when only white males served on Washington's juries in the 1957 and 1959 trials. Now, in 1970, no white males were selected.

The right to a trial by a jury was a time-honored cornerstone of Anglo-American law, stretching back to the Magna Carta of 1215 and guaranteed centuries later by the Sixth Amendment of the Constitution: "In all criminal prosecutions, the accused shall enjoy the right to a speedy and public trial, by an impartial jury of the State and district wherein the crime shall have been committed." Following the Civil War, the U.S. Congress passed legislation that made it a crime to "exclude or fail to summon any citizen" who possessed all legal qualifications to serve on a grand or petit jury in any court regardless of race. During the debate over what would become Section 4 of the Civil Rights Act of 1875, James Rapier, a black congressman from Alabama, declared that "after all, this question resolves itself into this: either I am a man or I am not a man." Within the decade, however, the U.S. Supreme Court declared other provisions of the act unconstitutional but preserved this section. "In salvaging the jury section," one historian later wrote, "the Court conferred upon that remnant the honor of being only one of the criminal statutes on civil rights to survive hostile decisions and congressional repeal" until the Civil Rights Act of 1957.

In 1880, the Supreme Court in *Strauder v. West Virginia* declared unconstitutional a West Virginia statute that excluded blacks from jury service. The law was nothing more than a "brand upon them and a discrimination against them" that denied equal protection. In a forceful opinion, Justice William Strong asked how the state could compel a black person to stand for trial by a jury from which every member of his race was excluded based on skin color. How was this "not a denial . . . of equal legal protection?" Nonetheless, states still had the right, the justices believed, to enact laws that set qualifications for potential jurors as long as they did not exclude based on race. One observer believed that these juror qualification laws included both objective and subjective standards. Objective standards required citizenship and a minimum age; disqualified convicted felons or the infirmed; and exempted doctors, ministers, lawyers, and other critical professionals. Subjective standards in Alabama required jurors who were "generally reputed to be honest and intelligent men . . . esteemed in the community for their integrity, good character and sound judgment." States throughout the South had these types of vaguely worded juror requirements that allowed white registrars and jury commissioners to exercise wide discretion in the selection process and thereby exclude blacks. They simply ignored the Supreme Court's ruling in *Carter v. Texas* in 1900, which held that any action by court officials to exclude blacks from grand juries in the criminal prosecution of black defendants violated the equal protection clause of the Fourteenth Amendment. The proper avenue to challenge racial exclusion was a motion to quash the indictment—a procedural move that Caliph Washington's lawyers submitted to the court but Judge Ed Ball denied.

In the decades following the *Carter* decision, the practice of racial exclusion remained mostly unchallenged until the case of one of the Scottsboro Boys reached the U.S. Supreme Court in 1935. Clarence Norris, one of the nine black boys accused of raping two white women near Scottsboro, Alabama, was tried and convicted by an all-white jury and sentenced to die in the state's electric chair. Lawyers appealed the guilty verdict on the grounds that Norris was denied equal protection because blacks were systematically excluded from jury service. In spite of overwhelming evidence to the contrary, the Alabama Supreme Court disagreed and reasoned that the listing of no names of eligible black jurors on the jury rolls did not mean they were excluded because of their race.

The U.S. Supreme Court reversed that decision. The evidence revealed that, for a generation or longer, Jackson County officials never called blacks for jury duty, even though many were qualified. This, the court ruled, "established the discrimination which the Constitution forbids." At the circuit court trial, Norris's lawyers filed a motion to quash the indictment based on this exclusion, and the judge denied it. The U.S. Supreme Court, however, believed it should have been granted. In writing the opinion, Chief Justice Charles Evans Hughes noted:

> We think that this evidence failed to rebut the strong . . . case which the defendant had made. That showing as to the long-continued exclusion of Negroes from jury service, and as to the many Negroes qualified for that service, could not be met by mere generalities.

In spite of Hughes's strongly worded decision, Alabama officials, like those in other southern states, continued to find ways to exclude blacks from juries, including the all-white jury that convicted Clarence Norris a third time in 1937 and sentenced him to die in the electric chair at Kilby Prison. The next year Alabama governor Bibb Graves commuted the sentence to life. In 1946, Norris jumped parole, fled the state, and lived under his brother's name until pardoned by Governor George Wallace in 1976. In response, Norris said, "The lesson to black people, to my children, to everybody, is that you should always fight for your rights, even if it cost you your life. Stand up for your rights, even if it kills you. That's all that life consists of."

Not until the civil rights era in the South did the issue of race-based jury exclusion once again emerge as a key issue in the black quest for equality. It was a tactic of some southern lawyers defending black clients to raise the issue in hopes of gaining a reversal at some higher court—

something Caliph Washington's lawyers did in each of his first three trials. In 1959, the same year as Caliph's second trial, the Court of Appeals for the Fifth Circuit weighed into the exclusion issue in *Goldsby v. Harpole*, an appeal by a black Mississippi death row inmate convicted of murdering a white woman. The lower court denied Robert Lee Goldsby's writ of habeas corpus because the defendant failed to raise the issue in the jury trial and because claims of systematic jury exclusion went unproven by his lawyers. A three-judge panel reversed the ruling. Upon reviewing the statistical disparity between eligible black jurors and those actually on jury rolls, Judge Richard Rives believed that it was the duty of the judges of the Fifth Circuit, which comprised six states of the Deep South, to take "judicial notice" that most lawyers living in the South rarely ("almost to the point of never") raised the issue of race-based jury exclusion. One writer argued that the *Goldsby* decision provided the foundation for subsequent Fifth Circuit decisions over race-based jury exclusion.

In 1962, the Fifth reversed the capital rape conviction of Willie Seals, one of Caliph Washington's death row prison mates, because of jury exclusion in Mobile County. The court pointed out that 31 percent of the blacks in the county were qualified for jury service, but less than 2 percent were on the jury rolls. "Not only does the respondent fail to come forward with an adequate justification to explain this long-continued, wide discrepancy between the number of qualified Negroes in the County and their representation on the jury rolls," Judge Rives wrote, "but the evidence is practically conclusive that the method of selection at the time of Seals' trial and during the preceding years inevitably resulted in systematic exclusion of all but a token number of Negroes from the jury rolls." The presence of no blacks on the eighteen-man grand jury that indicted Seals, and of only two blacks on the venire of 110 persons from which the petit jury was selected that convicted and sentenced Seals to death, was not a "mere fortuitous accident."

Like Caliph Washington, Willie Seals faced challenges in fighting for justice under the Jim Crow legal system. On February 1, 1964, a Mobile jury convicted him again and sentenced him to life in prison, but that was overturned by the Alabama Supreme Court in 1968. On June

22, 1970, Seals's third trial was scheduled to begin, but the circuit court dismissed the charges when the victim of the alleged attack failed to appear in court. While Caliph still awaited his chance at freedom, Willie Seals walked free.

In 1965, Robert Swain, another death row inmate, saw his appeal based on jury exclusion receive an unsympathetic hearing before the U.S. Supreme Court. In writing for the majority in the six-to-three decision, Justice Byron White concluded that Swain failed to prove racial exclusion in the jury that tried him and argued that the defendant must provide more evidence to prove such discrimination. Moreover, White emphasized that the defendants in criminal cases were not entitled to demand that the trial jury or jury roles include a proportionate number of their particular race. It was "wholly obvious" to White and the other justices in the majority, including Hugo Black, that Alabama had not totally excluded blacks from either the grand or the petit jury panels in *Swain v. Alabama*, as was the case thirty years earlier in *Norris v. Alabama*. "An imperfect system of selection of jury panels," White wrote, "is not equivalent to purposeful racial discrimination."

On the Talladega County grand jury that indicted Swain, five blacks were called as part of the thirty-three-member panel, and two served on the eighteen-man grand jury. Eight blacks were summoned as part of the petit jury venire, but two were excused, and six were struck by the prosecutor. Swain's attorneys argued that the prosecutor was racially motivated in striking the potential black jurors, and this action violated their client's constitutional rights. Justice White disagreed. He argued that the fundamental right to challenge and strike jurors was centuries old and needed to be preserved. "To subject the prosecutor's challenge in any particular case to the demands and traditional standards of the equal protection clause would entail a radical change in the nature and operation of the challenge," he wrote. Under this revision, the prosecutor's judgment would be under constant scrutiny and many challenges would be banned.

The majority opinion brought a passionate dissent from Justice Arthur Goldberg. "I deplore the court's departure from its holdings in *Strauder* and *Norris*," he wrote. By affirming Swain's conviction, the court condoned "highly discriminatory procedures" used to exclude blacks from serving on juries in Talladega County. In addition, the court added to the heavy burden of proof required to prove exclusion and created barriers against efforts to end such practices that serve to "nullify the command" of the equal protection clause. Once the justices released their opinions, one critic described the *Swain* decision as inconsistent with earlier Supreme Court pronouncements and called the Fifth Circuit the "wiser and bolder" court for its ruling in *Goldsby*.

As the *Swain* case worked its way through the court system, Orzell Billingsley, Jr., and Chuck Morgan plotted their own challenge to the jury selection process through a case involving Orzell's father. Born in 1899, Orzell Billingsley, Sr., was an iron ore miner who spent most of his career working in U.S. Steel Mines located in Wenonah, along Red Mountain, northeast of Bessemer. He was one of the first black men promoted to mine foreman by TCI (U.S. Steel), a position usually reserved for whites, but the pay, however, was still low, and he supplemented his income by selling bootleg whiskey to black folks in southwestern Birmingham. One evening in the early 1960s, as Chuck Morgan told the story, Billingsley was walking on a road near his home when he was hit, and seriously injured, by a car driven by a drunken black man. Orzell Sr. asked the man to pay for his medical expenses, but the driver refused, claiming that he purchased the moonshine from Billingsley and the "injured victim was the real culprit."

Lawyer Billingsley helped his father file suit in circuit court. The elder Orzell knew he would face an all-white jury, and the younger Orzell believed that these twelve men would most likely decide in favor of the driver. This pessimism, as Chuck Morgan later wrote, was because most whites believed most any amusing tale, ironic story, or moral lesson that one black man told about another. He added:

Besides, whites would consider Mr. Billingsley's injuries less serious than would blacks. That was one effect of white man's justice. Another was different standards of punishment for crimes: crimes by blacks against whites called for the harshest penalties; whites against whites, lighter sentences; whites against blacks, lighter still; and since, to whites, black lives were worthless, for crimes by blacks against blacks the penalties were wrist slaps.

A mixed-race jury, Morgan supposed, would see the case in a much different context than twelve white men. Morgan believed that the "rusty and unused" statutes that prohibited racial exclusion "slumbered in the law books while tens of thousands of white grand and trial jurors interpreted, judged, and often ended the lives of blacks."

Morgan and the younger Billingsley thought the circumstances provided a good opportunity to challenge race-based jury exclusion through a class action lawsuit filed in federal court with Orzell Sr. and local civil rights leaders Abraham Woods, J. S. Phifer, and C. Herbert Oliver serving as plaintiff representatives of the black community in Jefferson County. Their federal civil suit ended up in the courtroom of Judge Harlan Hobart Grooms, a fair-minded jurist who ruled frequently in favor of civil rights. They hoped Grooms would issue an injunction and force Jefferson County to select juries from a fair cross section of the population, which was 29 percent black in the county, and end the practice of exclusion. Although Grooms found a disparity between the percentage of blacks living in Jefferson County and those who actually served as jurors, he nonetheless ruled that the lawyers provided the court with "insufficient evidence to support a finding of improper conduct or constitutional wrongdoing."

Billingsley and Morgan appealed Grooms's decision to the Fifth Circuit in New Orleans, and the case was considered *en banc*, or before all the judges of the court, which included Elbert Tuttle (chief), John Robert Brown, John Minor Wisdom, Walter P. Gewin, Griffin Bell, William Homer Thornberry, and James Plemon Coleman. Alabamian Walter Gewin would compose the court's decision released on April 5, 1966. The judge described *Billingsley v. Clayton* as a jury exclusion case but "not one of the usual type." Most of these cases brought before the court arose from conviction in a criminal case in which black defendants claimed that the systematic exclusion of blacks from the juries violated their constitutional rights. Nonetheless, the judges would consider many of the same issues, and the lawyers would have upon them the burden of proving that the jury commissioners in Jefferson County intentionally excluded blacks from jury service. If Billingsley and Morgan could do this, Gewin concluded, their client "would be entitled to relief on that ground."

The attorneys, however, failed to prove their argument to the court, and in turn, the judges of the Fifth affirmed the lower court decision. Even a sympathetic U.S. Justice Department's "friend of the court" brief emphasized that the "difficult problem" in the case was that the racial composition of the jury boxes, the "critical link" in the evidence, was missing. "As the record stands," justice officials concluded, "this Court could conclude that the plaintiff had failed in his proof, since the racial composition of the jury boxes was not proved."

And that was what Judge Gewin concluded: "Rather than systematic exclusion (which also embraces token systematic inclusion) of Negroes from the jury rolls of Jefferson County, we are convinced that the record fails to show a lack of good faith on the part of jury officials to obtain qualified negroes for jury service," he wrote. Echoing the *Swain* decision, the judge believed that the system had not "worked perfectly in every instance," but the poison of racism had not entered into the selection process according to the evidence given to the court. "The record reflects a good faith, bona fide effort on the part of the Board to give the Negro citizens of Jefferson County at least an equal, if not a privileged opportunity, to be called for jury service."

The judges believed that evidence suggested that a larger percentage of the black community was either uninterested or never seized the opportunity for jury service. "The techniques used by the Jury Board have made the opportunity available," Gewin wrote. Nonetheless, most of the evidence the judges used in rendering this decision was from the Birmingham Division of the Jefferson County Court. The Bessemer Division was another matter.

After highlighting the efforts of inclusion by the jury board in Birmingham, Gewin was critical of the process of exclusion by Bessemer officials. He pointed to testimony by Judge Ed Ball, who admitted in open court that racial segregation was common practice in the Bessemer court. Although Bessemer used the same system as Birmingham, few blacks were ever called for service in the Cutoff. When blacks were summoned, Ball seemed to suggest, they were placed on a petit jury that was never called to court. "The record is silent," Gewin wrote, "as to exactly how such a racial determination is made." The judge, however, would have found no paper trail of the unwritten rule of jury exclusion in the Cutoff. The record *did* show that blacks seldom, if ever, sat on juries, petit or grand, in the Bessemer Division. Gewin pointed out that the last black man to serve on a grand jury in Bessemer was almost a decade before, in 1957—ironically, on the panel that indicted Caliph Washington. "We do not approve the situation which the record shows to exist in the Bessemer Division," he concluded. And although the judges had affirmed the lower court ruling, this did not "preclude the granting of relief" in future court cases in which plaintiffs provided "adequate proof" of race-based jury exclusion.

Although technically another setback in the legal quest to end exclusion, the *Billingsley* decision encouraged several offspring cases directed at the Bessemer Cutoff. In 1969, another three-judge panel considered yet another appeal regarding jury exclusion in Bessemer. The judges considering *Salary v. Wilson* included Emett Choate of Florida and Walter P. Gewin and John Cooper Godbold, both of Alabama. Godbold, who was appointed by President Lyndon Johnson to replace retiring judge Richard Rives on the Fifth, would write the opinion. In it, the judge concluded that the *Salary* case was the opposite of the *Billingsley* case. In *Billingsley*, the lawyers failed to prove charges of racial discrimination in the jury selection process, but in *Salary*, the attorneys achieved, in the minds of these three judges, the necessary burden of proof.

The plaintiff's lawyers (Billingsley and Morgan were not involved) introduced clear statistical information that compared the number of blacks (20,238) and whites (16,158) eligible for jury service in 1967.

In contrast, the jury roll that year contained 10,501 whites (87.1 percent) and 1,549 blacks (12.9 percent). The year before, 1966, less than 7 percent of blacks were called. The judges concluded that this made a clear case of racial discrimination and placed the burden on the jury board of "coming forward with a constitutionally acceptable explanation for the racial disparities." They failed to do so. In *Billingsley*, the Fifth believed that in Jefferson County overall, the jury board acted in good faith in compiling the jury roll, but that case considered Birmingham and Bessemer together. In examining Bessemer alone, the three judges came to a different conclusion: "Good faith, or lack of an improper motive," Godbold wrote, "is not a defense to the failure of jury board members to discharge the affirmative constitutional duties cast upon them." This compelled the judges to remand the case back to Alabama, for the northern district court to issue orders that required Bessemer officials to gather jury rolls that would not exclude blacks. The court would carefully monitor compliance.

In response, the jury board in Bessemer hired four black canvassers to work the predominantly black neighborhoods to add names to the jury lists. Their door-to-door efforts won the confidence of the community and greatly increased the number of blacks as potential jurors. "I noticed a lot better cooperation by the negro community than we had in the past," said John C. Wilson, president of the jury board. "Therefore we were able to secure more names." On August 26, 1969, the jury board refilled the jury box, and the number of blacks jumped from 12.9 percent to an average of 25 percent to 35 percent. In an affidavit filed to the court, Ronnie Barron, an investigator for the district attorney, reported that on April 6, 1970, eighty jurors were present in court (fifty-five white and twenty-five black) and seven whites and five blacks were selected to sit on the case of *State of Alabama v. Caliph Washington*.

IN MANY WAYS, during the thirteen years since Washington's first trial, Bessemer became a different town. Under the leadership of Mayor Jess Lanier, the city participated in major urban renewal projects that saw over 70 percent of the city's slums, including Caliph's old home in Thompson Town, torn down and replaced with public housing. In place of the outdated Bessemer General, a new hospital opened, as did five new schools, three new fire stations, and a new police headquarters. The city's population grew only slightly (1.1 percent) from to 33,054 to 33,671 between 1960 and 1970, but the percentage of black residents fell from almost 60 percent at the time of Cowboy Clark's death in 1957 to 52.3 percent in 1970. The decline was due to blacks leaving the city and Mayor Lanier's annexation of white areas—by the time he left office in 1974, Bessemer's land mass had tripled in size.

The city's white power structure remained unchanged. The colorful mayor Jesse Eugene Lanier continued to dominate local government as the leader of the old-school political machine that ruled Bessemer. While one friend described him as the "Moby Dick of Alabama politics," other admirers called him "Big Daddy" for the benevolent paternalism he exhibited to his white constituents. Lanier's detractors, however, labeled him a "small town Huey P. Long," a crook, and a dictator. "I'm not a crook," he once said. "When you get into politics you are going to make enemies who want to cut on you." Lanier had little use for courting the emerging black vote and remained a steadfast segregationist and a George Wallace–supporting states' rights politician, insulated from the outside realities of a changing South. Journalist John I. Jones from the *Birmingham News* believed Lanier and the other Bessemer city commissioners (Tom Ashley and Ed Porter) saw the town as a "self-contained entity" that was "geographically sealed off" from the rest of the country. "One senses," Jones added, "that they feel some sort of monster forever haunts its borders, posing a threat to their pocketbooks, security, and peace of mind."

This was the dogged persistence of what journalist W. J. Cash called the "savage ideal" in the South—defined as a widespread orthodox conformity on issues that appeared to challenge the status quo (especially those related to race) and a uniform hostility to criticism, dissent, change, or even compromise. Although Cash wrote *The Mind of the South* in the 1930s and published it in 1941, the "savage ideal," as journalist Edwin

M. Yoder argued in 1965, remained unchanged. "The race picture," he wrote, "though increasingly subject to federal legal pressure, is mostly as Cash saw it—status politics still intact. The South is still given, more than any single identifiable region, to unholy repression of wrong thinking." And as Jess Lanier once said, "That's the way it is in politics. There ain't no damn time for fence-straddling."

Attorneys David Hood (*left*) and Orzell Billingsley (*center*) consult with Caliph Washington at the beginning of the 1970 trial.

19

"HE STILL AIN'T DEAD"

IN BESSEMER, FEW people were fence-sitters when it came to Caliph Washington's guilt or innocence, and Washington's lawyers hoped that the racial and gender makeup of the jury would bring a "not guilty" verdict. The trial began with high expectations. Following opening remarks by Harry Pickens and Orzell Billingsley, Judge Ed Ball asked the district attorney to call his first witness. It was Furman Jones. For the first time since the 1957 trial, Jones, the prosecution's star witness, stood and walked to the front of the courtroom. With Jones having missed the 1959 trial, Bessemer officials made certain that he would testify this time. Two days before, Police Chief George Barron flew to South Carolina and brought him back.

Once Jones was sworn in, Pickens asked him to recount the first time he saw Caliph Washington and his conversations with the defendant on the Greyhound bus bound for Memphis over a dozen years earlier. "He [Caliph] said he had killed a policeman in Alabama," Jones recalled, "and he was trying to get away."

On cross-examination, U. W. Clemon asked Jones to be clear about what Washington told him that day on the bus: "Now, did he tell you that he had killed a policeman, or that he had *murdered* a policeman?" Jones said, "Killed." At the time, Washington offered Jones no specifics as to whether the killing was an accident or intentional. "So all you know about this case is that Caliph Washington told you that he killed a policeman and you did not ask where or how and he didn't tell you why or how?" That was all he knew, Jones testified.

The defense hoped to keep Jones around for further questioning, but Judge Ball argued that the witness had a civilian job, twelve children, and a sick wife in South Carolina. David Hood pleaded with the judge to keep the witness overnight while the defense presented evidence to contradict his testimony. Standing in front of the judge's bench, Hood gestured to the motionless Caliph Washington and said, "After all, we have a man here being tried for his life. The life or death of this defendant is at stake." Ball, however, excused the witness.

The next witness, former Mississippi highway patrolman J. W. Warren, recounted how he and his partner removed Caliph Washington from the bus and discovered Cowboy Clark's .38-caliber Smith and Wesson pistol in a brown paper sack near where the defendant was sitting. Pickens introduced into evidence the paper bag and the gun.

Pickens called Jones and Warren, as out-of-town witnesses, to testify first, which made for a confusing, disjointed beginning to the trial. Orzell Billingsley objected. "We don't know where Mr. Pickens is going," he said. The district attorney had not established that a killing or a homicide had occurred. "This could go on and on," Billingsley added, "and probably never prove a killing." Judge Ball overruled but said he would reverse himself if Pickens never connected the testimony of Warren and Jones to the killing.

U. W. Clemon's cross-examination of Warren revealed a striking generational difference between Clemon and David Hood and Orzell Billingsley. Although courageous in their own ways, the two older black attorneys were accustomed to working within the confines of the old Jim Crow legal system that led to a more genteel and deferential courtroom demeanor when questioning white witnesses. In contrast, Clemon was fearless, aggressive, and confrontational. "He spoke clearly and force-fully," Jack Drake recalled, "and took no shit" from opposing counsel or witnesses.

Clemon tried to get Warren to admit to abusing and threatening Caliph Washington. He pressed the lawman to concede that he hit Caliph across the head with the butt of a rifle. Warren said he did not.

"Before you left Byhalia, Mississippi," Clemon asked, "isn't it a fact that you turned on a side street and took Caliph out of the car and started to punch him until a white man came by?"

Warren said he did not.

"Did your partner hit him?" the attorney asked.

"Not to my knowledge," Warren answered.

Clemon peppered the witness with questions about his background: Are you a member of the Ku Klux Klan? Are you a member of the White Citizens' Council? Have you ever killed a black person in the line of duty?

Warren responded no to each question.

On into the afternoon, the prosecution called two more witnesses: for-mer Bank Pawn Shop employee M. F. Karr, who explained how he sold the .38 to Cowboy Clark, and retired Lipscomb police chief Thurman Avery, who recalled the bootlegger stakeout the night Clark died. After Judge Ball adjourned for the evening, the twelve-member jury was "locked up" at the Holiday Inn on the Bessemer Super Highway. That first day brought no real drama. The trial seemed scripted and artificial. "That's what hap-pens when you retry a case," Jack Drake recalled. The witnesses seemed to have memorized word for word the transcript from the earlier trials. "Everyone did what the prosecutor wanted them to do," Drake added.

WHEN THE TRIAL resumed, another packed courtroom of spectators lis-tened to witnesses describe the death of Cowboy Clark in graphic detail. On this second day of testimony, the first witness was James "Jimmy" Thompson, the former deputy coroner, who explained to the court the autopsy procedure and the type of wound Clark received. The prosecutor showed Thompson a series of photographs of Clark's dead body and asked him if they "reasonably and adequately" portrayed the wound—once the witness identified the photos, they were submitted as evidence and shown to the jury. This brought a strenuous objection from Clemon. The prosecution was using the graphic pictures, the attorney emphasized, to shock and "arouse the prejudice of the jury." Judge Ball allowed one of the pictures to show proof of Clark's death and the location of the bullet wound. "I don't think there is any need to put four or five pictures in evidence," Ball said. "The fact that one shows the wound is sufficient."

On cross-examination, David Hood carefully attacked Thompson's credibility as an expert in forensic sciences. Thompson, who was, at the time of the 1970 trial, an employee at the Continental Can Company in Fairfield, admitted that he had no college degree or any special training in forensic sciences to determine the cause of death of Cowboy Clark or any other human being. Thompson apparently received the job of deputy coroner for the Cutoff because his father was the politically powerful Bessemer commissioner of public safety, Herman Thompson.

During the autopsy, Thompson assisted pathologist Dr. L. H. Kwong, who once again testified that the sole cause of Clark's death was from a bullet wound, which caused uncontrollable bleeding inside the abdominal cavity. "Nobody can live with a massive hemorrhage like that plus the shock he sustained," Kwong added. He explained that the bullet entered Clark's body at a strange angle and that he removed it from the deceased's spine.

The state toxicologist Carl Rehling discussed the ballistics tests he made on the gun and the bullet almost thirteen years before. While questioning the toxicologist on cross-examination, David Hood was holding the gun in the direction of the judge's bench. Ball interrupted and said, "Would you please open that gun. I don't like it pointed at me like that." Hood apologized and complied. The attorney tried to determine if the ballistics tests would reveal whether the pistol was fired accidentally or intentionally. "I have no idea," Rehling answered. Nonetheless, he later emphasized that the gun was not fired while in a "personal contact struggle" between the two individuals, because of the lack of powder residue on Clark's shirt.

But the defense lawyers, as in the previous two trials, tried to show that the lack of powder burns on the shirt did not prove that the defendant grabbed the gun, backed away, and fired at Cowboy Clark—a key argument in the prosecutor's case. Hood contended that powder deposits could be easily dislodged by bleeding, rough handling, or improper shipping. Rehling agreed that this might have happened to Clark's shirt. However, Clark's shirt was lost during the appeals process and never found.

Following Rehling's testimony, the prosecution called to the stand several sheriff's deputies from the Cutoff and police officers from the city of Bessemer to recall the night Clark died, the capture of Caliph Washington, and the suspect's alleged confessions. Deputy Sheriff Walter Dean explained how he wrote down Caliph Washington's confession—a key piece of evidence in the state's prosecution. Vast changes had occurred in American law since 1957, and U. W. Clemon wanted to discuss those in front of the court. In response, Judge Ball sent the jury out of the courtroom, while the lawyers debated the points of law.

What Clemon hoped to show was that the atmosphere and environment in which Caliph made his statement was, as Justice Earl Warren wrote in the *Miranda* decision, "inherently intimidating" and worked to undermine the Fifth Amendment's prohibition on self-incrimination. In the presence of the jury, Dean claimed to have told Caliph he didn't have to make a statement if he didn't want to and that if he did talk, his words could be used against him in a criminal proceeding. Regardless, Dean admitted that he never told Caliph he had the right to consult a lawyer, or that he could stop talking during the interrogation, or that he could call his family. Clemon showed how intimidating it was for a young black suspect to be surrounded by five white lawmen. "Isn't it a fact, Mr. Dean," the attorney asked, "that you told Reverend Washington on that occasion, that you would kill him and that his head would look like a tomato if he didn't give you a statement?" Dean strongly denied the accusation.

Clemon also asked if the witness was familiar with the general atmosphere prevailing in the county at the time Caliph Washington was interrogated. Pickens, however, objected on the grounds that the question was "irrelevant, incompetent, and immaterial." Clemon argued that the basis for asking the question was to determine the "voluntariness" of the confession. "The Supreme Court and all the other courts say that where there is a general atmosphere conducive to . . . coercion, to have a confession made under those conditions does have a bearing as to whether or not the confession was voluntary." Ball overruled Pickens's objection and compelled the witness to answer. "At the time I took this confession," Dean answered, "and during that day prior to the taking of the confession, there was not to my knowledge any bad atmosphere concerning this case."

A few hours before Dean wrote down Washington's statement in Alabama, the suspect allegedly made an oral confession after his arrest in Mississippi to Bessemer police detective Lawton "Stud" Grimes. According to Grimes, Caliph said that while Clark was leading him to the patrol car after the arrest in that dark Bessemer alley, he grabbed the officer's gun, stepped back, and fired two or three times.

On cross-examination, Orzell Billingsley asked Grimes if he warned Caliph Washington about his right to remain silent or his right to an attorney. "I didn't tell him nothing," Grimes responded. "I told him he didn't have to answer my questions if he didn't want to." Billingsley then asked Grimes why he pressured Washington into making a statement.

GRIMES: "I wanted to know."
BILLINGSLEY: "Why?"
GRIMES: "I wanted to know why he killed that officer."
BILLINGSLEY: "That is what you wanted to know?"
GRIMES: "Yes."
BILLINGSLEY: "You couldn't wait until you got back to Bessemer to find out?"
GRIMES: "I didn't intend to."
BILLINGSLEY: "You didn't intend to wait? Why didn't you have this statement put in writing?"
GRIMES: "I didn't have time."
BILLINGSLEY: "What was your rush?"
GRIMES: "Wasn't no rush. I wasn't going to write it down."
BILLINGSLEY: "Well, how then do you remember it?"
GRIMES: "I just remember. I got a mind like anybody else."

When Grimes admitted that he did not remember testifying in the second Washington trial in 1959, Billingsley wanted to know why the witness could recollect vividly what Caliph said back in the summer of 1957 on a roadside in Mississippi, but he unable to recall his more recent testimony. What else had Grimes forgotten? The lawyer inquired.

BILLINGLSEY: "Didn't you beat Reverend Washington on the way from Mississippi to Bessemer?"

GRIMES: "I never laid a hand on him."

BILLINGSLEY: "Didn't you kill somebody you thought was Caliph Washington?"

GRIMES: "No."

BILLINGSLEY: "Didn't you tell Reverend Washington on his way back from Mississippi that you had his mother and father in jail and that he needed to talk before they could get out?"

GRIMES: "No."

BILLINGSLEY: "Is it not true that in Adamsville there were some hogs and chickens killed while you were out there?"

Before Grimes answered, Pickens objected and Ball sustained. When Billingsley asked who authorized Grimes to follow him and David Hood during the first trial, Pickens again objected and the judge sustained. "I want to say to this court," Billingsley continued, "that they say this confession was voluntary, but this officer [Grimes] followed the black lawyers in the trial all during the week to their homes and offices and wherever they went, and if he intimidated these lawyers in this matter, what do you think he did to this defendant?"

Judge Ball reiterated his sustain of the objection and added, "Mr. Billingsley, I don't want to argue with you." He then turned to the jury and told them not to consider the lawyer's statement.

With the jury out of the room, lawyer Clemon asked the judge to strike the statement made by Grimes on the grounds that it violated the defendant's rights, was taken without regard to the Fifth and Sixth Amendments to the Constitution, and went against the Supreme Court's *Miranda* and *Escobedo* decisions. Judge Ball, however, argued that the *Miranda* decision was applicable only for trials starting after June 13, 1966. The Caliph Washington trial, Ball countered, began on October 8,

1957, "many years before these cases were decided." Clemon, however, insisted that the trial began on April 6, 1970: "This is a new trial." His honor disagreed. "These proceedings began in October 1957, and this is not a new trial. This is a retrial of the same case."

On day three of the trial, prosecutor Harry Pickens called several witnesses who once lived in the old Thompson Town neighborhood near the crime scene. Each testified as to what they saw the evening of the shooting of Cowboy Clark. Mary Howard said she had trouble sleeping that evening. "I couldn't rest," she recalled, so she sat on the edge of her bed and was looking out the window when she saw cars approaching. At first, she didn't think much of it, because cars routinely sped down the narrow dirt road several times during the night, but when she saw the red light on top of the cars, she said, "That's the police and they got somebody." She woke her daughter, Ada Mae Howard, to come look, and that's when they realized that the car being chased belonged to Doug Washington. "Yes, look," Ada Mae said, "that's Caliph in that car." A few moments later, they heard a shot fired.

John Adams died since the last trial, but his onetime live-in girlfriend, sixty-eight-year-old Mary Davidson, returned to give her account of what happened that night in front of her house. When district attorney Pickens called her Mary, Orzell Billingsley objected to the prosecutor referring to her by her first name. The state should address black witnesses with appropriate courtesy titles, he argued. "I am a black person," he added, "and I really resent it, and I don't think it would put a member of the white race on the spot if they would call her by her proper name." Pickens agreed and referred to her as Mrs. Davidson (although she was unmarried). She testified that she saw Caliph with the gun and that he was about twelve feet away when he fired the fatal bullet. In the previous trial, she claimed she never saw the actual shooting but just heard the gunfire. "That was all I knowed," she said in 1957. But now she claimed that "Caliph stood there and the policeman come over and then he turned around and was going back toward his car, and the next thing I know Caliph walked out with the gun and I heard it fire. . . . I know he fired it. I didn't see no scuffling or nothing." She said Washington then fled into the night.

The suspect ended up at Elijah Honeycutt's house. Honeycutt

returned to testify that Caliph Washington knocked on his door and asked for a ride. "He said he wanted to see a girlfriend," Honeycutt said. "You know how soldiers do when they come home." He drove Washington into western Birmingham and let him out of the car. Honeycutt recalled that Caliph turned to him and said that he just killed a police officer. "I didn't believe him, because he didn't act like he had done such a thing, because he was smiling," he testified. Honeycutt said to Caliph, "Oh, get off man, you didn't do anything like that," and he turned around and drove back to Bessemer. "I didn't pay any attention to him." He found out the next day at work that Washington was the suspect in the death of a Lipscomb police officer.

Following Honeycutt's testimony and cross-examination, the state rested its case. Tensions were high as Billingsley, Clemon, Hood, and Drake prepared to make a defense of Caliph Washington. Before they could call their first witness, one of the white female jurors, Agalean Kirkland, had an "attack of nerves," Judge Ball announced, and was replaced with an alternate, Charlie Robinson, a black male. Sitting in the jury box now were seven white women, four black men, and one black woman. They watched and listened as Clemon called the first witness in defense of Caliph Washington.

Clemon called to the stand and questioned several character witnesses on behalf of the defendant—something not done in the first two trials and reflective of another shift in the criminal justice system. Under the old Jim Crow system, most attorneys never called character witnesses on behalf of black defendants because whites considered it a foregone conclusion that most blacks possessed low morals. But in this trial, teachers, preachers, neighbors, and community leaders (Cornelia Addison, Reverend Lucius Calvin Walker, Lula Belle Johnson, Bernice Jackson, Margaret Pettaway, and Bessie Mae Johnson) all came forward to testify that the defendant was a good man of high character. Orzell Billingsley even called Asbury Howard, still Bessemer's leading civil rights activist, to tell the court that Washington was a fine human being with a first-class temperament.

In contrast, witnesses also testified to the low moral character of Mary Davidson. "She is a public drunk," Lula Belle Johnson said. The night of the Cowboy Clark incident, several witnesses claimed Davidson and her boyfriend were drinking, fussing, and cussing. "I knocked on the door and asked them to hush," recalled Bessie Mae Johnson. She later saw Davidson playing with a big dog. "I knew when she played with this dog that she had been drinking. I said, 'You had a little nip, didn't you, Bum?' I used to call her Bum."

Next, Orzell Billingsley called Caliph's court-appointed attorney, Kermit "K. C." Edwards, to testify as an expert witness on the case. Edwards opined that he believed Clark died as a result of the accidental discharge of his weapon and that one of the bullets hit the car, ricocheted, and ripped through the officer's body—a plausible explanation, but one that Edwards was never able to piece together for juries in 1957 and 1959. In this new trial, Edwards identified himself as an attorney by profession, but he was disbarred years earlier, along with two other lawyers, for their "conduct in domestic relations proceedings." Nonetheless, Edwards continued to clandestinely practice law with his disbarred colleagues in a "quickie divorce mill," where out-of-state clients paid for divorces, which were in fact invalid. The scandal became public in 1970, when investigators discovered thousands of unrecorded divorce decrees in the offices of two corrupt judges who were participating in the scheme. In 1972, Edwards and the others were convicted in federal court for using the U.S. mail in a scheme to defraud and were sentenced by Judge Clarence Allgood to three years in prison.

Following Edwards's testimony, Clemon called witnesses to show alleged violence by white Bessemer police officers during the manhunt to find Caliph Washington. William "Burley" Merritt, Ernestine Merritt, and Hattie Cross testified that on Sunday morning, July 14, 1957, seven carloads of Bessemer police officers and sheriff's deputies showed up at their home in Adamsville and began a house-to-house search. Burley Merritt said he would never forget the "pretty rough" beating he received all over his face with the butt of a Winchester rifle. Instead of receiving medical attention, he was taken to the Bessemer jail, where police later forced him to sign a statement—although he could not read. When the prosecution objected to this line of questioning, lawyer Clemon said, "I think this goes to show the type of police officers that were involved in trying to capture or find Mr. Washington. Their conduct out there goes to show what they might have done to Mr. Washington."

When Jack Drake asked Hattie Cross if these police officers had beaten her and struck her mother in the head with the butt of a gun, the prosecutor objected. Judge Ed Ball sustained the request and asked Caliph's lawyers not to pursue this line of questioning. "You know that what the officers did to her is not admissible," he said.

Orzell Billingsley, however, explained to Ball that the defense wanted to "get these questions into the record" even if he ruled them inadmissible.

The judge sent the jury into the jury room, and he allowed Drake to state what he expected to prove by this line of questioning. Drake said:

I would like for the record to show that we had hoped to show by this witness that she was beaten and intimidated by the police from Lipscomb and Bessemer and others unknown to us; that her mother was beaten and otherwise intimidated, and that her mother later died from those injuries; that one Mr. Jessie Kyser was shot and killed in Adamsville on this date in question, and those actions and other actions to which this witness could tes- tify to was . . . part of the general pattern and scheme and harass- ment engaged in by the police of the city of Bessemer, and by the city of Lipscomb . . . to locate a witness and in doing so, to intimidate every black person in Jefferson County who had ever known Caliph Washington.

The prosecutor objected to Drake's statement as "irrelevant, incom- petent, and immaterial." Well aware of Stud Grimes's reputation, how- ever, Judge Ball agreed to allow the defense to put these points in the record. "Anything that Mr. Grimes did out there," Ball said. "I will let in." After all, the judge pointed out, Stud Grimes testified that nothing happened in Adamsville.

Clemon added that the defense also hoped to show through the tes- timony of these witnesses the "totality of the circumstances" in which every statement and confession was made by the black folks in this case. This would reveal to the court the atmosphere of fear, intimidation, and violence that gripped society at this time and compelled the defendant to seek refuge in another state. The prosecutor pointed out that if any harassment, beating, murders, or anything else had occurred in Adamsville, then the people had the right to report it, and the "people creating those offenses" would have been indicted in 1957. In response, Jack Drake said the defense would be happy to bring forward a great many witnesses from Jefferson County who would testify that black people would not have come forward with accusations in 1957. "They were afraid to have done that," Drake said.

With all these points in the trial records, Judge Ball brought back the jury, and Orzell Billingsley called the next witness: "We call Caliph Washington to the stand." For the first time in over a decade, he would recount his own version of the incident with Cowboy Clark.

Washington recalled how the chase began, when he thought night riders were after him, and he explained that as soon as he realized it was a police car, he stopped. In this retelling, Cowboy Clark was much meaner and rougher than how Washington described him in 1957 and 1959. "Get out of the car, nigger," he remembered Clark yelling. The defendant testified that the officer was looking for whiskey, and when the suspect wouldn't confess to having any in his car, Cowboy called him a "smart nigger" and a son of a bitch. "I denied knowing anything about any whiskey," Washington said, but Clark "kept talking about it" to the point that he grew so angry that he pulled his weapon and started to strike the suspect in the head with the butt of the gun.

Attorney Hood picked up Clark's gun and asked Washington to hold the weapon and demonstrate how it happened, but he refused. "I can't touch those," Washington said, but he went on to explain that he "threw his hands up" and grabbed Clark's hands as he was about to strike. "I was afraid," he said. "I was trying to keep from getting hit or shot." But the gun fired off three rapid shots, and Clark's grip grew weak. "It must have shot him," Washington said. "I don't know, because I was scared."

Judge Ball interrupted and adjourned the court until, Thursday, April 9, at 9:15 a.m. That next morning, Washington continued to testify. He explained how he fled the scene, got a ride from his friend, and stayed hidden in the woods. Caliph Washington told how his friend's stepfather, Tommy Lee Silmon, took him to Adamsville—absent from his testimony was the story about the mysterious stranger who drove Silmon's car. Washington described how he escaped to Mississippi. He denied ever sitting with, or even talking to, Furman Jones while on the bus. He said he fell asleep on the bus and was awakened by a woman who said there was a police roadblock ahead. Washington testified that the Mississippi lawmen took him off the bus, shook him down, beat him a little, and drove him to a service station. There, he said in this new version of the incident, the lawman put a bright light in his face, handcuffed his hands behind him, and threatened to kill him if he did not confess. When he refused to talk, they drove him to a secluded area in the woods. Caliph recounted the story from the 1959 trial:

> They were still holding me in the woods and fixing to lynch me up; trying to get me to run and said they were going to give me a break, but I said I didn't want to run, and this officer said, 'you run,' and he told me how he had hung a lot of black people up on a limb, and they were stringing me up on this car hood when another man came by—I don't know his name, but he had a little boy with him and he told them to take me in.

At the Mississippi Highway Patrol station, Washington said that he refused to talk to Stud Grimes. "He slapped me because I wouldn't talk to him," he testified. According to Washington, Grimes then said: "We have all these niggers in jail, your mother and father, and we are going to burn all of you. I want you to tell me what happened." Caliph refused.

Once he was back in Bessemer on July 15, 1957, he was taken to the courthouse and placed in a room, according to Washington, filled with angry cursing white lawmen with lots of guns and angry eyes. They never informed him, he recalled, that he had a right to remain silent and a right to an attorney. He could not call his family because they told him they were all in jail. Washington testified that the men forced him to answer the questions, while one of them wrote down his answers and then told him that they "would burn us all," if he did not sign. Tired, scared, and hungry, the defendant said that he initialed each page, and then signed the confession, without ever being allowed to read the document. He was then taken to the county jail in Bessemer.

On cross-examination, Harry Pickens peppered Washington with questions. Although he talked fast ("like a machine gun"), Pickens's tone was much more respectful and less authoritarian than that of his predecessor, Howard Sullinger. He skillfully revealed significant inconsistencies in Caliph's testimony from the two previous trials. When Pickens pointed out these gaps, Caliph said he was too afraid to tell the whole truth in 1957 and 1959.

PICKENS: "You were in a courtroom, weren't you?"
WASHINGTON: "But they threatened me all the time."
PICKENS: "The judge was on the bench, wasn't he?"
WASHINGTON: "I was afraid of all of them."
PICKENS: "Are you under any threat right now?"
WASHINGTON: "Ever since I been locked up."
PICKENS: "Right now?"
WASHINGTON: "Yes, sir."
PICKENS: "By whom?"
WASHINGTON: "You and the state for fourteen years. . . . You've threatened my life all the time with this charge."
PICKENS: "I have?"
WASHINGTON: "With this charge."
PICKENS: "Are you saying I have talked with you and threatened your life?"
WASHINGTON: "Not with those words."
PICKENS: "What do you mean? I don't understand."
WASHINGTON: "I mean, the law; with the law."

"You've been threatened with the law?" Judge Ball interjected.

"I mean," Washington replied, "you have had me here in confinement over and over, and you have violated my rights in this case and want to try me for my life again after holding me for four or five years without giving me a fair and impartial trial."

PICKENS: "You are getting a fair and impartial trial, aren't you?"

WASHINGTON: "I didn't even have a hearing when you brought me back in 1965."

PICKENS: "Have I threatened you?"

WASHINGTON: "You didn't turn me loose."

PICKENS: "I haven't threatened you, have I?"

WASHINGTON: "I am telling the truth and the record will show it."

Pickens moved on. He asked Caliph who he thought was chasing and shooting at him.

"Some of the white boys on the south side," he said, "used to shoot at us sometimes and throw brick and bottles."

Pickens pressed Caliph as to why he drove down to dark Exeter Alley instead of to the well-lit police station.

"They weren't going to protect me," he responded, "because they never do. Wasn't no use to go near the police station." After he pulled the car over down in that dark alley, Caliph said that he still had no idea he was being pursued by a police officer.

"He was in a police car with the blinker light going," Pickens said, "and he had on a gun belt with a gun hanging out of it and he had on a police shirt and a badge and you didn't know he was a policeman, is that right?"

Caliph said it was too dark to see.

Pickens questioned Washington about the arrest. He wanted to know what happened after Cowboy Clark led him to the patrol car and opened the door.

PICKENS: "You snatched his pistol at this time. Is that right?"

WASHINGTON: "No."

PICKENS: "Do you remember telling Mr. Grimes that you snatched this officer's pistol and shot him three times?"

WASHINGTON: "I didn't tell Mr. Grimes anything."

PICKENS: "Is Mr. Grimes lying about that?"

WASHINGTON: "What do you think?"

PICKENS: "I am asking you."

WASHINGTON: "That's what I want to know."

Pickens decided that his questioning was going nowhere, and he abruptly said: "All right, no further questions."

When Judge Ball asked Caliph's lawyers if they had any other questions, a confident David Hood proclaimed that the defense rested.

Ball seemed surprised. "You want to rest?"

The defense lawyers all agreed.

Following closing arguments by both sides, the judge gave the jury several oral charges. The jury could find Washington guilty of first- or second-degree murder, or first- or second-degree manslaughter. They could also find him not guilty. He told the jury that a lot of "extraneous matters" were injected into this trial and that as citizens they should return a verdict based upon the facts, not prejudice or bias. "This is not a race issue in this case," Ball said, and the jury should act as if they were blind to the race of the defendant, whether he was black or white. "Do not let your judgment be swayed by any preconceived ideas of the conflict in our modern society," he added, "or do not inject these matters into it when you are deliberating." The jury should decide based on what they heard from witnesses and other evidence. If they found that any witness was "knowingly and corruptly" giving false statements, then they had the right to use discretion and disregard that testimony.

In addition, based on evidence and testimony in this case, Caliph Washington fled the scene of the crime, which might suggest guilt. "The law takes up the proposition that the wicked flee, while the innocent is as brave as the lion," he said. In this case, the jury needed to ask what motivated his flight. Was it guilt? If the flight was caused by "fear for the defendant's own life," then a sense of guilt was not present, and it should not be considered as automatic evidence of guilt.

Judge Ball also instructed the jury not to consider the defendant's previous trials, verdicts, and reversals or how long the defendant was imprisoned. "These are all matters of law," he added, "and are not your concern."

When the judge finished his oral charges, and outside the hearing of the jury, U. W. Clemon objected to Ball's charging the jury not to consider the time Washington had been incarcerated and the number of reversals. "We think that those matters should be considered by the jury," Clemon said, "if the jury having determined that the defendant is guilty and is choosing between the death penalty or a sentence of life imprisonment." Ball noted the objection.

The jury retired to the jury room at 3:55 p.m. to consider Caliph Washington's guilt or innocence in the death of Cowboy Clark. They deliberated for ninety minutes before retiring for the evening. They resumed the next morning, Friday, April 10, at 9 a.m., for more deliberation. With the jury still out, the courtroom took on a festive atmosphere as Washington's friends and family sensed freedom coming. Speaking with a reporter, Caliph predicted that he would be found "not guilty or something like that" because he had such a strong belief in God. U. W. Clemon said that anything less than freedom for Caliph would bring an appeal.

After over two hours and thirty minutes of deliberating, word came that the jury had reached a verdict. A hush fell over the courtroom. Judge Ball warned the crowd about any emotional outbursts. The jury returned to the jury box. It was 11:30 a.m. The judge then asked Caliph Washington to rise and listen to the verdict.

The foreman of the jury, Peggy Haynes, a white office worker from Hueytown, said, "We the jury, find the defendant guilty of murder in the second degree as charged in the indictment, and we fix his punishment at forty years imprisonment in the penitentiary."

Caliph showed little emotion.

The spectators sat stunned. A low murmuring of voices echoed through the courtroom. Sheriff's deputies stepped forward and handcuffed Washington's wrists behind his back and whisked him from the courtroom.

"Then suddenly," a newspaper reporter observed, "a cry rocked the small courtroom and a bedlam of emotion broke out." At least a dozen deputies, some with helmets and night sticks, prevented Washington's family and friends from following him into the hallways. In a few seconds, with Caliph out of sight, the deputies allowed everyone else to leave. Most of the spectators moved into the corridor just beyond the courtroom doors and stood holding each other and weeping and shouting their opposition to the verdict. "They don't have any heart," cried one woman as tears coursed down her face. Another woman fainted on the marble floor and had to be carried away. Caliph's mother collapsed and was taken to the hospital in an ambulance. Someone yelled, "Reverend Caliph; my God; he still ain't dead!"

David Hood was also thankful that Washington was no longer living under the shadow the death penalty—even if this verdict were reversed and he was tried again, a jury was prohibited from sentencing him for anything more than second-degree murder. A confident Orzell Billingsley said, "There's no doubt we'll get it reversed. There were too many errors made by the court. It's just a matter of appealing."

Judge Ball, however, disagreed. "I took extreme caution to give the defendant as fair and impartial trial as is possible," he said. "I don't want it to be reversed and come back on me. I tried to keep it clean of any errors. This in my judgment was done." The judge, however, seemed saddened that none of Caliph Washington's previous time served, almost thirteen years, would count against the forty-year sentence. He told a newspaper reporter after the trial that perhaps the Alabama Pardon and Parole Board would look at the case and consider giving him parole. "I think he could probably apply for parole about eight years from now," Ball said.

A more immediate concern for Judge Ball, however, was the issue of bail for Washington. The judge told a journalist that he believed that forty years was too lengthy a sentence to grant a person bail. Nonetheless, he pledged to set a bond amount, which, given the sentence, would be a large sum of money, but first he would need to consult the other district judges. "I've been very liberal with this fellow [Washington]," he said, "but after conviction, it's a different matter."

That Friday evening following the verdict, tensions continued to run high. Several of the black jurors reported receiving death threats. Dora Beverly Mauldin, a maid from Bessemer and the only black female on the jury, reported that a woman called and said, "We are going to get you," and threatened to beat her for issuing that verdict. Mauldin, who endured having her Bessemer home bombed in 1957, remained unflappable. Alfonso Gaston of Fairfield also received a call from a woman who asked if he was a member of the jury that convicted Caliph Washington. When he said, yes, the caller promised to make him pay for what he had done.

On Saturday, the day after the verdict, Judge Ball announced that state law prohibited him from setting bail for Caliph Washington. "I spent the morning today and checked the state statutes," he said, and discovered that in Alabama, anybody sentenced to more than twenty years cannot be allowed bail. Washington's ten days of freedom seemed only to make going back to prison that much more difficult.

But Washington would not return to the Jefferson County Jail to await an appeal of the verdict. Immediately following the trial, Judge Ball signed an order transferring him to a state facility. "The court being further informed that the said defendant," read the order, "has created a security problem . . . and it would be to the best interest of all concerned if said defendant were transferred to the Medical and Diagnostic Center, Mt. Meigs, Alabama, for safe keeping . . . [and] where he shall be confined for the duration of his sentence."

The Mt. Meigs Medical and Diagnostic Center in Montgomery had just opened in January 1970 as part of the state's efforts to replace the old Kilby Prison. At Mt. Meigs's receiving center, Washington was fingerprinted, photographed, and assigned a new number, S-513. His information card listed his height as five feet eight inches and his weight as 250 pounds—seventy-five pounds more than he weighed when he went through the classification center at Kilby at age seventeen. On April 10, 1970, prison officials described the now-thirty-year-old man as having a dark complexion, black hair, brown eyes, and a "very stocky" build.

Perhaps since he was deemed a "security problem," Mt. Meigs officials placed Caliph in a quarantine cell. On Monday, April 13, 1970, he expressed his feelings of frustration and isolation in a prayer that he wrote out in the form of a letter:

Dear Jesus, I write this letter to you, because, I am away from my beloved back home, and "oh God!" how I'll like to be back in their presence. I miss the cheer of your spirit which worketh within each of them. Jesus, send me home with them again to stay, and to carry thou word to all that you wish for me to. I do remember the dream dear Jesus, where you showed me about this very thing, and I did not tell anyone until it happened. But I should had, because, it make people think you are not just, when you are the only true God to us all. I know Lord that you has saved me out of all of my trouble. I only fear you dear Jesus. My many praise are to you for the being so wonderful to me. I have enjoyed the short stay you given me for I know in due time it shall be long. Bless all that trust in you and are praying for your children. Help us Jesus in all we do. Set me free dear Jesus, for you said that anything I shall ask in your name you would do it. So this is my plea, and stand by me. Your beloved son and servant, Rev. Caliph Washington.

Three days later, on April 16, Washington wrote to Ralph Galt and complained about the isolation. He could not understand why they sent him to Mt. Meigs right after the trial, so far away from his family and friends. "They told me it was for safekeeping," he wrote. "I don't like it here at all, because, I can't write like I want to or nothing." He hoped that his attorneys could get him out on bond or moved back to the jail or anywhere but where he was. "But the attorneys has [sic] worked so slow on this case," he wrote. "I only hope they shall put some speed on now." Even so, Caliph said he had his trust in God and he had faith that "all things will work out well soon."

On April 20, prison officials removed Washington from his quarantine and placed him in cell A-23 in the A Cellblock. The prison floor commander told the guards to not let the "subject . . . out of his cell for any reason" and to carry all meals to him in A-23. Caliph could never leave the cell unless a request was approved by warden Glen Thompson, Captain W. L. Trawick, or associate warden Joseph E. Bonnett. Ironically, in 1957, Bonnett was the guard at Kilby who processed Washington when he first came to the prison.

Even outside solitary, Caliph was unhappy with the conditions of the new facility—cold food, dirty clothing and linens, no exercise, and poor medical treatment. Mt. Meigs was a new prison, but many of the guards remained surly and cruel. He and his fellow inmates wrote a letter to state officials requesting that the board make significant changes in the procedures. "It is very difficult to eat cold grits," they wrote, "and no one enjoys a cold meal and later a hot drink." Associate warden Bonnett wrote that Caliph and the other inmates in this cellblock enjoyed "stirring things up" and that the prison had more than its fair share of the state's most incorrigible prisoners. "I believe," he added, "that there exists a 'hard core' of agitators" in this area. Despite these observations, Bonnett improved the living conditions in the cellblock and ensured that prisoners had hot food, clean clothes, towels, and sheets, outdoor exercise, and frequent medical visits. For Caliph it was a small civil rights victory behind the walls of an Alabama prison.

Nonetheless, while he adjusted to these new surroundings at Mt. Meigs, his lawyers filed notice of appeal with the Alabama Court of Criminal Appeals—the same court that denied his habeas corpus writ in 1969.

Caliph Washington and Christine Luna in 1972.

20

"SET ME FREE DEAR JESUS"

T HE JUDGES OF the Alabama Court of Criminal Appeals, Anna Lola Price, Aubrey Cates, and Reneau P. Almon, announced their decision in *Caliph Washington v. Alabama* on January 12, 1971. One of the state's most learned and scholarly judges, Cates wrote the decision of the court. Born in 1909, Aubrey Marion Cates, Jr., was the son of an attorney who maintained a thriving practice in Louisville, Kentucky. The younger Cates earned an undergraduate degree from the University of Louisville in 1929 and subsequently studied as a Rhodes Scholar at Oxford University, where he earned his law degree in 1932 from the Honour School of Jurisprudence. Cates's legal career was remarkable, enhanced by the fact he truly enjoyed the law because it required thinking and offered good opportunities for public service and private profit. Following a brief stint as a law clerk in Louisville, Cates went to work in 1933 as a staff attorney for the Public Works Administration, a New Deal program designed to provide building jobs for the nation's unemployed. For the next seven years, he worked in the PWA offices in Washington, D.C., San Francisco,

Louisville, and Montgomery and, during the early 1940s, he served as one of the attorneys for the Office of Price Administration, where he worked alongside another young attorney, Richard M. Nixon. Following active duty in the U.S. Navy, he returned to Montgomery and remained in private practice until elected to the court of appeals in 1956 (later the court of criminal appeals), where he gained a reputation, as one attorney said, as perhaps the state's "most splendidly educated jurist whoever sat on an Alabama court."

Cates's opinions reflected a distinguished background, and were direct and learned, yet they contained, as another lawyer recalled, an "intensely human" element. "He was always alert," a colleague once wrote, "as an appellate judge in criminal proceedings, to the constitutional rights of all citizens, even those charged with crime." His opinions were thoroughly researched, at times abundantly filled with classical references, and often exhibited his near "encyclopedic knowledge of constitutional precedents."

In writing the Caliph Washington decision, Judge Aubrey Cates referenced many of the recent court decisions related to race-based jury exclusion and recent efforts by Bessemer officials to include blacks on Washington's petit jury in 1970. According to Cates, however, the issue was not the jury inclusion of 1970 but the jury of exclusion of 1957. When the Alabama Supreme Court overturned Washington's first conviction back in 1957, the judges made no ruling on the issue of jury exclusion and simply noted that the defense failed to show discrimination in the filling of the jury box in August 1957. Judge Thomas Lawson emphasized that the burden was on Caliph Washington to prove discrimination and that he "must be given an opportunity to produce relevant, legal evidence, if he can, which tends to prove racial discrimination."

In the circuit court trial in 1970, the defense again raised the issue of exclusion in the form of a motion to quash the indictment and refill the jury box. When Judge Ball denied that motion, Cates wrote, the court disallowed Washington the opportunity to "prove allegations of systematic exclusion as to [the] grand jury which had handed down indictment." In Cates's direct language, Judge Ball was in error. "Accordingly," Aubrey Cates continued, "the judgment . . . is reversed and the cause is remanded to the court below." For the third time, a higher court overturned Caliph Washington's murder conviction.

When Caliph received word of the court overturning his third conviction the next day, he pulled out the eight-month-old prayer he wrote to Jesus ("Set me free dear Jesus") and scrawled on the back, "Answered on January 13, 1971." Once again he hoped for a quick release, but it did not come. Orzell Billingsley and David Hood prepared a petition for a writ of habeas corpus with over thirteen years of well-worn arguments about rights denied and justice delayed. Caliph Washington was no criminal, they added, but a good man from a "reputable family" who was now a "Minister of the Gospel of Jesus Christ." They asked Judge Ball to grant the writ and order the warden of Mt. Meigs to bring the petitioner to Ball's courtroom together with the reasons for his imprisonment. The court should then order him released from confinement and declare his imprisonment unconstitutional and void. Hood filed the writ with Judge Ball on January 19.

The response was predictable and contained no surprises, as district attorney Harry Pickens objected to the "place, time, and method" of the writ but gave no opinion as to its merits. He filed a "plea in abatement" and argued that because Washington was being held at Mt. Meigs in Montgomery County and not in Bessemer, the petition should be heard by a judge there and not in Jefferson County. "The petition shows on its face," he wrote, "that the court does not have jurisdiction of the body of the petitioner." On January 28, Judge Ball agreed and transferred the petition to Montgomery County.

In the state capital on February 2, the Alabama Court of Criminal Appeals denied the state's request for a rehearing. Next, assistant attorney general David Clark asked the Alabama Supreme Court to review the case (writ of certiorari), but Justice Thomas "Buster" Lawson, who was soon to retire after thirty years on the state's high court, denied the writ on February 25. Yet Caliph Washington still waited at Mt. Meigs for the circuit court in Montgomery to act on the petition for the writ of habeas.

The petition ended up in the courtroom of Judge Richard Perrino Emmet. The boy-faced thirty-nine-year-old Dick Emmet was one of Montgomery's most popular political figures. "He knows the citizens of

Montgomery County," a journalist wrote in 1967, "from the janitor to the bank president, who their relatives are, where they went to school, and what they're doing, and he greets them warmly when they come to his court." Following graduation from the University of Alabama School of Law in 1956, Emmet maintained a private practice in Montgomery until 1960, when he was elected to a newly created family court judgeship. There Emmet developed a keen interest in helping youthful offenders, juvenile delinquents, and abandoned children—a passion he maintained after being elected to the circuit court a few years later.

When Emmet received the petition for habeas from Orzell Billingsley and David Hood, he suddenly became acquainted with the painful and frustrating legal journey of a seventeen-year-old youth accused of murder in 1957. The legal merit of the petition impressed the judge, and he ordered James Hagen, the warden at Mt. Meigs, to bring Caliph Washington to his courtroom in the Montgomery County Courthouse. The date was March 16, 1971, the time 2:30 p.m.

History does not record what happened at the hearing, but the next day, March 17, Judge Emmet granted the relief that Caliph Washington "prayed for in his petition" before the court and long prayed for on his knees before his God. In a dramatic if not stunning decision, the judge ordered Washington released on a $5,000 bond. Later that day, D. A. Brooks, the shift commander at Mt. Meigs, released him to Orzell Billingsley and made note that the attorney had in his possession a signed bond by the proper authorities. Just after noon, Washington and Billingsley walked out of the doors of the prison system's receiving station and drove back to Bessemer. Caliph Washington carried his possessions in a brown paper sack. For the first time, he would ride home from Montgomery a free man.

TIRED AND WEARY, he arrived at his parent's home and was greeted by hugs and kisses from his mother and sisters. "I could have cried all over the world when I knew that my son was free," Aslee Washington said. The characteristically modest man told a newspaper reporter that he was not bitter about the time he served. "Sure I missed the things I would have had and been able to do if I'd been free," he said, "but I found out that I wanted to help other people as well as myself and I became a minister." Those years confined in prison and at times so close to death gave him a strong faith in God, and he reported that he was going to make up for lost time by "preaching the gospel" to those folks who would listen. Caliph Washington was free, but as he told the journalist on that day in March 1971, he did not know for how long.

Even with this lingering threat, Washington enjoyed his freedom. "It seems like I'm breathing fresh air for the first time in fourteen years," he said. Members of the defense committee gave him money to start a new life, provided him with a job at a local vending company, paid his legal bills, and continued to hold fundraisers. Washington began preaching in small churches in the Bessemer area, sharing God's plan of salvation and his own story of personal redemption.

But while he believed God had washed his sins away and given him a new start on life, Bessemer officials thought otherwise. District attorney Harry Pickens made new plans to "most definitely" put Washington on trial for a fourth time. "Time really hasn't changed what happened in 1957," Pickens told a reporter in March 1971.

For months to come, Pickens and other Bessemer officials held the threat of the fourth trial over the freed man's head. They warned him not to leave the area. To keep him close by, county officials denied his request for a driver's license. He relied on friends, family, and neighborhood teenagers to take him where he needed to go, just as long as they drove slowly, no doubt recalling the 1957 incident that resulted in his arrest. "You could always tell when Caliph was coming down the road because there was a whole line of cars behind him," one friend later recalled.

One of Washington's frequent destinations was the nearby campus of Miles College in Fairfield, where he took courses through ECHO (Educational and Cultural Help Organization). While there, he struck up a friendship with one of the teaching assistants, Christine Luna, a twenty-four-year-old worker with the VISTA (Volunteers in Service to America) program, part of Lyndon Johnson's "war on poverty." It was apparent from the beginning of their relationship that Luna and Washington could not have been more different. She was a small, pale Italian-American with long, straight dark hair, and was a devout Roman Catholic from Long Island, New York, who had received a solid education and worked as a registered occupational therapist. He was a hefty, dark African-American with a budding afro, and was a devout Baptist from Bessemer, Alabama, who had a limited formal education that he received through correspondence courses while behind bars.

Yet the minister and the therapist found common bonds through their strong Christian faith, their compassion for the downtrodden, and their individual efforts to overcome adversity and suffering. Luna struggled, to a small extent, with cerebral palsy, which affected her gait and balance. Washington suffered through thirteen years of imprisonment and gained his freedom but was living under the threat of a new trial and more prison time. Before they met, Luna read a small article about Washington's release, and she did not imagine him being such a large, powerful man. She was surprised at the way he introduced himself. "He asked for my phone number first," she later said, "before he even asked me my name."

In spite of her preconceived notions, Christine accepted Caliph's invitations, and the pair began an interracial dating relationship in the Bessemer Cutoff of 1971—where fears of race mixing and miscegenation ran deep in the community. For most residents, both black and white, it was an unusual, if not improbable, sight. Only four years earlier, in June 1967, the U.S. Supreme Court invalidated all laws prohibiting mixed race marriage in *Loving v. Virginia*, but Alabama continued to enforce its laws until a 1970 district court ended the practice in *United States v. Brittain*. Even then, the long-standing statute in the Alabama Constitution of 1901 prohibited the legislature from ever passing any laws to "authorize or legalize any marriage between any white person and a Negro, or descendant of a Negro." Although it went unenforced, the miscegenation prohibition remained on the books until Alabama voters annulled the law in 2000—the last state in the nation to do so.

FOR GENERATIONS, THE notion of a black man and a white woman remained an existential threat to southern society and provided justification for segregation, violence, and incarceration. During the 1970s, the social stigma of interracial courtship and marriage in Alabama compelled some people to fix their eyes upon Washington and Luna. "I was used to people staring at me," she later recalled, "and talking about me . . . and the way I walked." While he never lived in fear, Washington recognized, at some level, that someone staring might be an official from Bessemer who would remember him, arrest him, and place him on trial for a fourth time.

Nonetheless, he remained a free man the remainder of 1971, but the threat of indictment lingered in the shadows. In January 1972, Judge Ed Ball convened a new grand jury, and Harry Pickens brought the 1957 murder of James Clark before the eighteen citizens of the Bessemer Cutoff. Pickens summoned a host of witnesses to testify that a suspect ("whose name to the grand jury is otherwise unknown") murdered Clark. Witnesses included Bessemer police chief George Barron, former Lipscomb police chief Thurman Avery, Bessemer police officer O. E. Kendrick, sheriff's deputies Walter Dean and A. J. Wood, and "eyewitness" Mary Davidson. On January 14, 1972, the grand jury indicted Caliph Washington for "unlawfully and with malice aforethought" killing James Clark by shooting him with a pistol. Jefferson County sheriff Mel Bailey issued an arrest warrant, and on January 21, two sheriff's deputies arrived at the Washington home at 2232 Fifteenth Street North in the Pipe Shop community of Bessemer. They arrested Washington and took him across town to the Jefferson County Jail—back to where it started almost fifteen years before.

Within a few hours, however, attorney David Hood secured a $5,000 bond, and an emotionally ravaged thirty-two-year-old Caliph Washington returned home. On January 28, 1972, Caliph was arraigned in Judge Ball's courtroom, where he pleaded not guilty. Attorneys Orzell Billingsley and David Hood objected to the arraignment and argued that the court was without jurisdiction. "To arraign the defendant," Hood wrote, ". . . constitutes cruel, unusual, and unjust punishment."

In darker moments, Caliph Washington predicted that the prosecutors would never give up until they saw him back in jail for life. "They can't let me go free," he said at the time, "because that would be saying they held me unfairly." Yet his faith brought forth hope. "I pray that their minds will be opened and they'll see things differently." In reality, this latest action by Bessemer officials seemed part of an epic struggle for justice, fairness, and equality. "My problem began when I was born," he once said. A fair and just trial could not be had in Bessemer, he believed, because of the racist attitudes and actions of police officers and jurors from 1957 onward.

Orzell Billingsley, the champion of forgotten black men, vowed to fight for Washington's release all the way to the U.S. Supreme Court, because his client was not guilty. "Heretofore," he said, "we've only received illegal trials at the Bessemer Circuit Court, but we'll get by that and get him free." He and Hood filed a petition for removal to Federal Judge Clarence Allgood to have Washington's case moved from the country court in Bessemer to the federal court in Birmingham. The attorneys had to prove to the federal court that this action was warranted. They restated the same well-worn arguments: (1) as an indigent, Caliph had been denied his right to counsel; (2) the state had violated the defendant's right to a speedy trial; (3) his years of confinement without trial was cruel and unusual punishment; (4) the selection of grand and petit jurors was discriminatory and violated the due process clause; and (5) Washington had been denied civil rights guaranteed under the Civil Rights Act of 1964 and the U.S. Constitution.

While awaiting a decision, Judge Ball moved Caliph's fourth trial to March 8. On February 23, 1972, Judge Allgood denied the petition and sent the case back to Bessemer for trial. In response, Hood filed a motion for emergency relief to Judge Allgood and requested a stay on any trial of Caliph Washington while an appeal was heard by the U.S. Court of Appeals for the Fifth Circuit. Allgood denied the motion. The trial could go forward.

But on March 8, 1972, the day the trial was scheduled to begin, Judge Ball decided, for unclear reasons, to move it to May 22, 1972. In the meantime, the Fifth Circuit dismissed the appeal of Judge Allgood's decision because Washington's lawyers failed to "timely docket the appeal within the time fixed by the rules." Regardless, the trial never began on May 22 or in the months to follow. On October 12, 1972, Judge

Ball wrote that legal action in Caliph Washington's case was still pending before the Fifth Circuit on the matter of "remandment" of his cause. "It is hereby ordered," he wrote, "that this case not be reset until this matter is resolved or upon the request of the district attorney." The Fifth Circuit, however, took no further action, leaving the decision to try Caliph Washington a fourth time up to Harry Pickens.

As 1972 yielded to 1973, a period in which the dark clouds of Watergate began to shadow the nation, Pickens had still scheduled no trial. That same year Governor George Wallace appointed him to a circuit judgeship in the Bessemer Cutoff. "I'll miss being a district attorney," Pickens said at the time, but the new job would carry a great responsibility to the public that required "more dedication on my part than ever." When Pickens left the district attorney's office, he passed along the case file for the fourth trial of Caliph Washington to his successor in the Bessemer Cutoff, Dan Reynolds. Years later, U. W. Clemon said he believed the district attorney's office was looking for a way to save face in the Washington matter. "But it became clear," he added, "that they were not going to save face, but they were still reluctant to dismiss the case." So the case stayed active—leaving Caliph Washington with no closure.

THE YEAR 1974 saw the first resignation of an American president, and locally it was the year that Jess "Big Daddy" Lanier closed his political career and chose not seek reelection as mayor of Bessemer following eighteen years in the position. "The city needs a rest from me," he said, "and I need a rest from it." Before the election, Bessemer's commissioner of public improvements, Tom Ashley, resigned after a grand jury indicted him for "misconduct of a public officer." Apparently, Ashley ordered Bessemer city workers to perform jobs, billed the city for the work, and then pocketed the funds. Lanier's retirement and Ashley's resignation marked the beginning of slow, simmering political unrest that would boil over by the end of the decade.

Jess Lanier picked fellow city commissioner, Ed Porter, as his successor, but the political drama would come over who would succeed Porter as commissioner of public safety and govern Chief Barron and the Bessemer Police Department. In an unusual role reversal, Aubrey "Snuffy" Garrett, a ten-year veteran of the force, won the closely contested election in 1974 and found himself serving as boss to his former boss. Garrett later claimed that the main reason he resigned from the police force to run for the commission was because Barron was a tyrannical bully. "Barron was not a very well-liked person," he wrote, "and his reputation had been fractured by years of underhanded incidents." Another Bessemer policeman recalled that if someone refused to do what Barron asked, or even disagreed with something he said, "he would have your home staked out and put under surveillance on a 24-hour basis until he felt you abided by his wishes. He was a very cruel man." After the election, Garrett remembered telling Barron that he could keep his job as chief if he stopped taking payoffs and bribes from the various forces of illegal activity in Bessemer. Barron agreed, but the new commissioner believed from that day forward the chief began working toward "how he could cause my defeat in four years."

The 1978 election proved a brutal contest between Garrett and the man he defeated four years before, Max Williams—a used car salesman and the former police chief in the nearby municipality of Brownsville. Williams, with his dark curly hair and homespun humor, described himself as the "common man's man, compassionate above all." But threats of physical violence and intimidation on both sides marred the election. Garrett later claimed that George Barron and his wife worked behind the scenes to sabotage his campaign by spreading rumors in the Italian and black communities that Snuffy Garrett hated "dagos" and "niggers." In addition, Garrett believed that the chief enlisted black taxicab and jitney drivers around town to transport black voters to the polls on election day with marked ballots. Someone, he claimed, paid black preachers thousands of dollars to endorse Williams in front of their congregations.

When the election results came in, Williams won. But he alienated many voters in a campaign that divided the city and the police department, which he would now oversee. He believed that leaders in the Bessemer Police Department had done little to clean up the vice that still ran rampant throughout Bessemer. The city was as it always had been—corrupt, vice ridden, and violent. The new commissioner decided to change that by forming his own vice squad that would report directly to him and not to Chief Barron. "He told me he'd run the vice squad," Barron later said, "and I could run the rest of the department and what the vice squad did was essentially none of my business." Williams used a small area on the third floor of the city hall—just down the hall from his office, but far from the police station—to house the squad. Officers in the police department divided over the issue between the Barron loyalists and the Williams faction—some stayed out of the fray and maintained a professional decorum. Almost immediately, Williams later claimed, he began receiving death threats.

IT WAS JUST one year after the bitterly contested election that Dan Reynolds, in 1979, took Harold Pickens's place as a circuit judge and handed the Caliph Washington file to William A. "Pete" Short, who became district attorney on April 27, 1979. Five days later, however, Short's attention would focus on the most "horrible, unthinkable" event in Bessemer's violence-filled history.

Just after 7 a.m. on May 2, Gene Lint, the executive assistant to the mayor, stopped at the Bessemer Post Office and picked up the mail—an errand he did every weekday morning before going to his office in City Hall. A package in the mail that day was stamped return to sender with the office of the new commissioner of public safety, Max Williams, written as the return address. Lint brought the package into Max Williams's office, where Clifford Hill, a Bessemer police officer, was chatting with the commissioner.

Lint placed the box in front of Williams, who was sitting behind his desk. He struggled to open the tightly taped package. Hill stepped forward, pulled out a pocket knife, and said, "Let me see it." As he sliced through the tape, the package exploded. It was 7:39 a.m. Hill died instantly. Barely able to see and missing his left hand, Williams cried out, "Oh God! Who could do anything like this? Help me!" At the moment of the explosion, Lint recalled, "Everything went black. I couldn't see anything. I couldn't hear anything." Inside that package that he unwittingly delivered was dynamite, nails, screws, and BBs—designed to inflict maximum pain and suffering—and a frequent bomb-making technique of the Klan.

The blast shattered the windows and littered the street with broken glass. Police and firemen quickly sealed off the area. Those working in downtown looked on in horror. A few hours later, investigators looking for clues discovered Max Williams's fingers on top of a nearby building. The explosion that morning also shattered a strange quietude that had settled over the city in recent years. All the heavy industry that once dominated the local economy and added to the city's dirty appearance had all gone silent. Mills and plants with locked gates stood rusting. A ubiquitous canopy of kudzu covered the remains of once vibrant iron ore mines. Unemployment in the Marvel City hovered at 22.5 percent. Racial and economic tensions still ran high, but that was the norm in Bessemer.

According to most accounts, the investigation of the bombing was mishandled. FBI agents urged Bessemer officials to work methodically and thoroughly to track down the culprit or culprits. (Perhaps they remembered how state and local officials botched the investigation into the bombing of the Sixteenth Street Baptist Church in 1963.) But Chief Barron took charge of the investigation and made a haphazard rush to judgment, announcing that the bombing was a result of the bitter commissioner election in 1978. "You've got to remember," he said, "that we went through a pretty hot election here about eight months ago." According to Snuffy Garrett, this placed the blame on him and other former Bessemer police officers, including Tom Fullman and Carter Roberts. Barron chose the "direction for the investigation," Garrett argued, which required that divisive local politics provoked the assassination attempt on Max Williams.

This explosion produced a new level of mayhem and violence in Bessemer's long troubled history. Some locals believed that the bombing would have never occurred if the "strong-armed political boss" Jess Lanier still served as mayor, kept city employees under control, and kept any controversies out of the local newspapers. Nonetheless, within days of the opening of the investigation, Chief Barron announced a major break in the case and said the name of the suspect "won't be a surprise." Behind

the scenes, Garrett and Roberts gained immunity and helped investigators build the case against Tom Fullman, who was arrested and charged
with murder in the death of Clifford Hill. In Barron's mind, the arrest
closed the case. Max Williams, however, was convinced that the act was
not the work of one man alone but was part of a broader conspiracy.

When the first trial of the suspect ended in a hung jury in the fall of
1979, Williams's criticism of Barron boiled over into the public sphere.
When a jury in the second trial acquitted Fullman and the state cleared
all charges against him, Williams fired Barron. "I'm conducting an intense
investigation of the bombing," Williams announced, "and Chief Barron
has stood in my way and I feel his removal will be instrumental for me
to move forward in my investigation." A few weeks later, the Jefferson
County Personnel Board reinstated Barron as chief, but he soon retired,
citing health concerns.

The bombing became one of the great mysteries in Bessemer's long
history of violence, graft, and labor dispute. A reporter for the *Birmingham News* wrote that perhaps Max Williams, an outsider and newcomer
to Bessemer hardball politics, was "onto something somebody didn't
want him involved in." In 1981, two years after the bombing, Tommy
Thedford, one of Williams's vice squad officers and the ranking black
police officer in Bessemer, was shot and killed while trying to recover
stolen property. Some suggested that Thedford was "set up" to be killed.

Two weeks later, Max Williams and several other officers on the vice
squad were indicted by a federal grand jury for civil rights violations,
including torturing prisoners with cattle prods and beating suspects with
rubber hoses. At the trial, a number of witnesses came forward to testify
of the sadistic cruelty of Williams's small band of lawmen, who called
their torture sessions with black prisoners "prayer meetings." Vice squad
agents allegedly picked up seventeen-year-old William Kenneth Kennard, the same age Caliph Washington was in 1957, and tortured him by
holding a cattle prod to his groin until he confessed to a robbery he did
not commit. The officers repeated the same questions to the high school
junior over and over again. "I told [them] I didn't know anything and he
began shocking me," he said. "I hollered and screamed." Kennard's fingerprints matched none of the prints at the crime scene. Although an all-

white jury acquitted the commissioner of public safety and the officers of these charges, the political damage to Max Williams was devastating.

WITH AN EVER-FRAUGHT atmosphere of scheming, backbiting, corruption, and violence, the truth about the bombing of city hall and other enigmatic crimes may never be known. On the day George Barron retired in 1981, he told a *Birmingham News* reporter that he sensed an "uneasiness about Bessemer" that he had never felt in his over-thirty-five-year career as a policeman. "In the last three years, we've had a city hall blown away, two people maimed, two police officers killed, four officers indicted, a fire chief demoted, and a police chief resign. That sounds mighty abnormal to me." For Bessemer residents, the storm cloud lingering over the city was the unsolved bombing that led to, as one journalist wrote, an "endless variety of dark conspiracies involving crooked politicians, the mafia, a jealous husband, or a bizarre plot to control local government."

In 1990, four Bessemer police officers reopened the investigation but, according to the *Birmingham News*, their supervisors quickly stopped the inquiry for unclear reasons. In 2005, the United States Postal Inspector Service renewed their examination of the case in hopes of using new DNA analysis on the reconstructed bomb, but county officials in Bessemer explained that they had no materials, and no one seemed to know what happened to the evidence. The same was true in the Caliph Washington case—gone was Cowboy Clark's pearl handled pistol and everything else associated with the almost fifty-year-old incident. Earl Carter, the circuit clerk in Bessemer, searched throughout the courthouse, including the old county jail cells where Washington spent five years of his life and that were now used as storage. No evidence for the city hall bombing or the Washington case were found; both cases remained open in the judicial system.

Over thirty years after the bombing, in 2012, Aubrey "Snuffy" Garrett, who remained a key suspect, offered a different theory on who was to blame: it was George Barron who sent the bomb to Max Williams and tried to pin the blame on Snuffy Garrett. According to Garrett, Barron had his eye on the commissioner of public safety's seat in the election of 1982, and by killing Williams and sending Snuffy to prison for the crime, he eliminated his top two contenders for the position. The investigation into the crime was conducted more like a "cover-up than an investigation designed to uncover the real culprit." Nonetheless, Garrett chose not run against Max Williams in 1982, but George Barron did, and in the mind of Snuffy Garrett, that proved his head-scratching theory true.

In the end, both Barron and Williams lost the election to another former Bessemer police officer, J. I. "Joe" Jones. An embittered Williams continued to hope that "someone would pay for this someday," but no one ever did. The year following his defeat, George Barron, who was in poor health, died and was buried at Highland Memorial Gardens—a cemetery with the lush green grass of a well-manicured golf course. For months after the burial, according to Garrett, grass failed to grow over Barron's grave, much to the embarrassment of the cemetery's ground-keeper. It was later revealed that a member of Max Williams's vice unit stopped by every evening to pay his respects to Barron by urinating on the grass.

Reverend Caliph Washington returned to
Atmore Prison to minister to the inmates.

CONCLUSION
THE SALVATION CLUB

The trumpet sounds within-a my soul;
I ain't got long to stay here.

—"STEAL AWAY"

T HE BLACK MAJORITY in Bessemer stood by and watched as the white minority power structure tore itself apart. Asbury Howard said blacks throughout Bessemer saw the May 2, 1979, bombing as nothing more than "white folks doing it to each other." As the white political establishment crumbled during the 1970s and 1980s, Asbury Howard emerged as a pivotal leader in black political empowerment in the Jefferson County Cutoff. As the longtime president of the Bessemer Voters League, Howard fought for decades to end the repressive "understanding tests" and other restrictions on black voters in the city. The Voting Rights Act of 1965 prohibited those practices, and black voter registration boomed, opening the door for dramatic changes in Bessemer and other predominantly black municipalities around the state. Yet at the state level, rural whites continued to hold disproportionate power in the Alabama House and Senate. For decades, these representatives and senators balked at the idea of reapportionment based on population, leaving the composition of the Alabama legislature virtually unchanged since

1900. When mass growth in urban areas began to alter the demographic composition of the state, legislators maintained the system of inequality. The state's urban residents, especially in Jefferson County, were notoriously underrepresented.

In the early 1960s, a series of legal challenges to Alabama's apportionment system worked its way through the court system and culminated in the 1964 U.S. Supreme Court decision in *Reynolds v. Sims*. Although less than 25 percent of the Alabama population lived in rural areas, rural senators and representatives made up a majority of the state legislature. With votes in less populated rural areas having more weight than votes in urban areas, the litigants argued that Alabama's method of apportionment violated the equal protection clause. Ultimately, the Supreme Court justices agreed and established the notion of "one man, one vote." Writing the opinion, Chief Justice Earl Warren concluded, "An individual's right to vote for state legislators is unconstitutionally impaired when its weight is in a substantial fashion diluted when compared with votes of citizens living in other parts of the state." This opened an avenue for black political empowerment at the state level, but it took until 1970 before Thomas Reed and Fred Gray, the first two blacks since Reconstruction, were elected to the Alabama House of Representatives.

Predictably, the state of Alabama continued to delay, defy, and obfuscate court orders regarding apportionment, but in 1972, a three-judge panel composed of Frank Johnson, Richard Rives, and Daniel Thomas forced the state to comply based on the "one man, one vote" doctrine. "This court [acted] only when confronted with totally inadequate legislative response to, or complete disregard for, its constitutional mandate." A writer for the *Montgomery Advertiser* declared that the legislature was "the worst legislature in years—some say the worst ever." Nonetheless, the judges' reapportionment plan was implemented in time for the 1974 elections, and fifteen blacks won seats in the Alabama legislature, including U. W. Clemon, who became the state's first black senator in a century. In the statehouse, voters in the newly created 49th District, which included the Bessemer Cutoff and parts of Tuscaloosa County, overwhelmingly elected Asbury Howard as their representative.

During the late 1960s and early 1970s, Howard, the onetime Communist labor radical, carefully reinvented himself as Bessemer's nonviolent civil rights statesman. "I've never been a Communist in the whole history of my life," he said in 1968, and no one in Bessemer could truthfully claim that "I ever was." Evidence, however, suggested otherwise. Even with a long record of violent confrontations ("meet fire with fire"), he explained in the 1970s that he embraced Martin Luther King's philosophy of nonviolence. "Dr. King said that . . . we should out-suffer that man that attacks us," Howard added, "and that by not striking back we would work on his conscience." The man who once believed that violent labor unrest and civil rights activism were one and the same now separated the two issues.

Still, his colleagues in the Alabama House knew of Asbury Howard's reputation, and one later commented that he was the "the closest thing to a Communist that you could ever find in Alabama politics." But during the legislative session, Howard was subdued, neither sponsoring much legislation nor joining in many floor fights over controversial bills—even as the rural-versus-urban conflict grew increasingly volatile during the 1970s. But as the astute Alabama political writer Tommy Stevenson observed in 1982, every so often when the chamber was mired in a controversy or fighting over a bill, Howard would take the microphone and "in the booming voice of a tent evangelist" bring everyone in line with a "what-the-heck-is-going-on-around-here-anyway" sermon. "And in those rousing outbursts," Stevenson added, "everyone can get a glimpse of the power of a man who has traveled a long, tough road to get where he is today."

Howard quietly won reelection in 1978 and continued to be cautious in his approach to representing the people of his district. His successes throughout his career, he argued, were due to "my pressing hard, fighting hard, but realizing that it's going to take a long time to change things. If you think change is going to come overnight, you better stop fighting now." In 1982, as the white establishment crumbled in Bessemer, he urged caution. "We've got to be a little patient," he said, "[and] wait for things to change and time our actions right." He won reelection again that same year, but several months later, the U.S. Justice Department approved a new plan to reapportion the districts to reflect ongoing shifts in Alabama's population. The Alabama Democratic Party, which still dominated state politics, decided against holding new elections for the redrawn districts and appointed nominees for all the house and senate districts. Most of the sitting members of the legislature were renominated, but a few, including Howard, found themselves unceremoniously dumped by the party. In Howard's place, the Democrats nominated Bobbie McDowell, a younger black activist politician whom Howard handily beat at the polls in 1982. As one political observer wrote, Howard had done nothing wrong to be so "ignominiously shoved aside by the movement he helped create." The party had simply "bowed to the new political realities in giving the seat" to someone with energy and vigor. Asbury Howard returned to Bessemer and lived quietly until his death in September 1986.

HOWARD LIVED JUST long enough to see dramatic changes in Bessemer's political landscape. In 1983 and 1984, a group of black citizens and the U.S. Department of Justice challenged the legality of the "at large system" of electing the three city commissioners. They argued that this violated the Voting Rights Act of 1965 and "resulted in blacks having less opportunity to participate in the political process and to elect candidates of their choice." As part of a consent decree in 1985, Bessemer officials agreed to change the city form of government from long-outdated city commission to mayor–city council in time for the municipal elections the following year.

On August 3, 1986, blacks, who now made up 55 percent of voter registrations, went to the polls with the opportunity to elect a full slate of black candidates running for mayor and seats on the new city council. While Ed Porter was reelected for a fourth term, Bessie Pippens, a retired schoolteacher, became the first woman and first black elected to public office in Bessemer. "I would not like to dwell on my being the first," she said at the time. "It means my job is going to be harder." A few weeks later, three other black candidates—Quitman Mitchell, James McWilliams, and Thomas Tolbert—all won their respective runoff elections and gave blacks a majority on the new city council.

In 1990, Ed Porter chose not to run for a fifth term as mayor—as blacks now made up 58.4 percent of the city's population—opening the door for Councilman Quitman Mitchell to win election as the city's first black mayor. Quitman said his goal was "to make sure this city runs hard, runs long, and runs fair." Most of the whites gave up and moved away, so that by 2015, the proportion of white residents dropped to its lowest point since 1940, with blacks making up 80 percent of the population.

But even with increased equality, the end of legal segregation, and black political empowerment, Bessemer remained what it always had been: a place with one of the highest crime rates in the nation; a city with such endemic poverty that many of its citizens had no hope.

ALMOST A FULL century after she first appeared in Bessemer, Hazel the Mummy made her last visits to the city in 1994 and 1995. Her disappearance coincided with the fading of the old political order as the white establishment lost hope and abandoned the Marvel City. Nearly a century earlier, the notorious murderess had seen suicide as her only way out of the darkness of Bessemer. Hazel's death illustrated the hopelessness many people, both white but especially black, felt in this gritty industrial town. Beyond the legend, the real story of her life was just as unnervingly tragic.

In the days leading up to the Christmas of 1906, newspapers reported that a "carnival of crime" occurred in Birmingham and Bessemer. In less than forty-eight hours, the "tragedies were unusually fruitful," with seven murders, two accidental deaths, one deadly assault (the victim was not expected to live), and two suicides. Among the dead was one Maggie Farris of Bessemer, who took her own life by drinking arsenic. The date, manner of death, and last name all pointed to Hazel. Her corpse was taken to Vermillion & Adams Furniture Store in downtown, where the owner William E. C. Vermillion, the city's amateur undertaker, placed her in a coffin to await family to claim her body. But they never came. When her corpse mummified, Vermillion decided to recoup some of his costs by propping her coffin in a corner and, in carnival-style fashion, charging curious locals a dime to view the body.

Yet, Bessemer's leaders were unhappy with Vermillion's mummy, and following a lengthy debate, the city council passed an ordinance in October 1907 that required the burial of all bodies soon after death. As the *Montgomery Advertiser* reported, Vermillion sold Maggie Farris, shipped her remains on the Alabama Great Southern Railroad to Meridian, Mississippi, and ended the ill feelings aroused by her presence in the Marvel City. By most accounts, Orlando Clayton Brooks, an elusive twenty-three-year-old traveling salesman and would-be entertainer, paid Vermillion $25 for the corpse. Soon after purchasing Ms. Farris, Brooks purportedly stored the body in Nashville while he traveled to Louisville, Kentucky, and searched in vain for the family of the mummified murderess. It was all a farce. No mass shooting of four police officers occurred on August 16, 1905, as Brooks claimed, or any other date in early-twentieth-century Louisville. Brooks simply invented the story to attract thousands of paying customers curious to see a mummy.

In 1911, Brooks placed a classified advertisement in the *Tennessean* newspaper in Nashville inviting locals to come see the all-natural, non-petrified, and mummified human flesh of Hazel Farris for 10 cents. In the years that followed, he joined several traveling shows and toured the country as a carnival barker for "Hazel the Magnificent." During the quarter century following her death, Hazel Farris retained her youthful appearance, leading Brooks to ask prospective customers, "Is she dead or is she alive?" Hazel appeared to be a real-life sleeping beauty. When she was finally returned to Alabama, hundreds of citizens from Bessemer flocked to see what Brooks described as the "Great American Wonder" and an exhibit that helped scientists reclaim the lost art of Egyptian mummification. No doubt, Brooks wanted to make money from the American public's fascination with Egyptian mummies—a captivation that led to the popularity of mummy films, plays, news stories, and literature.

The most noteworthy of the latter was Bram Stoker's gothic horror novel *The Jewel of the Seven Stars*. When the central character first viewed the unwrapped mummy, he proclaimed:

Then, and then only, did the full horror of the whole thing burst upon me! There, in the full glare of the light, the whole material and sordid side of death seemed startlingly real. . . . I felt a rush of shame sweep over me. It was not right that we should be there, gazing with irreverent eyes on such unclad beauty: it was indecent; it was almost sacrilegious!

Unlike Stoker's fictional character, Orlando Clayton Brooks had no ethical misgivings about displaying Farris's mummified body and justified his exploitation as a moral exhibit for the good of science and humanity.

In 1917, *Billboard* magazine described Hazel Farris as a "mystifying attraction" and described Brooks as a "whirlwind wonder" on the entertainment circuit with Rutherford Traveling Shows. With his wife, Girlie "Alabama Blossom" Brooks, he performed three shows: the farcical play *Why Smith Left Home*, "Spidora" (an illusion featuring Girlie as a giant spider with a human's head), and "Hazel the Magnificent." For years, the couple traveled throughout the country, visiting hundreds of small towns with Hazel strapped to the running board of a Model T Ford. By the early 1930s, much like the ebullient roar of the 1920s, Hazel's beauty faded as her body dehydrated and took on a macabre leathery appearance. Brooks now traveled alone in a gray Oldsmobile with his mummy still strapped to the car, but what become of his wife, the lovely Alabama Blossom, was unknown. "Hazel is an old established show," O. C. Brooks wrote a few years later, "known to most all showmen and is such a wonderful drawing card and money getter that I can get on most any show." He later estimated earning well over a million dollars on Hazel, but he spent it all over the years. "I have been . . . perhaps a fool with money. I GET IT and I know I CAN GET IT," he wrote in 1942. "For that reason I won't realize the value of it until it's gone and the season ends."

In the years following World War II, age and alcohol caught up with Brooks, and his peripatetic travels with his self-enthroned "queen" grew less frequent. Destitute and living in squalor, he slept in an elevated bed above Hazel—his only possession of value. It was there that he died in his sleep in 1950. He left the mummy to Luther Brooks, a young nephew in Nashville who housed her in the family garage and displayed her from time to time in the 1950s and 1960s.

In 1974, a few curious Bessemer residents "rediscovered" the legend of "Hazel the Mummy" and negotiated with Brooks to bring her back to the Marvel City as a fundraiser for a new "hall of history" to commemorate the town's most renowned, and well-traveled, citizen.

Her arrival that October coincided with end of Mayor Jess Lanier's political career and the beginning of a period of unequaled discontent and upheaval in the city that would last for over a dozen years. For several years, each fall Hazel Farris returned to Bessemer, where she witnessed the passing of the old white power establishment and the painful decline of a city that was once the fourth largest in the state of Alabama. Six years after making her final visit in 1995, Maggie "Hazel" Farris's dehydrated corpse was cremated and mercifully laid to rest in Tennessee—an act that ended her strange mummified career as a sideshow attraction that began in Bessemer—the dark city where she took her own life and Bessemer stole her humanity.

HUMAN LIFE REMAINED cheap in Bessemer, symbolized none more so than by the travails of a young black man like Caliph Washington. After years of residing in the shadow of the big yellow chair, where he almost "rode the lightning" to eternity, Caliph Washington emerged from prison with a purpose, vision, and Job-like faith. His journey and mission reflected the words of the old Negro spiritual: "My Lord, He calls me. He calls me by lightning. He calls me by thunder. The trumpet sounds within my soul." It was as if he had been "called by lightning" to do God's work as a minister to the poor, the abandoned, and the hopeless.

He decided to invest his time in the lives of young black men and keep them from following the same path. In 1972, after saving up enough money from his vending job, he bought a mammoth fifteen-passenger Dodge Maxi Wagon van and drove through the most impoverished areas of Bessemer in search of those who were poor in spirit. When he saw black teenagers, he stopped and shared his redemption story and explained God's love to young men who had little hope of escaping Bessemer's relentless poverty. On one such excursion, as he drove near the Bessemer-Lipscomb dividing line—just a short distance from where he was arrested in 1957—he spied a teen playing basketball alone. He decided to stop the van and talk to him. The five-foot-three inch youngster was intimidated by the sight of this boulder of a man who introduced himself as Caliph Washington. The young man's name was Alphonso January. The sixth of twelve children in a single-parent home, January was slight and sickly, just recently having outgrown his childhood asthma.

Even with a big family, Alphonso was a shy loner with few friends. He listened when Caliph Washington said, "I want to tell you my story—about what happened to me—I don't want to see it happen to nobody else." Caliph recounted how he was arrested when he was just a little older than January; how he survived long years on death row; and how he found comfort through his belief in God. "The Lord was good to me," Washington said, as he shared his faith with the teenager. He encouraged January to accept this faith and give his life to Jesus Christ. "Being young then," January later recalled, "I wasn't thinking about the Lord. I just wanted to play basketball." Reverend Washington recognized that basketball would be a good way to affect the lives of black teens in the most impoverished areas of Bessemer, so he decided to form his own squad.

Caliph Washington called his team the Salvation Club, and like Jesus calling his disciples, he told Alphonso, "Come with me, we're going to make something out of you." With January as one of his first followers, he continued to drive through town and recruit teens to be "fishers of men" and shooters of hoops. Once he enlisted enough members to build the Salvation Club team, he began taking them to gyms in the area for games with other teams. He became the father to scores of fatherless young men, and he spent long hours bringing them to church and encouraging them to be disciplined and self-controlled and to keep away from drugs, alcohol, and foul language. Wherever he was—in the van, on the street, on a basketball court, in a grocery store, or at the mall—Washington was smiling, talking, sharing, and praying. "You don't have to be out here," he would tell a young man he just met. "There's a better way."

Apart from his ministry, Caliph Washington continued to make a living at the vending company and later at a television station. He accepted a part-time call to serve as pastor of the tiny St. John's Missionary Baptist

Church in Lipscomb—not far from where Thurman Avery and Cowboy Clark had their stakeout in 1957. On Sundays, he preached fearless Gospel-tugging sermons to his church members, including the Salvation Club teens and other young people from the community, and later with his wife and six children in the audience. Through his faith and ministry, he found peace and hope, a kind that only a man who climbed from an airtight cage of hopelessness could understand. A big man with a bigger faith, Washington explained that even through fifteen years of solitude, he was never alone. "God was always with me," he said. "His faith allowed him to move beyond bitterness," his son Michael Washington once said. "He could hear the voice of God in all he did."

As the twentieth century came to a fitful close, Caliph Washington had witnessed the fruits of the civil rights movement as blacks made tremendous strides towards equality and gains in political power and participation. But the horrors of years of sedentary confinement, where he had no exercise and poor nutrition, took its toll on his body—he was overweight and battled against diabetes and high blood pressure. As one friend recalled in more human terms, "Racism didn't kill him, but a bad diet did."

Caliph Washington died on May 24, 2001. "The things he did may not seem monumental," Christine Washington said later, "but they were things important to many people. Everything he did was with love." He was a man who "endured incredible suffering due to injustice," she added, and one who "let God work through him to bring a message of peace and reconciliation to others." She believed his legacy was in the "many souls God converted and called to the ministry through him. This legacy lives on in all of our lives."

EVEN THOUGH CALIPH Washington was finally free of this world, the charges against him were still alive. The case file continued to be passed down in Bessemer to each subsequent district attorney, and Judge Ball's case records remained in the office of each of his successors. A few weeks after Washington's death, Circuit Court Judge Mac Parsons pulled the box of old legal files from a high shelf in the outer office of his chambers in the Jefferson County Courthouse in Bessemer. The affable Parsons, who grew up in poverty near Bessemer, was a tireless advocate for the poor and homeless. The white judge read through the long neglected files related to the open indictment against Caliph Washington, which was still considered an active case in the judicial system. On June 21, 2001, with the lightning stroke of his pen, he dismissed the case that began over forty-four years earlier in that parched summer of 1957.

NOTE ON SOURCES

THE LIFE OF a poor, barely literate black man in Alabama during the civil rights protest era is difficult to reconstruct historically, but those associated with Caliph Washington left long paper trails. By far, the most important sources used in this book were the thousands of pages of trial transcripts located at the Alabama Department of Archives and History in Montgomery—particularly the three *State v. Washington* cases held in 1957, 1959, and 1970. Former U.S. Supreme Court Justice Oliver Wendell Holmes, Jr., once said that "Lawyers spend a great deal of their time shoveling smoke," perhaps suggesting that attorneys spend too much time in minutia and never moving the case towards a speedy conclusion. But for a historian, as opposed to an aggravated jurist, that "smoke" provided rich personal and legal details most researchers rarely find. For example, instead of driving a generic sedan, Caliph Washington is driving a two-tone, crystal-green-metallic-over-mist-green 1950 Chevrolet Styleline sedan. More importantly, we can read the words of witnesses, accusers, and the defendant. We might even gain a new appreciation of the probing questions of lawyers, but then again, maybe not.

These trial records, combined with newspaper sources and endless mounds of legal documents composed by lawyers, judges, and assorted paper-pushers, created tedious repetition in the citations. While rhetorical redundancies work well for baseball great Yogi Berra ("we made too many wrong mistakes"), they leave readers of footnotes dithering in a cockeyed monotony of repetitiveness—a frustration that led author Frank Sullivan to once write, "I'll be damned if I read any more of your footnotes."

With this devil lurking in the details, the author and the editors at Liveright agreed to omit the repetitive citations and the long "garlands of ibids" that were garnishing the notes in every chapter. An extensive bibliography follows this essay on sources, but the following are the vital sources in this manuscript:

All the court documents related to Caliph Washington are available at the Alabama Department of Archives and History, the Birmingham Public Library Department of Archives and Manuscripts, and the National Archives in East Point, Georgia. Other key legal documents are located in the Papers of the NAACP (Microfilm Edition, Part 23: Legal Department Case Files, 1956-1965), and in the American Civil Liberties Union Southern Regional Office Records in the McCain Library and Archives at the University of Southern Mississippi.

Fortunately, newspapers throughout the country provided coverage of the trials of Caliph Washington, but the three local papers, *Birmingham News*, *Birmingham Post-Herald*, and *Birmingham World* had the most extensive articles.

Great insight into the careers of George Barron, Lawton "Stud" Grimes, James Hammonds, Asbury Howard, and Rudy Pipolo can be found in the FBI's surveillance files obtained through Freedom of Information Act requests. The grand jury depositions in the Hammonds investigation provided significant details into the district attorney's nefarious schemes and illegal activities. These files are located in James Hammonds's Alabama State Bar Association membership file located in the state archives.

Many people gave generously of their time for interviews and conversations with the author, including Edith Boswell Clark, Mason Clark, U. W. Clemon, Helen Cooley, Chriss Doss, Wilson Fallin, Alphonso January, Camille Morgan, David Orange, Eileen Walbert, Christine Washington, Michael Washington, and Abraham Woods. Other interviews were also helpful, including those at W. S. Hoole Special Collections at the University of Alabama, Southern Oral History Program Collection at the University of North Carolina, United Steelworkers of America and Labor Oral History Collection at Pennsylvania State University Special Collections Library, and the oral histories located in Samford University Special Collection. The essential interview for this project was the lone oral history with Caliph Washington conducted by Horace Huntley in 1998. The transcript and video recording are located in the Birmingham Civil Rights Institute Archives.

Several memoirs offer a few scant details on Caliph Washington, including works by David Orange, *From Segregation to Civil Rights and Beyond: A Story of the Southland*; Wayne Greenhaw, *Fighting the Devil in Dixie: How Civil Rights Activists took on the Ku Klux Klan in Alabama*; and Charles Morgan, Jr., *One Man, One Voice*. Although Morgan used Washington's name to win a noteworthy legal victory, he did nothing to help win Washington's release from prison, but in this memoir he disingenuously takes some credit for his freedom. "And so it went," Morgan wrote, "beyond reason and prediction, in the struggle for equal justice."

No secondary works cover the life and trials of Caliph Washington. When he is briefly mentioned in a handful of these sources, it is usually in the context of the *Washington v. Lee* prison integration case. In addition, with so much focus on Birmingham and civil rights, Bessemer has been largely ignored by historians and writers—one reason for this is the surprising lack of primary sources related to the Marvel City's past. Robin D. G. Kelley's book *Hammer and Hoe: Alabama Communists during the Great Depression* provides a comprehensive look at the labor unrest in Bessemer.

Overall, black Bessemer, especially with Asbury Howard's leadership, fits somewhat into Jacquelyn Dowd Hall's notion of a "long civil rights movement" rooted in the racial liberalism of the New Deal era.

Although Hall's framework has limitations, it does provide some contextual links between radical racial unionism of the 1930s and the civil rights struggles of the 1950s and 1960s.

While many secondary sources helped with the history and context of the state of Alabama, none were more important than *Alabama: The History of a Deep South State* by William Warren Rogers, Robert David Ward, Leah Rawls Atkins, and Wayne Flynt; *Alabama Governors: A Political History of the State* edited by Samuel L. Webb and Margaret E. Armbrester; and the scholarly articles in the online *Encyclopedia of Alabama*.

Law review articles covered several legal issues—jury exclusion, capital punishment, law enforcement, imprisonment—that related directly or tangentially to Caliph Washington. The best source on the legal history of Alabama remains Tony A. Freyer's and Paul M. Pruitt Jr.'s article in the Fall 2001 *Alabama Law Review*, "Reaction and Reform: Transforming the Judiciary Under Alabama's Constitution, 1901–1975." In addition, articles in the periodical *Alabama Lawyer* helped shed light on the legal philosophy of several judges and lawyers during the civil rights era.

Several years ago, scholar Charles Eagles encouraged historians to "muster even greater imagination to write new histories" of the civil rights era in a more "detached, well-rounded, and balanced manner." *He Calls Me by Lightning* provides readers with imaginative insight into the life of a forgotten man who spent the civil rights era sitting behind bars in the jails and prisons of Alabama.

BIBLIOGRAPHY

MANUSCRIPT COLLECTIONS

Government Records Collections. Alabama Department of Archives and History. Montgomery, Alabama.

Alabama Attorney General's Office civil rights case files, 1940–1974.

Alabama Attorney General's Office correspondence, 1878–1996.

Alabama Board of Medical Examiners application for certificate of qualification to practice medicine, 1879–2012.

Alabama Department of Corrections state publications, 1845–2011.

Alabama Department of Corrections administrative files, 1885–1995.

Alabama Department of Corrections and Institutions records of punishment, 1928–1951.

Alabama Department of Corrections and Institutions death record of state convicts, 1939–1953.

Alabama Governor (1951–1955: Persons) administrative files, 1950–1955.

Alabama Governor (1955–1959: Folsom) administrative files, 1954–1959.

Alabama Governor (1959–1963: Patterson) administrative files, 1959–1963.

Alabama Governor (1971–1979: Wallace) administrative files, 1966–1979.

Alabama Governor, Administrative assistants' files, 1961–1972 and n.d.

Alabama Governor, Administrative files, 1958–1968.

Alabama Governor, Administrative files, 1962–1978.

Alabama Governor, Administrative files—miscellaneous, 1963–1979.

Alabama Governor (1959–1963: Patterson) appointments files, 1956–1962.

Alabama Governor appointments files, 1963–2011.

Alabama Governor (1939–1943: Dixon) clemency hearing case files, 1939–1942.

Alabama Governor (1943–1947: Sparks) clemency hearing case files, 1943–1946.

Alabama Governor (1947–1951: Folsom) clemency hearing case files, 1947–1950.

Alabama Governor (1951–1955: Persons) clemency hearing case files, 1952–1954.

Alabama Governor clemency hearing case files, 1951–1962.

Alabama Governor death penalty case files, 1939–2003.

Alabama Governor executive orders denying commutation of a death sentence, 1951–1959.

Alabama Governor executive orders for transfer of convicts to state asylums, 1931–1994.

Alabama Governor legal advisors' files, 1963–1972.

Alabama Governor legal case files, 1963–2008.

Alabama Governor public relations files, 1954–1970.

Alabama Governor's record of death case reprieves and commutations, 1939–1946.

Alabama Governor state institutions files, 1963–1979.

Alabama State Bar Association membership files, 1920–2004.

Alabama State Board of Medical Examiners examination questions, 1907–1969.

Alabama Supreme Court cases files, 1820–2011.

Public Information subject files—surname files, 1901–2010.

Private Records Collections. Alabama Department of Archives and History. Montgomery, Ala.

    Charles Morgan papers, unprocessed.

    Frank Murray Dixon papers, LPR33.

    George C. Wallace collection, LPR124.

    Hugh Maddox papers, LPR103.

    James Elisha Folsom papers, LPR34.

American Civil Liberties Union. Southern Regional Office Records. McCain Library and Archives, University of Southern Mississippi. Hattiesburg, Mississippi.

Bessemer Police Force. "Procedural General Order Manual, 1961." Bessemer Hall of History. Bessemer, Ala.

Concerned White Citizens of Alabama Collection. Birmingham Civil Rights Institute Archives. Birmingham, Ala.

Department of Archives and Manuscripts. Birmingham Public Library. Birmingham, Ala.

    Alabama. Tenth Judicial Circuit Court Grand Jury Records.

    Aerial Maps of Jefferson County.

    Orzell Billingsley Jr. Papers.

Dickinson, Horace. "Musings of a Country Cop." Special Collection. Samford University Library. Birmingham, Ala.

Federal Court Records. National Archives and Records Administration. East Point, Georgia.

Forensic Case File (Caliph Washington/James B. Clark). Alabama Department of Forensic Sciences (formerly Alabama Department of Toxicology and Criminal Investigation). Auburn, Ala.

Hazel the Mummy Clipping Files. Bessemer Hall of History. Bessemer, Ala.

Howard, Asbury. United Steelworkers of America and Labor Oral History Collection. Pennsylvania State University Special Collections Library. University Park, Pennsylvania.

Jefferson County Circuit Court Records (Bessemer Division). Jefferson County (Alabama) Jefferson County Records Facility (Ketona). Tarrant, Ala.

Newspaper Clipping Files. Department of Southern History and Literature. Birmingham Public Library. Birmingham, Ala.

Papers of the NAACP. Microfilm Edition. Part 23: Legal Department Case Files, 1956–1965. Bethesda, Maryland, 1997.

"Provisional Anatomical Diagnoses of Mr. James B. Clark." Jefferson County Coroner/Medical Examiner Office, July 12, 1957. Birmingham, Ala.

St. Paul Lutheran Files. St. Paul Lutheran Church. Birmingham, Ala.

Washington, Caliph. Military Personnel Records. National Personnel Records Center. St. Louis, Missouri.

———. Prison Records. Alabama Department of Corrections. Montgomery, Ala.

———. Prison Writings. Copies in possession of author.

PUBLISHED PRIMARY SOURCES

A Circular of Information about Bessemer City, Alabama (Bessemer Land and Improvement Co). New York: South Publishing Company, 1889. Special Collection. Samford University. Birmingham, Ala.

African American Heritage Hymnal. Chicago: GIA Publications, Inc., 2001.

"Bessemer, Alabama (Bessemer Land & Improvement Co.)." New York: South Publishing Company, 1891.

The Bessemer Weekly: Special Illustrated Edition, May 18, 1901. Copy in possession of author.

Engineering and Mining Journal. Vol. 90. New York: Hill Publishing Company, 1910.

"From the Rough: The Bessemer Story, 1887–1962." Copy in possession of author.

Lake, Clancy. "*Birmingham News* Report on Alabama's Prisons (1959)." Copy in possession of author.

Lucas, Fielding. *Geographic, Statistical, and Historical Map of Alabama.* Philadelphia: Carey & Lea, ca. 1822.

"Report of the Osborne Association, Inc. on the Alabama Prison System: Summary of Findings." New York: Osborne Association, Inc., 1949.

Seay, Noble H. *Report of Cases Argued and Determined in the Supreme Court of Alabama During the October Terms, 1926–1927, 1927–1928.* Vol. 217. St. Paul, Minn.: West Publishing Company, 1928.

Transactions of the American Institute of Mining Engineers. Vol. 19. New York: American Institute of Mining Engineers, 1891.

Younger, William C. *Alabama Appellate Courts.* Montgomery: Alabama Supreme Court Library, 1973.

GOVERNMENT DOCUMENTS

Alabama Official and Statistical Register. Alabama Department of Archives and History. Montgomery, Ala. *1907, 1915, 1919, 1927, 1931, 1935, 1943, 1947, 1951, 1959, 1963, 1967, 1971, 1975, 1979.*

Code of Alabama, 1940, 1953.

Code of the City of Bessemer, Alabama, 1954.

Congressional Record: Containing the Proceedings and Debates of the Forty-Third Congress, Second Session. Vol. 3. Washington, D.C.: Government Printing Office, 1875.

Conscientious Objection. Special Monograph, No. 10, Vol. 11. Washington D.C.: Government Printing Office, 1950.

Constitution of the State of Alabama, 1901.

Official Proceeding of the Constitutional Convention of the State of Alabama, May 21, 1901 to September 3, 1901. Wetumpka: Wetumpka Printing Co., 1940.

Simpson, Thomas. "Geologic and Hydrologic Studies in the Birmingham Red-Iron-Ore District Alabama." Geological Survey Professional Paper 473-C. Washington D.C.: Government Printing Office, 1965.

United States Bureau of the Census. Fifteenth Census of the United States, 1930.

————. Sixteenth Census of the United States, 1940.

————. Seventeenth Census of the United States, 1950.

————. Eighteenth Census of the United States, 1960.

————. Nineteenth Census of the United States, 1970.

————. Twentieth Census of the United States, 1980.

————. Twenty-First Census of the United States, 1990.

————. Twenty-Second Census of the United States, 2000.

————. Twenty-Third Census of the United States, 2010.

United States Congress. House Un-American Activities Committee Hearings, 1959. Washington D.C.: Government Printing Office, 1959.

United States Department of Justice. Federal Bureau of Investigation (FBI). Surveillance Files.

Bapbomb.

Barron, George.

Bessemer Voters League.

Billingsley, Orzell.

Grimes, Lawton "Stud."

Hammonds, James.

Howard, Asbury.

Howard, Asbury Jr.

Liuzza, Viola.

Pipolo, Rudy.

Washington, Caliph.

United States Statutes at Large. Act of March 1, 1875 (Civil Rights Act of 1875), Ch. 114.

COURT CASES

Batson v. Kentucky, 476 U.S. 79 (1986)

Beecher v. Alabama, 88 Sup. Ct. 189 (1967)

Billingsley v. Clayton, 359 F.2d 13 (1966)

Boggs v. State, 116 So. 2d 903, 209 (1959)

Boles v. Stevenson, 13 L.Ed. 2d 109 (1964)

Bowen v. State, 145 So. 2d 421 (1962)

Browder v. Gayle, 352 U.S. 903 (1956)

Brown v. Allen, 73 S. Ct. 397 (1953)

Carter v. Texas, 177 U.S. 442 (1900)

Cassell v. Texas, 339 U.S. 282 (1950)

Chessman v. Teets, 354 U.S. 156 (1957)

Cobern v. State, 142 So. 2d 869 (1962)

Coleman v. Alabama, 377 U.S. 129 (1964)

Clark v. State, 25 Ala. App. 30 (1932)

Dickey v. Florida, 398 U.S. 30 (1970)

Dockery v. State, 114 So. 2d 394 (1959)

Edwards v. Sard, 250 F. Supp. 977 (1966)

Escobedo v. Illinois, 378 U.S. 478 (1964)

Evans v. State, 461 U.S. 1301 (1983)

Fikes v. Alabama, 352 U.S. 191 (1957)

Francis v. Resweber, 329 U.S. 459 (1947)

Furman v. Georgia, 408 U.S. 238 (1972)

Gideon v. Wainwright, 372 U.S. 335 (1963)

Goldsby v. Harpole, 263 F.2d 71 (1959)

Gosa v. State, 139 So. 2d 321 (1961)

Hamilton v. State, 368 U.S. 52 (1957)

Hampton v. Oklahoma, 368 F.2d 9 (1966)

Holman v. Washington, 364 F.2d 618 (1966)

Jacks v. Sullinger, 284 Ala. 223 (1969)

Jackson v. Denno, 378 U.S. 368 (1964)

Jackson v. Goodwin, 400 F.2d 529 (1968)

Johnson v. State, 133 So. 2d 53 (1961)

Jordan v. Fitzharris, 257 F. Supp. 674 (1966)

Lee v. Washington, 390 U.S. 333 (1968)

Loving v. Virginia, 388 U.S. 1 (1967)

Manning v. State, 116 So. 360 (1928)

Miranda v. Arizona, 384 U.S. 436 (1966)

Needel v. Scafati, 412 F.2d 761 (1969)

Norris v. Alabama, 294 U.S. 587 (1935)

Parker v. State, 94 So. 2d 209 (1956)

Patterson v. Alabama, 294 U.S. 600 (1935)

People v. Dorado, 62 Cal.2d 338 (1965)

Phillips v. State, 41 Ala. App. 393 (1961)

Pointer v. Texas, 380 U.S. 400 (1965)

Reeves v. State, 88 So. 2d 561 (1956)

Reynolds v. Sims, 377 U.S. 533 (1964)

Robinson v. California, 82 S. Ct. 1417 (1962)

Salary v. Wilson, 415 F.2d 467 (1969)

Salary v. Wilson, 313 F. Supp. 1037 (1970)

Salary v. Wilson, 493 F.2d 627 (1974)

South Highlands Infirmary v. Imperial Laundry Co., 149 So. 106 (1933)

State v. *Washington*, 6 Div 227 (1957)

State v. *Washington*, 6 Div 524 (1959)

State v. *Washington*, 6 Div 66 (1969)

State v. *Washington*, 6 Div 127 (1970)

Strauder v. West Virginia, 100 U.S. 303 (1880)

Swain v. State, 275 Ala. 508 (1962)

Swain v. State, 380 U.S. 202 (1969)

Talley v. Stephens, 247 F. Supp. 683 (1965)

Thomas v. Texas, 29 S. Ct. 393 (1909)

Trop v. Dulles, 356 U.S. 86 (1958)

United States Security Life Insurance v. Clark, 40 Ala. App 542 (1959)

U.S. v. Brittain, 319 F. Supp. 1058 (N.D. Ala. 1970)

U. S. ex. rel. Seals v. Wiman, 304 F.2d. 53 (1962)

Walker v. Birmingham, 388 U.S. 307 (1967)

Walker v. State, 114 So. 2d 402 (Ala. 1959)

Washington v. Holman, 245 F. Supp. 116 (1965)

Washington v. Lee, 263 F. Supp. 327 (1966)

Washington v. State, 269 Ala. 146, 112 So. 2d 179 (1959)

Washington v. State, 274 Ala. 386, 148 So. 2d 206 (1962)

Washington v. State, 45 Ala. App. 173, 227 So. 2d 805 (1969)

Washington v. State, 46 Ala. App. 539, 245 So. 2d 824 (1971)

White v. Crook, 251 F. Supp. 401 (1966)

DIRECTORIES

Bessemer City Directory, 1911, 1913, 1916, 1920, 1924, 1938, 1940, 1946, 1948, 1951, 1953, 1955, 1957, 1959, 1960, 1961, 1963.

Birmingham Suburban Directory, 1965–1969, 1971–1980, 1982–1985.

Montgomery City Directory, 1957–1972.

Martindale's American Law Dictionary, 1906, 1908, 1910, 1915, 1917, 1919, 1927.

Hubbell's Legal Directory, 1913, 1922.

Polk's Birmingham City Directory, 1923.

Alabama Blue Book and Social Register, 1929. Birmingham: Blue Book Publishing, 1929.

The Book of Birmingham and Alabama. Birmingham: *Birmingham Ledger,* 1914.

BOOKS

Allison, Thomas. *Moonshine Memories.* Montgomery: New South Books, 2014.

Armes, Ethel. *The Story of Coal and Iron in Alabama.* Birmingham: Birmingham Chamber of Commerce, 1910.

Ashmore, Susan Youngblood. *Carry It On: The War on Poverty and the Civil Rights Movement in Alabama, 1964–1972.* Athens: University of Georgia Press, 2008.

Atkins, Leah Rawls. *The Valley and the Hills: An Illustrated History of Birmingham and Jefferson County.* Windsor Publishing, 1981.

Auerbach, Jerold S. *Labor and Liberty: The La Follette Committee and the New Deal.* Indianapolis: Bobbs-Merrill, 1966.

Ayer, N. W, and Sons. *The Story of the States.* Philadelphia: N. W. Ayer & Son, 1916.

Baker, Gordon E. *The Reapportionment Revolution: Representation, Political Power, and the Supreme Court.* New York: Random House, 1967.

Banner, Stuart. *The Death Penalty: An American History.* Cambridge: Harvard University Press, 2002.

Barefield, Marilyn Davis, comp. *Bessemer, Yesterday and Today, 1887–1888.* Birmingham: Southern University Press, 1986.

Barkan, Elliot Robert, ed. *Immigrants in American History: Arrival, Adaptation, and Integration.* Volume 1. Santa Barbara, Calif.: ABC-Clio, 2013.

Bartley, Numan V. *The Rise of Massive Resistance: Race and Politics in the South During the 1950s.* Baton Rouge: Louisiana State University Press, 1997.

Bass, Jack. *Unlikely Heroes.* Tuscaloosa: University of Alabama Press, 1990.

————. *Taming the Storm: The Life and Times of Judge Frank M. Johnson, Jr., and the South's Fight over Civil Rights*. New York: Doubleday, 1993.

Bass, Jack, and Walter DeVries. *The Transformation of Southern Politics: Social Change and Political Consequence Since 1945*. Athens: University of Georgia Press, 1995.

Bass, S. Jonathan. *Blessed Are the Peacemakers: Martin Luther King, Jr., Eight White Religious Leaders, and the "Letter from Birmingham Jail."* Baton Rouge: Louisiana State University Press, 2001.

Bennett, Linda, and Genevieve Ames. *The American Experience with Alcohol: Contrasting Cultural Perspectives*. New York: Springer Science+Business Media, 1985.

Blackmon, Daniel. *Slavery by Another Name: The Re-Enslavement of Black Americans from the Civil War to World War II*. New York: Anchor, 2009.

Bodenhamer, David J., and James W. Ely Jr., eds. *Ambivalent Legacy: A Legal History of the South*. Jackson: University Press of Mississippi, 1984.

Branch, Taylor. *Parting the Waters: America in the King Years, 1954–1963*. New York: Simon and Schuster, 1989.

————. *Pillar of Fire: America in the King Years, 1963–65*. New York: Simon and Schuster, 1989.

————. *At Canaan's Edge: America in the King Years, 1965–68*. New York: Simon and Schuster, 1989.

Brandon, Craig. *The Electric Chair: An Unnatural American History*. Jefferson, N.C.: McFarland, 2009.

Brooks, Jennifer. *Defining the Peace: Race, World War Two Veterans, and the Remaking of Southern Political Tradition*. Chapel Hill: University of North Carolina Press, 2004.

Brown, Richard Maxwell. *Strain of Violence: Historical Studies of American Violence and Vigilantism*. New York: Oxford University Press, 1975.

Brown, William Garrott. *The South at Work: Observations from 1904*. Columbia: University of South Carolina Press, 2014.

Burnett, Jason. *Early Bessemer*. Charleston, S.C.: Arcadia Publishing, 2011.

Carlton, David. *Confronting Southern Poverty in the Great Depression: The Report on Economic Conditions of the South with Related Documents*. New York: Bedford Books, 1996.

Carr, Jess. *The Second Oldest Profession: An Informal History of Moonshining in America*. Englewood Cliffs, N.J.: Prentice-Hall, 1972.

Carter, Dan. *Scottsboro: A Tragedy of the American South*. Baton Rouge: Louisiana State University Press, 1979.

————. *The Politics of Rage: George Wallace, the Origins of the New Conservatism, and the Transformation of American Politics*. Baton Rouge: Louisiana State University Press, 2000.

Carter, Donald A. *Forging the Shield: The U.S. Army in Europe, 1951–1961*. Washington D.C.: Government Printing Office, 2015.

Cash, W. J. *The Mind of the South*. New York: Vintage Press, 1941.

Cason, Clarence. *Ninety Degrees in the Shade*. Tuscaloosa: University of Alabama Press, 2004.

Cobb, James C. *Away Down South: A History of Southern Identity*. New York: Oxford University Press, 2005.

Cortner, Richard C. *The Apportionment Cases*. Knoxville: University of Tennessee Press, 1970.

Couch, William Terry. *Culture in the South*. Chapel Hill: North Carolina Press, 1934.

Cowie, Susan D., and Tom Johnson. *The Mummy in Fact, Fiction and Film*. Jefferson, N.C.: McFarland Press, 2002.

Crider, Beverly. *Legends and Lore of Birmingham and Central Alabama*. Charleston, S.C.: The History Press, 2014.

Cruikshank, George M. *A History of Birmingham and Its Environs: A Narrative Account of Their Historical Progress, Their People, and Their Principal Interests, Volume 2*. Birmingham, Ala.: Lewis Publishing Company, 1920.

Curtin, Mary Ellen. *Black Prisoners and Their World, Alabama 1865–1900*. Charlottesville: University Press of Virginia, 2000.

Daniel, Pete. *Standing at the Crossroads: Southern Life in the Twentieth Century*. Baltimore: Johns Hopkins University Press, 1996.

Dray, Philip. *At the Hands of Persons Unknown: The Lynching of Black America*. New York: Modern Library, 2002.

Dunbar, Paul Laurence. *The Complete Poems of Paul Laurence Dunbar*. New York: Dodd, Mead and Company, 1922.

Egerton, John. *Speak Now Against the Day: The Generation Before the Civil Rights Movement in the South*. Chapel Hill: University of North Carolina Press, 1994.

Fallin, Wilson Jr. *Uplifting the People: Three Centuries of Black Baptists in Alabama*. Tuscaloosa: University of Alabama Press, 2007.

Fairclough, Adam. *Better Day Coming: Blacks and Equality, 1890–2000*. New York: Penguin Books, 2001.

Fischer, David Hackett. *Albion's Seed: Four British Folkways in America* (America: a cultural history). New York: Oxford University Press, 1989.

Fitzgerald, Maurice J. *Handbook of Criminal Investigation*. New York: Greenberg Publisher, 1951.

Flynt, Wayne. *Poor but Proud: Alabama's Poor Whites*. Tuscaloosa: University of Alabama Press, 1989.

Frederick, Jeff. *Stand Up for Alabama: Governor George Wallace*. Tuscaloosa: University of Alabama Press, 2007.

Freyer, Tony, and Timothy Dixon. *Democracy and Judicial Independence: A History of the Federal Courts of Alabama, 1820–1994*. Brooklyn, N.Y.: Carlson, 1995.

Friedman, Lawrence M. *Crime and Punishment in American History*. New York: Basic Books, 1993.

Garrett, Aubrey. *Bessemer Bombing: How Absolute Power Corrupts*. Bloomington, Ind.: Xlibris Corporation, 2012.

Garrow, David. *Bearing the Cross: Martin Luther King, Jr., and the Southern Christian Leadership Conference*. New York: Vintage Books, 1986.

Gibson-Graham, J. K. *Re/presenting Class: Essays in Postmodern Marxism*. Durham, N.C.: Duke University Press, 2001.

Goldstein, Robert Justin. *Political Repression in Modern America from 1870 to 1976*. Urbana: University of Illinois Press, 2001.

Goodman, James. *Stories of Scottsboro*. New York: Pantheon Books, 1994.

Goluboff, Risa. *Vagrant Nation: Police Power, Constitutional Change, and the Making of the 1960s*. New York: Oxford University Press, 2016.

Grantham, Dewey. *The South in Modern America: A Region at Odds*. New York: Harper, 1995.

Green, Hardy. *The Company Town: The Industrial Edens and Satanic Mills That Shaped the American Economy*. New York: Basic Books, 2010.

Greenhaw, Wayne. *Fighting the Devil in Dixie: How Civil Rights Activists Took on the Ku Klux Klan in Alabama*. Chicago: Lawrence Hill Books, 2011.

Gurr, Ted Robert, ed. *Violence in America, Volume 2: Protest, Rebellion, Reform*. Newbury Park, Calif.: Sage Publications, 1989.

Harris, Carl V. *Political Power in Birmingham, 1871–1921*. Knoxville: University of Tennessee Press, 1977.

Harvey, Paul. *Freedom's Coming: Religious Culture and the Shaping of the South from the Civil War through the Civil Rights Era*. Chapel Hill: University of North Carolina Press, 2012.

Hayman, John. *Bitter Harvest: Richmond Flowers and the Civil Rights Revolution*. Montgomery: Black Belt Press, 1996.

Hobson, Fred. *But Now I See: The White Southern Racial Conversion Narrative*. Baton Rouge: Louisiana State University Press, 1999.

Hudson, Hosea. *The Narrative of Hosea Hudson: The Life and Times of a Black Radical*. New York: W. W. Norton & Company, 1993.

Huntley, Horace, and David Montgomery, eds. *Black Workers' Struggle for Equality in Birmingham*. Champaign, Ill.: University of Illinois Press, 2004.

Ingram, John. *Biographical Dictionary of American Business Leaders*. Vol. 1. Westport, Conn.: Greenwood Press, 1983.

Isom, Chervis. *The Newspaper Boy: Coming of Age in Birmingham, Alabama, During the Civil Rights Era*. Birmingham, Ala.: The Working Writer Discover Group, 2013.

Jackson, Harvey H. *Inside Alabama: A Personal History of My State*. Tuscaloosa: University of Alabama Press, 2004.

Johnson, Frank M. *Defending Constitutional Rights*. Tony Freyer, ed. Athens: University of Georgia Press, 2001.

Kelley, Mark. *A Powerful Presence: The Birmingham Regional Chamber of Commerce and the History of Birmingham*. Birmingham, Ala.: Birmingham Regional Chamber of Commerce, 2008.

Kelley, Robin D. G. *Hammer and Hoe: Alabama Communists during the Great Depression*. Chapel Hill: University of North Carolina Press, 1990.

Kennedy, Randall. *Race, Crime, and the Law*. New York: Vintage Books, 1998.

Kennedy, Stetson. *Southern Exposure*. New York: Doubleday & Company, 1946.

Kimball, Herbert H. *The Meteorological Aspect of the Smoke Problem*. Pittsburgh, Penn.: University of Pittsburgh, 1913.

Kellner, Esther. *Moonshine: Its History and Folklore*. New York: Weathervane Books, 1971.

Key, V. O. *Southern Politics in State and Nation*. Knoxville: University of Tennessee Press, 1984.

Klarman, Michael J. *From Jim Crow to Civil Rights: The Supreme Court and the Struggle for Racial Equality*. New York: Oxford University Press, 2004.

Levine, Lawrence. *Black Culture, Black Consciousness: Afro-American Folk Thought from Slavery to Freedom*. New York: Oxford University Press, 1978.

Leyburn, James G. *The Scotch-Irish: A Social History*. Raleigh: University of North Carolina Press, 1962.

Lipscomb, Bonnie. *Bessemer Portraits: Stories of Marvel City People*. Bessemer, Ala.: Kean Advertising Direct Mail, 1992.

Litwack, Leon F. *Trouble in Mind: Black Southerners in the Age of Jim Crow*. New York: Vintage Books, 1998.

Lomax, John A. *Cowboy Songs and Other Frontier Ballads*. New York: Sturgis & Walton Company, 1911.

Mazzari, Louis. *Southern Modernist: Arthur Raper from the New Deal to the Cold War*. Baton Rouge: Louisiana State University Press, 2006.

McDowell, Deborah E. *Leaving Pipe Shop: Memories of Kin*. New York: Scribner, 1996.

McKiven, Henry M. *Iron and Steel: Class, Race, and Community in Birmingham, Alabama, 1875–1920*. Chapel Hill: University of North Carolina Press, 1995.

Meltsner, Michael. *Cruel and Unusual: The Supreme Court and Capital Punishment*. New York: Random House, 1973.

Minchin, Timothy. *Fighting Against the Odds: A History of Southern Labor since World War II*. Gainesville: University Press of Florida, 2006.

Morgan, Charles Jr. *One Man, One Voice*. New York: Holt, Rinehart, and Winston, 1979.

Myrdal, Gunnar. *An American Dilemma, Volume 2: The Negro Problem and Modern Democracy*. New York: Harper & Row, 1944.

Noggle, Burl. *The Fleming Lectures, 1937–1990: A Historiographical Essay*. Baton Rouge: Louisiana State University Press, 1992.

Orange, David. *From Segregation to Civil Rights and Beyond: A Story of the Southland*. Baltimore: PublishAmerica, 2004.

Owen, Marie Bankhead. *The Story of Alabama: A History of the State*. Volume V. New York: Lewis Historical Publishing Company, Inc., 1949.

Owen, Thomas McAdory, ed. *John Owen's Journal of His Removal from Virginia to Alabama in 1818*. Baltimore: Friedenwald Company, 1897.

Packer, George. *Blood of the Liberals*. New York: Farrar, Straus and Giroux, 2000.

Painter, Nell Irvin. *A Narrative of Hosea Hudson: His Life as a Negro Communist in the South*. Cambridge: Harvard University Press, 1979.

Patterson, Haywood, and Earl Conrad. *Scottsboro Boy*. Garden City, N.Y.: Doubleday & Company, 1950.

Patterson, William L., ed. *We Charge Genocide: The Historic Petition to the United Nations for Relief from a Crime of the United States Government against the Negro People*. New York: Civil Rights Congress, 1951.

Permaloff, Anne, and Carl Grafton. *Big Mules and Branchheads: James E. Folsom and Political Power in Alabama*. Athens: University of Georgia Press, 2008.

Peters, William. *The Southern Temper*. New York: Doubleday & Company, 1959.

Pierce, Daniel. *Real NASCAR: White Lightning, Red Clay, and Big Bill France*. Chapel Hill: University of North Carolina Press, 2010.

Quigley, Christine. *Modern Mummies: The Preservation of the Human Body in the Twentieth Century*. Jefferson, N.C.: McFarland Press, 1998.

Ray, Louise Crenshaw. *The Color of Steel.* Chapel Hill: University of North Carolina Press, 1932.

Read, Frank T., and Lucy S. McGough. *Let Them Be Judged: The Judicial Integration of the Deep South.* Metuchen, N.J.: The Scarecrow Press, Inc., 1978.

Rogers, William Warren, Robert David Ward, Leah Rawls Atkins, and Wayne Flynt. *Alabama: The History of a Deep South State.* Tuscaloosa: University of Alabama Press, 1994.

Salmond, John. *Southern Struggles: The Southern Labor Movement and the Civil Rights Struggle.* Gainesville: University Press of Florida, 2004.

Schissler, Hanna, ed. *The Miracle Years: A Cultural History of West Germany, 1949–1968.* Princeton, N.J.: Princeton University Press, 2001.

Shields, Charles J. *Mockingbird; A Portrait of Harper Lee.* New York: Henry Holt and Company, 2006.

Siegel, Barry. *Manifest Injustice: The True Story of a Convicted Murderer and the Lawyers who Fought for His Freedom.* New York: Henry Holt and Company,

Sikora, Frank. *The Judge: The Life & Opinions of Alabama's Frank M. Johnson, Jr.* Montgomery: New South Books, 2007.

Smith, J. Clay Jr. *Emancipation: The Making of the Black Lawyer, 1844–1944.* Philadelphia: University of Pennsylvania Press, 1999.

Stock, Catherine McNicol. *Rural Radicals: Righteous Rage in the American Grain.* Ithaca, N.Y.: Cornell University Press, 1996.

Stoker, Bram. *The Jewel of Seven Stars.* New York: W. R. Caldwell and Company, 1904.

Sterling, Robin. *People and Things from the Blount County, Alabama Southern Democrat 1928–1933.* Raleigh, N.C.: Lulu, 2013.

Suitts, Steve. *Hugo Black of Alabama: How His Roots and Early Career Shaped the Great Champion of the Constitution.* Montgomery: New South Books, 2005.

Stewart, Bruce. *Blood in the Hills: A History of Violence in Appalachia.* Lexington: University Press of Kentucky, 2012.

Thomas, Ronald. *Detective Fiction and the Rise of Forensic Science.* Cambridge, Mass.: Cambridge University Press, 1999.

Thompson, Holland. *The New South: A Chronicle of Social and Industrial Evolution.* New Haven, Conn.: Yale University Press, 1919.

Thornton, J. Mills III. *Dividing Lines: Municipal Politics and the Struggle for Civil Rights in Montgomery, Birmingham, and Selma.* Tuscaloosa: University of Alabama Press, 2002.

Tindall, George Brown. *The Emergence of the New South, 1913–1945.* Baton Rouge: Louisiana State University Press, 1967.

Tuck, Stephen G. N. *We Ain't What We Ought to Be: The Black Freedom Struggle from Emancipation to Obama*. Cambridge: Harvard University Press, 2010.

Vandiver, Margaret. *Lethal Punishment: Lynchings and Legal Executions in the South*. New Brunswick, N.J.: Rutgers University Press, 2006.

Walker, James H. *Things Remembered! Stories about Western Jefferson County, Alabama*. McCalla, Ala.: Instant Heirloom Books, 2003.

Walker, Samuel. *Popular Justice: A History of American Criminal Justice*. New York: Oxford University Press, 1998.

Ward, Robert D., and William W. Rogers. *Labor Revolt in Alabama: The Great Strike of 1894*. Tuscaloosa: University of Alabama Press, 1965.

Warren, Gwendolin Sims. *Ev'ry Time I Feel the Spirit: 101 Best-Loved Psalms, Gospel Hymns, and Spiritual Songs of the African-American Church*. New York: Henry Holt and Company, 1997.

Warren, Robert Penn. *All the King's Men*. New York: Harcourt Books, 1996.

Watson, Katherine D. *Forensic Medicine in Western Society: A History*. New York: Routledge Press, 2010.

Webb, Samuel L., and Margaret E. Armbrester. *Alabama Governors: A Political History of the State*. Tuscaloosa: University of Alabama Press, 2014.

Webb, Walter Prescott. *Divided We Stand: The Crisis of a Frontierless Democracy*. New York: Farrar & Rinehart, 1937.

Westley, William A. *Violence and the Police: A Sociological Study of Law, Custom and Morality*. Cambridge, Mass.: MIT Press 1971.

Williams, Yohuru, and Jama Lazerow. *Liberated Territory: Untold Local Perspectives on the Black Panther Party*. Raleigh, N.C.: Duke University Press, 2008.

Wilson, William Julius. *The Truly Disadvantaged: The Inner City, the Underclass, and Public Policy*. Chicago: University of Chicago Press, 1987.

Wood, Amy Louise. *Lynching and Spectacle: Witnessing Racial Violence in America*. Chapel Hill: University of North Carolina Press, 2011.

Wood, Florence Hawkins. *Building Birmingham and Jefferson County*. Birmingham, Ala.: Birmingham Printing Company, 1941.

Woodward, C. Vann. *The Strange Career of Jim Crow*. New York: Oxford University Press, 2001.

Wyatt-Brown, Bertram. *Southern Honor: Ethics and Behavior in the Old South*. New York: Oxford University Press, 1982.

Yarbrough, Tinsley E. *Judge Frank Johnson and Human Rights in Alabama*. Tuscaloosa: University of Alabama Press, 1981.

ARTICLES

Beau, Hugo Adam, and Michael L. Radelet. "Miscarriages of Justice in Potentially Capital Cases." *Stanford Law Review* 40, no. 1 (November 1987): 21–179.

Brittain, Joseph M. "Some Reflections on Negro Suffrage and Politics in Alabama—Past and Present." *Journal of Negro History* 47, no. 2 (April 1962): 127–138.

Brownell, Blaine. "Birmingham, Alabama: New South City in the 1920s." *Journal of Southern History* 38, no. 1 (February 1972): 21–48.

Dumas, Royal. "The Muddled Mettle of Jurisprudence: Race and Procedure in Alabama's Appellate Courts, 1901–1930." *Alabama Law Review*, 58, no. 2 (Spring 2007): 417–442.

Feldman, Glenn. "Soft Opposition: Elite Acquiescence and Klan-Sponsored Terrorism in Alabama, 1946–1950." *Historical Journal* 40, no. 3 (1997): 753–777.

Fellman, David. "Cruel and Unusual Punishments." *Journal of Politics* 19, no. 1 (February 1954): 34–45.

Flynt, Wayne. "The Ethics of Democratic Persuasion and the Birmingham Crisis." *Southern Speech Journal* 35, no. 1 (Fall 1969): 40–53.

Forman, James Jr. "Juries and Race in the Nineteenth Century." *Yale Law Journal* 113, no. 4 (January 2004): 895–938.

Freyer, Tony A., and Paul M. Pruitt Jr. "Reaction and Reform: Transforming the Judiciary Under Alabama's Constitution, 1901–1975." *Alabama Law Review* 53, no. 1 (Fall 2001): 77–133.

Forde-Mazrui, Kim. "Learning Law through the Lens of Race." *Journal of Law & Politics* 21, no. 1 (Winter 2005): 1–30.

Fuller, Justin. "From Iron to Steel: Alabama's Industrial Evolution." *Alabama Review* 17, no. 2 (April 1964): 137–148.

———. "Boom Towns and Blast Furnaces: Town Promotion in Alabama, 1885–1893." *Alabama Review* 29, no. 3 (January 1976): 37–48.

———. "Henry F. DeBardeleben, Industrialist of the New South." *Alabama Review* 39, no. 13, no. 1 (January 1986): 3–18.

Hall, Jacquelyn Dowd. "The Long Civil Rights Movement and the Political Uses of the Past." *Journal of American History* 91, no. 4 (March 2005): 1233–1263.

Ingalls, Robert P. "Antiradical Violence in Birmingham during the 1930s." *Journal of Southern History* 47, no. 4 (November 1981): 521–544.

———. "Lynching and Establishment Violence in Tampa, 1858–1935." *Journal of Southern History* 53, no. 4 (November 1987): 613–644.

Johnson, Charles S. "Southern Race Relations Conference." *Journal of Negro Education* 12, no. 1 (Winter 1943): 133–139.

Kuhn, Roger S. "Jury Discrimination: The Next Phase." *Southern California Law Review* 41, no. 2 (Winter 1968): 235–328.

Lanier, Charles S., and James R. Acker. "Capital Punishment: The Moratorium Movement, and Empirical Questions." *Psychology, Public Policy & Law* 10, no. 4 (December 2004): 577–617.

Lee, Allison Herren, William W. Shakely, J. Robert Brown Jr. "Judge Warren L. Jones and the Supreme Court of Dixie." *Louisiana Law Review* 59, no. 1 (Fall 1998): 209–252.

Linder, Douglas O. "Without Fear or Favor: Judge James Edwin Horton and the Trial of the 'Scottsboro Boys.' " *University of Missouri at Kansas City Law Review* 68 (Summer 2000): 549–583.

Martin, John Andrew. "The Fifth Circuit and Jury Selection Cases: The Negro Defendant and His Peerless Jury." *Houston Law Review* 4, no. 3 (Winter 1966): 448–466.

"Negro Defendants and Southern Lawyers: Review in Federal Habeas Corpus of Systematic Exclusion of Negroes from Juries." *Yale Law Journal* 72, no. 3 (January 1963): 559–573.

Ogletree, Charles J. Jr. "Black Man's Burden: Race and the Death Penalty in America." *Oregon Law Review* 81, no 1. (Spring 2002): 15–38.

Plachno, Larry. "Greyhound Buses through the Years, Part II." *National Bus Trader* (October 2002): 27–34.

Pellegrino, Anthony. "*Batson v. Kentucky*, Its Kin and a Solution to the Problem of Race-Based Peremptory Challenges (or Jury Selection)." *Temple Law Review* 76, no. 4 (Winter 2003): 901–921.

Schmidt, Benno C. Jr. "Juries, Jurisdiction, and Race Discrimination: The Lost Promise of *Strauder v. West Virginia*." *Texas Law Review* 61, no. 8 (May 1983): 1401–1499.

Shores, A. D. "The Negro at the Bar." *National Bar Journal* 2 (1944): 266–272.

Stevenson, Bryan A., and Ruth E. Friedman. "Deliberate Indifference: Judicial Tolerance of Racial Bias in Criminal Justice." *Washington and Lee Law Review* 51, no. 2 (March 1994): 509–527.

Sydnor, Charles S. "The Southerner and the Laws." *Journal of Southern History* 6, no. 1 (February 1940): 3–23.

Trulson, Chad R., James W. Marquart, Craig Hemmens, and Leo Carroll. "Racial Desegregation in Prisons. *Prison Journal* 88, no. 2 (June 2008): 270–299.

Vines, Kenneth N. "Federal District Judges and Race Relations Cases in the South." *Journal of Politics* 26, no. 2 (May 1964): 337–357.

Westley, William A. "Violence and the Police." *American Journal of Sociology* 59, no. 1 (July 1953): 34–41.

Wiecek, William M. "Synoptic of United States Supreme Court Decisions Affecting the Rights of African-Americans, 1873–1940." *Barry Law Review* 4, no. 1 (Fall 2003): 21–38.

Wyatt-Brown, Bertram. "The Civil Rights Act of 1875." *Western Political Quarterly* 18, no. 4 (December 1965): 763–775.

ELECTRONIC SOURCES

"Alabama Department of Corrections History," Alabama Department of Corrections; http://www.doc.state.al.us/history.htm (accessed June 4, 2005).

Bass, Jack. "Frank M. Johnson Jr." Encyclopedia of Alabama. July 26, 2007; http://www.encyclopediaofalabama.org/article/h-1253 (accessed March 1, 2009).

Bennett, James R. "Alabama Department of Labor." Encyclopedia of Alabama. June 13, 2008; http://www.encyclopediaofalabama.org/article/h-1577 (accessed December 17, 2010).

Bergstresser, Jack. "Iron and Steel Production in Birmingham." Encyclopedia of Alabama. August 12, 2008; http://www.encyclopediaofalabama.org/article/h-1638 (accessed June 5, 2009).

Brown, Steven P. "*NAACP v. Alabama*." Encyclopedia of Alabama. March 21, 2008; http://www.encyclopediaofalabama.org/article/h-3259 (accessed January 7, 2015).

———. "*Reynolds v. Sims*." Encyclopedia of Alabama. February 10, 2009; http://www.encyclopediaofalabama.org/article/h-3259 (accessed January 7, 2015).

Carr, Brad. "Alabama State Bar." Encyclopedia of Alabama. November 9, 2008; http://www.encyclopediaofalabama.org/article/h-1860 (accessed January 7, 2011).

Curtin, Mary Ellen. "Convict-Lease System." Encyclopedia of Alabama. September 12, 2007; http://www.encyclopediaofalabama.org/article/h-1346 (accessed March 21, 2016).

Day, James Sanders. "Coal Mining." Encyclopedia of Alabama. February 18, 2008; http://www.encyclopediaofalabama.org/article/h-1473 (accessed March 23, 2016).

———. "Henry DeBardeleben." Encyclopedia of Alabama. May 5, 2015; http://www.encyclopediaofalabama.org/article/h-3675 (accessed March 25, 2016).

Doss, Faye. "Bessemer." Encyclopedia of Alabama. December 9, 2010; http://www.encyclopediaofalabama.org/article/h-2996 (accessed January 17, 2011).

Downs, Matthew L. "Great Depression in Alabama." Encyclopedia of Alabama. July 10, 2014; http://www.encyclopediaofalabama.org/article/h-3608 (accessed December 28, 2015).

———. "Massive Resistance." Encyclopedia of Alabama. July 28, 2014; http://www.encyclopediaofalabama.org/article/h-3618 (accessed January 7, 2015).

Draper, Alan. "Alabama AFL-CIO." Encyclopedia of Alabama. June 3, 2008; http://www.encyclopediaofalabama.org/article/h-1559 (accessed December 17, 2010).

Eskew, Glenn T. "George C. Wallace." Encyclopedia of Alabama. September 8, 2008; http://www.encyclopediaofalabama.org/article/h-1676 (accessed April 29, 2016).

Fair, Bryan K. "U.W. Clemon." Encyclopedia of Alabama. August 11, 2008; http://www.encyclopediaofalabama.org/article/h-1633 (accessed March 3, 2011).

Fallin, Wilson Jr. "Black Baptists in Alabama." Encyclopedia of Alabama. July 7, 2007; http://www.encyclopediaofalabama.org/article/h-1243 (accessed January 9, 2011).

Grady, Alan. "Albert L. Patterson." Encyclopedia of Alabama. January 15, 2008; http://www.encyclopediaofalabama.org/face/Article.jsp?id=h-1250 (accessed May 21, 2013).

Grady, Henry. "The New South." December 22, 1886. Bartelby; http://www.bartelby.com/268/10/17.html (accessed March 20, 2009).

Gryski, Gerard. "U.S. District Courts in Alabama." Encyclopedia of Alabama. September 3, 2008; http://www.encyclopediaofalabama.org/article/h-1673 (accessed April 21, 2016).

"Haywood Patterson," Scottsboro Trial Project, University of Missouri at Kansas City Law School; http://www.law.umkc.edu/faculty/projects/FTrials/scottsboro/SB_bPATT.html (accessed June 22, 2005).

Hebert, Keith S. "Ku Klux Klan in Alabama from 1915–1930." Encyclopedia of Alabama. February 22, 2012; http://www.encyclopediaofalabama.org/article/h-3221 (accessed February 4, 2015).

———. "Ku Klux Klan in Contemporary Alabama." Encyclopedia of Alabama. August 15, 2012; http://www.encyclopediaofalabama.org/article/h-3291 (accessed February 4, 2015).

Holt, Robert J. "752nd Tank Battalion Historical Narrative"; http://www.752ndtank.com/narrative.html (accessed January 5, 2005).

Huntley, Horace. "International Union of Mine, Mill, and Smelter Workers in Alabama." Encyclopedia of Alabama. May 28, 2009; http://www.encyclopediaofalabama.org/article/h-1044 (accessed January 11, 2016).

Jensen, Ove. "Battle of Horseshoe Bend." Encyclopedia of Alabama. February 26, 2007; http://www.encyclopediaofalabama.org/article/h-1044 (accessed January 3, 2016).

Kaetz, James. "Adamsville." Encyclopedia of Alabama. February 16, 2012; http://www.encyclopediaofalabama.org/article/h-3217 (accessed January 11, 2014).

———. "Aliceville." Encyclopedia of Alabama. May 30, 2012; http://www.encyclopediaofalabama.org/article/h-3260 (accessed January 11, 2014).

———. "Atmore." Encyclopedia of Alabama. July 15, 2011; http://www.encyclopediaofalabama.org/article/h-3217 (accessed January 11, 2014).

———. "Autherine Lucy." Encyclopedia of Alabama. November 9, 2009; http://www.encyclopediaofalabama.org/article/h-2489 (accessed May 3, 2016).

———. "Mount Vernon." Encyclopedia of Alabama. May 30, 2012; http://www.encyclopediaofalabama.org/article/h-3259 (accessed March 23, 2016).

Kelly, Brian. "Birmingham District Coal Strike of 1908." Encyclopedia of Alabama. February 22, 2008; http://www.encyclopediaofalabama.org/article/h-1478 (accessed January 14, 2016).

Key, Barclay. "Fred Gray." Encyclopedia of Alabama. April 15, 2008; http://www.encyclopediaofalabama.org/article/h-1510 (accessed April 19, 2016).

Ledet, Shannon Emeigh, and Richard Ledet. "Alabama House of Representatives." Encyclopedia of Alabama. January 6, 2015; http://www.encyclopediaofalabama.org/article/h-3649 (accessed January 23, 2016).

———. "Alabama Senate." Encyclopedia of Alabama. January 6, 2015; http://www.encyclopediaofalabama.org/article/h-3740 (accessed January 23, 2016).

Lee, J. Lawrence. "Alabama Railroads." Encyclopedia of Alabama. August 10, 2009; http://www.encyclopediaofalabama.org/article/h-2390 (accessed February 9, 2011).

Lewis, David W. "Birmingham Iron and Steel Companies." Encyclopedia of Alabama. July 8, 2008; http://www.encyclopediaofalabama.org/article/h-1597 (accessed January 14, 2016).

Lewis, Herbert J. "Jim." "Daniel Pratt." Encyclopedia of Alabama. June 12, 2007; http://www.encyclopediaofalabama.org/article/h-1207 (accessed January 9, 2011).

Maloney, Christopher. "Lipscomb." Encyclopedia of Alabama. May 14, 2013; http://www.encyclopediaofalabama.org/article/h-3455 (accessed April 19, 2016).

———. "Reform." Encyclopedia of Alabama. May 15, 2013; http://www.encyclopediaofalabama.org/article/h-3456 (accessed April 19, 2016).

———. "Treaty of Fort Jackson." Encyclopedia of Alabama. February 28, 2011;

http://www.encyclopediaofalabama.org/article/h-3026 (accessed April 19, 2016).

McKiven, Henry M. Jr. "United Mine Workers." Encyclopedia of Alabama. October 12, 2010; http://www.encyclopediaofalabama.org/article/h-2948 (accessed January 14, 2016).

McRae, David. "Free State of Winston." Encyclopedia of Alabama. June 5, 2008; http://www.encyclopediaofalabama.org/article/h-1850 (accessed April 18, 2016).

Roberts, Charles Kenneth. "*Patterson v. Alabama*." Encyclopedia of Alabama. January 7, 2009; http://www.encyclopediaofalabama.org/article/h-1899 (accessed January 7, 2015).

Schaefer, Robert M. "State Courts of Alabama." Encyclopedia of Alabama. October 7, 2010; http://www.encyclopediaofalabama.org/article/h-2947 (accessed January 25, 2011).

Schmidt, Greg. "Scottsboro." Encyclopedia of Alabama. May 6, 2009; http://www.encyclopediaofalabama.org/article/h-2129 (accessed March 30, 2015).

Schuppe, Jon. "Civil Rights Act Anniversary: Survivors Recall Attack During Alabama Sit-In." June 30, 2014; http://www.nbcnews.com/news/us-news/civil-rights-act-anniversary-survivors-recall-attack-during-alabama-sit-n142066 (accessed September 19, 2016).

Siebenthaler, Donna J. "Jefferson County." Encyclopedia of Alabama. October 16, 2007; http://www.encyclopediaofalabama.org/article/h-1370 (accessed January 15, 2011).

———. "Pickens County." Encyclopedia of Alabama. July 6, 2007; http://www.encyclopediaofalabama.org/article/h-1207 (accessed January 9, 2011).

Stewart, Robert C. "Bessemer Hall of History." Encyclopedia of Alabama. June 13, 2013; http://www.encyclopediaofalabama.org/article/h-3464 (accessed April 12, 2016).

"Sir Henry Bessemer, F.R.S., an Autobiography"; http://www.history.rochester.edu/ehp-book/shb/pface.htm (accessed November 26, 2011).

Suitts, Steve. "Hugo L. Black." Encyclopedia of Alabama. November 16, 2008; http://www.encyclopediaofalabama.org/article/h-1848 (accessed January 11, 2011).

Ward, Robert David. "Banner Mine Tragedy of 1911." Encyclopedia of Alabama. March 21, 2007; http://www.encyclopediaofalabama.org/article/h-1135 (accessed January 17, 2011).

Weaver, Bill. "Bryce Hospital (Alabama Insane Hospital)." Encyclopedia of Ala-

bama. June 5, 2008; http://www.encyclopediaofalabama.org/article/h-1564
    (accessed March 23, 2016).
———. "Peter Bryce." Encyclopedia of Alabama. March 14, 2007; http://www
    .encyclopediaofalabama.org/article/h-1109 (accessed March 23, 2016).
Wilson, Claire M. "Eutaw." Encyclopedia of Alabama. December 4, 2009;
    http://www.encyclopediaofalabama.org/article/h-2501 (accessed April 17,
    2016).
Woodham, Rebecca. "Arthur Davis Shores." Encyclopedia of Alabama. August
    16, 2008; http://www.encyclopediaofalabama.org/article/h-1644 (accessed
    March 17, 2016).

UNPUBLISHED MATERIALS

Bailey, Barbara Connell. "Ten Trying Years: A History of Bessemer, Alabama,
    1929–1939." Master's thesis, Samford University, 1977.
Davis, Christopher. "In the Pursuit of the Goal: A Biography of the Life of Ralph
    Galt." Bachelor's thesis, Samford University, 2003.
Frederick, Jeffery J. "Command and Control: George Wallace, Governor of Ala-
    bama 1963–1972." Ph.D. diss., Auburn University, 2003.
Galt, Ralph. "Memoirs of Ralph Galt or What Some Missionaries Do in Their
    Spare Time," copy in possession of author.
Grimes, Lawton Jr. "History of the Bessemer Police Department," copy in pos-
    session of author.
Lee, Frank. "Historical Review of the Alabama Prison System." Alabama Depart-
    ment of Archives and History, Montgomery, Ala.
Pye, David Kenneth. "Legal Subversives: African American Lawyers in the Jim
    Crow South." Ph.D. diss., UC San Diego, 2010.
Uhlmann, Jennifer Ruthanne. "The Communist Civil Rights Movement: Legal
    Activism in the United States, 1919–1946." Ph.D. diss., UCLA, 2007.

NEWSPAPERS/PERIODICALS

ABA Journal
Alabama Citizen
Alabama Journal
Alabama: The News Magazine of the Deep South
Anniston Star
Atlanta Journal-Constitution

Alabama Lawyer
Atlantic Weekly
Augusta Chronicle (Georgia)
Baltimore Afro-American (Maryland)
Bessemer Advertiser
Bessemer Tribune
Bessemer Tribune-Advertiser
Bessemer Weekly
Bessemer Workman
Birmingham Age-Herald
Birmingham Business Journal
Birmingham News
Birmingham Post-Herald
Birmingham World
Cincinnati Enquirer (Ohio)
Courier-Journal (Kentucky)
Crisis
Delta Democratic-Times (Mississippi)
Dothan Eagle (Alabama)
Ebony
Eugene Guard (Oregon)
Florence Times Daily
Galveston Daily News (Texas)
Garnett Journal (Kansas)
Greensboro Daily News (North Carolina)
Indianapolis Star (Indiana)
Jet
Lexington Herald (Kentucky)
Macon Telegraph (Georgia)
Marietta Journal (Georgia)
Mobile Press
Mobile Register
Montgomery Advertiser
Nation
National Police Journal
New York Clipper
New York Herald
New York Times

Oregonian (Portland)

Palm Beach Post (Florida)

Printers' Ink (New York)

Richmond Times Dispatch (Virginia)

San Bernardino County Sun (California)

Searchlight (Alabama)

Southern Courier

Southern Workman

St. Louis Republic (Missouri)

St. Petersburg Times (Florida)

Time

Times-Picayune (New Orleans)

Tuscaloosa News

Twin-City Daily Sentinel (North Carolina)

Waco Morning News (Texas)

INTERVIEWS/CONVERSATIONS

Ausbun, Danny. Oral interview by John T. Carson, n.d. Transcript in possession of author.

Chandler, King. Oral interview by Brenda and Steve McCallum. May 23, 1983. W. S. Hoole Special Collections. University of Alabama. Tuscaloosa, Ala.

Clark, Edith Boswell. Telephone conversation with author, June 19, 2006.

Clark, Mason. Telephone conversation with author, June 27, 2006.

Clayton, Bobby. Oral interview by Cliff Kuhn. July 17, 1984. W. S. Hoole Special Collections. University of Alabama. Tuscaloosa, Ala.

Clemon, U. W. Conversation with author, February 11, 2007.

———. Oral interview by Jack Bass. July 17, 1974. Southern Oral History Program Collection. University of North Carolina. Chapel Hill, N.C.

Cooley, Helen. Conversation with author, September 3, 2006.

Doss, Chriss H. Oral interview by author. June 4, 2005. Transcript in possession of author.

Ellalee, Elam. Interview by Marlene Rikard. August 21, 1979. Samford University Special Collection. Birmingham, Ala.

Emmons, Thelma. Oral interview by Brenda McCallum. August 26, 1984. W. S. Hoole Special Collections. University of Alabama. Tuscaloosa, Ala.

Emmons, Thelma Coleman. Interview by Marlene Rikard, March 3, 1980. Samford University Special Collection. Birmingham, Ala.

Fallin, Wilson. Interview by author. August 3, 2006. Transcript in possession of author.

Grace, Jesse. Oral interview by Cliff Kuhn. July 16, 1984. W. S. Hoole Special Collections. University of Alabama. Tuscaloosa, Ala.

Harris, Leola. Oral interview by Brenda McCallum. June 25, 1984. W. S. Hoole Special Collections. University of Alabama. Tuscaloosa, Ala.

Howard, Asbury. Oral interview by Jack Spiese. March 27, 1968. United Steelworkers of America and Labor Oral History Collection. Pennsylvania State University Special Collections Library. University Park, Penn.

Johnson, Frank M. Oral interview by Jack Bass and Walter DeVries, July 10, 1974. Southern Oral History Program Collection. University of North Carolina. Chapel Hill, N.C.

Morgan, Camille. Conversation with author, May 18, 2006.

Morgan, Charles. Oral interview by Andrew M. Manis, May 24, 1989. Birmingham Public Library Department of Archives and Manuscripts. Birmingham, Ala.

Orange, David. Oral interview by author, March 11, 2006. Transcript in possession of author.

Robinson, Mittie. Interview by Marlene Rikard, January 19, 1981. Samford University Special Collection. Birmingham, Ala.

Shores, Arthur. Oral interview by Jack Bass. July 17, 1974. Southern Oral History Program Collection. University of North Carolina. Chapel Hill, N.C.

Smith, Dorothy. Telephone conversation with author, June 30, 2006.

Smith, Katherine. Oral interview by Peggy Hamrick. October 18, 1984. W. S. Hoole Special Collections. University of Alabama. Tuscaloosa, Ala.

Walbert, Eileen. Oral interview by Horace Huntley. February 3, 1995. Birmingham Civil Rights Institute Archives. Birmingham, Ala.

———. Telephone conversation with author, April 27, 2004.

Wallace, George C. Oral interview by Jack Bass and Walter DeVries. July 15, 1974. Southern Oral History Program Collection. University of North Carolina. Chapel Hill, N.C.

Washington, Caliph. Oral interview by Horace Huntley. July 22, 1998. Birmingham Civil Rights Institute Archives. Birmingham, Ala.

Washington, Christine Luna. Oral interview by author. January 28, 2004. Transcription in possession of author.

Washington, Michael. Oral interview by author. June 24, 2005. Transcription in possession of author.

Woods, Abraham. Telephone conversation with author, January 13, 2005.

ACKNOWLEDGMENTS

I have been blessed throughout this project with invaluable and generous support. I would like to express my deep gratitude to Scott Cook of W. W. Norton, who took this manuscript's prospectus to New York and convinced the editors that this was a worthwhile project. Those editors, Bob Weil, William Menaker, and Marie Pantojan, edited, polished, and strengthened the manuscript.

Several friends, all writers and scholars, generously agreed to critique the entire manuscript, including the erudite historian John Mayfield, who helped me understand this civil rights–era story in the broader context of southern honor and manhood; and the exceptional jurist William Pryor, who patiently guided me through the complex web of legal analysis. Thanks also to Margaret Armbrester for her vital criticisms at various stages of the project.

Most importantly, I offer a hearty word of thanks to my friend and mentor Tennant McWilliams. Over thirty years ago, he challenged me, during a close reading of Robert Penn Warren's *All the King's Men*, to take up the "burden" of history and pursue a career as a scholar. Since then, he has served as a patient guide, enthusiastic encourager, steady advisor, and creative critic of this simple first-generation college graduate.

I am blessed to work at a university with such exceptional students. I mention just a few who inspired me throughout the project—this is, by no means, a complete list: Haley Aaron, Maria Aguilera, Jessica Barton, Kitty Rogers Brown, Lauren Doss, Jenna Edwards, JohnMark Edwards, Chris Fite, Charlie Graham, Deidre Downs Gunn, Amy Harold, Mary-Wilkes Harris, Jordan Jones Hays, Holly Howell, Bryan Kessler, Ryan Lally, Hunter Martiniere, Christina Mosley, David Murphy, Evan Musgraves, Tara White Odum, Bradley Patton, Thomas Richie, Chris Shaeffer, Celia Stewart Rouse, Brittany Stancombe, Mary Kathryn Covert Steel, Nicole Hardy Swann, Ricky Thrash, Chase Trautwein, Kim Addington Watkins, Jerrod Williams, and Lauren Ziemer. Three former students provided essential assistance early on in the project: Chris Davis, Ashley Grantham Martin, and Thomas Richie.

While she attended Cumberland School of Law, Lindsey Wade Bridges served as a crackerjack research assistant who tracked down people and resources that provided key information for each chapter in this book.

I also recognize the support of Laura Anderson, Marilyn Ball Armbrester, Leah Atkins, Albert Brewer, Earl Carter, Culpepper Clark, James C. Cobb, Helen Cooley, Harriet Amos Doss, Jack Drake, Charles Eagles, J. M. Edwards, Cynthia Fleming, Lawton Grimes, Jr., Horace Huntley, Chervis Isom, Alphonso January, Mike Logan, Hugh Maddox, Tom Noon, Keith B. Norman, David Orange, Craig Pascoe, June Reese, Jeff Roberts, Maury Smith, Robert Smith, Caroline Summers, Scott Walker, and Dawna Walsh. Thanks also to Eason Balch, Bob Corley, Glenn Eskew, James Hall, James Noles, Sylvia Rodrigue, Brad Walker, and Tony Wanamaker.

In addition, I am particularly beholden to Wilson Fallin for his invaluable and generous support—thanks for opening closed doors in Bessemer.

The man of many hats (historian, preacher, attorney, librarian, politician) and tales, Chriss H. Doss, spent hours and hours regaling me with stories about Bessemer and its colorful lawyers, judges, and politicians. He knew most of them. Doss's winsome descriptions and wise pontifications provided vibrant details throughout the manuscript.

I would like to express my deepest appreciation to the faculty and staff in the Department of History, especially Ivy Alexander for her vital role in the completion of this project. I also express my gratitude to a few of my friends and colleagues at Samford University, including John Carroll, David Chapman, William Collins, Roderick Davis, Julie Steward Fuller, Mike Hardin, Emily Hynds, Michelle Little, Glenda Martin, Susan Wells Murphy, Jodi Newton, William Nunnelley, Marlene Rikard, Jason Wallace, Clark Watson, and Andrew Westmoreland. I am especially indebted to Erin Stewart Mauldin for her vigorous editing and vital suggestions during the early stages of the manuscript.

A special word of thanks to James L. Baggett of the Birmingham Public Library Department of Archives and Manuscripts for his patient friendship and steady advice throughout this project. I also recognize the assistance of Mary Beth Newbill, Elizabeth Veatch, and Don Vesey.

The rich and abundant sources for this manuscript came from the vast collections at the Alabama Department of Archives and History in Montgomery, Alabama. While many of the archivists at the facility assisted my research efforts, I acknowledge the exceptional work of Norwood Kerr for his pivotal role in this project's development. In addition, I thank former student Meredith McDonough of the ADAH for uncovering several photographs included in this book.

I also recognize the invaluable contributions of the library staff at Samford University, especially Gale Barton, Cheryl Cecil, Rachel Cohen, Kimmetha Herndon, Lori Northrup, Jennifer Taylor, Carla Waddell, and Elizabeth Wells. Thanks also to Ed Craig of the Beeson Law Library at Samford University, Paul Pruitt, Jr., at the Bounds Law Library at the University of Alabama, Tim Lewis at the Alabama Supreme Court and State Law Library, Gary Gerlach at the now-closed Jefferson County (Alabama) Records Storage Facility, the staff at the National Archives in East Point, Georgia, and the volunteers at the Bessemer Hall of History.

I offer a heartfelt thank you for the grace and friendship extended to me by the family of Caliph Washington, especially Reverend C. Michael Washington and Christine Luna Washington. Mrs. Washington shared with me a Bible passage from Romans 12 that her husband read every Sunday: "If possible, so far as it depends on you, live peaceably with all. . . . 'If your enemy is hungry, feed him; if he is thirsty, give him something to drink; for by so doing you will heap burning coals on his head.' Do not be overcome by evil, but overcome evil with good."

This project would not have been completed without the support of my family, especially my in-laws, Lee and Donna Synnott, my aunt Dorothy Burroughs, and my mother, Faye Bass. I also remember those family members who have passed on before me, including my grandmother Lillian Bass, my father Samuel J. Bass, Jr., and my uncle G. W. Burroughs.

I am blessed beyond measure for the love and laughter of my three children: Kathleen, Caroline, and Nathaniel. Lastly, I am humbled by the grace extended to me by my wife Jennifer Bass. Thank you for your love and your unfailing support on our journey together.

ILLUSTRATION CREDITS

he played a pivotal role in each of Caliph Washington's trials. Courtesy of the Department of Special Collections, Stanford University Libraries

90 Bessemer's notorious lawman Lawton "Stud" Grimes talks with Caliph Washington after his arrest. Grimes later claimed that Washington confessed to him about murdering Cowboy Clark. The Birmingham News, Alabama Media Group/AL.com © 2016

106 A *Birmingham News* photographer captures a heart-tugging image of Florence Clark the day following her husband's death. The Birmingham News, Alabama Media Group/AL.com © 2016

120 Asbury Howard (*third from left*) with leaders of the International Union of Mine, Mill and Smelter Workers in 1954. Ira Gay Sealy/The Denver Post via Getty Images

136 In the second trial, Caliph Washington claimed that Mississippi state troopers tried to hang and shoot him. The Birmingham News, Alabama Media Group/AL.com © 2016

148 Alabama's Kilby Prison in Montgomery, where Caliph Washington waited on death row. Alabama Department of Archives and History, Montgomery, Alabama

162 Alabama's electric chair, dubbed "Big Yellow Mama." AL.com Archive/ Advance Media

182 Federal judge Frank M. Johnson ordered Caliph Washington released from Kilby Prison in July 1965. Alabama Department of Archives and History, Montgomery, Alabama

200 While charming and charismatic, district attorney James D. Hammonds had a dark side that included quid pro quo schemes and violence against political and personal opponents. Courtesy of Jeanette Creighton

216 In a bitter irony, ACLU attorney Charles "Chuck" Morgan used Caliph Washington to integrate Alabama's prisons, but he did little to help Washington gain his release. Library of Congress

234 This *Birmingham News* editorial cartoon depicts the state of Alabama making another stand against integration—this time in the prison system. Birmingham, Ala. Public Library Archives

252 Civil rights demonstrators sing during a protest at the Jefferson County Jail in Bessemer in 1967. Standing on the first step are Fred Shuttlesworth (*left*) and Asbury Howard (*right*). Alabama Department of Archives and History, Montgomery, Alabama

INSERT

S. Lawson, J. Ed Livingston, Robert T. Simpson. Back row, left to right: Pelham J. Merrill, Davis F. Stakely, John L. Goodwyn, and James S. Coleman. Alabama Department of Archives and History, Montgomery, Alabama

[9]   Asbury Howard hoped to display Jack Hamm's cartoon in Bessemer, but instead he found himself arrested, tried, and beaten. Jack Hamm / Dawna Hamm Walsh

[10]   Alabama governor George C. Wallace granted Caliph Washington thirteen stays of execution in 1963. Alabama Department of Archives and History, Montgomery, Alabama

[11]   The power of prayer sustained Caliph Washington during years of prison isolation and, once he was a free man, throughout his ministry. Here Washington offers a prayer at a wedding during the 1990s. Courtesy of Christine Washington

[12]   Caliph and Christine Washington and their six children. Courtesy of Christine Washington

INDEX

Page numbers in *italics* refer to illustrations.

ABOUT THE AUTHOR

S. JONATHAN BASS is a professor of history at Samford University in Birmingham, Alabama, and the author of the Pulitzer Prize–nominated *Blessed Are the Peacemakers: Martin Luther King, Jr., Eight White Religious Leaders and the "Letter from Birmingham Jail."* Reared in the industrial suburb of Fairfield, Alabama, Bass is a frequent speaker on race, religion, and culture and was recognized by the National Urban League with an Interracial Friendship Award. He holds a PhD in history from the University of Tennessee, Knoxville, and lives in Birmingham with his wife, Jennifer, and their three children, Kathleen, Caroline, and Nathaniel.